Discover Book-keeping and Accoun

Discover Book-keeping and Accounts

David Spurling

General Editor: Geoffrey Whitehead

Pitman

PITMAN PUBLISHING
128 Long Acre, London WC2E 9AN

© David Spurling 1988

First published in Great Britain 1988

British Library Cataloguing in Publication Data
Spurling, David
  Discover book-keeping and accounts for GCSE.
  1. Accounting
  I. Title II. Whitehead, Geoffrey
  657   HF5635

ISBN 0 273 02870 7

Printed and bound in Great Britain

Contents

Foreword

Book-keeping and accounts are essential elements in any business activity. We need at least some understanding of them for even the smallest business and as a business grows they assume an increasing importance not only in ensuring that the enterprise is soundly based financially but also in detecting where its weaknesses are and anticipating difficulties.

In writing this book the author has aimed it particularly at the simplest examinations and has kept the subject matter practical and down-to-earth so far as that is possible. At the same time an understanding of basic principles is essential if practical affairs are to be kept on the right lines and the book does teach all the principles of double-entry book-keeping, the concepts of accounting and the accounting ratios which enable us to check our records whether they are a sole trader's account, partnership accounts, limited company accounts or the accounts of non-profit-making clubs and societies. All the syllabuses used in schools and colleges for elementary accounts are covered adequately including the syllabuses of all the GCSE bodies.

As general editor I must thank the author for his forbearance in dealing with my adjustments to his original text and his patience in seeking to meet the many detailed points that arise in such a comprehensive review of traditional and modern book-keeping and accounting systems.

Geoffrey Whitehead
General Editor

Acknowledgements

George Vyner Ltd, Simplex House, Mytholmbridge Mills, Holmfirth, Huddersfield, HD7 2DA

Barclays Bank PLC for permission to reproduce a specimen cheque

Micro-Retailer Systems Ltd for permission to reproduce their Micro-simplex computerised account system

Kalamazoo Business Systems for permission to reproduce their simultaneous entry systems

All names used in this book are entirely imaginary and are not intended to represent actual firms or companies in any respect whatsoever.

Coverage of syllabus topics in this book

Examination Boards
L = London and East Anglia   S = Southern   M = Midland   N = Northern   W = Welsh

Topic	L	S	M	N	W
Books of Original Entry					
Opening Journal entries	•	•	•	•	•
All types of Journal entries	•	•	•	•	•
Purchases Day Book	•	•	•	•	•
Sales Day Book	•	•	•	•	•
Purchases Returns Book	•	•	•	•	•
Sales Returns Book	•	•	•	•	•
Cash Book	•	•	•	•	•
Petty Cash Book	•	•	•	•	•
Club Receipts and Payments Book	•	•	•	•	•
Contra entries	•	•	•	•	•
Bank Reconciliation Statements	•	•	•	•	•
VAT entries	•	•	•	•	•
VAT Return					
One-book accounting -Simplex System	•	•	•		
Simultaneous records					•
The Ledger					
T form accounts	•	•	•	•	•
Running-balance accounts	•	•	•	•	•
Balancing-off	•	•	•	•	•
Interpretation of entries	•	•	•	•	•
Debtors Accounts	•	•	•	•	•
Creditors Accounts	•	•	•	•	•
Personal Accounts	•	•	•	•	•
Nominal Accounts	•	•	•	•	•
Real Accounts (assets)	•	•	•	•	•
Assets & Liabilities	•	•	•	•	•
Losses & Profits	•	•	•	•	•
Stock Accounts (FIFO, LIFO & AVCO)	•	•	•	•	•
Suspense Accounts	•	•	•	•	•
Control Accounts	•	•	•	•	•
Capital and Revenue Expenditure	•	•	•	•	•
Depreciation	•	•	•	•	•
Straight-line method	•	•	•	•	•
Diminishing-balance method	•	•	•	•	•
Revaluation method	•	•	•	•	•
Household Accounts					•

Topic	L	S	M	N	W
Final Accounts of Sole Traders					
Trading Account	•	•	•	•	•
Net Sales & Net Purchases	•	•	•	•	•
Valuation of Stock	•	•	•	•	•
Gross profit and gross loss	•	•	•	•	•
Cost of stock sold	•	•	•	•	•
Cost of sales	•	•	•	•	•
Trading Accounts in vertical style					
Profit and Loss Account	•	•	•	•	•
Profit and Loss Account in vertical style					
Balance Sheets	•	•	•	•	•
Fixed assets	•	•	•	•	•
Current assets	•	•	•	•	•
Capital	•	•	•	•	•
Long-term liabilities	•	•	•	•	•
Current liabilities	•	•	•	•	•
Adjustments-all types	•	•	•	•	•
Partnership Accounts	•	•	•	•	•
Appropriation Accounts	•	•	•	•	•
Current Accounts	•	•	•	•	•
Balance Sheets	•	•	•	•	•
Limited Company Accounts	•	•	•	•	•
Appropriation Accounts	•	•	•	•	•
Balance Sheets	•	•	•	•	•
Balance Sheets in vertical style	•	•	•	•	•
Non-profit-making Club Accounts	•	•	•	•	•
Receipts and Payments	•	•	•	•	•
Income and Expenditure Accounts	•	•	•	•	•
Balance Sheets	•	•	•	•	•
Accumulated Funds	•	•	•	•	•
Incomplete Records	•	•	•	•	•
Manufacturing Accounts	•	•	•	•	•
Departmental Accounts	•				
Interpretation of Accounts	•	•	•	•	•
Gross Profit Percentage	•	•	•	•	•
Net Profit Percentage	•	•	•	•	•

Coverage of syllabus topics in this book

Topic	L	S	M	N	W	Topic	L	S	M	N	W
Trial Balance	•	•	•	•	•	Debtors to Sales Ratio	•	•	•	•	•
Preparation of	•	•	•	•	•	Bad debts to Debtors Ratio	•				•
Purpose of	•	•	•	•	•	Net working capital	•	•	•	•	•
Exact nature of	•	•	•	•	•	Current Ratio		•	•	•	•
Failure to agree	•	•	•	•	•	Acid-test Ratio		•	•	•	•
Errors that do not show up:	•	•	•	•	•	Rate of Stock Turnover	•	•	•	•	
Original errors	•	•	•	•	•	Expense Ratios			•		
Compensating errors	•	•	•	•	•	Return on Capital Employed		•	•	•	•
Errors of omission	•	•	•	•	•	Return on Capital Invested		•	•	•	•
Errors of commission	•	•	•	•	•	Net current assets	•	•	•	•	•
Errors of principle	•	•	•	•	•	**Concepts of Accounting**					
Documents						Business entity	•		•	•	•
Invoices	•	•	•	•	•	Ownership	•		•	•	•
Credit notes	•	•	•	•	•	Stewardship	•				•
Debit notes	•	•	•	•	•	Going concern (continuity)			•	•	•
Petty cash vouchers	•	•	•	•	•	Consistency			•	•	
Statements	•	•	•	•	•	Objectivity			•		•
Cheques	•	•	•	•	•	Prudence (conservatism)			•	•	•
Bank giro transfers	•	•	•	•	•	Materiality			•	•	•
Sources and applications of			•	•		Accruals (matching)		•	•	•	•
funds						Stable-money		•	•	•	•
Cash budgets	•		•	•		Duality			•	•	•
						Financial control and			•	•	•
						Purpose of	•		•	•	•
						Purchase of a business	•				
						Goodwill and					

1 Accounting for business receipts in small businesses

1.1 What is business?

Business is any activity which creates wealth. Wealth is not money, but an abundance of goods and services. Robinson Crusoe found a box of gold on the wreck of his ship, but it didn't make him wealthy. He couldn't eat it, drink it, wear it, live in it or get it to take care of him when he was sick. Food, clothing, housing, fuel, shelter, education, entertainment — these are real wealth. It is business activity that makes them all available. This business activity may be carried on by private persons, such as sole traders, partnerships and companies (private enterprise) or by public enterprises such as Central Government, local authorities or nationalised corporations.

In this book we study one special branch of business, the accounting records. If you want to know more about business itself you should read *Discover Business and Commerce* by the same author, also published by Pitman Publishing. Here we are learning about the financial records of a business. These were always kept in **books of account**, so that the name 'book-keeping' came to be applied to this special type of work. Today many businesses have been computerised, and very few of their records are kept in books, because the computer stores them all in its memory. However, we can still call them up on to the screen of our **visual display unit (VDU)** in the old form, so we can look at each 'page' of our book-keeping records on the screen if we wish to do so.

The other name for book-keeping is 'accounting'. This name comes from the word **account**, which is a very old name for the pages in the main book of account, the **ledger**. In medieval counting-houses there was only one book — the ledger — which lay on a ledge under the window where the light was good. Each page in the book kept a record of the business's activities with one person — say Mr Smith or Mrs Jones. This account of dealings with each person gave us the name 'account', and the words 'accounting' and 'accountant'. An accountant is a person skilled in accounting, and the author hopes very much that every reader will eventually become a qualified accountant.

1.2 Cash activities in business

We can't be in business even for one day without handling cash. People come into the shop and pay cash, or into the garage for petrol and pay cash. On the very first day of a new business we transfer money into a special 'account' at the bank, so that the business has its own 'Bank Account'.

Of course, we may also be paid by cheque, and some people pay by credit card, but these are just ways of paying cash rather more safely than in coins or bank notes. In most small businesses we just treat them as cash in the book-keeping records, though we have to go to the bank every day and pay in the cheques, and the duplicate copies of the credit card vouchers. Until we do that the cheques and vouchers are as good as cash, and we put them in the till with the ordinary coins and notes.

1.3 Recording cash receipts

There is a great deal to learn in book-keeping, but let us make a start by understanding how cash received is recorded on the books. In a busy supermarket, for example, the cashiers who take the money at the checkout cannot enter it in any books. The till records the amount of the items sold, works out the total to be charged to the customer and the cashier takes the money and puts it into the till, giving change if necessary. The tills get so full of cash that in some supermarkets it is collected every hour, with the whole bundles of notes being put into a bag for each till and taken to the Accounts Department.

We will imagine a smaller shop than this, which only 'cashes up' the till once at the end of the day. How does such a shop record cash takings?

At the start of the day the cashier needs some change, and this is called the **cash float**. Usually it is a nice round sum, say £25, made up of two £5 notes, and the rest in £1, 50 pence, 20 pence, 10 pence, 5 pence, 2 pence and 1 pence coins. As money is added through the day the till collects it all together, and at the end of the day the till is 'cashed up'. This means we count the cash, but first of all we take out and put on one side the float that we need for tomorrow morning. The float is not part of the day's takings, so it must be removed before we start to count. Assuming this has been done, we can then count the takings. Example 1.1 illustrates this, and the piece of paper we need to keep our daily record.

EXAMPLE 1.1

Mary Jones runs a small general shop in her village. At the end of the day she counts up the takings, after removing the float from the till. She finds she has 4 × £20 notes, 17 × £10 notes, 16 × £5 notes, 37 × £1 coins, 18 × 50 pence coins, 42 × 20p coins, 5 × 10p coins, 7 × 5p coins, 31 × 2p coins and 11 pennies. What are the total takings?

Mary records them on a list as follows:

		£ p
£20 ×	4=	80.00
£10 ×	17=	170.00
£ 5 ×	16=	80.00
£ 1 ×	37=	37.00
50p ×	18=	9.00

$$20p \times 42 = \quad 8.40$$
$$10p \times 5 = \quad 0.50$$
$$5p \times 7 = \quad 0.35$$
$$2p \times 31 = \quad 0.62$$
$$1p \times 11 = \quad 0.11$$

Total   £385.98

The figure which Mary will record for her daily takings is therefore £385.98. Most of the takings will be paid into the bank next day.

You should now try working out the cash takings for each of the businesses named below.

1.4 Exercises: cashing up at the end of the day

1 At the end of the day, after removing the float, Mary West finds that her takings are as follows: 1 × £50 note, 3 × £20 notes, 11 × £10 notes, 16 × £5 notes, 27 × £1 coins, 13 × 50p coins, 22 × 20p coins, 17 × 10p coins 15 × 5p coins, 8 × 2p coins and 19 pennies. Work out the takings for the day.

2 At the end of the day, after removing the float, George Overton finds that his takings are as follows: 3 × £50 notes, 17 × £20 notes, 21 × £10 notes, 9 × £5 notes, 181 × £1 coins, 17 × 50p coins, 13 × 20p coins, 42 × 10p coins, 12 × 5p coins, 9 × 2p coins and 23 pennies. Work out the takings for the day.

3 At the end of the day, after removing the float, Sandra Patel finds that her takings are as follows: 2 × £50 notes, 5 × £20 notes, 38 × £10 notes, 27 × £5 notes, 19 × £1 coins, 42 × 50p coins, 63 × 20p coins, 12 × 10p coins, 18 × 5p coins, 32 × 2p coins and 14 pennies. Work out the takings for the day.

4 At the end of the day, after removing the float, Haji Muhammadu finds that his takings are as follows: 3 × £50 notes, 42 × £20 notes, 46 × £10 notes, 27 × £5 notes, 35 × £1 coins, 37 × 50p coins, 25 × 20p coins, 62 × 10p coins, 13 × 5p coins, 19 × 2p coins and 37 pennies. Work out the takings for the day.

1.5 Cheques and credit card vouchers

These days many people do not pay in cash, but pay by cheque, or with credit cards. The trader treats the cheque, or the credit card voucher, just as if it was cash takings from the point of view of the book-keeping records, since the sales made in this way are still part of the daily takings and will eventually be used to work out the profits of the business.

When taking cheques in payment the shopkeeper has to be careful, for cheque books are often stolen or misused by their true owners. It is unwise to accept a cheque unless a cheque guarantee card is also presented. When a cheque is written out on business premises and a cheque card is also presented the shopkeeper can compare the signature on the card with the signature on the cheque. If they are the same the shopkeeper writes the number of the cheque card on the back of the cheque and the bank will then honour the cheque to the limit (at present) of £50, even if there are no funds in the account.

Similarly, when a customer pays by credit card the voucher which is made out is embossed with the details on the card in a simple machine process, and the bank will then honour the voucher and pay the trader. Both cheques and vouchers are simply treated as cash and placed in the till until the end of the day, when the 'cashing up' procedure takes place.

Fig. 1.1 shows a typical cheque, which is explained in the notes below.

Fig. 1.1 A crossed cheque

Notes
1 The cheque is an order to a banker to pay money to a named person.
2 The banker in this case is Barclays, High Street, Caxton, London.
3 They are ordered to pay Symphonia Musicale (Camside) Ltd, £2096.84. This is written both in words and figures.
4 The cheque is signed by A. Trader, who is called the drawer of the cheque.
5 20–99–93 is the computer code for the Caxton branch which will have to pay the money.
6 The computer codes at the bottom of the cheque show the cheque number, the branch number and the account number of A. Trader.

1.6 Recording cash takings on a weekly basis

Many small firms use very simple book-keeping systems, where sales and purchases figures are recorded every day, but gradually build up the figures for each week, month, quarter and year. This is important because it is the annual figures which are used to work out the profits of the business and let the proprietor (and the income tax authorities) know how much profit has been made.

One simple system, the owners of which have kindly allowed the author to use their rulings, is the Simplex System. Example 1.2 shows how the sales figures are recorded. The sales of a business are also called the 'takings' of the business and must be recorded daily.

EXAMPLE 1.2   Peter Fleming sells goods for cash, and also accepts cheques if they are backed by a cheque guarantee card. Here are his takings for the week commencing 1 January. Record them in a suitable 'Daily Takings' record:

Cash takings: Monday £174.52; Tuesday £203.25; Wednesday £381.54; Thursday £326.75; Friday £405.96 and Saturday £627.54.

Sales paid for by cheque: Monday £85.26; Tuesday £136.95; Wednesday £32.65; Thursday £272.50; Friday £195.36; Saturday £127.35.

On Wednesday he also received a Tax Refund of £85.00, which was not part of his ordinary takings.

RECEIPTS						
Day	Date	Gross Daily Takings (cash) Col 1		Gross Daily Takings (cheques) Col 2		Other Receipts Col 3
Sunday	: 1 Jan	—	—	—	—	
Monday	: 2 "	174	52	85	26	
Tuesday	: 3 "	203	25	136	95	
Wednesday	: 4 "	381	54	32	65	85	00
Thursday	: 5 "	326	75	272	50	
Friday	: 6 "	405	96	195	36	
Saturday	: 7 "	627	54	127	35	
Totals		2119	56	850	07	85	00

(Courtesy of George Vyner Ltd, Huddersfield)

Fig. 1.2 Recording daily takings

Notes

1 Each day's cash takings are recorded in the 'cash' column.

2 Each day's takings in the form of cheques or credit card vouchers are recorded in the 'cheques' column.

3 Any receipt which is not a sale of goods, for example the Tax Refund, is recorded in the 'Other Receipts' column.

4 If the two totals of Columns 1 and 2 are added together they give the total sales for the week. This is an important figure, as we shall see, when it comes to working out the profits of the business.

1.7 Exercises: recording weekly takings

In these exercises you may either head up columns of an ordinary exercise book as shown in Fig. 1.2 or use duplicated copies of the illustrations provided on page 12.

1 M Lockyer sells goods for cash. He also accepts cheques if they are backed by a cheque guarantee card, and credit card payments for all major credit card companies. He treats the vouchers from these as if they are cheques. Here are his takings for the week. Record them in a suitable 'Daily Takings' record.

Cash sales: Monday £84.52; Tuesday £176.35; Wednesday £58.60; Thursday £232.72; Friday £324.80 and Saturday £426.50.

Sales paid for by cheque or credit card voucher were as follows:
Monday £49.25; Tuesday £98.26; Wednesday £37.65; Thursday £242.60; Friday £195.96; Saturday £238.45.

On Thursday Lockyer received a loan from the bank of £500. Enter this in the 'other receipts' column.

2 K Shah sells goods for cash, and also accepts cheques if they are backed by a cheque guarantee card. He also takes credit card payments for all major credit card companies. He treats the vouchers from these as if they were cheques. Here are his takings for the week. Record them in a suitable 'Daily Takings' record.

Cash sales: Monday £273.60; Tuesday £429.25; Wednesday £382.65; Thursday £497.63; Friday £485.95; and Saturday £399.60.
Sales paid for by cheque or credit card voucher were as follows:
Monday £72.65; Tuesday £143.24; Wednesday £286.72; Thursday £328.65; Friday £427.62; Saturday £559.65.

On Friday Shah received a refund of carriage costs from Fastjobs Ltd, of £17.54. Enter this in the 'Other receipts' section.

3 Anne Bailey sells goods for cash. She also accepts cheques if they are backed by a cheque guarantee card. Here are her takings for the week. Record them in a suitable 'Daily Takings' record.

Cash sales: Monday £138.41; Tuesday £195.21; Wednesday £85.60; Thursday £497.25; Friday £426.71 and Saturday £527.53.
Sales paid for by cheque were as follows:
Monday £137.25; Tuesday £142.65; Wednesday £156.72; Thursday £195.40; Friday £178.86 and Saturday £328.49.

On Tuesday Anne received an allowance of £160 from the Enterprise Allowance Authorities. Enter this in the 'Other receipts' section.

4 Mervyn Pyke sells goods for cash, and also accepts cheques if they are backed by a cheque guarantee card. Here are his takings for the week. Record them in a suitable 'Daily Takings' record. Sales in cash each day were as follows:

Monday £98.72; Tuesday £148.65; Wednesday £395.65; Thursday £528.65; Friday £472.65 and Saturday £501.25.
Sales paid for by cheque were as follows:
Monday £39.26; Tuesday £127.32; Wednesday £165.86; Thursday £132.78; Friday £42.75; Saturday £198.86.

On Friday Mervyn put £1000 extra capital into the business. Enter this in the 'Other receipts' section.

1.8 Self-assessment questions

In every chapter you will find some self-assessment questions. If you have studied the chapter properly you will be able to answer the questions easily, either mentally or in written work. If you have any difficulty you should refer to the Answers to Self-Assessment Questions, which is the very last section in each chapter. (*Note: For the answers to the book-keeping exercises you must turn to the back of the book.*)

1 What is business?
2 What is the main book of account?
3 What do we call the pages in this book?
4 What is 'cashing-up'?
5 What is a cheque?
6 What do we call the person who is to be paid the amount of money written on the cheque?

7 What do we call the person who is writing out the cheque?

8 What do we call the daily takings of a business?

1.9 A project on daily takings

Using your own home district as the area for investigation, make a collection of till receipts for items purchased by your family. Write against at least one item on the receipt what it was you purchased. Try to obtain receipts from a wide variety of shops, and if possible discover the name of the till being used. If a shopkeeper does not use a machine that dispenses till receipts ask for a bill for your purchase — explaining that you need it for your accountancy studies.

1.10 Answers to self-assessment questions

1 Business is any activity that creates wealth. It may be private enterprise or public enterprise activity.

2 The ledger is the main book of account.

3 Each page in the ledger is called an account.

4 Cashing-up is a process done each night to find the total takings for the day. After removing the float from the till the contents are counted and made ready to pay into the bank next day.

5 A cheque is an order to a banker to pay money.

6 The person to be paid is called the payee.

7 The person who writes out the cheque is called the drawer.

8 They are called the 'sales' of the business.

2 Accounting for payments in small businesses

2.1 Payments for business stock

Business payments fall into two main classes; payments for business stock and payments other than for stock. When we sell goods to our customers, as we have already seen, the receipts are the daily takings of our business, called in book-keeping the 'Sales' of the business. Of course we cannot sell anything unless we have purchased it beforehand (or purchased the raw materials to manufacture it). The 'Purchases' of the business are what we pay for business stock to sell again, or for raw materials if we are a manufacturer. Other purchases are not called 'purchases', but are called 'overhead expenses'. So postage stamps, petrol for a motor van, wrapping paper, etc., are not purchases but overhead expenses of the business. Here we will deal with true purchases, that is 'Payments for Business Stock'.

Many small business using simple systems of book-keeping, such as the Simplex System, record payments for business stock each week, and carry the totals to summaries which build up into quarterly and eventually annual totals. Example 2.1 shows a record of this sort.

EXAMPLE 2.1

Thomas Walford buys goods for resale as follows:

July 5 Paid to M. Aubrey by cheque no. 211046: £56.80.
Also to S. A. Abujama in cash £25.84.
July 6 Paid to Super Biscuits PLC by cheque no. 211047: £385.56.
July 8 Paid in cash to A. Farmer £37.80 for fresh vegetables.
Also to Cornwall Florist Co. Ltd, by cheque no. 211049: £138.50 for flowers.
July 10 Paid to A. Smallholder £28.50 cash for potatoes supplied.
Also by cheque to M. Shah for fruit £125.60, cheque no. 211051.

Record these items in the Payments for Business Stock section of a Simplex Account book (see opposite).

2.2 Exercises in recording payments for business stock

To do these exercises you may either copy the layout shown in Fig. 2.1 in an ordinary exercise book or use a duplicated copy of the special rulings shown on page 12.

1 M. Fox records on his payments page under the heading 'Payments for Business Stock' the following items during the week:

July 7 Paid to R. Cross by cheque £25.84 (cheque no. 126354) and to S. Tims in cash £5.60.

July 8 Paid to McNab Biscuit Co., by cheque £85.50 (cheque no. 126355) and to Prepared Foods Ltd, £48.50 by cheque (no. 126356).

July 9 Paid to Ace Pizza Co., by cheque £27.25 (no. 126358) and to the Ashborne Water Co. Ltd, in cash £25.85.

July 13 Paid to R. Cross by cheque £17.25 (no. 126361).

Enter these items and total the 'cash' and 'cheque' columns.

PAYMENTS FOR BUSINESS STOCK		Amount Paid			
Date or Chq. No.	To Whom Paid	By Cash Col 7		By Cheque Col 8	
211046	M. AUBREY			56	80
JULY 5	S. A. ABUJAMA	25	84		
211047	SUPER BISCUITS PLC			385	56
JULY 8	A. FARMER	37	80		
211049	CORNWALL FLORIST Co LTD			138	50
JULY 10	A. SMALLHOLDER	28	50		
211051	M. SHAH			125	60
	Totals	92	14	706	46

(Courtesy of George Vyner Ltd, Huddersfield)

Fig. 2.1 Recording payments for business stock

Notes
1 The entries are self-explanatory.
2 Where a payment has been made by cheque it is helpful to put the cheque number in — it then can be followed through on the bank statement when we get one at the end of the month.
3 If the two totals are added together it gives the total purchases for the week, which is a very important figure when we come to working out the profits of the business.

2 C. Boyer records on his payments page under the heading 'Payments for Business Stock' the following items during the week:

August 14 Paid to R. Longstaff by cheque £27.55 (no. 381178) and to B. Laker by cheque £13.50 (no. 381179).

August 16 Paid to R. Boyd in cash the sum of £25.78 for materials supplied.

August 18 A delivery from Moncrief PLC is valued at £48.50 but returns amounting to £7.25 are given by Boyer to the van driver. The net amount is paid in cash.

Enter these items and total the 'cash' and 'cheque' columns.

3 M. Lynch records on her payments page under the heading 'Payments for Business Stock' the following items during the week:

October 7   Paid to R. Britain by cheque £28.74 (no. 179595) and to S. Thames in cash £5.46.

October 8   Paid to Water Biscuit Co. Ltd, by cheque £88.50 (no. 179596) and to Novel Foods Ltd, £48.50 by cheque (no. 179598).

October 9   Paid to M. Lush by cheque £112.00 (no. 179599) and to Fresh Vegetables Ltd, in cash £7.35.

October 13 Paid to M. Lawson by cheque £14.25 (no. 179600).

Enter these items and total the 'cash' and 'cheque' columns.

4 P. Singh records on his payments page under the heading 'Payments for Business Stock' the following items during the week:

May 24   Paid to R. Carey by cheque £24.25 (no. 171956) and to K. Mayman by cheque £27.20 (no. 171957).

May 26   Paid to M. Bull in cash the sum of £18.25.

May 28   A delivery from T. Lark is valued at £42.80 but returns amounting to £5.00 are given by Singh to the van driver. The net amount is paid in cash.

Enter these items and total the 'cash' and 'cheques' columns.

2.3 Payments for overheads

The second class of payments all businesses need to record are the payments for overheads such as rent, rates, light and heat, etc. We shall see later that large firms make these payments through a book called the Three Column Cash Book, or for small items they need a Petty Cash Book. We shall learn how to keep these books. For the present let us just look at a very simple system, the Simplex system already referred to, and see how it records these transactions. Example 2.2 illustrates these entries.

EXAMPLE 2.2

Ken Smart is in business as a signwriter. In a particular week he pays for the following overhead expenses in cash: rent £35.00; postages 27p, 42p £1.80 and £3.42; petrol £12.25; insurance £25.00. He pays by cheque for an easel (capital item) £68.50, and for paper £18.50. He also draws out for himself (drawings) £60.00 by cheque.

Record these items in the 'Payments other than for stock' section of a simple accounting system.

2.4 Exercises in recording 'Payments other than for stock'

For these exercises you may either head up columns in an ordinary exercise book or use duplicated copies of the ruling shown in Fig. 2.3.

1 Tom Cross is in business as a greengrocer. In a particular week he pays the following items in cash: rent £45; postages 27p, 32p, 46p and £1.40; petrol £8.75 and insurance £15.20. He also pays wages £87.50 in cash. He pays by cheque for a weighing machine (a capital item) £69.75 and for sundries £8.50. He also draws for his own use the sum of £60.00 by cheque. Enter the above items and total the two columns to find the total 'Cash' and 'Cheque' payments.

PAYMENTS OTHER THAN FOR STOCK				
Nature of Payment	By Cash Col 9		By Cheque Col 10	
Rent	35	00		
Rates				
Light and Heat				
Carriage				
Postages 27p, 42p, £1·80, £3·42	5	91		
Paper			18	50
Motor Expenses (PETROL)	12	25		
—do— (SERVICING)				
Travelling				
Cleaning				
Printing & Stationery				
Repairs & Renewals				
Insurance (Business)	25	00		
Advertising				
Telephone				
Wages (Wife)				
Wages (Employees)				
Sundries				
Private Pension Contributions				
Inland Revenue (PAYE + NI)				
Drawings for Self (see Note. 10)			60	00
—do—				
—do—				
Capital Items (see note 7) EASEL			68	50
Totals	78	16	147	00

(Courtesy of George Vyner Ltd, Huddersfield)

Fig. 2.2 *Recording overhead expenses*

Notes

1 The items are recorded as shown, in either the cash or cheque columns.

2 The totals of the two columns are used to work out the balance of cash which should be in hand at the end of the week, and the balance of money that should be in the bank. These records are not shown here.

3 All these various expenses are collected together in summaries at the back of the Simplex account book to build up total figures for rent, rates, etc. These can be used to work out the profits of the business at the end of the year. How this can be done is explained later (*see* Chapters 20, 21 and 22).

2 Mary Adele is in business as a fashion designer. In one particular week she pays the following items in cash: postages £2.47 and £1.32; art materials (sundries) £4.65 and travelling £12.50. She also pays wages £82.50 in cash. She pays by cheque for stationery £27.42 and a telephone bill for £281.74. She also draws for herself the sum of £100 in cash. Enter the above items and total the two columns to find the total 'Cash' and 'Cheque' payments.

3 K. Ahura starts in business as a chiropodist. In the first week he pays the following items in cash: postages 27p, 32p, 66p and £1.46; advertising £32.50 and sundries 25p. He also pays travelling expenses £13.28 in cash. He pays by cheque for rates £48.50, and for stationery £42.54p, and also draws for his own use the sum of £85.00 by cheque. Enter the above items and total the two columns to find the total 'Cash' and 'Cheque' payments.

RECEIPTS				
Day	Date	Gross Daily Takings (cash) Col 1	Gross Daily Takings (cheques) Col 2	Other Receipts Col 3
Sunday	:			
Monday	:			
Tuesday	:			
Wednesday	:			
Thursday	:			
Friday	:			
Saturday	:			
	Totals			

PAYMENTS FOR BUSINESS STOCK		Amount Paid	
Date or Chq. No.	To Whom Paid	By Cash Col 7	By Cheque Col 8
	Totals		

a

(Courtesy of George Vyner Ltd, Huddersfield)

Fig. 2.3

PAYMENTS OTHER THAN FOR STOCK		
Nature of Payment	Amount Paid	
	By Cash Col 9	By Cheque Col 10
Rent		
Rates		
Light and Heat		
Carriage		
Postages		
Paper		
Motor Expenses	17 54	
—do—		
Travelling		
Cleaning		
Printing & Stationery		35 80
Repairs & Renewals		
Insurance (Business)		
Advertising	2 50	
Telephone		
Wages (Wife)		
Wages (Employees)		
Sundries		
Private Pension Contributions		
Inland Revenue (PAYE + NI)		
Drawings for Self (see Note. 10)		
—do—		
—do—		
Capital Items (see note 7)		
Totals		

b

Fig. 2.3 a (opposite) and b (above) may be duplicated for classroom use

4 Sally Brown operates as a hairdresser from her own home. In the week under consideration she pays out in cash, motor expenses (petrol) £17.54, postage 18p and £1.98, advertising £2.50 and telephone expenses £2.40. She pays by cheque for stationery £35.80 and a drier (capital item) £184.60. She also draws a cheque for her personal use (drawings) £80.00. Record these items and total the cash and bank columns.

2.5 Working out the profits of a small business

The main purpose of keeping accounts is to work out the profits of the business. We need to do this for several reasons. First, it tells us whether it is worthwhile being in business at all. If we cannot make a profit but only sustain losses, we shall finish up in the bankruptcy courts. Second, the Inland Revenue Department (the tax authorities) require book-keeping records so that they can assess the business for tax purposes. Everyone in the country pays some taxes (unless they are in the very poorest sector) and the Inland Revenue has a duty to collect the tax due from businesses.

At this stage it is too early to learn how the profits of a business are calculated but the simple cash and cheque records we have been learning about can easily be used to work the profits out. It is done in two stages.

Stage I Finding the profit on trading (the Gross Profit)
Sales (daily takings) *less* Purchases (payments for business stock) = Gross Profit
Stage II Deducting the overheads to give the clear profit
Gross Profits *less* overheads = Net Profit

Having said this we will leave the actual calculations of the profits until later in our course of studies.

2.6 Computerised book-keeping for small businesses

Schools and colleges who possess a micro-computer might like to see these very simple records in computerised form. The software for this simple system is available from Micro Retailer Systems Ltd, Cheshire House, Exchange Close, Castle Street, Macclesfield, Cheshire SK11 6UX and is available for most makes of computer. It can be very instructive both in accountancy and computer appreciation.

2.7 Self-assessment questions

1 What are 'purchases' in book-keeping?
2 What are 'sales' in book-keeping?
3 What are 'overheads' in book-keeping?
4 Name five overheads.
5 What is gross profit?
6 What is net profit?
7 What is a capital item?

2.8 Project: a study of purchases and overheads

If we wish to understand book-keeping properly it is no good just sitting in a classroom. We have to think about business all the time. For this project you should go, as an individual, into a busy supermarket near your home. Draw up a list of the following things:

1 Ten purchases of the supermarket (items of business stock which it is obvious the supermarket must buy if they are to sell them on the shelves).

2 Five capital items, that is pieces of equipment which the supermarket buys to use in the business, not to sell again.

3 Ten overhead expenses it is obvious that the management has to meet to run the business — for example lighting will mean they have to pay an electricity bill once a quarter.

   (a) Write a short report on these items which includes your three lists.

   (b) Taking one item from each list try to estimate what the management will pay for the item each week, using your own experience of what things cost. Write a short explanation of your estimate.

For example: Tins of baked beans sell for 22 pence.

   They must be making a good profit — usually at least one third — so say 8 pence is profit. This means the baked beans cost 14 pence per tin.

   Suppose they sell 500 tins a day; that is £40 a day. If they open six days a week that makes £240 just to buy the baked beans.

2.9 Answers to self-assessment questions

1 Purchases are the items we buy to sell again, or the raw materials we buy to manufacture into finished goods.

2 Sales are the takings achieved by our business when we trade. Takings are usually collected together in a till.

3 Overheads are the expenses we pay out apart from purchases (payments other than for business stock).

4 Rent, rates, postage, telephone expenses, advertising, etc.

5 It is the profit on trading activities. We find it by finding the difference in value between what we purchased and what we sold.

6 It is the profit found after the overheads have been deducted from the gross profit to give us the clear profit on our business.

7 A capital item is a piece of equipment, machine or tool which is purchased not for resale but to use in the business, such as a till, a filing cabinet, a display cabinet in a supermarket, etc.

3 The Ledger — the main book of account

3.1 The origin of the Ledger

In the old-fashioned counting houses the book-keeper worked in front of the window, with the books of account on a ledge, open in front of him. The chief book was the ledger — the book lying on the ledge. There was another book called the Journal, or day book, but the ledger was — and still is — the main book of account.

The book-keeper worked all day making entries in the ledger as they occurred. If Mr Smith called to obtain some goods the entry was made in Mr Smith's account there and then. What exactly do ledger accounts look like?

3.2 A traditional ledger account

All the ledger consists of is a book full of ruled pages, all ruled exactly alike, called 'Accounts'. **An account is a page in a ledger.** They are doubled sided — each account is a double page — or leaf — in the book. Each page is numbered, and these numbers are called 'folio numbers' because the Latin word for a leaf is *folium*. Suppose you say 'I have an account at Barclay's Bank', all you mean is that you have a page in their ledger. Any transaction you do with the Bank will be recorded on your account. If you put money in they will record the deposit, and if you take money out they will record the withdrawal. And the account number they give you will be your 'folio' number.

We must now see how ledger paper is ruled. This is shown in Fig. 3.1, and described in the notes which follow it. Study these now.

Tom Bell A/c. 2047 High Street, Ipswich, Suffolk Tel. (0473) 579614										L19
Dr Date	Details	F	£	p	Date	Details	F	£		Cr p
19. . Oct 1	Balance	b/d	27	50	19. .					
	This side is the debit side. Debit the A/c that receives goods, or services, or money					This side is the credit side. Credit the A/c that gives goods, or services, or money				

Fig. 3.1 An account in the ledger

Notes

1 The top line of each page in the ledger runs the full width of the page and has room for the name of the account.

2 If it is a personal account the name will be the name of the person concerned, with the address and telephone number.

3 In the top right-hand corner is the folio number, which in this example is L19 (page 19 in the Ledger).

4 The page is then divided down the middle, either with a thick line, or in this case, with three lines very close together.

5 The left-hand half of the page shows the date, the word 'Balance', which is the amount brought down from last month. b/d in the folio column (F) means 'brought down' from last month.

6 The amount is £27.50. Notice this side of the page has Dr printed at the top and this stands for 'debtor'. Tom Bell is a debtor for £27.50. A debtor is a person who owes you money, and this would be for goods or services supplied last month. Notice the explanation — this side is the debit side. We debit the account that receives goods, or services or money.

7 The other side of the page has exactly the same rulings, but it is called the credit side. It has Cr at the top, which stands for creditor. If the person named at the top gives goods or services or money we make the entry on the credit side of the account.

We must now develop Fig. 3.1 to show what Tom Bell's account might look like in the month of October.

EXAMPLE 3.1

During October the following transactions took place with Tom Bell, who is one of our debtors, and has an opening balance of £27.50 as shown in Fig. 3.1.

October 7   Bell orders goods from us value £210.35. These are dispatched the same day.

October 9   Bell returns some goods to us from the previous month since they were not up to the sample offered. The value was £5.00.

October 15 Bells sends a cheque for £21.38 being payment for the previous month's items, less the returns already received and discount of £1.12.

October 29 Bell orders more goods, value £59.50, which are dispatched the same day.

Whenever we make entries in the ledger for a debtor we have to think carefully and follow the basic rule:

Debit the account which receives goods, services or money.
Credit the account which gives goods, services or money.

Shortened this rule reads:

Debit the receiver; credit the giver.

In every case we think what happened to the person, or thing, that is named at the top of the account, in this case Tom Bell.

October 7   Bell has been sent goods worth £210.35. Is he the receiver of these goods, or the giver? Clearly he is the receiver. Debit the receiver. You will see this has been done in Fig. 3.2. As the transaction was a sales transaction we write the word Sales in the details column. The folio numbers will be explained later. For the present ignore them.

October 9   Bell returns some goods. Is he receiving them or giving them back? Clearly he is the giver. Credit the giver — so this entry goes on the right hand side of the account.

October 15 This is a more difficult entry. Bell sends us a cheque for £21.38. Clearly he is giving us money, so we must credit the giver. However, we are also allowing him to pay us less than the full amount, because he is paying promptly. This is called a **settlement discount**. It is an encouragement to customers to pay promptly. You might say 'Well this time he hasn't given us anything'. This is true, but we must credit his account if the debt from last month is to be fully written off. Credit him with £1.12. Note that we write 'Bank' in the details column, because the cheque will go in the Bank Account, and we call the discount 'Discount allowed' because we have allowed him to keep that amount of discount.

October 29 This is the same as the entry on 7 October. Bell is ordering more goods.

When the end of the month comes we sort out the account and make it clearer by a process known as 'balancing-off' the account. Looking at it on the last day of October we can't really see who owes whom how much. To sort it out we add up the two sides as follows:

Debit side: This totals	£297.35
Credit side: This totals	£ 27.50
Difference (balance)	£269.85

This difference is what Tom Bell owes us on the last day of October for goods supplied. To balance the books we put £269.85 on the credit side, to make the two

Dr Date		Details	F	£	p	Date	Details	F	£	Cr p
19. .						19. .				
Oct	1	Balance	b/d	27	50	Oct 9	Sales returns		5	—
	7	Sales		210	35	15	Bank		21	38
	29	"		59	50	15	Discount allowed		1	12
						31	Balance	c/d	269	85
			£	297	35			£	297	35
Nov	1	Balance	b/d	269	85					

Tom Bell A/c. 2047 High Street, Ipswich, Suffolk Tel. (0473) 579614 — L19

Fig. 3.2 A debtor's account

Notes
1 The debtor is a debtor at the start of the month, because there is a debit balance on the account.
2 The month is only written once on each side (Oct).
3 The dates then run down the page in the column provided.
4 Wherever possible to save time ditto marks are used (as under Sales).
5 When balancing off the totals are written on the same line. In this example one line was left blank on the left hand side. To prevent mistakes (someone might try to write figures on this line) it is filled up with a neat Z
6 It is usual to use red lines for underlining totals, and for the Z lines.
7 When we carry down the balance we write c/d in the 'carried down' folio column and b/d in the 'brought down' folio column. Other folio columns are explained later.
8 Although the Z entries are used to fill up the gaps between sides as shown in the example these are difficult to insert in a printed book and will not be inserted in future exercises.

sides balance. Then we bring this balance down to show what is owing on the first day of the new month.

Follow these ideas carefully by looking at Fig. 3.2 and reading the notes below it.

Now try some of the debtors' ledger exercises below. You will need ruled ledger paper which is obtainable from any good stationer's shop. In a real office you would of course have a separate page for each account in the ledger. This would be too expensive for schools and colleges, so we just do one exercise, rule a line right across the page and start another new exercise. Practice makes perfect — try to do them all.

As you do each exercise you have to read each entry, decide whether to debit or credit it, and make the entry on the correct side of the paper, as shown in the example given in Fig. 3.2.

3.3 Exercises: debtors' accounts

1 Mr D. Black is one of our debtors. In our debtors' ledger the folio number of his account is DL14. On 1.1.19. . there is a debit balance of £120.15 on this account.

Head the account correctly; make the opening balance entry and then the entries listed below:

Jan 3   D. Black sent us a cheque for £120.15 to settle his account in full.
Jan 4   We sell Black goods worth £25.50.
Jan 5   Black is sent further goods valued at £45.10.
Jan 15 Goods sent to Black worth £65.60.
Jan 18 Black returns goods to the value of £20.60 (wrong colour).
Jan 22 We sell Black goods to the value of £30.75.
Jan 25 We send Black more goods valued at £20.45.
Jan 31 The account is balanced off and the balance brought down ready for 1 February.

2 Mrs E. Noir is one of our customers. Her folio number in our ledger is DL16. On 1 February 19. . the debit balance on her account is £150.00. Open her account and enter the following items:

Feb 2   We sent Noir goods valued at £50.75.
Feb 3   Noir pays the amount owing us as on 1 February by cheque less 10% discount we have allowed her.
Feb 4   Noir buys further goods invoiced at £40.25.
Feb 7   She returns some of the goods bought on 2 February valued at £10.50.
Feb 14 We send her further goods worth £60.45. We also charge a further £4.20 for delivery (carriage).
Feb 28 Balance off the account and bring the balance down.

3 Miss B. Schwarz has a ledger account with us, folio DL20. Open this account with a debit balance of £50.60 on 1 March 19. . and enter the following items:

Mar 2   Goods sent to her were invoiced at £25.00.
Mar 3   Schwarz was sent more goods valued at £40.10.
Mar 5   She returns goods valued at £10.20.

Mar 8 We receive her cheque for the balance owing to us on 1 March less £2.50 discount.

Mar 9 Schwarz was sent goods valued at £90.20.

Mar 10 We charge her £3.40 carriage and £2.60 insurance for goods sent to date.

Mar 12 We sell her goods, invoiced at £10.25.

Mar 16 She returns goods (wrong size), valued at £7.75.

Mar 27 Invoiced for further supplies £14.35.

Mar 31 Balance her account ready for April, and bring down the balance.

4 T. Zwart is one of our debtors and his account in our ledger is page DL26. Make the following entries, beginning on 1 April 19. .

Apr 1 Balance owing by Zwart £70.75.

Apr 2 Zwart is supplied with goods valued at £25.25.

Apr 3 Zwart sends in a cheque for £67.95 in full settlement of the amount outstanding on 1 April 19.

Apr 16 Zwart is sent goods £55.40 and is charged for carriage £2.45.

Apr 17 Goods returned to us valued at £9.20.

Apr 23 Zwart orders further goods valued at £29.30.

Apr 30 Balance off the account and bring down the balance, as at 1 May 19. .

5 On 1 May 19. . , S. Davies, a customer, has a debit balance of £165.75 on his ledger account DL34. After opening this account enter the following items:

May 3 We supplied Davies with £54.30 worth of goods.

May 5 Davies buys some more goods invoiced at £80.45 for goods and £6.50 for delivery charges.

May 7 We received Davies' cheque for £157.50 which was in full settlement of his debt owed on 1 May.

May 10 More goods purchased were invoiced to a total of £39.55.

May 12 Davies returned some goods (faulty) for which we sent him a credit note, £17.65.

May 19 We sent Davies goods on account valued at £35.00 and there was an insurance charge of £1.20 on these.

May 31 The account is balanced off, and the balance brought down to 1 June.

3.4 A traditional creditor's account

A creditor is a person to whom we owe money, because he/she has supplied us with goods or services.

Following the basic rule, that you always credit the account of a person who gives goods, services or money, the creditor's account is credited with the value of the goods or services supplied. If the creditor receives money (because we pay for the goods or services) or if he/she receives goods which have been returned for some reason, the account will be debited. Figure 3.3 shows a typical creditor's account.

Now try some of the exercises below. Once again, in each case, read the entry; decide whether you are going to credit the account or debit it; make the entry neatly on the correct side, and balance the account off at the end of the month.

Mohammed Haji, 27, Zanzibar Street, Dodoba, Tanganyika   L84

19. .			£	19. .			£
Mar	5	Bank	4 081.01	Mar	1	Balance b/d	4 185.65
	5	Discount			13	Purchases	4 250.50
		Received	104.64		27	Purchases	3 827.70
	16	Purchases					
		returns	426.32				
	31	Balance c/d	7 651.88				
			£12 263.85				£12 263.85
				19. .		F	£
				Apr	1	Balance b/d	7 651.88

Fig. 3.3 A creditor's account

Notes
1 On 1 March Haji is a creditor for £4185.65.
2 On 5 March we pay him this money (but we deduct discount of £104.64).
3 On 13 March we purchase more goods — credit Haji — the giver of the goods.
4 On 16 March we have returns of £426.32. It is very unlikely we would return anything all the way to Tanganyika. What probably happened was that we complained to Haji by telex about the quality of the goods received. He sent us a document (called a credit note) saying he would make an allowance on the price of £426.32. This reduces our debt to him, so it must be debited on his account — we pretend he has received back some of the goods.
5 On 27 March we purchased more goods — credit the giver — Haji.
6 On 31 March the account is balanced off and the balance brought down.
7 Of course, in a real office the folio columns would have been completed with the cross references showing the source of each entry to the account. These have to be ignored in practice exercises, but you can invent sensible ones if you like — like CB11 for 'Cash Book, page 11' on 5 March — since the Bank Account is actually kept in the Cash Book.
8 Note, that in text books, to save expense, we do not draw all the lines for a specimen ledger page. We expect the student to follow the work without the ruled lines. Although the Z appears in the spare line, to remind you about this way of preventing errors in a real book of accounts, we shall not put the Z's in, in future.

3.5 Exercises: creditors' accounts

1 Mr C. Reid is one of our suppliers. The folio number of his account is CL18. On 1 January 19. . there is a credit balance of £240.30 on his account. Head the account correctly, make the opening balance entry and then the entries listed below:

19. .
Jan 2   C. Reid supplies goods valued at £51.90.
Jan 3   We send Reid a cheque for £240.30.
Jan 4   Reid supplies more goods worth £90.20.
Jan 6   We return goods to Reid (sub-standard quality) £41.20.
Jan 28 We purchase more goods from Reid, £30.75.
Jan 31 The account is balanced off and the balance brought down ready for 1 February.

2 Mr R. Glover is one of our creditors and on 1 February 19. . the credit balance on his account is £735.60. His account is CL19. After opening his account make the following entries:

19. .
Feb 2   We took delivery of goods valued at £483.00.
Feb 4   We pay Glover by cheque the balance we owed on 31 January.
Feb 9   Glover supplies more goods at a value of £247.60.
Feb 10 We return goods to Glover (imperfect) £24.50.
Feb 23 Received another of Glover's deliveries: goods £975.75, Insurance £9.75.
Feb 24 Goods returned to Glover to a value of £30.20.
Feb 28 Balance off this account and bring down the balance.

3 E. Roth, a creditor, has an account on our ledger, page CL21. There is a credit balance of £535.65 on 1 March 19. . . Open this account and after entering the balance continue with the following items:

19. .
Mar 5   We bought goods from Roth worth £450.90 and are charged £20.70 for carriage.
Mar 6   We send Roth a cheque for £508.87 in full settlement of the balance owing on 1 March.
Mar 12 Details on invoice for an order received today were: £290.40 for goods, £15.90 for delivery.
Mar 14 Some of these goods were returned, value £80.50.
Mar 31 The account is balanced and the balance brought down.

4 Mr D. Rankin is a creditor of ours. His account in our ledger is CL24. On 1 April 19. . it showed a credit balance of £890.50. Open this account and continue with the entries below:

19. .
Apr 4   We pay Rankin by cheque the balance owing on 1 April less £17.80 discount allowed.
Apr 11 We purchased goods. Details on invoice were goods £635.40, Carriage £20.45, Insurance £6.35.
Apr 15 A credit note of £30.40 received for goods returned to D. Rankin.
Apr 20 Rankin sent us goods and invoiced us for £30.40.
Apr 26 Took delivery of goods from Rankin, value £100.25.
Apr 30 We balance the account off ready for May, and bring the balance down.

5 Mrs S. Grainger has an account in our ledger the folio of which is CL28. She is one of our suppliers with a credit balance of £83.35 on 1 May 19. . Open her account and enter the following transactions:

19. .
May 9   We buy goods on credit from her, valued at £63.15.
May 16 She supplies us with more goods, invoiced at £46.45.
May 20 Received goods valued at £135.20 and we were charged for delivery £2.35.
May 21 We return some articles (wrong size and colour) worth £10.40.
May 31 We settle the balance of our April purchases and purchases up to 9 May, deducting our usual 5% discount (£146.50 − £7.32) by cheque. The account is then balanced off.

3.6 Computerised (running balance) ledger accounts

Although traditional accounts are the most useful — especially in really understanding double entry — the most likely type of accounts we shall see as ordinary citizens these days are computerised ledger accounts printed out from the memory bank of a computer. These are in 'running balance' style, which simply means that every time we make an entry on the account the computer adds on (or takes away) the new figure to give the running balance on the account. This can be a bit tedious if we have to do it in our books ourselves, but it gives the computer no trouble, since it is working at a speed of several thousand calculations a second.

Let us therefore look at Fig. 3.4 which shows a running balance account. Read the notes below it.

R Miller, 227 High Street, Shoreside, Hampshire					
Date	Type	Ref No	Debits	Credits	Balance
1 Jan 19 ..	—	—	—	—	427.55 Dr
4 Jan 19 ..	Inv	1375	386.50	—	814.05 Dr
11 Jan 19 ..	Inv	1421	727.36	—	1541.41 Dr
27 Jan 19 ..	Chq	217216	—	427.55	1113.86 Dr
31 Jan 19 ..	C/N	172	—	63.86	1050.00 Dr

Inv = Invoice   Chq = Cheque   C/N = Credit note

Fig. 3.4 A running balance account

Notes

1 Since the account has debit balances all the way down R. Miller is almost certainly a debtor and this is a page from the Debtor's Ledger.

2 A debit entry means further goods have been supplied and invoiced to the debtor. An invoice is a document made out when one person sells goods to, or performs services for, another. This increases the running balance.

3 A credit entry reduces the balance payable — either because money was paid to clear some of the debt (£427.55 owing on 1 January) or because some goods were returned and a credit note was issued.

4 The final amount shown in the balance column is the amount payable at 31 January 19. . .

3.7 Exercises: running balance accounts

In the following exercises you are asked to copy out the first line given to you and then carry on with the exercise making the entries in the correct column and working out the running balance on each line.

1 A. Martin, 1227 Robin Hood's Road, Worksop, Nottinghamshire

Date	Type	Ref No	Debits	Credits	Balance
1 Jan 19. .	—	—	—	—	526.34 Dr

The following events then happen:

8 Jan An invoice number 1286 is sent to Martin to a total value of £326.50; for goods he is buying from us.

17 Jan A credit note (Ref No 158) is sent to Martin to a value of £126.34 for goods returned as unsatisfactory (wrong colour).

23 Jan Martin pays by cheque (No 163561) £526.34, the balance outstanding at 1 January.

24 Jan A charge is made by us for £10.26 on a debit note (D/N) No 126 for delivery charges on the goods delivered on 8 January.

31 Jan An invoice number 1299 is sent to Martin for further goods supplied to a total value of £426.50.

2 M. Senior, 2146 Holmfirth Road, Huddersfield

Date	Type	Ref No	Debits	Credits	Balance
1 May 19. .	—	—	—	—	342.37 Dr

The following events then happen:

4 May An invoice number 4136 is sent to Senior to a total value of £524.60 for goods supplied to him.

7 May A further invoice No 4195 is sent to Senior to a value of £386.50 for goods supplied to him at this date.

8 May Our credit controller points out that Senior has exceeded his credit limit of £1000. Senior pays by cheque (No 52461) the balance owing at the start of the month to reduce his debt.

10 May A credit note is sent to Senior to a value of £12.50 for containers returned. No further transactions occur in May.

3 M. Wabenze, 2174 Harbour Street, Zanzibar

Date	Type	Ref No	Debits	Credits	Balance
1 July 19. .	—	—	—	—	495.00 Cr

The following events then happen:

4 July An invoice number 2476 is sent to us by Wabenze to a total value of £575.55 for goods supplied. (Careful: This increases our debt to him — he is a creditor.)

5 July A credit note (No 139) is sent to us by Wabenze to a value of £125.80 for goods returned (poor quality).

18 July We pay Wabenze by cheque (No 51327) £470.25 and he allows us discount of £24.75, thus settling the balance owing on 1 July.

29 July A charge is made by Wabenze for insurance for the goods sent on 4 July. It is charged to us on a debit note (careful) £23.50.

31 July We pay by cheque No 51375 to clear the balance outstanding on the account.

4 R. Carless, 2175 Leigh Road, Preston, Lancashire

Date	Type	Ref No	Debits	Credits	Balance
1 Aug 19. .	—	—	—	—	1365.56 Cr

The following events then happen:

4 Aug An invoice number 1459 is sent to us by Carless to a total value of £826.50.

5 Aug A debit note is sent to us for £16.25 for the carriage of the goods delivered the previous day. It is debit note No 415.

16 Aug We pay Carless by cheque (No 141526) £1365.56 to clear the balance on the account at 1 August.

27 Aug An invoice number 1485 is sent to us by Carless to a total value of £526.35 for goods supplied to us.

29 Aug A credit note (No 514) is sent to us by Carless to a value of £48.50 for goods returned as unsatisfactory.

3.8 Self-assessment questions

1 Where did the word 'ledger' originate?
2 Debit the account if . . . . *continue*.
3 Credit the account if . . . . *continue*.
4 What is the layout of a traditional ledger page?
5 What is a debtor?
6 What is a creditor?
7 What is a running balance account?

3.9 A project: 'Thinking about debtors'

A. Builder writes to your firm, which is called Building Supplies Ltd, and asks if he can become your customer for all sorts of supplies required in his business, which is mainly concerned with doing minor alterations to customers' premises, adding rooms, porches, etc., and also doing repairs and redecorations. What sort of problems might arise with such a customer and what sort of precautions might you take before agreeing to supply him?

Write a short report as if you were your firm's credit controller advising management of the likely problems and what precautions you would take.

3.10 Answers to self-assessment questions

1 It lay on a ledge in the medieval counting houses, under a window where the light was good.
2 . . . . it receives goods, or services, or money.
3 . . . . it gives goods, or services, or money.
4 It is divided into two halves by a central line, to give a debit side (the left-hand side) and a credit side (the right-hand side).
5 A debtor is a person who owes us money because he has received goods, or services from us.
6 A creditor is a person to whom we owe money because he has supplied us with goods or services.
7 It is an account (usually a computerised account) where the computer works out the balance every time an entry is made. Consequently the page is not divided down the middle, but the debit and credit sides lie alongside one another.

4 More about the Ledger: Cash and Bank Accounts

4.1 Real Accounts

In Chapter 3 we learned how to keep simple **personal accounts** — the accounts of debtors and creditors. We must now learn about **real accounts**. These are accounts where we record the real things a business owns — which are called **assets**.

Listing the commonest assets we would have accounts for:
- (a) Land and Buildings
- (b) Plant and Machinery
- (c) Furniture and Fittings
- (d) Motor Vehicles
- (e) Typewriters and Office Machinery
- (f) Stock
- (g) Cash at Bank
- (h) Cash in Hand

Whenever we keep the records of assets we obey the rule:

Always debit the asset account if you spend money to aquire it.

This is because the asset account has *received* the value of the buildings, machinery, etc., so it is just another way of saying 'debit the receiver'.

The simplest asset accounts to consider for the moment are the Cash Account and the Bank Account. These accounts receive money as soon as we start up in business, and everything we buy after that is bought with the money in these two accounts. Later we will see how other asset accounts are opened.

4.2 The Cash Account

The Cash Account is one of the busiest accounts. As soon as the business begins we put money into the Cash Account. This money is part of our capital (the money we contribute to start the business). Naturally, as the Cash Account receives the money we debit the account with this capital. As we spend money from the account we credit it — the Cash Account is giving the money away in exchange for postage, fares, assets of various kinds, wages etc. If debtors pay us money in cash we debit the Cash Account, and if we pay our creditors we credit the Cash Account. Figure 4.1 is a simple Cash Account. The notes below it explain the entries.

Cash Account **L7**

19. .		F	£	19. .		F	£
Jan 1	Capital	L1	250.00	Jan 2	Postage	L9	4.50
2	Sales	L10	56.85	4	Purchases	L11	28.25
3	"	L10	72.65	5	Sundry		
4	"	L10	132.80		Expenses	L12	1.95
5	"	L10	140.52	6	Cleaning		
6	"	L10	236.25		Materials	L13	7.32
7	"	L10	325.80	8	Bank	L8	795.26
8	R Deeping	L15	8.25	8	Travelling		
					Exp.	L14	7.65
				8	Balance	c/d	378.19
			£1223.12				£1223.12
19. .			£				
Jan 9	Balance	b/d	378.19				

Fig. 4.1 A simple Cash Account

Notes:

1 The business started on 1 January and £250 cash was contributed as part of the capital. This is debited in the account.

2 On the 2nd, 3rd, 4th, 5th, 6th and 7th of January we had cash sales to enter on the debit side because the cash was received in the tills.

3 The only other debit entry was cash received from R Deeping, who must have been a debtor who settled his debt in cash.

4 On the credit side are the expenses which we paid in cash. On 2 January — postage; on 6 January — cleaning materials; on 8 January — travelling expenses.

5 The words 'sundry expenses' refer to a general account where many small expenses can be collected together — such things as string, wrapping paper, tea for the employees, etc., might be collected together in this way.

6 Purchases is a rather special account, as we have already seen — because it refers to all the things we buy to sell again. Thus postage stamps are not 'purchases' even though we do purchase them. 'Purchases' has a special meaning in business — and it is the opposite of 'Sales'. It is very important, because later we find our profits by finding the difference between 'purchases' and 'sales'.

7 The only other item on the credit side is the item 'Bank'. This refers to the banking of surplus cash — to reduce the chances of theft. Most firms bank every day, and most supermarkets bank every hour, to give the maximum safety. It is never wise to keep too much 'takings' in the tills, or in a safe in the office.

8 Notice that where possible ditto marks are used to save time.

9 Notice the folio numbers in the column headed 'F'. These are explained in the main text.

4.3 Folio numbers and double entries

We shall see in Chapter 5 that the whole book-keeping system is based upon double-entries, in fact the full name of book-keeping is *Double-Entry Book-keeping*. What does this mean? Simply that there are always two accounts which are affected by any transaction, because for every account that gives goods or services or money there must be another account that receives goods or services or money. You can't have a giver without a receiver, and you can't have a receiver without a giver.

It follows that when you do book-keeping you must learn to think all the time in double entries. There are lots of people who do accounting (particularly people like computer programmers) who have not been trained in book-keeping and don't think in double entries. It causes endless trouble, and sooner or later they have to come back to someone who does think in double entries to sort out the problem.

Consider a few simple double entries:

1 *The purchase of an asset.* Joan Brown buys a pressing machine for her dressmaking business, paying by cheque. Which account receives the machine? Answer — the Machinery Account — debit it. Which account gave the money? Answer — the Bank Account — credit it. There is the double entry; debit Machinery Account, credit Bank Account. If we do a double entry both accounts will be correct. The Machinery Account will give a true account of the machines Joan owns, and the Bank Acount will show how much money she has left at the bank after paying for the new machine.

2 *The purchase of stock for re-sale.* We know that stock for re-sale is called purchases. Man Lee purchases chickens for his take-away business from Free Range Poultry Co. He pays monthly for all supplies (in other words he is given the normal trader's credit). Which account receives the chickens? Answer — Purchases Account — debit it. Which account gives the chickens? The Free Range Poultry Co.'s Account; credit it. So the double entry is: debit Purchases Account, credit Free Range Poultry Co. Account.

Like all accounts these four accounts will have a folio number; that is, a page number in the ledger. If we wish to trace the double entry easily we can write in as we make each entry the place where the double entry can be found. This is what we write in the folio column of the account, as in Fig. 4.1. The double entry for cash contributed as capital will be found in the Capital Account, on page 1 in the Ledger. The Sales Account is page 10 in the ledger and will be credited with all the amounts debited in the Cash Account; £56.85, £72.65, etc.

You should now try some of the simple Cash Account exercises in 4.4 below. Remember that the words you write in the details column should always be the name of a sensible account. Thus 'stamps' would go in the Postage Account, so write Postage in the details column. Takings is the money we take when we sell things and the entry would be made in the Sales Account. You will gradually get used to the sort of words used for account headings.

4.4 Exercises: simple Cash Accounts

1 For the first day of A. J. Smith's business his Cash Account had the following entries. Make these entries in his account.

19. .

Jul 1 Starting contribution of capital £100.00
    Paid for key cutting £3.85

Jul 1 Paid for goods for re-sale £27.25
Paid for rent £25.00
Paid for minor repairs £6.95
Paid for carriage charges £10.00
Paid to M. Layside £14.72
Paid for cleaning materials £4.26
Received for sales for the day £138.25
Balance off the account at the end of the day and bring down the balance ready for 2 July.

2 For the first day of M. Astroseal's business his Cash Account had the following entries. Make these entries in his account.

19..

Aug 1 Starting contribution of capital £85.00
Paid for repairs to door £10.50
Paid for goods for re-sale £32.25
Sales for the day £162.25
Paid for minor office equipment £8.20
Paid carriage charges £3.50
Paid for postage stamps £3.20
Paid for goods for re-sale £17.38
Balance off the account at the end of the day and bring down the balance ready for 2 August.

3 Enter the following items in the Cash Account of Peter Lewis, a builders' merchant. Some suggested names of accounts for the details columns have been written below the exercise to help you.

19..

Jul 1 Began business with capital of £300.00. Paid for account book (stationery) £6.50, office equipment £27.30, stamps £3.20. Takings in cash £85.00.
2 Takings in cash £163.00. Purchases for re-sale £132.50. Paid for cleaning materials £7.25.
3 Paid for stationery £4.25. Paid R. Levinson £22.85. Paid for repairs to front steps £13.50. Cash takings £133.40.
4 Paid for sundry expenses £3.60. Paid to charity £1.50. Paid M. Green £42.50. Cash takings £133.25
5 Paid rent £18.50. Paid to Bank £500. Daily takings £198.20.

(Suggested accounts: Capital Account, Sales Account, Stationery Account, Office Equipment Account, Postage Account, Purchases Account, Sundry Expenses Account, R. Levinson Account, Repairs Accounts, M. Green Account, Rent Account, Bank Account.)

4 Enter the following items in P. Grant's Cash Account. Invent your own details for the details column and balance off the account at the end of the week.

19..

Aug 4 Balance of cash in hand (debit) £37.25. Purchased goods for re-sale £28.50. Paid travelling expenses £3.25. Takings in cash £268.56.
5 Paid R. Molesworth £23.25. Paid for small tools (Equipment A/c) £6.38. Rent £30.00. Railway freight charges £7.95. Takings in cash £325.20.
6 M. Constable paid us £7.95. Paid postage £4.25. Sundry expenses £3.00. Minor repairs £12.60. Takings in cash £182.50.
7 Purchased goods for re-sale for cash £37.50. Postage £3.25. Paid to bank £400. Crockery for kitchen use £5.60. Takings in cash £395.80.

8 Paid for export documents £11.28. Advertising costs £17.30. Paid to Bank £400. Takings in cash £425.60.

9 Bought scales for postal department £8.25. Paid R. London £8.00. M. Taylor paid to us £17.35. Takings in cash £366.29. Paid to Bank £800.

5 Enter the following items in R. Elsegood's Cash Account. Using suitable details for the details column make all the entries and then balance off for the week.

19..

June 4 Balance of cash in hand (debit) £48.25. Purchased goods for resale £30.00. Paid travelling expenses £8.25. Takings in cash £290.00.

5 Paid Express Printers £14.95. Paid for office equipment £7.05. Rent £28.00. Railway freight charges £10.50. Takings in cash £300.50.

6 M. Crozier paid to us £62.50. Paid postage £12.50. Sundry expenses £7.95. Minor repairs £12.05. Takings in cash £328.50.

7 Purchased goods for resale for cash £158.50. Postage £10.00. Cleaning materials £20.00. Takings in cash £150.00.

8 Paid for export documents £12.50. Advertising costs £17.50. Paid to Bank £400. Takings in cash £280.00.

4.5 Simple Bank Accounts

The Bank Account is another of our 'real' accounts. We do actually own the money in the bank, and it is one of the assets of the business. Here we shall just consider it as a separate account in the ledger, but later we shall learn that in real life it is either kept in computerised form or it is kept in a special part of the ledger called the **Three Column Cash Book**.

There are one or two special points to know about Bank Accounts. These are:

1 We keep our account in the usual way; we debit the Bank Account when it receives money and we credit it when it gives away money — debit the receiver, credit the giver.

2 At the same time the bank where we actually bank our money is keeping our account in its books. The two accounts (our one in our books and their one in their books) are keeping the same records, but from opposite points of view. Suppose we work for Robinson & Co. If we receive a cheque we put it on the debit side of our Bank Account. When we go down to the Bank and pay the cheque into the Bank, they say 'Ah, now we must credit this cheque in Robinsons and Co's account because they have given us this money to look after'. When the bank manager says 'You are in credit' he means he owes you money — so really it means you are in debit on your own real account. Try to get this clear in your head — what the bank says is spoken from their point of view. From your point of view it is the opposite.

3 Usually we have to have a cheque in mind when we make an entry in the Bank Account. If we receive a cheque we debit it in the account, and if we write out a cheque to pay someone some money we credit it in the account. There are one or two occasions when we don't need a cheque. These occur when the bank sends us a bank statement. Sometimes on the bank statement we find that the bank has deducted **bank charges** or **standing orders** or **debit transfers**, while at other times it may

have collected money for us by **credit transfers** (bank giros) for dividends, interest received etc. When we discover such an entry on a bank statement we must enter it in our Bank Account on the correct side. These are explained more fully later on — in the chapter on **Bank Reconciliation Statements**.

4 Another point is that we frequently have money banked from the tills — busy supermarkets may bank every hour to reduce risks. Such money has to be debited in the Bank Account — debit the receiver. The word 'cash' is written in the details column. Also sometimes we draw cash from the bank to put into the cash box or till. This has to be credited in the Bank Account, and the word 'cash' is written in the details column.

Let us now look at a simple Bank Account.

Bank Account

19..			£	19..			£
Jan 1	Balance	b/d	1 275.97	Jan 1	R. Barber	L3	127.24
1	R. Salmon	L1	155.29	1	Office	L2	
3	Cash	L9	1 325.60		equipment		174.25
5	Cash	L9	1 475.60	2	M.	L5	
6	Dividends	L15	27.25		Blackburn		55.30
	Rec'd			3	Cambridge-	L6	
					shire C.C.		230.55
				4	M. Brandon	L29	426.25
				5	R. Knight	L8	72.70
				6	Deposit A/c	L13	2 000.00
				6	Balance	c/d	1 173.42
			£4 259.71				£4 259.71
			£				
Jan 8	Balance	b/d	1 173.42				

Fig. 4.2 A simple Bank Account

Notes
1 R. Salmon paid us £155.29 on 1 January.
2 The items of cash on 3rd and 5th were moneys banked from the cash account.
3 The item Dividends Received is one of those items we would find entered on the Bank Statement.
4 Money was paid to creditors on the 1st, 2nd, 3rd, 4th and 5th.
5 The item on 2 January is the purchase of an asset.
6 The item 'Deposit A/c' is the transfer of £2000 to a separate account which will earn interest (interest is not earned on ordinary current accounts).
7 The account is balanced off and brought down to start the new week (assuming that the 7th is a Sunday). Note that it is absolutely wrong to fail to bring the balance down — leaving the impression that the account is clear. A Bank Account — and every other real account — must have a balance on the debit side (although it is possible for a Bank Account to have a credit balance, and be 'overdrawn'). A debit balance shows you how much of the asset you have at the start of the next trading period.

You should now try some of the simple Bank Account exercises in Section 4.6 below.

4.6 Exercises: simple Bank Accounts

 1 P. Hammersley has a Bank Account, the folio number of which is L12. On 17 March 19.. it has a balance in the bank (a debit balance) of £1705.39. Enter this balance and then make the following subsequent entries.
(a) Paid T. Hall £42.50 by cheque.
(b) Paid City Council £195.80 by cheque for rates due.
(c) Eclipse & Co., paid us £45.00 by cheque for work undertaken in February.
(d) Paid H. Ecott £176.50 by cheque for supplies delivered in February.
(e) Cash takings paid into bank £480.75.
(f) Bank notified us that they had deducted £52.50 for interest and charges.
Balance off the account at the end of the day and bring down the balance for 18 March.

 2 B. L. Hamilton has a Bank Account, the folio number of which is L2. On 25 June 19.. it has a balance in the bank of £1385.20. Enter this balance and then make the following subsequent entries. Then balance off the account and bring the balance down ready for 26 June.
(a) Paid P. King £175.50 by cheque.
(b) Paid A. Landlord £120.00 by cheque for rent due.
(c) P. Knebworth paid us £456.00 for work undertaken in May.
(d) Paid M. Kirk £176.50 for supplies delivered in May.
(e) Cash takings paid into bank £680.85.
(f) Bank notified us that they had credited us with £72.50 interest on a gilt edged security. (Be careful — if the bank say they have credited us it is a *debit* in our account.)

 3 J. Rix's Bank Account has a debit balance on Monday 1 December 19.. of £4275.32. Enter the following items and balance off the amount at the end of the week bringing down the balance for the following week. The folio number of this account is L19.

Dec 1 Paid by cheque to B. Howlett £196.85. Paid by cheque to F. Roach £27.72. Banked takings £842.50 from tills.
Dec 2 C. Ridley paid us £242.25 by cheque. Paid City Council by cheque for rates £384.46. Banked takings from tills £796.80.
Dec 3 Paid to M. Roberts £42.95 by cheque. A. H. Ripley paid us £27.98. Banked takings from tills £1427.55.
Dec 4 Paid N. Robertson £416.50 by cheque. Paid T. Logan £27.84 by cheque. F. Robertson paid us £173.25 by cheque. Banked takings from tills £848.28.
Dec 5 Paid M. Childs £42.65 by cheque. Paid Royal Hotel Ltd £129.25 by cheque. Banked takings from tills £1127.26. Bank notified receipt of dividend from United Coal Supplies Ltd £143.63. Transferred to Deposit Account £5000.00.

 4 J. Lindsell's Bank Account has a debit balance on Monday 1 December of £1429.72. Enter the following items and balance off the account at the end of the week. The folio number of this account is L9.

Dec 1 Paid by cheque to T. Hooper £176.95. Paid by cheque to Linton Social Centre £12.95. Banked takings £385.55 from tills.
Dec 2 G. Little paid us £42.95 by cheque. Paid City Council by cheque for rates £835.75. Banked takings from tills £586.95.
Dec 3 Paid to M. Martin £72.49 by cheque. W. Marsh paid us £38.95. Banked takings from tills £427.25.

Dec 4 Paid E. D. Mason £136.24 by cheque. Paid W. S. Noakes £42.50 by cheque. E. Nesbit paid us £327.25 by cheque. Banked takings from tills £425.00.

Dec 5 Drew cash for wages £325.30 by cheque. Paid G. Nice £326.25 by cheque. Banked takings from tills £1084.44.

4.7 Self-assessment questions

1 What is a personal account?

2 What is a real account?

3 What are the rules for making entries on real accounts (asset accounts)?

4 What are the special features of Cash Accounts and Bank Accounts?

5 What is a folio number?

6 Where would a folio number appear, apart from in the top right hand corner of the page for which it is the number?

7 How do we decide what word to write in the details column when we make an entry in an account.

4.8 A project on till receipts

Till receipts can be quite instructive for a book-keeper, and it is well worthwhile making a small collection of them. Take an A4 sheet of paper, fold it in half lengthways, and then in half again to give four long strips. Obtain a till receipt, preferably from four different shops, and glue or clip one in each part of the page. Then explain each mark on the slip. For example the date will be easy to explain. You may find markings like TL for 'total' and AT for 'amount tendered' and CH for 'change'. You may find codings for the class of merchandise — a supervisor in the shop will tell you what they mean if you are in any difficulty.

4.9 Answers to self-assessment questions

1 A personal account is an account for one of the people we deal with, who may be debtors or creditors. They may be sole traders, partnerships or limited companies.

2 A real account is an account where we keep a record of one of the assets of the business — things you can really touch, such as Plant and Machinery, Land and Buildings, Stock, etc.

3 The rules are 'Debit the asset account if you spend money on purchasing the asset. Credit the asset account if you sell it because it is of no further use, or if it declines in value due to 'fair wear and tear' — depreciation.

4 Cash Accounts and Bank Accounts are very busy accounts since we receive and pay money many times a day — whereas we are unlikely to deal with a debtor or creditor more than once or twice a month.

5 A folio number is a page number in a book such as the ledger. Every account has a folio number.

6 Besides the page number in the top corner of a page the folio number may be written in the folio column of a book to show where the other half of a double entry can be found.

7 In the details column we always write a sensible name for the account where the double entry is to be found — so that if we pay cash for stamps we would write 'Postage' because the double entry will be in the Postage Account.

5 More about the Ledger: nominal accounts

5.1 What are nominal accounts?

We have seen that in the old-fashioned counting houses the book-keeper worked in front of the window, with the chief book of account, the ledger, open on a ledger in front of him.

Every page in the ledger is called an account, and has its own folio number, or page number.

Some of these accounts will be personal accounts, like the debtors' and creditors' accounts we kept in Chapter 3. Some of them will be real accounts, like the Cash Account and the Bank Account we learned to keep in Chapter 4. In this chapter we need to learn how to keep the third type of account. These are called nominal accounts, because the money we record on them is not really available, it is there 'in name only', which is what the word 'nominal' means.

Some of these accounts where the money is there 'in name only' will be losses of the business, other will be profits of the business. A few examples will illustrate what we mean by the money on these accounts being there 'in name only.'

5.2 Nominal accounts which are losses of the business

EXAMPLE 5.1

On 15 July 19. . Tom Sawyer pays the air freight of £18.50 on a parcel to Harare. Do the double entry if he pays in cash.

Clearly the Cash Account has given £18.50 to the freight forwarder who is undertaking to dispatch the package. We shall credit the Cash Account. Which account has received £18.50? It can only be an account such as Carriage Paid Account, which is one of the expenses of the business. Although we must debit this account there is nothing to show for it really — this is clearly not a **real account**. It is a **nominal account**, where the money is debited 'in name only'. It has actually been spent on sending the parcel to Harare. The ledger entries will be as shown in Fig. 5.1.

Cash A/c				L1
	19. .			£
	July 15 Carriage Paid	L39	18.50

Carriage Paid A/c			L39
19. .		£	
July 15 Cash	L1	18.50	

Fig. 5.1 A double entry for one of the expenses of the business

Every time we spend money, either in cash or by cheque, on an expense of the business we shall have an entry in the accounts debiting the expense account concerned. It happens with rents, rates, light and heat, advertising, stationery, postage, cleaning expenses, etc., etc. All these accounts are losses of the business. They are very important when it comes to working out the profits at the end of the year. Notice that all loss accounts are debit entries, because the item named at the top of the page (such as Carriage Paid) has received some expenditure upon it, while the Cash Account, or perhaps the Bank Account has given the money for the purpose concerned.

EXAMPLE 5.2

On 24 April 19. . Jean Jardine who runs an exhaust centre makes out a cheque for £325.25 for telephone expenses. What will the double entry be?

Clearly the Bank Account has given the money so we must credit the giver — credit the Bank Account. The account receiving the £325.25 is the Telephone Expenses Account, which is a nominal account. The money is recorded 'in name only', the actual money has gone to British Telecom. It is one of the losses of the business.

Telephone Expenses A/c					L47
19.			£		
Apr 24	Bank	L2	325.25		

Bank A/c					L2
			19. .		£
			Apr 24	Telephone	
				Expenses	L47 325.25

Fig. 5.2 Another 'loss' account

Note
For convenience, when doing classroom exercises, it is usual to abbreviate the word 'account' into A/c. Every account is a proper noun, not a common noun, and should therefore have capital letters. Hence the use of capital T, E and A in Telephone Expenses Account.

5.3 Nominal accounts which are profits of the business

Just as we can have nominal accounts which are losses of the business we can also have nominal accounts which are profits of the business. For example Rent Received Account, Commission Received Account, Interest Received Account, Fees Received Account and Subscriptions Received Account are all profits of the organisations where such accounts appear. Thus a property company would record most of its profits in a Rent Received Account, while a firm of lawyers would record most of its earnings in a Fees Received Account.

Consider Examples 5.3 and 5.4 which are about profits earned.

EXAMPLE 5.3

Migdal and Maloney own a garage business. They agree to display a car on the forecourt for sale. The owner is an Australian student returning home shortly. The agreed commission is 10%. The car fetches £2350 in cash. What will be the double entry if the sale is made on 11 July 19. .? The actual money received is kept separate from other garage receipts and only the commission is to be entered in the books.

Ten per cent of £2350 is £235.00. Therefore Cash Account receives £235.00. What account is giving this money to the cash box? It must be the Commission Received Account, which has given the service to the Australian student, and earned £235.00. The double entry is shown in Fig. 5.3.

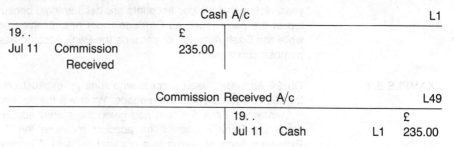

Cash A/c   L1

19. .		£		
Jul 11	Commission	235.00		
	Received			

Commission Received A/c   L49

			19. .		£
			Jul 11	Cash	L1 235.00

Fig. 5.3 A nominal account which is a profit of the business

EXAMPLE 5.4

Short-term Tenancies Ltd let rooms to students. On 1 June Peter Mead pays rent £80.00 for the month by cheque. Show the double entry for this in the books of Short-term Tenancies Ltd.

Since the Bank Account will receive the £80.00 we must debit the £80.00 in the Bank Account. Which account shall we credit? It will be Rent Received Account, and we regard it as the account which gave the service to the student. This account is a nominal account where the money is recorded in name only (the actual money is at the bank). It will collect all the money earned for renting properties, and at the end of the year will be used to calculate the profits of the business.

Bank A/c   L2

19. .		£		
June 1	Rent Received L61	80.00		

Rent Received A/c   L61

			19. .		£
			June 1	Bank	L2 80.00

Fig. 5.4 Another 'profit' account

5.4 Exercises on nominal accounts

1 Shear Magic is a hairdressing salon in a university town. The accountant pays the half yearly rate of £880 by cheque on 1 April 19. . . Show the double entry.

2 Anglia Micros PLC is a computer company whose chief accountant receives a cheque for £385.00 commission on the sale of second-hand computers for a liquidator who is handling the affairs of a bankrupt company. Show the double entry for this profit. The cheque arrives on 30 May 19. . .

3 'Herb of Life' is a health food store in a seaside town. The accountant pays the following bills on 1 June 19. . by cheque:
(a) telephone expenses £325.50 (b) advertising £86.50 (c) van repairs £66.25. Show the double entries in the accounts in each case.

4 Gusher Extinguishers PLC specialises in putting out burning oil wells. On 4 May 19. . their accountant receives a cheque for £325 000.00% for a successful action in Saudi Arabia. This is to go in Fees Received Account. He also writes a cheque for £84 000.00 concerned with helicopter hire during the action. Show the double entries for both these matters. All aviation expenses are entered in Aviation Expenses Account.

5.5 Recapitulation: the three classes of account

We have now studied the three main types of account; personal accounts, nominal accounts and real accounts.

We can summarise as follows.

Personal Accounts

These are the accounts of individuals, firms and companies with whom we deal. They will all be either debtors, or creditors, but there are a few special cases. In particular the **Capital Account** is the personal account of the proprietor and shows how much capital has been given to the business. It has a credit balance, because the proprietor is a creditor of the business — the business owes back to the proprietor everything that has been invested in it. A rather similar account — the **Drawings Account** — shows how much the owner has drawn out of the profits to support his/her family. It always has a debit balance because the proprietor has received the profit for his/her personal use. These accounts are explained more fully later.

Nominal Accounts

These are the accounts of the real things the business owns, such as it has actually either been spent (Loss Accounts such as Light and Heat Account, etc.) or it may have been gained (Profit Accounts such as Rent Received Account). The actual money — is kept either in the cash box or in a Bank Account, and is not a nominal item but a real thing. The nominal record of expenses and profits made in these nominal accounts is used at the end of the year to work out the profits of the business.

Real Accounts

These are the accounts of the real things the business owns, such as Furniture and Fittings Account, Motor Vehicles Account, etc. These are the **assets** of the business, purchased for use in the business. A real account always has a debit balance.

These are the three classes of accounts, personal accounts, nominal accounts and real accounts. No matter how large a firm is, all the accounts come into one of these classes. One public company has about 8 million accounts and sends out milions of accounts each month, yet all these accounts come into one of the three classes.

5.6 Self-assessment questions

1 Name five nominal accounts which are losses.
2 Name three nominal accounts which are profits.
3 What are the three types of accounts?
4 Which type of account is Land and Buildings Account?
5 Which type of account is R. Thompkin's Account?
6 If R. Thompkins account has a balance on the right hand side is he a debtor or a creditor?
7 You are shown an account in a ledger which is called the Discount Received Account. Would you expect the account to have entries on the left hand side or the right hand side?

5.7 A project on profits and losses of a business

In your spare time go and stand in front of the following businesses (if you can find them fairly convenient to your home). Then in *each* case draw up a list of five expenses you would expect to find given an account in the books of the business. Also a list of three profits you would expect to find in the accounts of the business.

Of course it would be possible to do this very easily by writing down such things as Postage Account (everyone sends letters) or Sales Account (many people sell things at a profit). The object of the exercise is not just to come up with the names of a few accounts, it is to think hard about the business concerned. For example most Insurance Brokers would have an account 'Motor Cycle Accident Claims Account', but not many other businesses would have this sort of expense to worry about.

The types of business suggested are:
(a) a newsagent, confectioner and tobacconist
(b) an insurance broker
(c) a doctor, dentist or similar professional in the health field
(d) a garage
(e) a bank
(f) any business which particularly interests you in your own locality. Present your project in the form of a double A4 folder with the front cover reading 'Nominal Accounts' and giving your name and class, or group. Inside give the names of each business, the type of business it is and your list of losses and profits.

5.8 Answers to self-assessment questions

1 There could be many of them but let us say Rent Account, Rates Account, Repairs and Redecorations Account, Petrol and Oil Account, Stationery Account.
2 There could be many but let us say Sales Account, Fees Received Account and Commission Received Account.
3 Personal, nominal and real accounts.
4 Land and Buildings Account is a real account — you can really touch the land and buildings.
5 R. Thompkin's Account would be a Personal Account.

6 If R. Thompkins' Account has a balance on the right hand side he must be a creditor, because that is the credit side of the account. We owe him money.
7 Discount Received is one of the profits of a business and profits are always credited, so I would expect the entries to be on the right hand side of the account.

6 Some concepts of accounting

6.1 What is a concept of accounting?

A concept is an idea. Every science or art is based upon a set of concepts or ideas. Some of these basic concepts go back into the dawn of history, like the legal concept of sealing documents with a red wax seal which was difficult to imitate, to prove their authenticity. Thousands of seals have been found in the ruins of ancient cities like Knossos in Crete, or Ur in Ancient Babylon. Accounting concepts do not perhaps go back as far as that, but most of them were well understood in the Middle Ages, and the first real book-keeping book appeared in 1494. It was written by an Italian Mathematician called Pacioli, and was called Summa, which means 'amounts' of money.

We can't learn all the concepts of accounting at this stage because we don't know yet enough about book-keeping, but it is helpful to make a start. Let us therefore begin with three concepts:

1 the concept of business entity
2 the concept of stewardship
3 the concept of duality.

6.2 The concept of business entity

In accounting we must always keep the concept of business entity in mind. The business is a separate thing (a separate entity), quite distinct from the *owner* of the business. When we keep accounts for John Smith's business we look on it as a totally separate organisation from John Smith himself. He is just the owner of the business, and the person entitled to receive any profits the business makes — or of course he has to suffer the losses if the business makes a loss.

Similarly if Patricia Brown and Maira Malik set up in business as partners in a fashion house the partnership business is regarded as a separate entity from either of the partners. We would be keeping the books of the partnership, not of either Patricia Brown or Maira Malik. If a business is a limited company, trading under a name which has been registered with the Registrar of Companies — for example Monsoon Fabrics Ltd — then the book-keeper will be keeping the books of the company and not the books of the shareholders. Some companies have millions of shareholders who have contributed a 'share' of the capital but do not know anything else about the business at all.

Capital Accounts

Of course the owner, or owners, must come into the picture somewhere. The owner is the person who provides the capital of the business. Consider Example 6.1.

EXAMPLE 6.1

Janet Campbell sets up in business on 1 April 19. . marketing Scottish knitwear. She starts with capital of £500 from her personal savings which she puts into the business bank account. What will be the double entry for this opening transaction?

As with all other transactions we have a receiver and a giver. The Bank Account is receiving the money so we debit the Bank Account. Janet Campbell is contributing the capital, so she is the giver and we must credit the giver. It is usual to call this account the Capital Account, but just to show who is the capitalist (i.e. the owner who has provided the capital) we write the owner's name in the heading of the Account too. The entries would therefore be as shown in Fig. 6.1. Note that the accounts have been done in a simple form called T accounts.

Bank A/c   L1

19. .			£	
Apr 1	Capital	L2	500.00	

Capital A/c (Janet Campbell)   L2

			19. .			£
			Apr 1	Bank	L1	500.00

Fig. 6.1 Opening the accounts of a new business

Notes
1 Notice that, as always when making book-keeping entries, we must have a proper double entry, with a debit entry exactly balancing a credit entry.
2 Notice that in the details column we write the name of the account where the other half of the double entry can be found and we also put the folio number in the folio column.
3 Remember — the concept of business entity holds that we always keep the accounts of the business, not the accounts of the owner of the business, although she must have a mention — in the Capital Account.

Taking a slightly more difficult case, consider Example 6.2.

EXAMPLE 6.2

Paul Lee-Fong sets up in business on 1 July 19. . as an orchid grower and florist with the following assets.

	£
Cash in hand	125
Cash at bank	1625
Motor-car (½ only of £4700)	2350
Shop fittings	455
Greenhouses	2000
Stock	3230
Total assets	£9785

He has a loan from the bank outstanding for £3000. Work out the capital contributed by Paul Lee-Fong and do the opening entries in his accounts.

From the example we can see that the total value of the assets introduced is £9785, but £3000 of this has been borrowed from the bank. Therefore the value contributed by Lee-Fong is £6785. Here we can see a very important point about capital. Capital is not necessarily money, because we can contribute other things besides money to the business. Lee-Fong has contributed fittings, greenhouses, stock and half the value of a motor car. This sounds strange, but it is a way the Inland Revenue Department

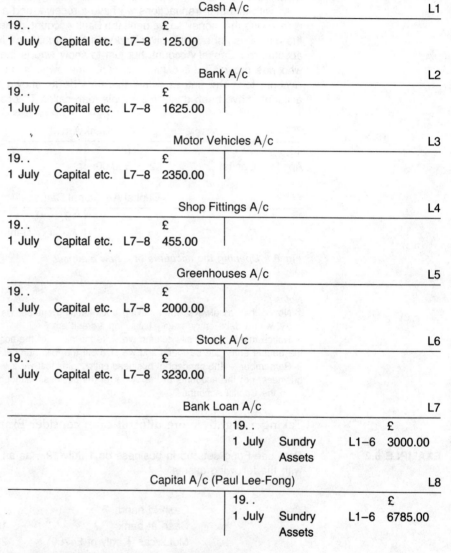

Cash A/c · L1

19..			£	
1 July	Capital etc.	L7–8	125.00	

Bank A/c · L2

19..			£	
1 July	Capital etc.	L7–8	1625.00	

Motor Vehicles A/c · L3

19..			£	
1 July	Capital etc.	L7–8	2350.00	

Shop Fittings A/c · L4

19..			£	
1 July	Capital etc.	L7–8	455.00	

Greenhouses A/c · L5

19..			£	
1 July	Capital etc.	L7–8	2000.00	

Stock A/c · L6

19..			£	
1 July	Capital etc.	L7–8	3230.00	

Bank Loan A/c · L7

				19..			£
				1 July	Sundry Assets	L1–6	3000.00

Capital A/c (Paul Lee-Fong) · · · · · · · · · · · · · · · · L8

				19..			£
				1 July	Sundry Assets	L1–6	6785.00

Fig. 6.2 Opening accounts for a number of items

Notes

1 If you check carefully you will find that the total of the accounts which have been debited exactly balances the total of the accounts which have been credited, so that we do have a perfect double entry.

2 The accounts of the business are now open and other transactions such as buying and selling can begin.

treats vehicles which are partly used for business and partly for domestic purposes. We are keeping the books of the business, so only half the value of the car is allowed to appear on the Motor Vehicles Account.

When we take these items onto the books of the business all the accounts that are receiving value (Cash Account, Bank Account, Motor Vehicles Account, Shop Fittings Account, Greenhouses Account and Stock Account) have to be debited. These items are the assets of the business.

There are two accounts which are giving value. The Bank has loaned us £3000 which is credited in Bank Loan Account and the proprietor's Capital Account has to be credited with £6785. The result is shown in Fig. 6.2.

6.3 Exercises on the contribution of capital by the proprietor

These exercises should preferably be done on proper ledger paper, but if necessary you may use a sheet of plain paper and do T accounts similar to Figs 6.1 and 6.2.

1 Clive Ralston sets up in business as a hairdresser on 1 January 19. . with capital of £1000 which he places in a bank account opened for the purpose. Show the ledger entries for the start of the business.

2 Edward Shah sets up in business as an exhaust replacement mechanic. He has capital of cash, £500, and money at the bank £4500. Show the ledger entries for the start of the business.

3 Margaret Green is a computer programmer who decides to set up as a freelance programmer. She brings into the business cash £155, bank moneys £3825, computer equipment already in her possession of £1750 and furniture and fittings £360. Show the ledger accounts to open the business.

4 Abdul Muhammadu decides to set up as a picture restorer in the fine art field. He contributes furniture £850, a van £1250, art materials and small tools £360 and cash at the bank £621.65. Open the ledger accounts for his business.

6.4 The concept of stewardship

A steward is a person who looks after something for someone else. For example most golf clubs have a steward who is responsible for the club premises, ensures that the lounges and bars are clean and well supplied, deals with the admission of new members, etc. Clearly the book-keeper or accountant of any organisation is in this sort of responsible position and must take care of the money, cheque books, etc. on a day-to-day basis. Every now and again some sort of reckoning or report must be drawn up and presented by the steward to those entitled to receive it. In the case of a sole trader, or partnership, it will be the owner or partners to whom the report will be made. In the case of a limited company the report will be made to the shareholders at a meeting called the

Annual General Meeting (AGM). This will also be the case for a club or society like the golf club mentioned above, but the Annual General Meeting will be one where the members of the club can consider the book-keeping records presented by the treasurer.

The accounts prepared in accordance with the concept of stewardship are called the Final Accounts of the business. They go under a variety of names, but for trading businesses we have already seen that they are called the Trading Account and the Profit and Loss Account; a Balance Sheet as at the end of the trading period is also prepared.

For clubs and societies we prepare a Receipts and Payments Account, followed by an Income and Expenditure Account and a Balance Sheet.

For professional firms, such as lawyers, architects, medical and dental practices, etc. we prepare a Revenue Account which shows the fees received and the expenses incurred, and a Balance Sheet.

Much of this book is about the preparation of these final accounts, which allow us to report to the owners of the business in accordance with the concept of stewardship. We shall meet all of the accounts named as we continue our studies.

6.5 The concept of duality

This basic concept of accounting is one we have already considered and become familiar with. This is the idea that there is a dual nature to every transaction. Whatever business activity occurs there must be one account that is debited and another account that is credited. Sometimes a perfect double entry requires more than two accounts, but those accounts that are to be debited must be debited altogether with the same amount as those accounts that are to be credited. Consider Example 6.3.

EXAMPLE 6.3

On 9 October 19. . Farmer Giles goes to a sale at another farm, the owner of which is retiring. He takes £600 in notes as he believes there may be items that will be useful to him. In fact he buys farm machinery for £450, pigs for £120, cattle for £730 and fertiliser for £320. The auctioneer agrees to take a cheque for the balance owing after the £600 has been paid in cash.

(a) What would be the value of the cheque?

(b) What would be the entries in the various accounts?

Calculations:

Items purchased	£
Farm machinery	450
Pigs	120
Cattle	730
Fertiliser	320
	1620
Less Cash paid	600
Balance by cheque	£1020

Four accounts have received value; debit these accounts.

Two accounts, Cash Account and Bank Account have given value. Credit these accounts.

In the accounts shown below the entries have been made, but note that some imaginery balances have been invented to show that the accounts are already open and running. It would be unrealistic to pretend that the accounts were clear, because this is not the first day of Farmer Giles' business.

Farm Machinery A/c   **L29**

19..			£
1 Oct	Balance	b/d	8954.00
9	Cash and Bank	L1 & 2	450.00

Pigs A/c   **L31**

19..			£
1 Oct	Balance	b/d	725.60
9	Cash and Bank	L1 & 2	120.00

Cattle A/c   **L34**

19..			£
1 Oct	Balance	b/d	5872.50
9	Cash and Bank	L1 & 2	730.00

Fertiliser A/c   **L48**

19..			£
1 Oct	Balance	b/d	847.50
9	Cash and Bank	L1 & 2	320.00

Cash A/c   **L1**

19..			£	19..			£
9 Oct	Balance	b/d	632.00	9 Oct	Machinery etc.	L29 etc.	600.00

Bank A/c   **L2**

19..			£	19..			£
9 Oct	Balance	b/d	4257.55	9 Oct	Machinery etc.	L29 etc.	1020.00

Fig. 6.3 Double entries for bids at an auction

Notes
1 Notice that all the accounts dealt with were asset accounts — accounts for things that the farmer owns. Asset Accounts always have debit balances, because always at some time in the past they have received value.
2 Those accounts which have to be debited because the account has received value again today are debited to increase the value of the asset on the books.
3 By contrast the Cash Account and Bank Account have given value (the farmer has less cash in hand, and less money in the bank) so these accounts must be credited.
4 A perfect double entry for today's entries has been made, but of course the balances we invented are not a perfect balance — to get a perfect balance on them we should need to show every account in Farmer Giles' books.

6.6 Questions on double entry

1 Tom Brown buys goods for re-sale for his business on 17 July 19. . valued at £500. He pays by cheque. What would be the double entry?

2 Mary Morgan sells a motor vehicle on 23 October 19. . which is surplus to requirements. The price is £580 cash. What will be the double entry if that is the value of the motor on her books at the time?

3 On 1 May 19. . Kenneth Ogawa pays £27.50 cash for freight charges on packages sent to his home in Nigeria. What will be the double entry?

4 Peter Ogbourn buys a roadside cafe business for £3500 on 27 May 19. . . He pays by cheque and receives a van valued at £2300, stocks of food £125, stocks of cigarettes £495 and small equipment £580. What will be the entries in the accounts.

5 Vishnu Patel is a dentist. He buys a machine for his surgery on 1 May 19. . valued at £3850. It is supplied on credit by Dental Hygiene Ltd. Show the ledger entries
(a) on purchasing the machine
(b) on 27 May after its trial period when he pays for it by cheque.

6.7 Self-assessment questions

1 What is a concept of accounting?
2 Give three examples.
3 Explain the concept of business entity.
4 Alison Bradley is a fashion designer who sets up in business on her own account selling 'prêt à porter' fashions. What will her account in the books of the business be called?
5 Explain the concept of stewardship.
6 What sort of accounts does the 'steward' prepare for an ordinary trading business?
7 What is the concept of duality?

6.8 A project on business organisation

Figure 6.4 is an organisation chart of a small business showing the personnel and the types of activity they perform. Drawing on any experience you have of part-time or full-time employment draw up a similar chart for any firm or company you are familiar with, and attempt an answer to the questions listed below the diagram. Your presentation should take the form of a double page A4 folder with the organisation chart on the front of the folder and a short description of the personnel, the jobs each person does, the sources of supply and the types of people who form the customers of the firm or company.

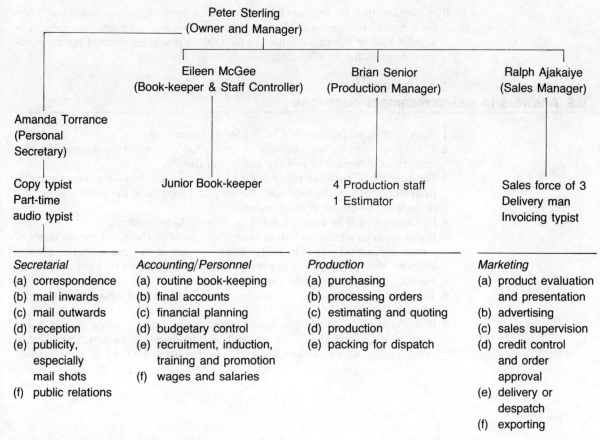

Secretarial
(a) correspondence
(b) mail inwards
(c) mail outwards
(d) reception
(e) publicity,
    especially
    mail shots
(f) public relations

Accounting/Personnel
(a) routine book-keeping
(b) final accounts
(c) financial planning
(d) budgetary control
(e) recruitment, induction,
    training and promotion
(f) wages and salaries

Production
(a) purchasing
(b) processing orders
(c) estimating and quoting
(d) production
(e) packing for dispatch

Marketing
(a) product evaluation
    and presentation
(b) advertising
(c) sales supervision
(d) credit control
    and order
    approval
(e) delivery or
    despatch
(f) exporting

Fig. 6.4 An organisation chart

Questions to be answered in the project

1 Is the organisation a sole trader (one man/woman business) a partnership or a limited company?
2 Is it in any sense a part of a larger organisation, for example a branch or agency of a bigger company?
3 If so what is the proper legal name of that larger organisation?
4 How many people are employed and are they full-time or part-time?
5 What separate functions (production, sales, accounting, etc.) can you distinguish?
6 Where does real authority lie within the organisation you are studying?
7 You might like to estimate the capital tied up in the business, by guessing
   (a) the value of the premises
   (b) the value of the stock
   (c) the value of the machinery, tools and equipment in use
   (d) the value of any motor vehicles. Don't enquire too closely about actual values or the owner/s may think you are some sort of commercial spy. If questioned explain that you require information for educational purposes only.

8 In commenting on the functions or work performed by any individual keep your remarks impersonal. Remember even the most unimportant person is usually vital to the organisation — the biggest machines depend on the operation of even the smallest cog.

6.9 Answers to self-assessment questions

1 A concept of accounting is a basic idea in accounting.

2 The three examples we have met so far are the concept of business entity, the concept of stewardship and the concept of duality.

3 The concept of business entity is the idea that the business is a separate entity from the owner of the business. We keep the records of the business, not the records of the owner of the business.

4 Her account will be called 'Capital Account (Alison Bradley).'

5 It is a concept which holds that everyone who is in charge of the accounts of a business should report back at regular intervals to the true owner or owners to show how the business is progressing and to establish that the accounting records have been properly kept.

6 The accountant draws up a Trading Account, Profit and Loss Account and a Balance Sheet.

7 It is the concept of 'double entry' book-keeping, which holds that in book-keeping there will always be two entries for every transaction, one account being debited as it receives value and the other being credited as it gives value.

7 Book-keeping to the Trial Balance — 1 Direct entries to the accounts

7.1 What is a Trial Balance?

We have already learned that book-keeping records are kept on the principle known as the double-entry system. This means that every entry that is made affects two accounts, debiting one account (which is receiving value) and crediting another account (which is giving value).

If we carry out entries for all the various transactions that take place, for hundreds or perhaps thousands of transactions, we shall have to debit and credit a great array of accounts, and it would be quite understandable if we made a mistake here and there. We must have a method of checking whether we have made a mistake, and the method is known as a Trial Balance. What we do is to take out a list of all the balances on the various accounts. Some of them will have debit balances, and some of them will have credit balances, but if we have done our double entries properly we should find that the total of the debit balances and the total of the credit balances come to the same figure. We will look at a simple example first in Fig. 7.1.

Capital A/c			L1
19..	£	19..	£
		Jan 1 Sundry	
		Assets	2500.00

Cash A/c			L2
19..	£	19..	£
Jan 1 Capital	200.00	Jan 1 Telephone	40.00

Bank A/c			L3
19..	£	19..	£
Jan 1 Capital	1300.00	Jan 2 Rent	160.00
		Jan 3 Light and	
		Heat	46.00

Furniture and Fittings A/c			L4
19..	£	19..	£
Jan 1 Capital	1000.00		

Rent A/c			L
19..	£	19..	£
Jan 2 Bank	160.00		

Light and Heat A/c			L
19..	£	19..	£
Jan 3	46.00		

P. Smith A/c			L
19..	£	19..	£
Jan 4 Sales	365.00		

T. Jones A/c			L
19..	£	19..	£
		Jan 4 Purchases	850.00

Purchases A/c			L
19..	£	19..	
Jan 4 T. Jones	850.00		

Sales A/c			L
19..	£	19..	£
		Jan 4 P. Smith	365.00

Fig. 7.1 Some typical ledger entries

Notes
1 We started on 1 January with capital of £2500.00, made up of cash £200.00, money in the bank £1300.00 and Furniture and Fittings of £1000.00. These entries make a perfect double entry (spread across four accounts L1–L4). Check that there are £2500.00 debits and £2500.00 credits.
2 We then spend some cash getting the telephone installed, and paid by cheque for Rent and Light and Heat. Check the double entries for these three items. Is anything wrong? If you think there is wait a minute and we'll sort it out.
3 On 4 January we purchased some goods on credit from T. Jones and we sold some goods on credit to P. Smith. Check these double entries. Now return to the main text, at the sub-heading 'Have we made any mistakes?'

Have we made any mistakes? One of the double entries in Fig. 7.1 is not complete. In a real business with hundreds of accounts it is very easy to make a slip and to do some part of a double entry incorrectly. To find out whether our book-keeping is correct we take out a Trial Balance of the books. This means that we draw up a list of all the accounts, and the balances on them at the time the Trial Balance is taken out, and if we have done our book-keeping correctly the totals will agree. If they don't agree — if the Trial Balance does not balance — we have made a mistake and must find it. This Trial Balance has been drawn up in Fig. 7.2, and explained alongside the figures and in the notes below.

Trial Balance as at 4 January 19. .

	Dr £	Cr £	*Notes*
Capital A/c		2500.00	A credit balance
Cash A/c	160.00		After tidying up — a debit balance
Bank A/c	1094.00		After tidying up — a debit balance
Furniture and Fittings A/c	1000.00		A debit balance
Rent A/c	160.00		A debit balance
Light and Heat A/c	46.00		A debit balance
P. Smith A/c	365.00		Smith is a debtor
T. Jones A/c		850.00	Jones is a creditor
Purchases A/c	850.00		A debit balance
Sales A/c		365.00	A credit balance
	£3675.00	3715.00	

Fig. 7.2 A Trial Balance that does not balance

Notes
1 Notice that the Trial Balance always states in the heading the date when it was taken out. The words 'as at' always introduce this date.
2 It is clear we have made a mistake on our double entries, for the Trial Balance does not balance. What can be wrong?
3 Taking one side from the other we find that there is £40.00 difference. Is there an item of £40.00 on the books anywhere? Yes, there is! There is £40.00 paid out for the telephone installation, but we have not done a proper double entry for this. We need an entry on the debit side of the Telephone Account, which has received £40.00 of value.
4 If we open a telephone account and put £40 on the debit side, our Trial Balance will then agree, as shown in Fig. 7.3.

Trial Balance as at 4 January 19. .

	Dr £	Cr £
Capital A/c		2500.00
Cash A/c	160.00	
Bank A/c	1094.00	
Furniture and Fittings	1000.00	
Rent A/c	160.00	
Light and Heat A/c	46.00	
P. Smith A/c	365.00	
T. Jones A/c		850.00
Purchases A/c	850.00	
Sales A/c		365.00
Telephone A/c	40.00	
	£3715.00	3715.00

Fig. 7.3 A Trial Balance that does agree

7.2 What does a Trial Balance actually prove?

A Trial Balance is a fairly good test of whether we are doing our double entries properly. If we are, and the Trial Balance agrees, we can say that *prima facie* (at a first glance) our double entry book-keeping is correct. We can't be absolutely sure, because there are some errors that don't show up on a Trial Balance. For example if we leave out a transaction altogether — both debit and credit entries — then the books will balance but there will still be an error (in fact two errors) on the books. These kinds of errors are explained later.

7.3 What to do if a Trial Balance does not agree

If a Trial Balance does not agree, like the one in Fig. 7.2 opposite, there is a sequence of events we can follow to investigate what has gone wrong. The procedure is as follows:

1 Check the addition of the two sides. It may just be an error in totalling the two sides.

2 Take the smaller side from the larger side, to find the difference between the two sides. In Fig. 7.2 the amount was £40. If we look through for an amount during the month of £40, or whatever the figure is, we may find we have left out one half of the double entry.

3 If this is no help we can divide the difference by two — which in this case comes to £20. Is there an item of £20 on the Trial Balance or

anywhere in the books. If so have we put it on the wrong side? You see, £20 left out of the debit side and put in on the credit side by mistake makes the debit side £20 too small and the credit side £20 too large, which makes the £40 difference between the sides. If we discover such an error and correct it the two sides will balance.

4 If this does not find the error we must check all the entries in the month to see if we have made a mistake anywhere. It is quite common to change two figures over — for example writing £94 for £49. Look carefully for this kind of error. An interesting clue here is that if the difference on the books divides by 9 it might be this kind of error.

We must now do an exercise in which we prepare the accounts of a business for one month, and then take out a Trial Balance to check the accuracy of our work. It is usual to do a Trial Balance monthly, although it could be done more frequently, but as balancing off the hundreds of accounts in a business is a great deal of work we can't do it too frequently. On the other hand, if we don't do at least a monthly check-up we have an awful lot of work to do to find the mistakes if we *have* made any.

7.4 A double-entry exercise to the Trial Balance

We must now try a simple double-entry exercise to the Trial Balance level. This is the first level of Accountancy knowledge and many people never go beyond this stage. Jobs are often advertised as follows: 'Book-keeper to the Trial Balance required', etc., etc., and with the modern systems of accountancy in use today — which are explained later in this book — it would be possible to take employment even if you had only studied book-keeping as far as the end of this chapter. Thinking in double entries is halfway to a job.

In this exercise we take each part of the activities of a business as they occur, say 'What would I do for the double entry?' and make it directly into the ledger accounts concerned. When we have done a complete month's entries we take out a Trial Balance to ensure that we have done all the entries correctly. Here is the exercise, and each transaction has an explanation in brackets after it, telling you what the double entry is. Follow each double entry carefully in the specimen ledger accounts, shown in Fig. 7.4. Notice that in each account the word used tells you which account to look in for the other half of the double entry. The folio numbers would also show these cross references, but because of lack of space they have been left out in the illustration. Notice also that wherever possible ditto marks are used in an account to save time.

EXAMPLE

Tom and Eileen Spriggs set up in business on 1 April 19. . as 'Beautiful Gardens'. They bring in as capital the following items: cash £50.00, cash at bank £950.00, a small van valued at £2300.00, tools and equipment £580.00, office equipment £320.00 and stock purchased during March £265.00. (These matters require an opening entry as shown in Section 7.1 above. The total capital contributed comes to £4465.00. Check these entries in Fig. 7.4 now.)

Transactions then took place as shown below:

April 4 Purchased roller mower £86.00 by cheque (Purchase of an asset. Debit Tools and Equipment A/c; credit Bank A/c).

      5 Purchased turf for re-sale for cash £27.50. (This is a purchase of business stock. Debit Purchases A/c; credit Cash A/c.)

      6 Takings for week £360.52 in cash. We have also done some landscaping work for £185.00 for Mrs E. Jones, who owes us for this work. (The first part is a routine receipt; debit Cash A/c and credit Sales A/c. The second part will earn us fees for work done and Mrs Jones is a debtor. Debit Mrs E. Jones A/c and credit Fees Receivable A/c.)

      9 Purchased plants and shrubs for re-sale £236.50, paying by cheque. (A routine expense — debit Purchases A/c and credit Bank A/c.)

   11 Paid postage £1.85 cash, telephone expenses £23.50 by cheque and motor van expenses £15.65 in cash. (Three routine expenses. In each case debit the expense account concerned and credit either Cash A/c or Bank A/c as appropriate.)

April 13 Takings for week £425.62 in cash. Mrs Jones pays the amount owing by cheque. (These are both routine receipts. Debit Cash A/c and credit Sales A/c; debit Bank A/c and credit Mrs Jones as she is giving us the money.)

   17 Purchase plants for re-sale, by cheque £328.56. (Debit Purchases A/c, credit Bank A/c.)

   19 Paid Rent for quarter £390.00 by cheque. (A routine expense, credit the Bank A/c which is giving the money and debit Rent A/c.) Paid £750.00 cash into bank. (Debit Bank A/c as it receives the money and credit Cash A/c as it gives it.)

   20 Sales for week in cash £1272.50. We also did work for R. Marshall to the value of £560.50, on the promise that he would pay on 30 April. (These two entries are similar to the entries on 6 April. Debit Cash A/c and credit Sales A/c for the first entry. Debit R. Marshall — the debtor — and credit Fees Receivable A/c for the second entry.)

   24 Paid salaries £636.50 by cheque. (Credit Bank A/c and debit Salaries A/c.) Paid cash into bank £1000.00. (Credit Cash A/c as it gives the money; debit Bank A/c as it receives the money.)

   27 Paid advertising expenses by cheque £36.50. (Credit Bank A/c as cheque goes out; debit the expense in Advertising Expenses A/c.)

   30 Cash sales for week £1380.24. Paid cash into bank £800.00. (Debit Cash A/c £1380.24 and credit Sales A/c. For the payment of cash into bank, credit Cash A/c as it gives the money and debit Bank A/c as it receives the money.) Drew cash for personal use, £600.00 from till. (This is called 'drawings' — the proprietor draws out money from the business for his/her personal use. It is really part of the profits he/she hopes to have made in the month. Credit Cash A/c as it gives the money and debit Drawings A/c to show that the proprietor has received £600.00 of the profits.

If you have followed all these entries in the specimen ledger accounts, it is now time to do the Trial Balance. We must of course balance off such accounts as need balancing off (because they have entries on both sides and it is impossible to see at a glance what the outstanding balance is on the account; this is true of Cash Account, Bank Account and Mrs E. Jones Account). We need not balance off accounts which have entries on only one side, but if there is more than one entry we would add them up and put the total in feintly in pencil, so that we can extract the figure to the

Cash A/c					L1
19..		£	19..		£
Apr 1	Capital	50.00	Apr 5	Purchases	27.50
6	Sales	360.52	11	Postage	1.85
13	Sales	425.62	11	Motor Van	
20	Sales	1272.50		Expenses	15.65
30	Sales	1380.24	19	Bank	750.00
			24	Bank	1000.00
			30	Bank	800.00
			30	Drawings	600.00

Bank A/c					L2
19..		£	19..		£
Apr 1	Capital	950.00	Apr 4	Tools etc	86.00
13	Mrs E	185.00	9	Purchases	236.50
	Jones				
19	Cash	750.00	11	Telephone	23.50
24	Cash	1000.00	17	Purchases	328.56
30	Cash	800.00	19	Rent	390.00
			24	Salaries	636.50
			27	Advertising	
				expenses	36.50

Motor Vehicles A/c			L3
19..		£	
Apr 1	Capital	2300.00	

Tools and Equipment A/c			L4
19..		£	
Apr 1	Capital	580.00	
4	Bank	86.00	

Office Equipment A/c			L5
19..		£	
Apr 1	Capital	320.00	

Stock A/c			L6
19..		£	
Apr 1	Capital	265.00	

Capital A/c			L7
	19..		£
	Apr 1 Sundry		
	Assets		4465.00

Sales A/c			L9
	19..		£
	Apr 6	Cash	360.52
	13	Cash	425.62
	20	Cash	1272.50
	30	Cash	1380.24

Purchases A/c			L8
19..		£	
Apr 5	Cash	27.50	
9	Bank	236.50	
17	Bank	328.56	

Fees Receivable A/c			L11
	19..		£
	Apr 6	Mrs E	
		Jones	185.00
	20	R Marshall	560.50

Mrs E. Jones A/c					L10
19..		£	19..		£
Apr 6	Fees		Apr 13	Bank	185.00
	Receivable	185.00			

Motor Van Expenses A/c			L14
19..		£	
Apr 11	Cash	15.65	

Postage A/c			L12
19..		£	
Apr 11	Cash	1.85	

R. Marshall A/c			L16
19..		£	
Apr 20	Fees		
	receivable	560.50	

Telephone Expenses A/c			L13
19..		£	
Apr 11	Bank	23.50	

Advertising Expenses A/c			L18
19..		£	
Apr 27	Bank	36.50	

Rent A/c			L15
19..		£	
Apr 19	Bank	390.00	

Drawings A/c			L19
19..		£	
Apr 30	Cash	600.00	

Salaries A/c			L17
19..		£	
Apr 24	Bank	636.50	

Fig. 7.4 Ledger accounts for the specimen enterprise

Note The accounts have deliberately not been balanced off; though this is essential before a Trial Balance is prepared.

Trial Balance easily. The Trial Balance then appears as shown in Fig. 7.5. Study the notes below the Trial Balance.

Trial Balance as at 30 April, 19. .

	Dr £	Cr £
Cash A/c	293.88	
Bank A/c	1947.44	
Motor Vehicles A/c	2300.00	
Tools and Equipment A/c	666.00	
Office Equipment A/c	320.00	
Stock A/c	265.00	
Capital A/c		4465.00
Purchases A/c	592.56	
Sales A/c		3438.88
Fees Receivable A/c		745.50
Postage A/c	1.85	
Telephone Expenses A/c	23.50	
Motor Van Expenses A/c	15.65	
Rent A/c	390.00	
R. Marshall A/c	560.50	
Salaries A/c	636.50	
Advertising Expenses A/c	36.50	
Drawings A/c	600.00	
	£8649.38	8649.38

Fig. 7.5 The Trial Balance at the end of the month

Notes
1 The Trial Balance agrees, the total of the debit entries equalling the total of the credit entries. This shows that all the double entries have been done correctly.
2 In the debit column balances you might like to notice that we have a number of asset accounts, a number of losses (expenses), one debtor (R. Marshall) and the proprietor's drawings.
3 In the credit column we have two profit accounts — the sales figures and the fees receivable, and one liability, the capital which the business owes back to the owner of the business.

You should now try some of the exercises to the Trial Balance in Section 7.5.

7.5 Exercises to the Trial Balance

1 Valerie Skilton starts to trade in costume jewellery on 2 January 19. ., with a capital of £5000.00 which she banks. Record this opening capital and do the double entries for the following transactions. Balance off the accounts where necessary and extract a Trial Balance as at 12 January 19. . .

2 Jan Buys stock for re-sale (Purchases A/c) for £180.00 (by cheque). Buys till for shop use (Fixtures and Fittings A/c) £240.00 by cheque.

4 Jan Buys second-hand rings etc. (Purchases A/c), for re-sale paying £235.00 by cheque. Draws £65.00 cash from bank for office cash box.

6 Jan Cash sales for week £325.00. Pays cleaner £12.50 cash (Cleaning Expenses A/c).

11 Jan Buys jewellery for re-sale £317.25, paying by cheque.

12 Jan Pays rent £120.00 by cheque. Pays wages for part-time helper £25.00 in cash. Draws money for personal use (Drawings A/c) £100.00 from bank. Cash sales for week £550.00.

2 On 1 June 19. . Michael Martin sets up in business as a courier in Newtown, with the following assets and liabilities: Motor cycle £1350.00, office equipment £220.00, specialist clothing £300.00 and cash at the bank £350.00. This £350.00 had been borrowed from his father, interest free (Loan Account), but is to be repaid at the rate of £25.00 per month. Open the necessary accounts to record these matters, including his capital contribution and then record the following transactions. He does his book-keeping once a week, on the dates shown. Take out a Trial Balance on 30 June to prove the accuracy of your work.

7 June Takings for week for various jobs (Fees Received A/c) £62.50 cash and £103.20 by cheque; Petrol and oil, £9.70 cash; extra lock-up container fitment for motor cycle £88.50 (cheque); rent £15.00 (cheque).

14 June Takings £85.70 (cash), £94.60 (cheques); Petrol and oil £8.25 cash; rent £15.00 (cheque); deposit on reserve motor cycle £100 (cheque). This motor cycle is to cost a total of £1450, of which interest payable is £270 and the machine £1180. The balance of the price is owed to H. P. Finance Co. Ltd.

21 June Takings £120 (cash) £136.00 (cheques); Petrol and oil £12.56 (cash); rent £15.00 (cheque); office expenses £14.25 (cheque). R. Watutsi owes £17.50 for work done on a job which will be completed next week.

28 June Takings £105.20 (cash), £104.00 (cheques). The cheques include R. Watutsi's £17.50 owing. Petrol and oil £13.04 (cash); Rent £15.00 (cheque); repayment of loan £25.00 cash. Paid £200.00 cash into bank.

3 On 1 July 19. . Abdul Kadar sets up in business as a typesetter with the following assets: Cash £250.00, Bank Balance £5600.00, office equipment £1450.00, delivery van £2300.00. Record these assets and his capital in the appropriate accounts and then do the double entries for the following transactions. On 31 July take out a Trial Balance to check the accuracy of your work.

July 1 Arranged loan £35 000.00 from Three Eyes Investment Ltd, by cheque. Purchased electronic typesetting equipment by cheque £40 000.00 (Typesetting Equipment A/c).

5 Purchased copier paper £25.36 in cash. Purchased toner for copying machine £8.56 cash (both to Printing Expenses A/c).

6 Takings for week Cash £86.00. He has also done work valued at £386.50 for Acme Publishing who will pay on 31 July.

10 Purchased cleaning materials £8.12, cash.

13 Takings for week Cash £102.50. Has also done work for George McCall Publishing £426.50 who will pay within one month.

16 Paid Insurance £50.00 by cheque. Paid Rent £120.00 by cheque.

20 Takings for week Cash £156.60, Cheques £135.50.

26 Paid for printing materials £17.25 cash.

27 Takings for week Cheques £396.50. Also work for Acme Publishing £586.00 who will pay by 27 August.

31 Acme Publishing paid by cheque £386.50.

4 On 2 January Mary Rowan set up in business as an employment agency and began to keep book-keeping records. She had an initial capital of £3600.00 made up of cash £200.00, cash at bank £1600.00, office furniture and equipment £550.00 and a car worth £2500.00 which was shared between business and domestic use so that only half the value was to be brought onto the books. Enter these items into the appropriate ledger accounts and then enter the following transactions, making a double entry in each case. Take out a Trial Balance on 31 January to prove that your entries are correct.

2 Jan Arranged a loan with Helpful Bank PLC for £5000 which was put into the Bank Account. Paid for advertising £160.00 (cheque); paid for office stationery £120.60 (cheque); paid for redecorations £230.24 (cheque).

3 Jan Paid telephone connection charges £86.50 (cheque).

6 Jan Takings for week £84.00 (cheque).

9 Jan Paid rent for quarter (cheque) £325.00; paid for petrol £13.60 (cash) of which only half is to be treated as a business expense.

13 Jan Takings for week cash £14.50, cheques £236.80.

19 Jan Paid Insurance £50.00 (cheque).

20 Jan Takings for week cash £28.00, cheques £296.50.

24 Jan Paid for petrol £12.84 (cash of which only half is for business use).

27 Jan Takings for week cash £18.50, cheques £276.25.

31 Jan Paid for advertising £198.50 (cheque).

7.6 Self-assessment questions

1 What do we call a page in the ledger?

2 For cross reference purposes each page is given a number. What is this number called?

3 Our business uses typewriters, motor vehicles, premises, machinery and a computer. What do we call these items?

4 What do we call accounts which record expenses of the business?

5 What do we call accounts that record assets of the business?

6 What do we call a person to whom we owe money?

7 What do we call a person who owes money to us?

8 We pay cash for repairs to the firm's lorry. There is a credit entry in the Cash Account. Where would the double entry appear?

9 We pay by cheque for a filing cabinet £150.00. The credit entry is in the Bank Account as the bank gives money. Where is the debit entry?

10 What does the Trial Balance actually prove?

7.7 Answers to self-assessment questions

1 An account.

2 A folio number.

3 They are assets of the business.

4 They are nominal accounts.

5 They are real accounts.

6 A creditor.

7 A debtor.

8 Motor Vehicles Repairs Account (or Motor Vehicle Expenses Account).

9 In the Office Equipment Account.

10 It proves that *prima facie* (at a first glance) we have done our book-keeping double entries correctly. However, there are *some* errors that do not show up on a Trial Balance. These are explained later.

8 Documents for purchases and sales

8.1 The use of documents

Almost every transaction that takes place is recognised by some sort of document. The great advantage of documents is that they constitute written evidence which can be produced in court if necessary, and it is usual to keep ordinary documents for six years — though more formal legal documents may be kept for 12 years after the contracts to which they refer have been completed. In the United Kingdom the VAT (Value Added Tax) regulations require VAT invoices to be kept for six years.

It follows that all business activities really start with some sort of document and all business records begin with the passing of documents from one party to another. The word 'party' here is used in the sense of a party to a contract. Any transaction — for example a sale of goods or a supply of services — is a contract, and there are two parties involved, though there may be more than two parties in certain circumstances. Documents passed between these parties trigger off all sorts of activities, order picking, packing, delivery, receipt into stores, accounting records and finally payment.

Each of these documents has to be studied and followed through in the activities of a business. Let us make a list of the common documents which deal with the routine activities of business. Less routine activities like exporting, may require dozens of other documents. For the moment we will list only the routine ones. These are as follows:

1 The invoice (but there will be at least four copies of this)
2 The debit note
3 The credit note
4 The statement
5 The cheque
6 The receipt
7 The petty cash voucher.

Each of these documents has its own place in the business activities and we must study it carefully and see what activities it leads to and what records it requires. Each needs a chapter to itself, especially as we have to study several different ways of dealing with it (traditional ways, labour-saving ways and computerised methods). However, there is a basic pattern for all of them which is worth studying first. This is best followed in diagrammatic form. Study Figure 8.1 closely and you will understand this general pattern.

1 Start here!

The original documents. The trouble with these is that they are loose bits of paper. They get in a muddle, blow out of windows etc. We need a permanent record of these, recording each day's documents.

2 This permanent record used to be kept in a book called the Day Book. The French word for 'day book' is 'Journal', so the documents were recorded in the Journal. Today we can use a bound book, but we may also use other methods, looseleaf sheets or computer printouts.

(a)
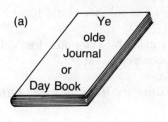
Ye olde Journal or Day Book

(b)
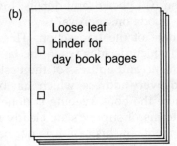
Loose leaf binder for day book pages

(c)
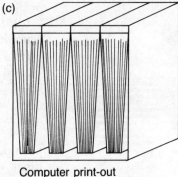
Computer print-out

3 These daily records then have to be sorted out and entered in accounting records for each person we deal with. The traditional book in which these records are kept is called the ledger. Each person has a page in the ledger called an 'Account'. The day book entries in (2) above were moved into the ledger. This is called 'posting' the ledger. Today we might use either:

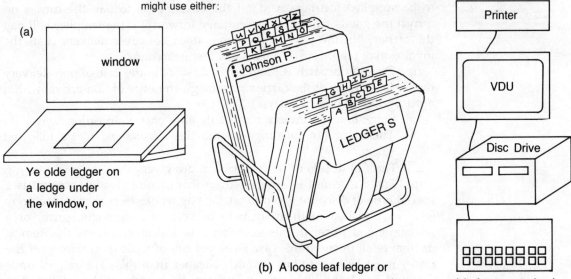

(a) Ye olde ledger on a ledge under the window, or

(b) A loose leaf ledger or

(c) A computerised ledger system

Fig. 8.1 Documents, day books and ledger accounts

8.2 The invoice

A typical invoice is shown in Fig. 8.2. An invoice is a business document made out whenever one person sells goods to another, though it is sometimes waived in the case of cash transactions and replaced by a petty cash voucher. If goods are supplied on credit, and the customer will pay later, the issue of an invoice recognises the transaction and leads to the book-keeping entries required in both firms, the supplier and the customer. It also — in the UK — leads to the VAT records (for value added tax which is payable on almost all supplies of goods or services).

Such a document should show the following details (the notes are coded to the same letters as those used in Fig. 8.2).

(a) The name of the document.

(b) Its serial number.

(c) The name and address of the supplier who is making out the set of invoices, in this case Lovely Homes PLC.

(d), (e) and (f) Other useful details. Instead of sale we could have had 'sample' or 'goods on approval'.

(g) The date of the transaction. This is also the tax point for Value Added Tax, which decides when the tax becomes payable.

(h) The name and address of the customer.

(i) The delivery address, which may be different from the Head Office address where the book-keeping is done.

(j) The terms of supply state clearly whether discount is allowed for prompt payment. In this case it is not because it says Terms Net (sometimes written Nett). The credit period is one month from the time the 'statement' arrives. A 'statement' is a list of the month's transactions which is sent out on the same date each month. In this case the customer then has one month to pay.

(k) Often the price of goods covers delivery and the goods are said to be supplied 'carriage paid'. If the customer is to pay the carrier on arrival the goods are said to be 'carriage forward'. If the supplier will pay the carrier, but the price of the goods does not cover delivery costs the invoice may read: Carriage for Customer's Account.

(l) Date of despatch is often advised, since in the case of non-delivery due to loss in transit the carrier must be given notice of non-arrival within a set period — often 28 days.

(m) Sometimes an invoice represents only part of an order.

(n) These column headings enable the calculations to be followed easily.

(o) The full details of the transaction are given.

(p) Trade discount is mentioned on this invoice. Trade Discount is a special type of discount given to retailers by wholesalers or manufacturers who supply them with an item to be sold at a catalogue price, or a recommended price. In this situation it is easiest to discuss the item at its final retail price (in this case £4.30 per roll of wallpaper). However the trader must be able to buy it much cheaper than this. The rate of trade discount has to be high since it is the profit margin of the retailer. The wallpaper is to be sold at £4.30, but the trader only pays 55% of this, since 45% of it (£1.935 per roll) is deducted as trade discount.

(q) Since VAT rates are liable to change on Budget Day in the UK this book has used an imaginary rate of 10%.

(r) The charge for the wallpaper to the trader is £2365.00.

(s) The VAT is added to this to give the total invoice value.

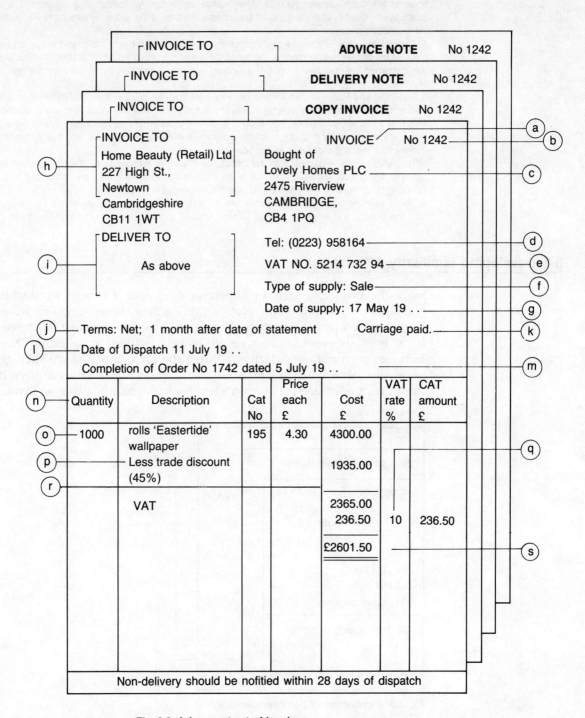

Fig. 8.2 A four-part set of invoices

Notes

1 An invoice is a document made out whenever one person (the supplier) supplies goods or services to another person (the customer).

2 There are usually at least four copies, and in many cases more.

3 Of these the top copy is the most important. It is sent to the customer and becomes the basis of his book-keeping records. The invoice as far as the customer is concerned is a 'purchases' invoice, and the supplier becomes a creditor, a person to whom money is owed for the goods supplied.

4 The second copy is almost equally important — it is retained by the seller and becomes the basis of his book-keeping records. As far as the seller is concerned this is a sales invoice, and the customer has become a debtor, a person who owes the supplier money for the goods supplied.

5 The third and fourth copies are the delivery note and the advice note. The delivery note is carried by the driver who is making a delivery. It has room for a signature from the customer. This may read something like 'Received in apparent good order and condition'. If the package or crate appears to be in good condition a signature will enable the driver to prove to his firm that he has made the delivery in a proper manner.

The advice note is packed with the goods, or it may be handed in by the driver when he delivers the goods. It tells the stores at the customer's end what they are supposed to be receiving and ensures that they can check the contents for correctness.

6 There may be other copies, for example, a 'gate copy' to allow the driver out of the gate with the goods, and a 'representative's copy' to send to the salesman who took the order.

8.3 Developing familiarity with invoices

Since the invoice is such an important document it is well worthwhile making a collection of them. Not that this is easy, because no-one wants to give up a copy of an invoice. They have to be kept by most businesses for at least six years, and so we are usually reduced to collecting them from our own domestic dealings. When the car is repaired we shall get an invoice, and when we make any large purchase, such as a piece of furniture, a television set or even a text book, we may be given an invoice

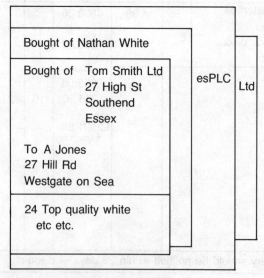

Fig. 8.3 A collection of purchases invoices

for it. Start to make a collection right away — or make a class collection if you are using this book in a school or college. As your collection grows you will notice one thing — which is illustrated in Fig. 8.3. Since the invoices you are collecting will be invoices for things purchased or services purchased, they will all have come from different firms — and will be different shapes, sizes, colours, etc. They will look a very jumbled and untidy collection. We cannot have a *neat* pack of purchases invoices. We shall never be able to make a collection of sales invoices for we can only do that within the firm, where the second copy of each invoice becomes a record of sales made to various customers. They will all be the same size, shape and colour, because they are the second copies of our invoices, and all come from our firm. So a collection of sales invoices is a neat pack, but of course we can only have such a collection within our own firm, if we are working in the Accounts Department. Figure 8.4 shows such a collection.

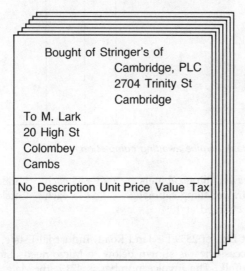

Fig. 8.4 A collection of sales invoices

8.4 Exercises: the completion of invoices

Here is a blank invoice. Rule up a similar one on a sheet of paper for each of the questions below (or copy the illustration on page 64) and then complete the invoice with the information given. If you are a typist you may of course type these invoices. In this book wherever VAT is mentioned it is deemed to be levied at the 10% rate, although the actual rate levied in the UK is specified in the Budget each year, and may therefore vary from time to time.

1 Wholesale suppliers PLC of 2185 Shore Street, Portsmouth, Hants, supply office equipment as shown below to Peter Gray Ltd, 3816 High Street, Southampton, Hants. The invoice number is 1216, the date is 7 May 19. . and the details of the goods supplied are as follows:

No. _____			Bought of _____ No: _____				
To _____ _____ _____			_____ _____ Date (Tax point) _____				
Quantity	Description	Cat. No	Unit Price	Cost		VAT rate	VAT amount

Fig. 8.5 A blank invoice awaiting completion

5 Four-drawer filing cabinets   @ £55 each   Catalogue No 213
4 Three-drawer filing cabinets   @ £45 each   Catalogue No 214
   VAT is charged at 10%

2 Micro-fast Ltd, of 2859 Leyland Road, Industrial Estate, Baldock, Herts, supply computer accessories as shown below to Micro-needs Ltd, of 3725 South Street, Ipswich, Suffolk. The invoice number is 4219, the date is 27 July 19. . and the details of the goods supplied, on which VAT is payable at 10% are as follows:

Cat. No X14   20   blank floppy disks   @ £17.50 per box of 10
Cat. No Y327   10   power point adaptors   @ £ 6.80 each

3 Orchid Wholesalers PLC of 2147 Airport Way, Bedok, Singapore, invoice gift wrapped supplies of orchids as shown below to Exotic Products Ltd, of 2143 High Street, Camden, London. The invoice number is 3417, the date is 20 May 19. . and the details of the goods supplied, on which VAT does not apply, are as follows:

100   special pack orchids (varieties)   @ S$5.80 each Cat No 9235
 50   vases for orchid display   @ S$7.50 each Cat No 7250

4 Shona Wholesale Supplies of 1864 Inyazura Road, Umtali, Zimbabwe, send wholesale supplies of cleaning materials as shown below to Freedom Stores of 2756 Mtoko Road, Harare. The invoice number is 1719, the date is 14 December 19. . and the details of the goods, on which VAT is not levied, are as follows:

1200 packets Shino washing powder	@ Z$1.25	Cat No 247
750 packets Whito washing machine powder	@ Z$2.50	Cat No 250

5 Answer these questions with short written answers:

(a) How many copies would there usually be in a set of invoices?

(b) Which are the two most important copies?

(c) What happens to the top copy of an invoice?

(d) What happens to the second copy of an invoice?

(e) The office boy comes down the corridor carrying a bunch of invoices on his way to the Accounts Department. It is a nice neat bunch of invoices, all coloured yellow, and the same size and shape. What copy of the invoices is he carrying? Who typed them out yesterday?

8.5 The debit note

A debit note is very similar to an invoice. As the name implies it is a document which is designed to debit someone's account, and this may happen in a number of circumstances. Suppose we have sent a customer an invoice for a certain goods but due to a typing error too little has been charged — for example £150 when we meant to charge £1500. Clearly we must correct this error. At the moment the customer will be debited with £150 (debit the receiver of goods) but it should read £1500. What is needed is a debit note for another £1350. When this is debited to the customer's account it will make the amount due up to the correct amount. The double entry for this £1350 will of course be in the Sales Account, because we have sold £1500 of goods, but only £150 will have been recorded.

A debit note is therefore used to correct errors on invoices, and is put through the accounting records as if it was an invoice (see Section 8.8).

8.6 The credit note

Obviously a credit note is the opposite of a debit note. It is a document used whenever we wish to credit someone's account. There are several reasons why we might want to do this. They are:

1 *When goods are returned for some reason* This may be because they were unsatisfactory or because they were sent '**on approval**' hoping the customer would buy them, but in fact he/she decides not to do so.

2 *When an overcharge has been made* We have seen that if an undercharge has been made we must debit the customer's account to increase it to the proper figure. If an overcharge has been made we must credit the customer's account to reduce the balance to its proper figure.

3 *Where an allowance is to be made* It often happens that an item which has been delivered to a customer proves to be unsatisfactory for some reason — such as damage in transit. It could be very expensive to collect the item again, repair it and re-deliver it, or replace it. If the customer can get the repair done locally and pays the charges it may be cheaper

to give an allowance on the purchase price and leave the customer to sort out the problem. We would do this with a credit note.

A typical credit note is shown in Fig. 8.6. Note that it would normally be printed in red, since this distinguishes a credit note clearly from an invoice or a debit note which are usually printed in black.

Special note re Trade Discount   When goods are returned after Trade Discount has been allowed on them there is a chance that the credit note will be made out at the full catalogue price and that the trade discount will be overlooked on the credit note. Suppose the retailer invoiced with wallpaper in Fig. 8.2 at a price of £4.30 per roll, less trade discount of 45%, returned some of the supplies and was given a credit note for the full catalogue price. He would actually be making a profit on the returned goods. We must be careful to make the credit note out only for the actual amount charged in the first place.

CREDIT NOTE

Credit to	Returned to	No 326
Home Beauty (Retail) Ltd	Lovely Homes PLC	
227 High Street	2475 Riverview	
Newtown	Cambridge	
Cambridgeshire	CB4 1PQ	
CB11 1WT	Tel: (0223) 958164	
	VAT No: 5214 732 94	
	Date: 23 May 19 . .	

Quantity	Description	Cat No	Price each £	Cost £	VAT rate %	Vat amount
100	rolls 'Eastertide' wallpaper	195	4.30	430		
	Less trade discount			193.50	10	23.65
				236.50		
	VAT			23.65		
				£260.15		
	(Damaged by water in transit)					

Fig. 8.6 A credit note (normally printed in red)

Notes
1 The red credit note contains all the details necessary to record the transaction, which is a returns transaction for goods damaged in transit.
2 Notice that the trade discount has been deducted to give the true price charged for the goods.

8.7 Exercises: the completion of credit notes

For these exercises you must either rule up a credit note like the one shown in Fig. 8.6 for each answer, or you could photo copy the illustration provided on page 68.

1 On 4 May 19. . Peter Higgins, of 24 Roundhouse Way, Billericay, Essex returns goods to M. Lawson Ltd, 224 Southlands Way, Wickford, Essex, because they are the wrong style. They consist of three dining tables at £86.50 each and 12 dining chairs at £35.50 each. VAT is charged at 10% and trade discount had been given on the original order of 50%.

Make out a suitable credit note inventing any other details you require such as telephone numbers, VAT numbers etc.

2 On 17 July 19. . Microchips (Singapore) PLC, of Harbourview, Singapore 0513, returns goods to Electronic Suppliers Ltd, 2475 Harrow Way, Wembley, Middlesex. They consist of 1000 metres of shielded twisted cable @ 32 pence per metre and 500 metres of High Frequency coaxial cable @ 62 pence per metre. VAT is not charged on this order and trade discount has been given on the original order of 25%.

Make out a suitable credit note inventing any other details you require such as telephone numbers, VAT numbers etc.

3 On 14 March 19. . M. Soave of 1275 Mombasa Road, Mtandura, Kenya, claims an allowance on goods supplied by Overseas Supplies PLC, 2457 Westway, Northolt, Middlesex. The allowance is for repairs to one replacement tractor engine, £395.00 (damaged in transit). VAT and trade discount do not arise on this order.

Make out a suitable credit note inventing any other details you require such as telephone numbers, VAT numbers etc.

4 On 11 February 19. . Roger Kitope, 2794 Mandela Way, Haringey, London returns goods to the Excelsior China Co. PLC, 2438 High Road, Stoke on Trent. They consist of
1 china dinner service £194.50 (damaged in transit)
1 decorated vase £18.75 (glaze faulty).
VAT is charged at 10% and trade discount had been given on the original order of 40%.

Make out a suitable credit note inventing any other details you require such as telephone numbers, VAT numbers etc.

8.8 Debit notes and returns

It is important to notice that credit notes are always made out when goods are returned to a supplier, and it is the supplier who makes out the credit note. If a customer who returns the goods wishes to send a document with them to claim the money for the return, it would be necessary to send a debit note, since the customer wants to debit the supplier with the goods he is receiving back. When he receives the debit note, the supplier responds to it with a credit note which can be entered into the books — the debit note is for advice purposes only.

8.9 Self-assessment questions

1 What is an invoice?
2 What details should an invoice show?
3 You are given a bunch of invoices. They are all different shapes, sizes and colours. What sort of invoices are they?
4 What is a credit note?
5 What colour is a credit note?
6 You are given a bunch of credit notes. They are all the same size and shape. What type of credit notes are they?

8.10 Project: designing a rubber stamp

You have been given the job of receiving and checking all invoices from suppliers. You are told that when the invoices arrive they will be routed through to you. You should then (a) send them to stores to enquire whether the goods have been received. You need a date of arrival, and the signature of someone in the stores. (b) Check that the price and terms of payment are correct according to the original order. (c) Check that the extensions on the invoice (i.e. the calculations, trade discount, VAT etc.) are correct. (d) Do the book-keeping entries and write the

	Credit Note				No:	
Credit to			Return to			
Quantity	Description	Cat No	Price £	Cost £	VAT rate	VAT amount

Tel.
VAT No.

Fig. 8.7 A blank credit note

(This may be photocopied for class use if required)

folio number of the account on the invoice. (e) Indicate that you agree that the invoice should be passed to the accountant for payment. He will then pay it in due course.

To do all this you decide to design and have made a rubber stamp that will enable you to cover the five points. Each point will have a space for the signature of the person who checked the point concerned. Design such a rubber stamp 5 cm deep and 10 cm wide.

8.11 Answers to self-assessment questions

1 An invoice is a business document made out whenever one person sells goods to another.
2 (a) The names and addresses of both parties to the transaction. (b) An exact description of the goods sold and the quantity, unit price and total value. (c) Any trade discount given and the VAT charged (if applicable). (d) The terms for payment and the time allowed before payment is due.
3 They must be purchases invoices, the top copies of invoices sent in by suppliers, since they have obviously come from a great many different firms.
4 A credit note, is a document made out whenever one person returns goods to another.
5 The printing is always in red.
6 They must be credit notes from our own office (since they are all the same shape and size) and recognise that sales have been returned to us — in other words they are Sales Returns credit notes.

9 Value Added Tax (VAT)

9.1 What is value added tax?

Before continuing our study of documents it is convenient at this point to learn about this tax which features on practically every business document in the UK. VAT is a tax added to almost everything we buy as consumers, though some items are only charged a VAT rate of 0%. This may sound a rather silly idea, but zero rated goods are necessities, such as food, children's clothing, educational materials of various sorts, gas, electricity and water supplies, etc. Most other consumer goods are charged at a rate known as the standard rate, which is fixed by the Chancellor of the Exchequer on Budget Day, and varies from time to time. It is also possible to have other rates, known as Higher Rates, on luxury items. For the sake of simplicity in this book we only refer to two rates; a standard rate of 10% and zero rate, 0%.

Like other taxes, VAT is simply a way the Government raises money to collect the funds it needs for the many things Governments supervise, such as defence, internal security (police, prisons, etc.), education, roads, public housing, etc.

9.2 Output tax and input tax — how VAT works

Every business with a turnover of more than a certain amount a year (£23 700 at present), has to register for VAT by filling up a form issued by HM Customs and Excise. They must then charge VAT to customers every time they supply goods or services. A supply is called an 'output' from the business and the tax on an output is called **output tax**. So if goods worth £1000 are sold to P. Smith on 1 February 19. ., and the VAT rate is 10% the trader adds £100 to the bill and the customer must pay £1100. When the customer pays the £1100 only the £1000 belongs to the trader for the goods sold, the other £100 is output tax for the VAT officer.

Imagine the double entry for this £1100 paid by cheque. The Bank Account is receiving the money so debit the Bank Account. The trader has given the goods to the customer so this will be credited to Sales Account £1000. The other £100 must be credited to the VAT Account because we owe HM Customs and Excise £100. This is shown in Fig. 9.1.

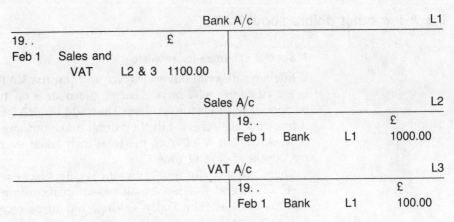

Fig. 9.1 Double entries for output tax on sales

At the same time as we are charging VAT (output tax) to all customers we are paying tax on all the supplies received from our suppliers. These supplies are called 'inputs' to the business and the tax on them is called **input tax**. Suppose we buy £800 of goods from A. Supplier Ltd, on 12 February 19. . and VAT is 10%, we shall pay £880 in total. This time the double entries will be as shown in Fig. 9.2, and explained in the notes below it.

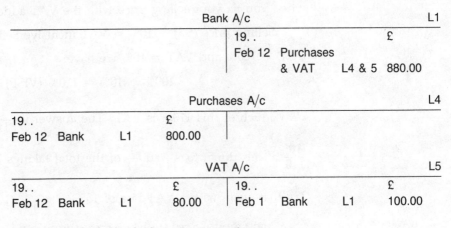

Fig. 9.2 Double entries for input tax on purchases

Notes
1 Bank Account is credited because it is giving the money.
2 Purchases Account is receiving the goods purchased which are worth £800; debit the receiver.
3 VAT Account has also received value of £80 paid out to the supplier who will eventually pay it over to the VAT officer. So the VAT officer has really received £80 from us.
4 For convenience the VAT from the previous entry is still shown on the VAT Account.
5 Notice therefore that what is owing on the VAT Account is actually only £20, because the input tax we pay is deducted from the output tax we collect and we only need to pay the balance of £20 to the VAT officer. In fact we only pay once every three months, so that in fact the VAT Account builds up to quite a large sum for most traders. Remember then:

VAT payable = Output tax − Input tax

9.3 A few other points about VAT

1 Special schemes for retailers

While we can write out an invoice and put the VAT on it we cannot give every customer who buys a bar of chocolate a tax invoice. There have to be special schemes for retailers. They add the VAT to the price and collect it from the customers, but they don't make out any invoices. All they do is work out the VAT from the total cash taken every day, when cashing up the till at closing time.

There are actually nine different retailers' schemes called A, B, C, D, E, F, G, H and J. They are all based on recording the daily figures for cash in the tills. The **Daily Takings** has to be recorded every day, and failure to do so is an offence. It is also an offence to understate the takings, because if you do that you are keeping some of the VAT (which belongs to the Government). Hence some pretty serious cases of VAT fraud appear in the newspapers. If you record your daily takings correctly the correct VAT will be in the total. But how much? That depends upon the **VAT fraction**.

2 VAT fractions

These are just a bit tricky. Using 10% as the VAT rate, what happens when you fix your selling price with the VAT added?

Selling price (SP) + 10% = VAT inclusive Selling Price (VISP)

If SP = 100% and VAT = 10% we have:

$$100\% + 10\% = 110\% \text{ (VISP)}$$

How much of this 110% is VAT? The answer is $\frac{10}{110}$ (not $\frac{10}{100}$):

$\frac{10}{110}$ cancels down to $\frac{1}{11}$ so $\frac{1}{11}$ of the total takings is VAT (not $\frac{1}{10}$).

Try that again with a VAT rate of 15%.

$$100\% \text{(SP)} + 15\% \text{ VAT} = 115\% \text{ (VISP)}$$

How much of the 115% is VAT? The answer is $\frac{15}{115}$ (not $\frac{15}{100}$):

so $\frac{15}{115} = \frac{3}{23}$ (cancelling by 5)

The VAT fraction is $\frac{3}{23}$ (not $\frac{15}{100}$).

Now, suppose you are a shopkeeper with takings over the three months of £27 800.50. If VAT is 10% how much of the takings is VAT? The answer is $\frac{1}{11}$.

$$
\begin{array}{r}
£ \\
11 \enspace \big|\, \overline{27\ 800.50} \\
2\ 527.318 \\
=\ \underline{\underline{£2\ 527.32}}
\end{array}
$$

This is your output tax figure. When you deduct your input tax from it (which you find from your supplier's invoices) you know how much to pay the VAT officer.

3 Saving up your VAT

You can see that even a small firm (in the case chosen I have taken a firm with takings of £300 a day) collects about £2500 of VAT in three months. It is not easy to find this money to pay the VAT officer on the due date if you do not save it up in a special bank account. Every trader must put VAT money away where it cannot be spent on other things. Sooner or later you have to pay it over to HM Customs and Excise. It is the Government's money, not yours.

4 A VAT Return

Most traders have to make out a VAT return every three months, and pay over what is owed to the VAT officer at that time. However, traders who deal mainly in zero rated items do not collect any output tax, but may pay out quite a lot of input tax on items they buy for use in the business. This means that the input tax is greater than the output tax and

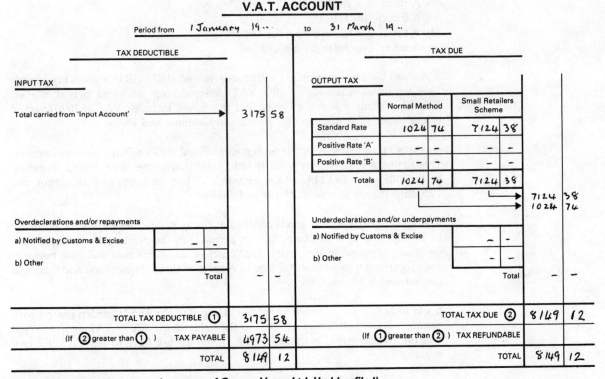

Fig. 9.3 A typical VAT return (courtesy of George Vyner Ltd, Huddersfiled)

the VAT office actually owes them money. To save hardship they are allowed to claim this every month, so they make out a monthly VAT return. Figure 9.3 shows a typical VAT return, from one of the special VAT accounting books used to record VAT calculations.

9.4 Self-assessment questions

1 What is value added tax?
2 When does the trader have to charge VAT?
3 How does the trader charge the tax?
4 What are zero-rated goods?
5 How does the trader calculate the tax due to Customs and Excise?
6 When is the tax paid?

9.5 Exercises on VAT

1 What will be the VAT charged on the following items with tax at a rate of 10%? (Answers correct to the nearest penny) (a) a car for £6850; (b) a typewriter at £525; (c) a machine at £3465; (d) a bar of chocolate at 18 pence; (e) a gallon of petrol at £1.65.

2 What will be the VAT charged on the following items with tax at a rate of 15%? (Answers correct to the nearest penny):
(a) An answering machine for £140
(b) A ridge tent for £37.50
(c) A bicycle for £66.50
(d) A set of garden furniture for £64.75
(e) A micro computer for £365.00.

3 A small business is supplied with goods valued at £37 280 in a given tax period. This figure is increased by 10% VAT. Sales during the same period totalled £97 680, according to the till rolls, and this figure included VAT at 10% charged to customers. Calculate the tax payable to Customs and Excise.

4 A small business is supplied with goods valued at £48 875 in a given tax period. This figure is increased by VAT at 15%. Sales during the same period according to the tills were £92 115, which included VAT at 15% charged as output tax. Calculate the tax due to Customs and Excise.

5 A grocer only deals in goods charged at the zero rate, but pays VAT on many items supplied to him. During the tax period (July–September, 19. .) he pays tax on goods supplied to him worth £7200, net of tax. What sum will pass between the grocer and Customs and Excise in respect of these transactions and who will pay whom? VAT rate 15%.

6 On 15 March 19. . Garden Supplies Ltd supply your firm (a garden centre) with paving stones, pottery wares, etc., to the value of £17 520 + VAT at 10%. What will the double entry in the ledger be, if you do not have to pay them for two months?

7 On 23 April 19. . you supply R. Akram and Co. with office furniture valued at £1080 + VAT at 15%. You give them 28 days credit. What will be the double entry in the accounts for these items?

9.6 Answers to self-assessment questions

1 Value added tax is a tax added to all the outputs of a business at a fixed rate per cent, which brings in tax money to the Government by raising the price of goods to consumers.

2 The trader charges VAT every time goods or services are supplied.

3 The tax is added to the invoice, if an invoice is made out, but for 'over the counter' cash trading it is added to the price of the goods.

4 Goods on which VAT is not charged — the rate is 0% — because they are essential items like food.

5 Tax due is calculated using the formula:

Tax due = Output tax collected − input tax paid

6 The tax is paid every three months for ordinary traders, but zero-rated traders (who are usually owed money because they don't collect tax) are allowed to claim the refund due every month.

10 Keeping permanent records of invoices and credit notes

10.1 The handling of documents

We have seen that documents are very important because they trigger off all sorts of activities within a firm. We have also said that they must be retained for six years. This is because under an Act of Parliament called the Limitation Act 1980 legal action on a simple contract can be commenced at any time up to six years after the contract was made. After six years it is said to be 'statute-barred' in other words Parliament will not allow a dispute in the Courts to start — since the exact details may have become too hazy in most people's minds for the truth to be arrived at.

Another point about documents is that they are loose bits of paper; they blow about, fall on the floor and may finish up in the waste-paper basket. If we can make a permanent record of the document we should do so, and if we can't and are going to keep the document itself we should supply folders, lever arch files or some other way of preserving the documents so that they do not get mislaid.

Keeping a permanent record of invoices for purchases and sales

We saw in Fig. 8.1 that methods of keeping a permanent record of invoices have changed greatly over the years. In medieval times, when firms were small and a single book-keeper could keep all the accounts for a firm, all invoices were entered in the Journal (Day Book) and posted from there into the main book of account, the Ledger. Later other methods were developed. Let us look at each of these methods in turn. They are:

Method 1 — ye olde Journal method
Method 2 — the specialised day book method
Method 3 — the simultaneous records method
Method 4 — computerised records

The first two are dealt with in this chapter. Simultaneous records are explained in Chapter 11 and computerised records in Chapter 12.

10.2 Method 1 — ye olde Journal method

The word 'journal' is simply the French word for 'day book', and the medieval way of doing book-keeping was as follows:

1 Whatever happens in business, make a record of it in the day book, or Journal.

2 Then post the day book to the Ledger, to get the entries into the accounts.

Although this method is never used today for purchases, sales, purchases returns or sales returns, it is still the only sort of day book that can be used for all the other things that happen, such as the purchase of assets, the depreciation of assets, writing off bad debts, etc.

The paper used is called Journal paper, and the Journal is always in real life a bound book. Since it is only used for the more tricky items in business this bound book is usually kept (and certainly supervised closely) by a senior book-keeper or accountant.

All that is necessary to do a journal entry is to think in 'double entries'. You decide what entries need to be made, on the basis of the evidence before you — which for students means 'the problem being set'. Having decided what accounts to debit and credit you record them in the journal entry, and write a short explanation called a 'Narration' in the details column. Consider Example 10.1.

EXAMPLE 10.1

On 1 May 19. . P. Brown purchases a new motor lorry for £38 000, of which the tyres are worth £4600. The supplier, Heavyfreight Motors PLC has agreed to give one month's credit.

What will the Journal entry be? Clearly the account that has received value is the Motor Lorry Account, but as tyres wear out very quickly it is usual to treat tyres as separate from the vehicle itself and the value of the tyres is usually placed in a special Tyres Account. These two accounts will therefore be debited (debit the receiver) and the supplier, Heavyfreight Motors PLC who has not yet been paid will be credited, because we credit the giver. Heavyfreight Motors PLC are our creditors for £38 000. The entries are shown in Fig. 10.1.

19 . .				£	£	J.17
May 1	Motor Vehicles a/c	Dr	L27	33 400.00		
	Tyres a/c	Dr	L35	4 600.00		
	Heavyfreight Motors PLC		L61		38 000.00	
	Being purchase of new motor					
	Lorry at this date (174 PEG)					

Fig. 10.1 *Permanent record of invoices in the Journal proper*

Notes
1 The entry gives a permanent record of the invoice, which could be shown in Court if necessary should the invoice be mislaid.
2 The narration usually starts with the word 'Being . . . . . .' and explains what has happened at this date.
3 The entries make a perfect double entry, but of course the only double entry that counts is a double entry in the ledger. When we post this entry into the ledger accounts we put the folio numbers in to show that the posting has been done, and remind us where to find the entry if we want to check it — page 27 in the Ledger for the Motor Vehicles Account, for example. These entries are shown in Fig. 10.2.

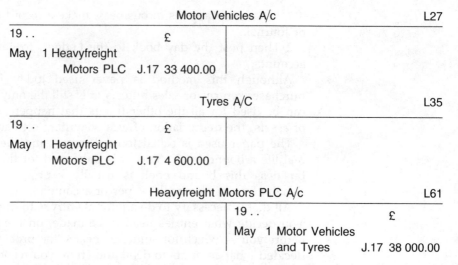

Fig. 10.2 *The entries in the Ledger, posted from the Journal*

Since this method is now only used for invoices that are to do with the purchase of assets of the business, and ordinary purchases of goods for re-sale are dealt with by the specialised day book method (see 10.4 below) we will practice these journal entries with some invoices about the purchase of assets.

10.3 Exercises: the purchase of assets of the business

1 On 14 January 19. ., we purchased two electronic typewriters for £850.00 altogether. Reference nos. were P12785 and C1734. They were purchased on credit from Electronic Office Supplies Ltd. Do the Journal Entry and post to the Ledger.

2 On 6 July 19. ., we purchased a new freezing cabinet, Serial No. 2178E from Shopfitters PLC for £420.00 on credit. Do the Journal Entry and post to the Ledger.

3 On 23 September 19. ., we purchased for cash at an auction sale the following items: weighing machine £85.00; cooking utensils £234.00; goods for resale (purchases) £120.00; electronic till £90.00. Do the Journal Entry and post to the Ledger. The weighing machine and cooking utensils are to be recorded in the Restaurant Equipment Account.

4 On 12 May 19. ., Hancock PLC purchased a new machine for £465.00 (Serial No. 24795) by cheque at an auction of property involved in a bankruptcy case. Do the Journal Entry and post it to the Ledger.

5 On 4 August 19. ., we purchased on credit desks and other office furniture to a total value of £845 from Mitre Furniture PLC. They also supplied computers to the value of £3000. Do the Journal Entry and post it to the Ledger.

6 On 1 August 19. ., Keis Muhammadu set up in business and purchased on credit from Business Materials Co. the following items: one office desk £218.50, four filing cabinets at £95.60 each and one electronic typewriter at £327.50. VAT at 10% was charged on all items. Show the Journal Entry and post it to the Ledger.

10.4 Method 2 — The specialised day book method

Why was the Journal method of recording invoices for purchases and sales and for recording credit notes for goods returned, so unsatisfactory?

The reason is that it was so wasteful of effort. All the purchases of goods are very much alike, consisting of the ordinary things our type of business trades in. Similarly all the sales invoices are very much alike, consisting of the same sort of items sold to different customers. There was no point in debiting every purchase to Purchases Account, or crediting every sale to Sales Account, with a separate Journal entry for each one. We might as well have a specialised day book for all the purchases (a Purchases Day Book) and a similar specialised book for sales (a Sales Day Book). Similarly we might as well put all the credit notes for purchases returned in a special Purchases Returns Book, and all the credit notes for sales returns in a special Sales Returns Book.

With the specialised day book method we remove all the ordinary trading items from the Journal, and put them instead in specialised journals (day books) for their particular class of goods, i.e. purchases, sales, purchases returns and sales returns. It used to be the case that the full document, whether it was an invoice or a credit note, was copied into the day book. Today we usually only show the name of the supplier (purchases) or the name of the customer (sales), and the main details, i.e. the total value of the goods, the VAT (if any) and any extra charges such as carriage charges, warehousing costs, etc. As all the entries are very much alike we can record them fairly quickly, using special columns for each item. The only tricky part then is the posting of these items to the ledger. The four illustrations Figs. 10.3, 10.5, 10.7 and 10.9 show some entries in the four books. Compare these four books and you will see how similar they are in layout. The only parts that are really different are the document numbers (the invoice and credit note numbers), and the folio numbers. These are explained below, but first study the four layouts carefully.

10.5 The Purchases Day Book

It is when we come to posting these books to the Ledger that we really begin to understand double entries. We have four books. To see what is happening in each case we must look at the postings to the Ledger and read the notes under each set of postings.

Purchases Day Book							PDB5
Date 19..	Supplier	Inv. No	Folio No	Goods £ :p	Carriage in £ :p	VAT (10%) £ :p	Total £ :p
May 4	M. Roberts Ltd	1754	CL5	180.20	4.50	18.47	203.17
5	Grover PLC	0221	CL7	68.54	—	6.85	75.39
9	Pinfold & Sons	0346	CL91	173.20	16.25	18.94	208.39
11	Abrahammadu Co.	1975	CL36	15.95	—	1.60	17.55
13	K. Chaira Co.	1864	CL29	166.27	—	16.63	182.90
25	Jones Bros	0021	CL81	1435.16	87.34	152.25	1674.75
28	R. Seager & Co.	0987	CL106	375.40	5.83	38.12	419.35
			£	2414.72	113.92	252.86	2781.50
				NL1	NL2	CL100	

Fig. 10.3 The Purchases Day Book

M. Roberts Ltd A/c — CL5

			£
19..			
May 4	Purchases	PDB5	203.17

Grover PLC A/c — CL7

			£
19..			
May 5	Purchases	PDB5	75.39

Pinfold and Sons A/c — CL91

			£
19..			
May 9	Purchases	PDB5	208.39

Abrahammadu Co. A/c — CL36

			£
19..			
May 11	Purchases	PDB5	17.55

K. Chaira Co. A/c — CL29

			£
19..			
May 13	Purchases	PDB5	182.90

Jones Bros A/c — CL81

			£
19..			
May 25	Purchases	PDB5	1674.75

R. Seager & Co. A/c — CL106

			£
19..			
May 28	Purchases	PDB5	419.35

Purchases A/c — NL1

			£
19..			
May 31	Sundry Creditors	PDB5	2414.72

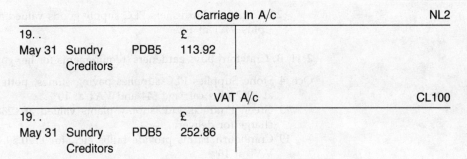

Fig. 10.4 Postings to the Ledgers from the Purchases Day Book

Notes
1 For convenience the Ledger is usually split up into several pieces so that different book-keepers can work on them. In this case we have the Creditors Ledger and the Nominal Ledger.
2 All the suppliers have given us supplies, so we credit the giver in each case. That makes them all creditors, in the Creditors Ledger, for the total amount owed.
3 Which accounts then are we to debit? The answer is that the purchases are debited in the Purchases Account (we have received the goods from our suppliers). Similarly the 'carriage in' is debited in the Carriage In Account, since this account has received the benefit of some expenditure. This is of course one of the losses of the business. Both these accounts are in the Nominal Ledger, because they are nominal accounts, that is accounts where the money is there in name only.
4 The VAT Account is a special case. Most businesses owe the VAT office money each quarter so that the VAT Account will be in the Creditors Ledger — the VAT officer is one of our creditors. However, we are debiting this account, not crediting it, because VAT on purchases is input tax, which we can reclaim from the VAT office. (See Chapter 9.)
5 If you check the totals you will find out that the debit entries exactly equal the credit entries, so we have done a proper double entry.
6 Note that the folio number in all these accounts is PDB5 (Purchases Day Book page five) whereas in the Purchases Day Book we insert the number of the account, CL5, CL7, etc., down to CL106. After that the other folio numbers are written under the total of the columns NL1 (Nominal Ledger page one) etc.

You should now try some of the exercises on the Purchases Day Book in 10.6 below.

10.6 Exercises on the Purchases Day Book

To do these exercises you should either rule up paper similar to Fig. 10.3 or use the illustration on page 90 to photocopy suitable paper.

1 R. E. Byworth buys furniture for re-sale to customers in his furniture store. The following details apply for the month of April. Record them and total the book for the month, checking the cross totals to see your work is correct. You need *not* post them to the Ledger.

April 4 R. Keeler supplies goods valued at £540 carriage paid (ie no carriage charges) but VAT is added at 10%.
 13 C. A. Projects Ltd, supply dining room furniture valued at £2250, plus carriage charges £85 and VAT at 10% on the total order.
 17 Coffee Tables Ltd, supply lounge furniture for £880 + carriage £45 and VAT at 10%.

29 Courtfield Furnishers PLC supply goods valued at £3460, carriage paid, plus VAT at 10%.

2 H. B. Crawford buys gardeners' requirements for her garden centre as follows:

Oct 4 Stone Supplies PLC supplies paving stones, pottery objects etc., valued at £962 plus carriage £44 and VAT at 10%.

13 Green Products Ltd, supply plants valued at £238 + VAT at 10%. No charge for delivery.

19 Cranbourn Farms provide bulbs etc., for £720.50 + carriage £38.50 and VAT at 10%.

27 De Carlo Supplies Ltd, provide garden furniture for £2380, plus carriage charges of £360 and VAT at 10%.

Record them in her Purchases Day Book. You need *not* post them to the Ledger.

3 Chris's Fashions buys fashion goods for re-sale to customers in her boutique. The following details apply for the month of May. Record them and total the book for the month, checking the cross totals to see your work is correct. You should then post them to the Ledger.

May 4 Monsoon PLC supplies goods valued at £540 carriage paid (i.e. no carriage charges) but VAT is added at 10%.

17 Swedish Couture Ltd, supply sportswear valued at £2080, plus carriage charges £65 and VAT at 10% on the total order.

19 Woolman & Co., supply knitted wear for £846.50 + carriage £32.50 and VAT at 10%.

27 Highland Crofters Ltd, supply goods valued at £3065, carriage paid, plus VAT at 10%.

4 M. Bhattacharya buys delicatessen items for his grocery as follows. Record them in his Purchases Day Book and post them to the Ledger.

Oct 7 Meat Supplies PLC supplies potted meats, curries, etc., valued at £262 plus carriage £14 and VAT at 10%.

13 Indian Produce PLC supplies foods valued at £218 + VAT at 10%, no charge for delivery.

23 Oriental Supplies provide canned products for £320.50 + carriage £18.50 and VAT at 10%.

31 M. Choudhary provides decorative and festival items for £290.60 plus carriage charges of £36.40 and VAT at 10%.

10.7 The Sales Day Book

Before looking at this illustration, can you visualise what entries are going to be made in this book. It may help you to answer the following questions:

1 What documents are going to be recorded in the Sales Day Book? (Answer — the sales invoices made out in our Invoicing Department yesterday.)

2 Will they be a neat bunch of invoices or will they be an untidy collection of invoices? (Answer — a neat bunch — they are the second

copies of our own invoices, the top copies were posted off to the customers yesterday.) They are all the same size, shape and colour.

3 Who is supplying the goods mentioned on the invoices? (Answer — we are. We are selling them to our customers and hope to be paid for them next month.)

Now look at the entries in Fig. 10.5, and the postings to the Ledger in Fig. 10.6.

Sales Day Book							SDB14
Date 19 ..	Customer	Inv. No	Folio No	Goods £ :p	Carriage out £ :p	VAT (10%) £ :p	Total £ :p
May 5	R. Lucas	1015	DL7	495.60	27.30	52.29	575.19
8	P. Boreham	1016	DL17	327.85	18.50	34.64	380.99
11	C. Shah	1017	DL95	86.42	—	8.64	95.06
23	D. Viet	1018	DL63	137.29	14.25	15.15	166.69
27	Cold foods Ltd	1019	DL64	1850.00	163.50	201.35	2214.85
31	Elder Corp. Ltd	1020	DL81	786.55	56.25	84.28	927.08
			£	3683.71	279.80	396.35	4359.86
				NL3	NL4	CL100	

Fig. 10.5 The Sales Day Book

R. Lucas A/c   DL7

19..			£	
May 5	Sales	SDB14	575.19	

P. Boreham A/c   DL17

19..			£	
May 8	Sales	SDB14	380.99	

C. Shah A/c   DL95

19..			£	
May 11	Sales	SDB14	95.06	

D. Viet A/c   DL63

19..			£	
May 23	Sales	SDB14	166.69	

Coldfoods Ltd A/c   DL64

19..			£	
May 27	Sales	SDB14	2214.85	

Elder Corporation A/c   DL81

19..			£	
May 31	Sales	SDB14	927.08	

Sales A/c   NL3

				£
	19. .			
	May 31	Sundry		
		Debtors	SDB14	3683.71

Carriage Out A/c   NL4

19. .			£	19. .			£
May 31	Sundry			May 31	Sundry		
	Carriers	CB 19	560.24		Debtors	SDB14	279.80

VAT A/c   CL100

19. .			£	19. .			£
May 31	Sundry			May 31	Sundry		
	Creditors	PDB5	252.86		Debtors	SDB14	396.35

Fig. 10.6 Postings to the Ledger from the Sales Day Book

Notes
1 All our customers are debtors who owe us for the goods they have received from us. We debit their accounts (debit the receiver). The debtors' accounts are usually kept in a separate part of the Ledger called the Debtors Ledger.
2 What accounts shall we credit? The Sales Account is our account where we record the goods we have 'given' to our customers, so the total of the 'Goods' column is credited to the Sales Account.
3 The Carriage Out Account needs a special mention. We have shown the figure on the left hand side for all the carriage paid out from the cash book — £560.64 during the month of May. That is nothing to do with posting the Sales Day Book but it lets us see why the Carriage Out total of £279.80 has been credited in the Carriage Out Account. Since we are charging some of our customers with the carriage on their goods this money — when it comes in — will reduce the losses we have suffered. So crediting the Carriage Out Account cuts the expenses on carriage for the month of May.
4 Similarly the VAT Account is credited with the total VAT we have charged our customers, £396.35. This is output tax which we have to pay to the VAT office, so consequently they are a creditor of ours. However, the amount we owe the VAT office is reduced by the input tax already recorded on the left hand side of the account, since this is the amount already paid by us to our suppliers (as shown in Fig. 10.4).
5 You should now try some of the exercises in 10.8 below.

10.8 Exercises on the Sales Day Book

1 M. Disart sells office supplies to customers, making no charge for carriage but VAT is added at 10% to all orders, except zero rated items. Transactions in the month of April were as follows:

April 4 He supplied goods to Geomechanical Co. Ltd, valued at £840.00, plus VAT.
       7 He supplied goods to Fishlock and Sons valued at £231.98, plus VAT.
       9 He supplied goods to Empson Consultancy Ltd, valued at £84.95, plus VAT.
     23 He supplied goods to Erith Building Services valued at £184.60. No VAT is chargeable as the goods were zero rated.

31 He supplied goods to Magpie Garages Ltd, valued at £3250, plus VAT.

Enter these items in a Sales Day Book using paper similar to that shown on page 90. You need not post the items to the Ledger.

2 Oaktree Preservation Ltd send out invoices to customers for their wood-preservation services making no charge for delivery of materials, but VAT is added at 10% to all invoices. Transactions in the month of June were as follows:

June 11 They supplied services to Chalk House Offices valued at £725.50, plus VAT.

June 17 They supplied services to Stately Homes PLC valued at £5950 plus VAT.

June 22 They supplied services to Rural Retreats Ltd, valued at £824.50, plus VAT.

June 25 They supplied services to Breckland Cottages Ltd, valued at £268.60, plus VAT.

June 30 Elizabethan Homes Ltd, requested services and were invoiced for work valued at £4980, plus VAT.

Enter these items in a Sales Day Book using paper similar to that shown on page 90. You need not post the items to the Ledger.

3 Kay Marshall sells fashion goods to customers, making a charge for carriage and adding VAT at 10% to all orders, except zero rated items. Transactions in the month of September were as follows:

Sept 5 She supplied goods to Young Fashions Ltd, valued at £485.60, plus carriage £34.40 and VAT on the total charge.

   7 She supplied goods to Top Drawer Man valued at £1756.50, plus carriage £72.50 and VAT on the total charge.

  11 She supplied goods to School-age Fashion Ltd, valued at £1405.00, plus carriage £84.00. No VAT payable on these items.

  21 She supplied goods to Teenager Ltd, valued at £865.50, plus carriage £36.40. No VAT payable.

  26 She supplied goods to Young Idea valued at £1486.60, plus carriage £106.20 and VAT.

Enter these items in a Sales Day Book using paper similar to that shown on page 90. You should then post the items to the Ledger.

4 Decor PLC sells gifts to gift shops, making a charge for carriage, and VAT is added at 10% to all orders. Transactions in the month of February were as follows:

Feb 7 They supplied goods to Decorations Ltd, valued at £580.50, plus carriage £33.30 and VAT.

  11 They supplied goods to Choice Gifts valued at £427.50, plus carriage £21.50 and VAT.

  18 They supplied goods to Orient Gift Shop valued at £1275.75, plus carriage £72.60 and VAT.

  25 They supplied goods to Country Images valued at £625.50, plus carriage £38.50 and VAT.

  29 They supplied goods to Shop-on-the-Green valued at £426.85, plus carriage £18.25 and VAT.

Enter these items in a Sales Day Book using paper similar to that shown on page 90. You should then post the items to the Ledger.

10.9 The Purchases Returns Book

When something we have purchased is unsatisfactory for some reason we return it and are given in exchange a credit note. This credit note (which is usually printed in red) acknowledges the return of the goods and is used to reduce our debt to the supplier. It is entered in the Purchases Returns Book — the special day book for credit notes for returns outwards.

Study the example shown in Fig. 10.7 and the postings to the Ledger shown in Fig. 10.8.

Purchases Returns Book							PRB3
Date 19 ..	Supplier	C/N No	Folio No	Goods £ :p	Carriage in £ :p	VAT (10%) £ :p	Total £ :p
May 11	M. Roberts Ltd	17	CL5	24.80	—	2.48	27.28
23	K. Chaira Co.	114	CL29	12.85	2.80	1.56	17.21
31	Jones Bros	89	CL81	85.60	8.24	9.38	103.22
			£	123.25	11.04	13.42	147.71
				NL5	NL2	CL100	

Fig. 10.7 The Purchases Returns Book

Notes
1 The documents being recorded are credit notes received from our suppliers for goods returned to them, perhaps because they were the wrong size, shape, colour, quality, etc.
2 If the incorrect goods have been supplied and carriage has been charged on them we would expect to be able to reclaim the carriage paid, since the supplier who sent the wrong goods must be expected to carry this expense.
3 The VAT item will of course be Input Tax which we are no longer to be charged, since the goods are being returned. When posted to the Ledger the entries will be as shown in Fig. 10.8.

M.˙ Roberts Ltd A/c		CL5
19.. £	19..	£
May 31 Purchases returns PRB3 27.28	May 4 Purchases PDB5	203.17

K. Chaira Co. A/c		CL29
19.. £	19..	£
May 31 Purchases returns PRB3 17.21	May 13 Purchases PDB5	182.90

Jones Bros A/c		CL81
19.. £	19..	£
May 31 Purchases returns PRB3 103.22	May 25 Purchases PDB5	1674.75

Purchases Returns A/c   NL5

19. .	£	19. .		£
		May 31 Sundry		
		creditors	PRB3	123.25

Carriage In A/c   NL2

19. .		£	19. .		£
May 31 Sundry			May 31 Sundry		
creditors	PDB5	113.92	creditors	PRB3	11.04

VAT A/c   CL100

19. .		£	19. .		£
May 31 Sundry			May 31 Sundry		
creditors	PDB5	252.86	debtors	SDB14	396.35
			May 31 Sundry		
			creditors	PRB3	13.42

Fig. 10.8 Postings to the Ledger from the Purchases Returns Book

Notes
1 It is a bit difficult to follow the double entries since the items from the Purchases Day Book and the Sales Day Book have been left in deliberately. It would be unrealistic to show returns if we had not recorded any purchases in the first place. We cannot return what we do not have.
2 You can follow the entries by looking for the folio numbers PRB3.
3 The three creditors have each been debited with the returns — because they have received back the goods returned.
4 Our account, the Purchases Returns Account has given back the goods and is credited with £123.25.
5 Carriage In has been reduced by the amount of the carriage, now payable by the supplier who sent the wrong goods.
6 VAT Account has also been credited — some of the Input Tax of £252.86 which we were claiming back from the VAT office has been allowed on the credit note and we can no longer claim it back.
7 If you add up the debits and the credits on the lines with PRB3 on them you will see that they make a perfect double entry.

10.10 Exercises on the Purchases Returns Book

1 Electronic Machines Ltd, returns items during the month of January to various suppliers as shown on the following credit notes:

Jan 11 Returned one Focus brand facsimile copier to Flowline Machines Ltd (damaged in transit). Price £485 + VAT at 10%.
    17 Returned five desk reader-printers to Arizus Microfilm (faulty). Price £400 each plus 10% VAT. Carriage £40 + VAT also to be refunded.
    24 Returned one desk telephone with answering machine to Microphones Ltd, price £140 + VAT at 10%.
    25 Returned one Magic colour copier to Oriental Products Ltd, (defective drum) price £780 + VAT at 10%. Carriage of £35 + VAT also to be refunded.

Record these items in their Purchases Returns Book and post them to the various Ledger Accounts. Invent suitable folio numbers as required.

2 Hilary Robbins returns items during the month of February to various suppliers as follows:

Feb 11 Credit note from Farouk Fabric Printers Ltd, for cloth valued at £85 + VAT at 10%.
    17 Credit note from Unit Eighteen for 24 sets of ladies sportswear to a total value of £108 plus carriage £8.50 and VAT at 10%.
    24 Credit note from Designer Fashions PLC for one Ski-suit at £285 plus VAT at 10%.
    25 Credit note from Scanning Designs Ltd, for beachwear valued at £86.50 + carriage £9.50 and VAT at 10%.

Record these items in her Purchases Returns Book and post them to the various ledger accounts. Invent suitable folio numbers as required.

3 Bureau Supplies Ltd, returns items during the month of March to various suppliers as follows:

March 11 Credit note from Klondyke Equipment Supplies for filing cabinets valued at £240 plus carriage £20 and VAT at 10%.
    17 Credit note from Thomas's Home Interiors for one desk £186 plus carriage £15 and VAT at 10%.
    24 Credit note from Boardrooms PLC for three dictation machines to a total value of £189.50 + VAT at 10%.
    25 Credit note from Enterprise Superstore for one electronic typewriter at £245 + VAT at 10%.

Record these items in their Purchases Returns Book and post them to the various ledger accounts. Invent suitable folio numbers as required.

10.11 The Sales Returns Book

When the things we have sold to our customers prove to be unsatisfactory for some reason, they return them and we issue a credit note to them to recognise the return of the goods supplied. Remember also that a firm that does not deal in goods, but supplies 'services', may issue a credit note to reduce the customer's bill, even though nothing has been

Sales Returns Book							SRB2
Date 19..	Customer	C/N No	Folio No	Goods £ :p	Carriage out £ :p	VAT (10%) £ :p	Total £ :p
May 9	R. Lucas	214	DL7	54.50	5.50	6.00	66.00
16	C. Shah	215	DL95	9.65	—	.96	10.61
29	P. Boreham	216	DL17	42.20	7.80	5.00	55.00
			£	106.35	13.30	11.96	131.61
				NL6	NL4	CL100	

Fig. 10.9 The Sales Returns Book

returned. This is called an 'allowance' and might be given if there was some dissatisfaction expressed by the customer.

Study the Sales Returns Book shown in Fig. 10.9 and the postings to the Ledger in Fig. 10.10. Once again the original sales to the customers have been inserted so the entries you need to consider most closely are those with the folio numbers SRB2.

R. Lucas A/c							DL7
19. .			£	19. .			£
May 5	Sales	SDB14	575.19	May 9	Sales returns	SRB2	66.00

C. Shah A/c							DL95
19. .			£	19. .			£
May 11	Sales	SDB14	95.06	May 16	Sales returns	SRB2	10.61

P. Boreham A/c							DL17
19. .			£	19. .			£
May 8	Sales	SDB14	380.99	May 29	Sales returns	SRB2	55.00

Sales Returns A/c					NL6
19. .			£		
May 31	Sundry debtors	SRB2	106.35		

Carriage Out A/c							NL4
19. .			£	19. .			£
May 31	Sundry carriers	CB19	560.24	May 31	Sundry debtors	SDB14	279.80
31	Sundry debtors	SRB2	13.30				

VAT A/c							CL100
19. .			£	19. .			£
May 31	Sundry creditors	PDB2	252.86	May 31	Sundry debtors	SDB14	396.35
31	Sundry debtors	SRB2	11.96	31	Sundry creditors	PRB3	13.42

Fig. 10.10 Postings from the Sales Returns Books

Notes
1 The returns entries are shown by the folio numbers SRB2.
2 The three debtors have been credited because they gave back the goods — credit the giver — and this reduces their debts to us.
3 The Sales Returns Account has received back the goods — debit the receiver.
4 The Carriage Out Account has been debited, because the carriage the debtors were to have

paid us has been reduced — we can't expect them to pay the carriage if we sent them the wrong goods. This increases the expense item, Carriage Out, one of the losses of the business.

5 The VAT Account is debited, because these customers are going to pay less tax to us (the output tax we have charged them) as a result of these returns. Therefore we shall owe the VAT office less tax. Now try the exercises in Section 10.12.

10.12 Exercises on the Sales Returns Book

1 Allison Chinawares PLC is returned items during the month of July 19. ., by dissatisfied customers as follows:

July 5 The Crockery Shop returns a dinner service of the wrong pattern valued at £98.50 plus carriage £5.50 and VAT at 10%.
    11 The Churchyard Crystal Co. returns specialist pottery items valued at £234 plus 10% VAT.
    29 Orient China Co. returns a tea service valued at £28.50 plus carriage £4.50 and VAT at 10%.

Record these items in their Sales Returns Book and post them to the the various ledger accounts. Invent suitable folio numbers as required.

2 Equipyu Computers Ltd issues credit notes during the month of October 19. as follows:

Oct 7 Digital Products Ltd return goods valued at £256 plus carriage charges of £24 and VAT at 10%.
    18 Hallmark Services Ltd return components valued at £176 plus VAT at 10%.
    28 Pegasus Products return accessories valued at £385 plus carriage charges £37.50 and VAT at 10%.
    29 Iambic Services Ltd return word processor software worth £282.50 plus VAT at 10%.

Record these items in their Sales Returns Book and post them to the various ledger accounts. Invent suitable folio numbers as required.

3 Double-glazing Ltd issues the following credit notes during the month of July to dissatisfied customers as follows:

July 4 A. Lang is given an allowance of £100 plus VAT at 10%.
    17 A. Ajakaiye is given an allowance of £250 plus VAT at 10%.
    30 M. Ellard is given an allowance of £50 and also is given credit for a replacement window surplus to requirements worth £86.50 plus carriage £5.50 and VAT on all these items at 10%.

Record these items in their Sales Returns Book and post them to the various ledger accounts. Invent suitable folio numbers as required.

Type of Day-book											Folio	
				£	p	£	p	£	p		£	p

Fig. 10.11

Note
This blank sheet may be reproduced by photocopier to enable the exercises in this chapter to be answered easily.

11 Simultaneous records systems

11.1 Business systems

The word 'systems' is very important in business. It is applied to any method of working or procedure that achieves the results that business desires in an economical and simple way. This may apply to a manual system of book-keeping such as we are chiefly interested in for elementary accounting or to a computerised system. You will almost certainly have seen advertisements for 'systems analysts' — people who can analyse any system of activity and translate it into computerised form, whether it is computerised accounting or hotel and holiday bookings or any field of production etc.

In this chapter we are looking at **simultaneous records systems**, or **three-in-one systems**; that is systems which enable us to produce three sets of records at the same time. Since most of these systems depend upon carbon copying, or perhaps on NCR paper records, we cannot usually do more than three things at once, since the carbon copy gets too faint. NCR paper is paper where **no carbon** is **required** — NCR. The paper itself is coated all over with transparent globules of very tiny size. The globules contain a transparent ink which, when the bubbles are burst by the pressure of a ball point pen, combines with the air to form a visible writing. Whether we use carbon paper or NCR paper the fact remains that if we have three pages, or three papers, one on top of the other, what we write on the top one will be reproduced on the other two below, and we will have prepared three records simultaneously. As an example we will consider the Sales Day Book which we have already studied in Chapter 10.

11.2 The three records for sales

When we sell goods to someone we make out a copy of the invoice. The top copy is sent to the customer and is entered in his/her Purchases Day Book. The second copy is our accounts copy, and goes to the Accounts Department, to be entered in our Sales Day Book. When it has been entered we post the entry to the Ledger, and at the end of the month we send out a Statement of Account, asking the customer to pay the total amount due. So here are three records that can easily be prepared simultaneously if we just devise a system that makes it possible.

Kalamazoo — a famous name in business systems. There are many firms offering simultaneous records systems today, but it is worth mentioning the most famous name in this field "Kalamazoo" because (a) it is an unusual name (actually it is the name of a city in the United States) and (b) many advertisements for employment do mention the system by name. Thus an advertisement reading 'Kalamazoo Wages Clerk required' refers to a person who can keep wages under the Kalamazoo simultaneous records system. Those who have studied this chapter on simultaneous records could easily master Kalamazoo Wages, and could take such a position and manage the work quite cheerfully after a little induction.

To return to our three records for sales, we have:

1 The Sales Day Book — the permanent record of sales invoices sent out day by day.

2 The Sales Ledger Accounts.

3 The monthly statement of account.

We are going to learn how to keep these simultaneously but first let us look at a statement of account.

11.3 Statements of account

A **statement of account** is a request for payment. Figure 11.1 shows a Kalamazoo monthly statement. It lists all the items sold to the customer — Ward & Co. Ltd — during the month of January. The statement is in running balance form. Every time the customer's account is debited because Ward & Co. Ltd have received supplies the balance on the account increases, and every time the account is credited (in this case when Ward & Co. paid the amount due at the start of the month) it reduces the balance on the account. A statement is sent out each month, and becomes payable, usually within 30 days.

What to do when you receive a 'statement' The actions to take on receiving a statement are:

1 Check the statement against your own records to see that you have received goods as stated, and listed in the debit column.

2 Check that all payments sent by you since last month have been recorded as received — they will be in the credit column.

3 Similarly any returns you have sent to them should have been entered in the credit column. (In this case there were none.)

4 Check the calculations and if correct pass the statement to the Accountant for payment. Very often a rubber stamp might be impressed on the statement reading 'Checked and passed for payment . . . . (signature)', or something similar.

11.4 Simultaneous records for sales

To make book-keeping entries simultaneously we have to lay one record on top of another. In the case of the Kalamazoo Sales Day Book system,

amount outstanding from previous months

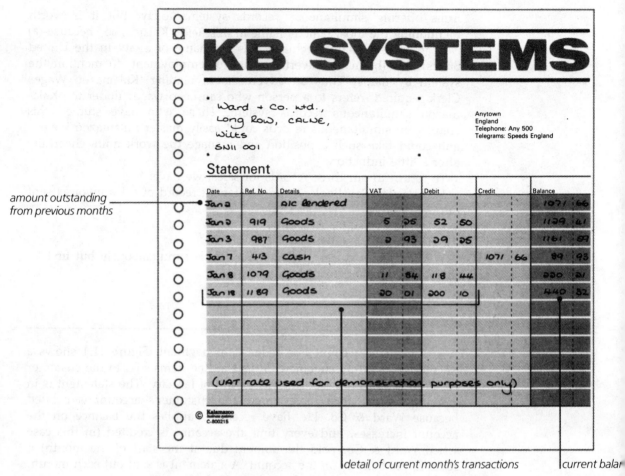

detail of current month's transactions | current balan

Fig. 11.1 A monthly statement

we first lay out the Sales Day Book page, which has holes punched down one side which engage with studs on the flat board called a **copywriter**. On top of this we lay a ledger card for the customer whose entry we are making and on top of the ledger card we lay the customer's monthly statement, which will be sent off at the end of the month. The statement is positioned so that the next clean line on the statement is over the top of the next clean line on the ledger and this is on top of the next clean line on the Day Book page. Now, any entry made on the Statement, which is NCR paper, will be copied onto the ledger card which is also coated with NCR globules and therefore is copied onto the Sales Day Book page. The result is that with one writing you have not only done the Sales Day Book entry but have also posted it to the ledger and updated the monthly statement ready for it to go out at the end of the month. You can see the layout in Fig. 11.2.

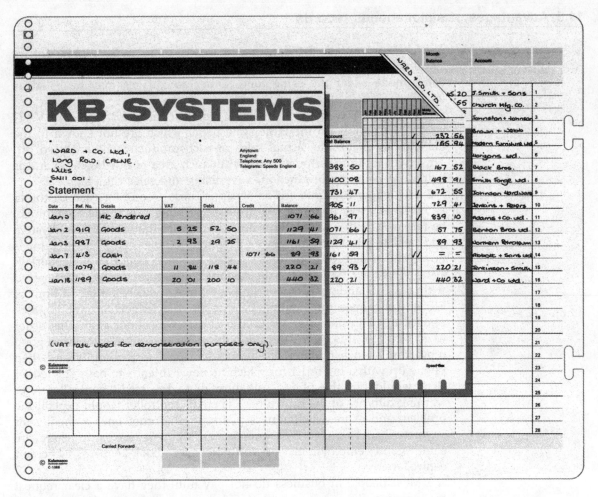

Fig. 11.2 Simultaneous entries

Notes

1 The Sales Day Book page is the largest sheet underneath the others. When it is full it is filed in a loose-leaf binder and becomes our Sales Day Book with every sales invoice recorded on it.

2 The ledger card (there is one for each customer) is the second sheet, which has the corner cut off, and little notches cut in the base of the card. These enable it to be stored in a special rack, and each account is moved along one notch so that every account can be seen at a glance — what is called a visible index system — the part saying 'Ward & Co. Ltd' is visible at all times.

3 The statement is on top, and is actually written on, and then it is stored with the ledger card until the end of the month. At the end of the month we take a new statement, head it up, write the first line — in this case Feb 1 A/c rendered £440.32. The new statement is put with the ledgercard; the old one is put in an envelope and posted off to the customer, who pays it in due course.

Clearly the whole system is very simple, and once established it can continue for years with very few problems indeed.

11.5 Advantages of simultaneous records

The chief advantage is of course that one entry makes three entries simultaneously; the statement, the ledger posting and Sales Day Book being made all at the same time. Other advantages may be listed as follows:

1 The Sales Day Book pages build up clear totals for sales and VAT, but extra columns on the large scale paper which are not shown in the illustration, enable the actual sales of each product to be analysed off. This gives us the 'customer activity' in each area of our business and is helpful in planning production, advertising and sales campaigns.

2 The ledger accounts are on separate cards — one for each customer — not in a heavy bound book or loose-leaf binder. A single account can be removed with a simple arm movement from the visible index system and held in the hand to answer telephone queries, etc. The account is never out of date (waiting to be posted by some junior book-keeper). It also shows the credit limit of the customer, which can easily be compared with the outstanding balance. Suppose Mr A. who has a credit limit of £1500 and whose outstanding balance on the ledger account is £500, phones up with an order for £2000. Clearly we cannot allow this order to go through. It is quite a common thing for a rogue to establish a good reputation with a number of small orders paid for promptly and then phone up with a big order for which he never intends to pay. The ledger clerk would put the phone call through to the **credit controller** after warning him/her of the difficulty. The credit controller would explain the problem and express willingness to supply the order once a cheque for payment had been received and cleared through the bank. There are some good employment opportunities for book-keepers as credit controllers.

3 Most people in business do not pay until they have a clear request for payment. If someone has not paid you for goods or services supplied ask yourself 'Have I actually demanded payment?'. If not, send a statement at once. With simultaneous records the statement is always ready to go out, up to date and ready for posting. It used to be the practice to send statements out on the last day of the month, but this clogs up the Post Office with millions of statements on the move. Most firms now send out about 4% of statements every day. This has two advantages; (a) the work of posting-off the statements is spread evenly over the month and (b) the cash flowing in as customers pay their accounts is also even. This is called **'cash flow smoothing'**.

11.6 Other simultaneous records

Of course, it isn't just the sales that appear on our ledger cards. We must have similar systems for purchases, for payments by debtors and for our payments to creditors. Other systems such as wages, stock records and income tax records lend themselves to this system of work.

Some of the commoner systems are:

1 *The Purchases Ledger system*   Here we have
(a) The remittance advice note placed on top of
(b) The Creditor's Ledger account placed on top of
(c) The Purchases Day Book

2 *The Sales Returns system*   with
(a) The statement placed on top of
(b) The Sales Ledger account placed on top of
(c) The Sales Returns Book

3 *The Purchases Returns system*   with
(a) The remittance advice note placed on top of
(b) The Creditors Ledger account placed on top of
(c) The Purchases Returns Book

4 *The wages system*   with
(a) The payslip placed on top of
(b) The employee's wages record card placed on top of
(c) The payroll sheet (which shows the payments to every one in the firm or company).

11.7 Self-assessment questions

1 What is the other name for simultaneous records systems?
2 What do we call the board the system rests on?
3 What is the purpose of the studs or other holding device on this board?
4 What is NCR paper?
5 What is the particular danger of NCR paper?
6 What is the most famous name in simultaneous record systems?
7 In a Sales Day Book system, what are the three records produced?

11.8 Exercises in simultaneous records

The reader will see that it is impossible to set exercises on this subject unless the student has all the equipment required, copywriter boards, sheets of day-book paper, ledger cards, statements, etc. These can be obtained at reasonable cost from the suppliers, for example Kalamazoo. Look in your local telephone directory for your local Kalamazoo supplier, or write to Kalamazoo Business Systems, Northfield, Birmingham, B31 2RW.

Perhaps the best system to afford for educational purposes is the Wages system.

11.9 Answers to self-assessment questions

1 Three-in-one systems.
2 A copywriter.
3 The studs (a) hold the papers firmly in position one above the other and (b) enable the position of the copies to be moved down one line each time an entry is made so that the next entry is always made on the next clean line.

4 NCR paper is 'no carbon required' paper — the paper itself is coated with microscopic ink globules which only release the ink when the pressure of a pen (preferably a ball point pen) bursts the bubbles and releases the ink.

5 You must never write on a whole pad of statements, ledger cards etc. Only use them one at a time. One young book-keeper scribbled a message on a pack reading 'Gone for a cup of tea'. It came out on every statement in the pack. The manageress was *not* pleased.

6 Kalamazoo.

7 (a) the statement; (b) the ledger card; (c) the Sales Day Book.

12 How a computer keeps Ledger Accounts

12.1 Computerised accounting

Today most large businesses, and many small ones, use some sort of computerised book-keeping system. We have already seen one small aspect of this in the section on running-balance accounts.

A computer is really a very hard-working idiot. By this we mean that it can only do very simple things, but it does them so incredibly quickly that it appears to be very clever. For example, even a slow computer can do ten million adding up sums in a second. There is nothing very clever about adding up, but to add up so fast that while you blink your eyes the answer is done leaves the computer well ahead of even a very intelligent human being.

The computer itself consists of a number of units, now reduced to very small size because of the miniaturisation which has been made possible by the use of silicon chips — tiny wafers of silicon onto which circuits have been printed. The chief unit is the **central processor unit (CPU)**. Other units are the **arithmetic unit**, the **memory unit** (or units), various registers which can store figures until required in a difficult calculation and a **peripheral control unit** which controls the various devices outside the computer, but linked to it. These are mentioned below. They are all input or output devices which can input data and programs to the computer, and output results in understandable form. A typical micro-computer configuration is shown in Fig. 12.1.

We don't need to understand how computers do accounts unless we are programming the machine to get it to do the work. All we need to consider is what the computer does, how we can use its abilities in business life and how the computer can be operated to do the things we want it to do.

The development of cheap micro-computers has brought computerised accounting within reach of every small business. It is possible to buy the essential units very cheaply, a computer, a keyboard communicator, a disc drive unit, a printer and a visual display unit, together with a set of programs on a single floppy disc which will do all the accounting activities we need. With these few items, and one more disc on which to save our data, we can make every type of entry we require, in such a simple way that it is almost impossible to make a mistake. If the computer is **user-friendly** it will ask us safeguarding questions all the time.

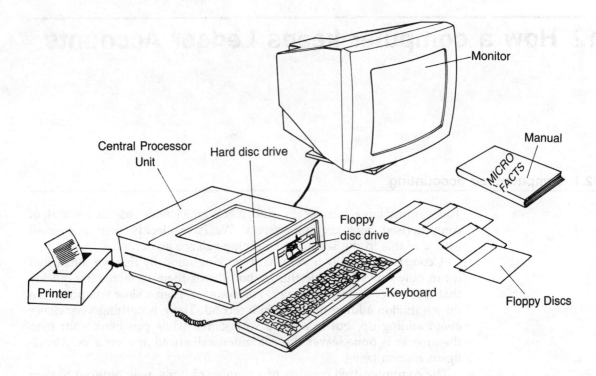

Fig. 12.1 A micro-computer configuration

For example:

    You are asking me to enter this invoice in the Sales Day Book.
    Is that right? Y/N

Y/N stands for Yes/No. If we touch the Y key the computer will then ask
    Are you sure? Y/N

If we touch the Y key again the computer will do all the necessary things
— enter the invoice in the Sales Day Book, post it to the Ledger, record
it on the statement in the computer's memory and flash up another
instruction such as

    Please enter the next invoice!

That is what we mean by a computer that is user-friendly.

    The system described in this chapter is based on the very simple
Simplex System described earlier. The programmes are available from
Micro Retailer Systems Ltd, Cheshire House, Exchange Close, Castle
Street, Macclesfield, Cheshire SK11 6UX (Tel: 0625 615000) from whom
they may be obtained for class or business use. There are many other
computerised accounting programs, some of which are more suitable for
large scale businesses. All such microcomputer programs are stored on
floppy discs which when inserted into a disc unit will load the first
program into the computer. The first thing we see is a 'menu' or list

of programs, which we can select to carry out the first piece of book-keeping we wish to do.

12.2 The main menu

The main menu of Micro-Simplex reads:

1 Weekly/daily Entries
2 Summaries
3 Unpaid Bills
4 Outstanding Invoices
5 Audit Trail
6 VAT Reporting
7 Profit and Loss Accounts
8 Stocks
9 Close Down
Select Menu Option

We respond to this invitation to select a menu option by keying in one of the nine numbers shown. Each of these numbers is a whole group of programs, for instance the 'VAT Reporting' option will let us do VAT by ten different methods — whichever one is appropriate for our business. If we press key 1 the Main Menu program will be removed from the computer and will be replaced by the group of programs in this subsidiary menu.

12.3 The weekly/daily entries menu

This reads as follows:

1 Receipts/Paid to Bank
2 Payments for Business Stock
3 Payments Other Than for Stock
4 Weekly Bank Report
5 Weekly Cash Report
6 Print Weekly Statement
7 Return to Main Menu
Select Menu Option

Suppose we press 3, requesting the Payments Other than for Stock. The line 'Select Menu Option' disappears to be replaced by a statement:

'Loading Payments Other than for Stock'

This is another example of a user-friendly computer. The computer tells the user all the time what it is doing, so that you are never in doubt. In a few seconds a layout for making an entry appears on the screen as shown in Fig. 12.2.

```
                    1234.56      SIMPLEX-64      123.45
          BANK                                               CASH

              PAYMENTS OTHER THAN FOR STOCK


          ANAL. CODE              17 MOTOR EXPENSES (1)

          DATE/CHEQUE             123456

          TO WHOM PAID            THE LOCAL GARAGE

          AMOUNT                  87.64

          VAT CONTENT             11.43


              THIS TRANSACTION NUMBER IS 58
```

Fig. 12.2 Visual display for the entry of payments of expenses

Notes

1 The whole display does not come up at once, but certain pieces of information appear first — for example the computer tells us that at the moment we have £1234.56 in the bank and £123.45 in the cash box or till.

2 It asks what analysis code we require by lighting up the screen with a blip of light (the cursor). As the payment is a motor expense we type in the code for this, which is 17. Computers use codes as a signal to the computer. At once the computer remembers that code 17 is Motor Expenses (1) and this appears. Also a cursor appears on the date cheque line. If we paid by cheque we type in the cheque number — this lets the computer know that the Bank balance is about to change. If we type in the date it tells the computer we paid in cash and the cash balance is going to alter.

3 The cursor has moved on to 'To whom paid'. We key in The Local Garage. The cursor moves on to the 'amount' line. We type in £87.64. The computer at once works out that the VAT content of this is £11.43 (by using the VAT fraction programmed into its memory). In this example the fraction is 3/23, because VAT is at 15%.

4 The computer now goes into its 'user-friendly' routine.

   Do you wish this expense to be entered? Y/N

We press the Y key

   Are you sure? Y/N

We press the Y key again.

5 The computer now does these things, in less than a second.

   (a) It enters the expense in the summary of expenses to increase the amount lost in the year on motor expenses. In other words it debits the Motor Vehicle Expenses Account.

   (b) It takes the £87.64 from the bank balance, so we have now spent the money.

   (c) It records the whole transaction on the 'audit trail'. This is a record of every entry made on the computer. It can be printed out so that the accountant (and the fraud squad if there is any dishonesty) can follow every entry made.

   (d) It gives us a transaction number — 58 — for this transaction. We write this on the document from which we have made the entry, and file it away. That document, we can now see, is the 58th entry on the audit trail. We can now move on to the next entry.

   Whatever program we select the same sort of simple, foolproof, user-friendly procedure will appear on the screen, to take us through the necessary entries.

12.4 Other points about computers

There are many points to learn about computers, but they are best learned in practical terms, actually watching a VDU (visual display unit) and seeing what the programmer has done to provide us with a full accounting service. This is called 'hands-on' experience, because we can have our hands on the keyboard and key in the responses, that are required. If you get the chance to get any 'hands-on' experience take it — you will soon find that it is easy to use computers. It is not quite so easy to program them.

Looking back at the two menus shown we can consider a few further points.

1 Unpaid bills

This module keeps a record of all the unpaid bills we have received. As soon as a statement arrives we key it in to the 'unpaid bills' module so that it is not forgotten. We also key in information about the length of time we have before the bill needs to be paid, and we can in some cases arrange to pay it by computer on the due date. When the bill is actually paid it is cleared from the unpaid bills module and the money is deducted from the Bank Account.

2 Close Down

When we finish using the computer at the end of the day, or at the end of our piece of book-keeping — since we probably only need 20 minutes work a day — the computer has to go through a close-down program. This takes any program which is loaded into the computer out of the computer's memory and back onto the program disc where it can be stored over-night. It also takes all the book-keeping records out of the computer onto a data disc, where they can be stored over-night. The computer then shows 'Closed Down'. We now make a copy of our data disc, and put it away in a safe place or preferably take it home. If anything happens to our data disc — a burglary, a fire or just someone messing about with our computer — we have a copy somewhere else which is true and correct. With all our book-keeping on one floppy disc we can't be too careful.

Note that since the 'close down' facility is on the main menu, every other menu has at the end the option 'Return to Main Menu'. You have to go from the subsidiary menu to the main menu so that you can go to 'Close Down' and get your records out of the computer.

3 Outstanding invoices

Just as we need to know which bills we have not paid yet, we need to know which of our customers have not paid us yet. As soon as we make out an invoice to a customer the amount goes on the 'Outstanding Invoices' module. The computer will print out a statement of account when instructed and when the payment is received it will clear the invoice from the 'Outstanding Invoice' list. If the customer does not pay in time the computer will print out a list of overdue accounts to remind us to get on the telephone and demand payment.

4 Stock Control

In many stores we have seen the cashier at the till rub an electronic pencil across a label called a bar-code consisting of vertical black and white lines. The computer reads the code and searches its memory for the price of the article, which it then rings up on the cash register. It also finds the stock records for the item being sold, and reduces the record of stock held by one unit. If the stock reaches the re-order point stored in computer's memory the computer will automatically print out an order for replacement stock in the Buying Department. It already knows all the suppliers' names and addresses, and all the reference numbers needed to order the item, and the EOQ, the economic order quantity, to buy a reasonable number at the cheapest possible price. Meanwhile, if the EFTPOS system is in use the computer will go directly into the customer's bank records and instruct the bank's computer to take the agreed sum of money out of the customer's account and put it in the store's bank account. EFTPOS stands for Electronic Funds Transfer at the Point of Sale, which pays the store automatically and instantly for the goods sold. This truly marvellous chain of events illustrates how 'clever' computers are.

5 The Final Profit and Loss Accounts

It is possible to program a computer to work out your profits not only once a year, or once a quarter, but every day if you wish it to do so. Not everyone does this, because the program is a long and involved one, whereas most people can do a set of final accounts in half an hour. You can't do this yet because we haven't got that far, but you will be able to by the time you get to the end of your course. In the meantime there are some fairly simple exercises to try using computerised accounts in Section 12.7 below.

12.5 Computerised running-balance accounts and examinations

In examinations it is rarely intended that students should produce an account in the running-balance style. If you do present such an account you will not lose any marks, but you will waste time, since unlike the computer you cannot add up or subtract in a few millionths of a second. As time is very important in examinations it is not advisable to do accounts in the running-balance style. They are only included here to show you how such accounts look — because when you open a Bank Account, or work in an office this is the sort of account you will usually see — especially for debtors and creditors. For examination purposes it is advisable to use T style accounts as used in Fig. 10.4, Fig. 10.6 etc, earlier in this book.

12.6 Self-assessment questions

1 What is a computer?
2 What is the main 'brain' of the computer?

3 What other elements does a computer include?
4 What are peripherals?
5 How is the data fed in for processing?
6 How do we choose a program of work?

12.7 Exercises on computerised accounts

1 The following account is sent to their customer, Alice Spriggs, by the Country Bank PLC. Answer the questions about it below. Do not copy out either the account or the questions, but simply give the answer in the form (a) . . . (b) . . . etc. (*Note*: Ch = Cheque; SO = Standing Order; Dep = Deposit)

Country Bank PLC, Llangarven Branch, 32 Market Hill, Llangarven
Miss Alice Spriggs, 42 Llangarven Way, Powys   Account number: 21743268

19. .	Details	Debit £	Credit £	Balance £
Jan 1	Balance brought forward			247.59 Cr
3	Ch 238716	20.00		227.59 Cr
4	Ch 238719	23.80		203.79 Cr
7	Ch 238717	16.75		187.04 Cr
11	SO 5294	65.20		121.84 Cr
18	Dep		220.50	342.34 Cr
25	Gilt edged interest (Bank of England)		12.75	355.09 Cr
27	Ch 238720	400.00		44.91 Dr
29	Dep		100.00	55.09 Cr
31	Balance carried forward			55.09 Cr

(a) What was the opening balance?
(b) What does this balance represent? (Has Miss Spriggs got money in the Bank or not?)
(c) What happened on the 3rd, 4th, 7th and 27th January?
(d) What happened on the 11th January?
(e) What do you think happened on the 25th January?
(f) What important effect did the entry on 27th January have on Miss Spriggs balance in the Bank?
(g) What was the final balance on 31st January?

2 This is an account in the computerised records of A. Trader of Norwich. Write (a) to (g) on a sheet of paper and answer the questions below.

R. Melhuish, 27, High Street, Chievely, Newmarket   A/C Number 127

19. .	Details	Debit £	Credit £	Balance £
Jan 1	Balance brought forward			429.77 Dr
3	Sales	138.27		568.04
5	Bank		408.28	159.76
5	Discount		21.49	138.27
17	Sales	86.25		224.52
23	Sales	139.45		363.97
31	Balance due, carried forward			363.97

(a) Was R. Melhuish a debtor or a creditor on 1 January 19. .?
(b) How much for, at that date?
(c) What happened on 3 January?
(d) What happened on 5 January?
(e) What percentage discount was given on the sum settled on 5 January?
(f) What was the closing balance on 31 January?
(g) Who owes it, to whom?

3 This is an account in the computerised records of Smart Edem, a Lagos importer. Write (a)–(g) on a sheet of paper and answer the questions below.

M. Laidlaw, 1337 Hill Street, Royston, Herts, England   A/C Number 576

19. .	Details	Debit £	Credit £	Balance £
May 1	Balance brought forward			21 785.00 Cr
9	Purchases		2 286.74	24 071.74
12	Bank	20 695.75		3 375.99
12	Discount	1 089.25		2 286.74
13	Purchases		24 427.25	26 713.99
25	Allowance	449.54		26 264.45
31	Balance to pay			26 264.45

(a) Is this the account of a debtor or a creditor?
(b) On 1 May who owed £21 785.00 to whom?
(c) What happened on 9 May?
(d) What happened on 12 May?
(e) What does the word 'allowance' mean on 25 May?
(f) Was the balance of £26 264.45 a debit balance or a credit balance?
(g) Who owed it to whom?

12.8 Problems and projects

1 Try to obtain a bank statement from some member of your family for a recent month. Note that many people do not like other people to know how much money they have in the bank, so if someone is kind enough to give you one of their monthly statements to put in your 'Accounts' file as a specimen you should keep it confidential and not show it to anyone you feel is untrustworthy.

2 Try to obtain an ordinary statement from a commercial firm. These will often be sent to parents — for example electricity and gas bills, telephone bills, etc. At one time they would always be sent back with the cheque so that they could be receipted. Since the Cheques Act 1957 this has not been necessary, and only a small tear-off counterfoil is sent in with the cheque. You should therefore try to collect a few of these statements and put them in your Accounts file. Notice the details given — the account number, addresses etc. Make sure you understand every *line* on the account.

12.9 Answers to self-assessment questions

1 A computer is an electronic device which can perform very simple activities very quickly, so that it can be used in many activities where calculations are required, or choices have to be made.

2 The 'brain' of the computer is the central processor unit (CPU).

3 The other elements are the memory, the arithmetic unit, various registers which can store numbers and the peripheral control unit.

4 Peripherals are other units surrounding the computer which perform certain functions, such as visual display units, printers, disc drive units, keyboards and similar input or output devices.

5 Originally data was fed in by punched cards or paper tape. Today it is fed in either by magnetic tape or from a disc.

6 Programs of work are selected from a 'menu' of choices. Keying in the number of the item on the menu loads the required program into the CPU ready for whatever instructions we might need to feed in.

13 The Three (or Four) Column Cash Book

13.1 The importance of cash in business

The chief activity of many businesses is the purchase and sale of goods, or the purchase of goods that eventually go into the provision of services. We have seen that such transactions require invoices, credit notes for returns, books of original entry (the day books) and of course many postings to the ledger accounts of debtors and creditors.

All these debtors must eventually pay for the goods and services supplied to them, and all our creditors require to be paid, so the records of payments in and payments out are obviously very important. There are also all the overheads of the business to be paid; rent, rates, light, heat, wages, salaries, motor expenses, repairs, redecorations etc, and from time to time we must also buy new assets such as machinery, furniture, fittings, etc. We must have a sound system for recording all such receipts and payments, especially as money is a great temptation to those who handle it, and theft of moneys handled is one of the commonest crimes. Never be tempted to take money from tills, cash boxes, club funds, etc. Theft is always viewed seriously by the Courts and the fines imposed, or the prison sentences, are severe. One of the chief concerns of every manager or proprietor is the cash flow. Cash flows into a business must be large enough to cover all flows out, and still leave something for profit, which is the reward of the owner of the business. Theft, of course, has a serious effect on cash flows and has caused the collapse of many firms and companies.

Other points about the handling of money are that it may be in cash form (coins and notes of the realm) or it may be handled in a more secure way by the use of cheques (orders to a banker to pay money). If we put our cash into a bank account and simply give written instructions to our banker to pay money to any creditor who sends us a monthly statement, we reduce the amount of cash handled and hence reduce the temptation to staff handling money.

13.2 Cash and discounts

The word 'discount' means a reduction in the money charged to a customer. In business there are three types of discount, trade discount, cash discount and settlement discounts. *Trade discount* is a rather special type of discount given by manufacturers and wholesalers to retail traders (hence the name). It has already been explained in Chapter 8 (see page 60). Trade discount is not recorded in the books of a business and there is no such thing as a Trade Discount Account. *Cash discount* is discount given to a customer who pays promptly in cash. It is a reduction in the marked price of an article to encourage a customer to buy, and again is not recorded in the accounts.

A *settlement discount* is a reduction in the total amount due on a monthly statement to encourage a customer to settle the account promptly. It is usually about 5%, but may be only 2½%. The aim in offering a settlement discount is to encourage cash flow into the business, since it may be better to have 95% of the sum due at once rather than wait for the full 100% at a later date. A person in financial difficulties may pay a bill where a discount is offered and hold back on a payment where there is no incentive. Because taking a settlement discount at the moment when we actually pay is very similar to taking a cash discount the latter term is sometimes used rather loosely when a settlement discount is really being referred to. In the Cash Book which we are about to study the discounts are really settlement discounts.

13.3 The Three Column Cash Book

The layout of the cash book illustrated in Fig. 13.1 is a three column one, with three columns on either side of the central line, which represents the middle of the two accounts recorded in this book, the Cash Account and the Bank Account. There are several important ideas behind this layout, which are as follows:

1 Although it is a bound book ruled as shown in Fig. 13.1 the Cash Book is really only two accounts — the Cash Account and the Bank Account. They have been removed from the ordinary ledger and given to a responsible member of staff, the cashier. Only the cashier makes entries in the Cash Book, since these two accounts deal with money and cheques, and could tempt a young or inexperienced member of staff, or be misused by an unprincipled employee. Most cashiers are required to take out a **fidelity bond** (an insurance policy on their faithful behaviour). If they misappropriate the funds the insurance company will compensate the employer (but not until the employee has been tried and convicted of an offence). The cashier does allow other members of staff to do the postings from the Cash Book to the various parts of the Ledger (which means they must enter the folio numbers in the Cash Book as they make the postings) but all the main entries are the work of the cashier.

2 We always say that every account is a separate page in the ledger, but with only two accounts in the whole book it would be tedious to keep turning the pages to go from the Cash Account to the Bank Account and vice versa, so the two accounts are laid side-by-side. They are nothing to do with one another, and you must be careful to make entries in the correct columns.

3 When accounts are settled the question of discount may arise and we therefore need a discount column on each side. The one on the left hand

Dr   **C.B.15**   **Cr**

Date	Details	£	Discount Allowed	Cash	Bank	Date	Details	£	Discount Received	Cash	Bank
19..			£	£	£	19..			£	£	£
June 4	Balance	b/d		328.54	13 725.66	June 5	Telephone Expenses (VAT £38.71)	L65			425.80
5	R. Green	L21	27.50		522.50	6	A. Supplier	L9	93.25		1 771.75
5	Sales (VAT £120.45)	L49		1 325.00		6	Rates	L66			386.50
6	M. Chara	L12		116.50		6	Office expenses (VAT £1.59)	L67		17.50	
6	Sales (VAT £102.68)	L49		1 129.50		7	Motor expenses (VAT £1.39)	L44		15.30	
7	Hellespont Aquaties PLC	L30			725.00	7	Repairs (VAT £2.26)	L45		24.86	
7	Sales (VAT £177.05)	L49		1 947.50		8	M. Lynch	L27	8.76		166.54
7	A. Malik	L57	1.92		36.58	8	Merit Fashions PLC	L28	36.74		1 432.76
8	Sales (VAT £260.23)	L49		2 862.50		8	Light and heat	L68			195.90
9	R. Houston	L24	2.22	86.40		9	Office Stationery (VAT £3.18)	L69		35.00	
9	Sales (VAT £284.09)	L49		3 125.00		9	Bank	C		8 500.00	
9	Cash	C			8 500.00	9	Travelling Expenses	L75		27.50	
10	Sales (VAT £298.86)	L49		3 287.50		9	Pretty wear Ltd	L18	78.20		1 485.80
						10	Motor expenses (VAT £1.50)	L44		16.50	
						10	Wages	L15		827.50	
						10	Balance	c/d		4 744.28	17 644.69
		£	31.64	14 208.44	23 509.74			£	216.95	14 208.44	23 509.74
June 11	Balance	b/d	L35	4744.28	17 644.69			L36			

Fig. 13.1 The Three Column Cash Book

Notes:

1 Remember that we have two completely separate accounts, the Cash Account and the Bank Account lying alongside one another. The Discount Allowed column and the Discount Received column do not make a third account, they are memorandum columns only (columns which help our memory).

2 *The debit side.* On the debit side we are receiving either cash or cheques. The first line shows the opening balance; in both cases a debit balance. Since both the Cash Account and the Bank Account are asset accounts, we would expect a debit balance (but it is possible to be overdrawn at the bank and consequently have a credit balance on the Cash Book for the Bank Account).

3 The sums paid by R. Green, M. Chara, Hellespont Aquatics PLC, A. Malik, and R. Houston are all payments by debtors who owed us money. Chara and Houston paid in cash, the others by cheque. Discount was given to Green, Malik and Houston.

4 Each day the tills were cashed up to find the total sales for the day and this was entered inthe Cash column. However some of this money was VAT (shown at 10%) so this was noted in each case. It would be possible to draw an extra line on the Cash Book to collect this VAT together if the accountant wished. (Remember that where VAT is 10% the VAT fraction is one eleventh — not one tenth.)

5 The only other entry on the debit side is the entry 'cash' on 9 June. This is called a 'contra entry'. Contra means opposite, and the 'C' in the folio column means that you will

find the other half of the double entry opposite. If you look across at the credit side of the Cash Book you will see it in the Cash column. The Cash Account has given money to the Bank Account which has received it on the debit side. This is explained a bit more fully in Section 13.5 below.

6 Note that in each case the wording to be written is the name of the account where the other half of the double entry will be found. However in the case of the six 'Sales' entries some of the double entry has to go in the VAT Account and only the rest of the money is really the true selling value of the goods. This is explained in Section 13.5 below.

7 *The credit side.* On the credit side we are paying money, either in cash or by cheque. The items paid to A. Supplier, M. Lynch, Merit Fashions PLC and Prettywear Ltd are all payments by cheque to suppliers. In each case we deducted discount from the statement before making out the cheque and thus saved ourselves useful amounts.

8 The items for rates, telephone expenses, office expenses, motor expenses, repairs, light and heat, stationery, travelling expenses and wages are all expenses of the business. They will be posted to the nominal accounts concerned and become losses of the business which must be taken into account when we work out the profits of the business at the end of the financial year.

Some of these expense items do involve VAT and a note of this has been made in the details column. Once again it would be possible if the accountant wished to rule in an extra column on the credit side and collect this VAT together.

9 At the end of the week in this example (but in a large firm

it could be done every day) the book is balanced off and the balances on the two accounts are brought down to start the new week. However the totals of the discount columns are not balanced off, since they are not an account. Instead these two totals are posted to the Discount Account as explained in the next Section. The spare lines on the debit side are ruled off with a Z ruling.

10 The final result is that the business concerned starts the new week with £4744.28 cash in hand and £17 644.69 in the bank.

side (where we are receiving money) is the discount allowed column, because we allow the customer who is paying to take a discount. The one on the right hand side (where we are giving money to our creditors) is called the discount received column because we are receiving a settlement discount when we pay the creditor. Note that these columns are not an account, they are only a couple of **memorandum columns**, where we make a memo of the discount allowed or the discount received.

Study the layout of Fig. 13.1 and the notes below it at this point.

13.4 Posting the Cash Book to the Ledger

Posting from one book to another means we have to complete the double entry as required. In each case where the Cash Account or the Bank Account receives money some other account must be giving it — so that every debit entry in the Cash Book requires a credit entry somewhere else. Similarly every credit entry in the Cash Book means the cashier is giving away money and some account must be receiving it. So every credit entry in the Cash Book requires a debit entry elsewhere. There is one tricky situation which is explained later about discount, and one pair of entries that does not need to be posted at all is the contra entry already described, where one half is in the Cash Account and the other half is in the Bank Account.

To save space only some of these postings have been shown in Fig. 13.2, but they cover all the typical postings to the Ledger.

	R. Green A/c						L21
19. .			£	19. .			£
May 14	Sales	SDB1	550.00	June 5	Bank	CB15	522.50
				5	Discount	CB15	27.50

Fig. 13.2 (a) A debtor's account

Notes
1 The debtor has cleared his account fully by paying £522.50 — the remainder is discount. The two credit entries here are the double entry for the payment on 5 June.
2 The Accounts of Chara, Hellespont Aquatics PLC, Malik and Houston would be credited in exactly the same way.

Sales A/c					L49
19 . .					£
June	5	Cash	CB15	1204.55	
	6	Cash	CB15	1026.82	
	7	Cash	CB15	1770.45	
	8	Cash	CB15	2602.27	
	9	Cash	CB15	2840.91	
	10	Cash	CB15	2988.64	

VAT A/c					L50
19 . .					£
June	5	Cash	CB15	120.45	
	6	Cash	CB15	102.68	
	7	Cash	CB15	177.05	
	8	Cash	CB15	260.23	
	9	Cash	CB15	284.09	
	10	Cash	CB15	298.86	

Fig. 13.2 (b) Posting the daily takings to Sales Account and VAT Account

Notes

1 In view of the fact that the sales (takings) included VAT (in this example at 10%) not all the money taken was for goods sold, some of it was output tax levied on customers on behalf of HM Customs and Excise. We therefore have to credit the VAT account since we owe this money to the VAT officer.

2 As a result the double entry for the Cash Account entry for Sales of £1325.00 on June 5 is in two parts, £1204.55 on the credit side of Sales Account and £120.45 on the credit side of VAT Account.

Telephone Expenses A/c				L65
19 . .			£	
June 5	Bank	CB15	387.09	

VAT A/c (really part of the Account shown above)				L50
19 . .			£	
June 5	Bank	CB15	38.71	

Fig. 13.2 (c) Posting the expenses accounts

Notes

1 The Telephone Expenses Account has received this share of the business's outlays in name only (a nominal account). It is one of the losses of the business. However, as part of the bill is VAT, which the business can reclaim as input tax we have to debit the Telephone Expenses Account with only £387.09, the other £38.71 being entered on the VAT account.

2 All the other postings for expenses (losses); rates, office expenses, motor expenses, repairs, light and heat, office stationery, travelling expenses and wages will be debited in their respective accounts and if they are affected by VAT the VAT input tax will be debited in the same way as shown above for the Telephone Expenses Account.

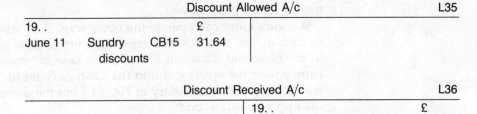

A. Supplier A/c   L49

19. .			£	19. .			£
June 6	Bank	CB15	1771.75	May 29	Purchases	PDB23	1865.00
6	Discount	CB15	93.25				

Fig. 13.2 (d) Posting a creditor's account

Notes
1 The supplier has been a creditor of ours for the last few days.
2 When we pay him the cheque he has to be debited, because he is receiving the money and the discount received from him also counts as an allowance, to clear the amount owing completely.
3 The accounts of M. Lynch, Merit Fashions PLC and Prettywear Ltd will be debited in exactly the same way.

Discount Allowed A/c   L35

19. .			£
June 11	Sundry discounts	CB15	31.64

Discount Received A/c   L36

				19. .			£
				June 11	Sundry discounts	CB15	216.95

Fig. 13.2 (e) Posting the totals of the discount columns

Notes
1 Up to now we have noticed that every debit entry in the Cash Book becomes a credit entry when posted to the ledger. Similarly every credit entry in the Cash Book becomes a debit entry in the ledger.
2 We now find that the totals of the discount columns are the only things that do not change sides. The total of the Discount Allowed is debited in the Discount Allowed Account (because it is a loss of the business and all losses are debits). The total of the Discount Received column is credited in the Discount Received Account (because it is a profit and all profits are credits). However, why are these two items the only things that do not change sides when the Cash Book is posted to the Ledger? The answer is that the double entry depends on it.
Look back at Fig. 13.1 and the item on 5 June R. Green £522.50 and £27.50 discount. Think about this double entry. It is as follows:

	Debits	*Credits*
R. Green's double entry		
Debit in the Bank A/c	£522.50	
(The £27.50 is only in a memorandum Column so we can't count that as an entry in an account)		
Credit in R. Green's Account together with discount (see page 111)		522.50 27.50

It is clear that these double entries do not balance. The £522.50 debit in the Bank Account is not large enough to balance the £550 in the account of R. Green. What we need is a *debit* entry for the discount, not another credit entry. So the £27.50 discount (which is actually mixed with other discounts to give a total of £31.64) has to be debited in Discount Allowed Account and must not cross over to the other side.
Similarly the discount received must stay on the credit side in the Discount Received Column, and not cross over to the other side. You can check this for yourself by checking the double entry for an item such as the cheque sent to A. Supplier on 6 June. Remember, the real test of an accountant is whether he/she can think in double entries. Try to work out this double entry now, and prove to yourself that you are becoming an accountant.

13.5 Contra entries in the Cash Book

We saw in the notes to Fig. 13.1 that certain entries in the Cash Book are called 'contra entries'. The word contra means 'opposite' (Latin) and indicates that the two halves of the double entry are opposite one another, one on the debit side of the Cash Book and the other on the credit side. Clearly no account can both receive and give in the same transaction, so we cannot have a contra entry on a single account, but in the Cash Book we have two accounts placed side by side for convenience. Therefore we can have one account receiving money as the other account gives it. In Fig. 13.1 this happened when we paid £8500 of shop takings (sales) into the bank for safe keeping. The Cash Account *gave* the money (credit the giver) to the Bank Account which received the money (debit the receiver).

A contra entry can operate the other way. For example if we are short of cash in the cash box and need £100 for general purposes we can go to the bank and draw out £100. In this case the money goes out of the bank (credit the giver) and into the Cash Account (debit the receiver). It would be similar to the entry in Fig. 13.1 but the accounts would be used the opposite way round.

You should now obtain some three column cash paper and try the exercises shown below. Only questions 4 and 5 include mention of VAT.

13.6 Exercises for the Three Column Cash Book

1 R. Fortescue keeps a three column cash book and in the first week in June the following entries appear. Make the entries, balance off the book and bring down the balance. You need not post to the ledger.

1 June Balances in hand: Cash £283.65; Bank £3824.25. Paid M. Patel £58.50 by cheque, after taking discount of £1.50. Sales for the day £428.55 cash.

2 June Paid rail fares £14.50 in cash. Paid R. Harcourt £170.62 by cheque after taking discount received £4.38. Sales for the day £825.65 cash.

3 June Paid cash into bank (contra entry) £1000. M. Hacker settled his account with a cheque for £361 after taking discount of £19. Sales for the day came to £852.35 cash.

4 June Paid telephone expenses £192.40 by cheque; postage £13.42 in cash and a small account in full to R. Hazeldine £17.35 in cash. Sales for the day £1120.95 cash.

5 June Paid wages £426.50 by cheque. D. Honour paid her account by cheque £162.50 (after taking discount of £8.55). Banked cash £2000 (contra entry). Paid T. Ikuzawa £546.50 by cheque (after taking discount of £14.01).

2 Mark Aylott keeps a three column Cash Book and in the week shown below the following entries appear. Make the entries, balance off the book and bring down the balance for the start of the following week. You need not post the entries to the ledger.

14 July Balances in hand: Cash £426.50; Bank £3928.60. Paid M. Aveling by cheque £117 in full settlement of a debt of £120, the balance being discount. Sales for the day £469.55 cash.

15 July   Paid rail fares £27.56 in cash. Paid Far East Printing Ltd £1425.50 by cheque after taking discount of £75.03. Sales for the day in cash £959.75.

16 July   Paid cash into bank (contra entry) £1000. U. Eco settled her account by cheque for £404.22 after taking discount of £21.28. Sales for the day £1125.75 in cash.

17 July   Paid rates for half year by cheque £426.50; postage £73.25 by cheque; sales for the day £1424.65 in cash. Paid B & B Windows £19.27 in cash.

18 July   Paid wages £358.55 in cash. Paid into bank (contra entry) £2200. M. Garcia paid her account by cheque £399.00 after taking discount of £21.00. Paid P. Boeteng £162.65 after taking discount of £8.56.

3 Man Lee imports and markets oriental items. He uses a three column cash book which in the week commencing 17 October 19. . has entries as listed below. Make these entries and post them to the ledger. Be particularly careful about the posting of the totals of the discount columns. (*Note*: the Bank Account is overdrawn on 17 October.)

17 October   Balances: cash in hand £284.50 Bank overdraft (credit balance) £172.56. Loan arranged from Trustful Bank PLC £3000 (debit the Bank Account — credit Loan Account). M. Short paid his account by cheque £163.50, in full. Home Furnishings PLC paid by cheque for supplies sent earlier £1726.50, after taking discount £90.87. Cash sales for day £1712.50.

18 October   Paid Eastern Supplies £2521.60 by cheque after taking discount £64.66. Paid for motor vehicle expenses £32.46 cash, and for repairs to premises £76.56 by cheque. Cash sales for day £1425.50.

19 October   Paid into bank from tills £2500.46. Paid for stationery £38.50 cash. Paid for cleaning expenses £47.62 cash. Paid M. Loe £385.62 by cheque after taking discount of £20.30. Cash sales for day £1386.50.

20 October   Paid Manilla Exporters Pty £2465 by cheque, being settlement in full of their account for £2594.74 for the previous month. Cash sales for day £1594.60.

21 October   Paid cash into bank £3000.00. Paid wages £286.50 in cash. Paid Telephone Expenses by cheque £328.65.

4 In this Cash Book exercise VAT is mentioned. You should be careful when doing the postings to extract any VAT input tax or output tax and take it to the VAT Account. You are asked to record the following entries and post them to the Ledger Accounts.

1 Jan 19. .   N. Hayden starts in business with cash of £500 and £3000 in his Bank Account. These amounts are his opening capital. He pays £104.60 for telephone installation costs (of which VAT was £9.51) and £50 each for gas and electricity (both to be recorded in Light and Heat Account). All three payments are by cheque. Takings for the day are £186.50 in cash, of which £16.95 is VAT.

2 Jan 19. .   Pays for goods for re-sale (purchases) £195.00 by cheque VAT £17.73. Pays Shopfitters Ltd a cheque for £184.60 for work done, after having taken discount of £9.72. Cash takings for day £295.50 of which VAT was £26.86.

3 Jan 19. .   Cash takings for day £426.56 of which VAT is £38.78. Paid to bank £1000 in cash.

4 Jan 19. .   H. Hayashi pays by cheque for goods supplied on 1 January £326.50 after taking £17.18 discount. Hayden pays cash for wrapping materials

£23.86 of which £2.17 is VAT and cleaning expenses £35.00 cash. Cash takings for day £495.56 of which £45.05 is VAT.

5 Jan 19. . Cash Sales £826.50 of which £75.14 is VAT. Paid to bank £1000 cash.

5 VAT is also mentioned in this exercise. Enter the items listed below in your three column Cash Book; balance the book at the end of the week and post it to the Ledger, being particularly careful about VAT entries and discount entries.

28 Feb 19. .   Balances in hand: Cash £184.56 Bank £1384.75. C. Khoo settled his account with a cheque for £146.50 after deducting discount of £7.71. Cash Sales for day £386.50 of which VAT was £35.14.

1 March 19. .   Paid for office stationery by cheque £138.40 of which VAT was £12.58. Paid fares in cash £11.74. Paid for motor expenses £23.52 in cash of which VAT was £2.14. M. Clarke paid her account, by cheque. It stood at £48.50 but she deducted £2.42 discount from it. Cash Sales £686.20 of which VAT was £62.38.

2 March 19. .   Cash takings £727.50 of which VAT was £66.14. Paid £1400 out of the cash box into the bank. Paid R. Malik £127.56 by cheque after deducting discount of £3.27.

3 March 19. .   The Bank of England sent a warrant (a cheque) for £18.50 for interest on gilt-edged securities. Paid advertising expenses by cheque £48.90 of which VAT is £4.45. Cash takings for day £828.75 of which VAT is £75.34.

4 March 19. .   Paid cleaning expenses £35.50 and wages £325.65 both in cash. Takings for day £1195.65 of which VAT was £108.70. Paid into bank from cash £1000.00.

13.7 Self-assessment questions

1 Which accounts appear in the Three Column Cash Book?
2 Are they personal, nominal or real accounts?
3 What is discount allowed, and which side of the Cash Book does it appear on?
4 What is discount received, and which side of the Cash Book does it appear on?
5 What is a contra entry?
6 Tom Smith is overdrawn at the bank by £250.38. On which side of his Cash Book will the balance of his Bank Account appear?

13.8 Paying-in books and paying-in slips

Most cashiers pay in cash and cheques received by the business every day. To do this you either need a **paying-in slip** or a **paying-in book**. Paying-in slips are available free of charge on the counter of any bank, but for convenience it is usual for the bank to supply books of paying in slips, or they are sometimes added to the backs of cheque books. They must have a tear-off slip which can be torn out by the bank's cashier when the deposit is accepted over the counter, leaving a counterfoil which can be receipted by the cashier as a proof of the deposit. It is usual to use both sides of the slip, the rear side giving plenty of room to record a list of cheques received. This is illustrated in Fig. 13.3.

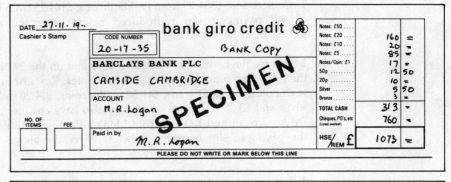

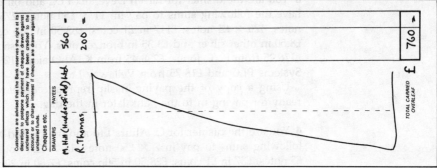

Fig. 13.3 A paying-in slip (showing both sides)

Notes

1 The cashier fills in the details of each class of note or coinage being banked — for example 8 × £20 notes must have been banked as the total value was £160.00. The bank's cashier will check each item to ensure it is correct, and also the total.

2 The cheques are listed in the space provided, and the total is carried over to the front of the slip.

3 Many paying-in slips already have the computer codes recorded on them so that the sums deposited can be credited to the customer's account in the bank's computer memory. In the illustration they are not encoded yet, but will be encoded during the day by the bank staff, at the point where the slip says — 'Please do not write or mark below this line.'

4 The cashier stamps and initials both the slip and the carbon copy. The slip is retained by the bank, and the paying-in book with its carbon copy is returned to the person lodging the payment. The slip taken by the bank's cashier becomes the basis for the bookkeeping, which is done by what is known as the **slip system**. The slips are encoded with the account details in magnetic ink, and when the total amount to be credited to the account has also been encoded in magnetic ink the slip can be passed through a 'reader' which can read the electronic data and will update the account within a few milliseconds. All bank branches are 'on-line' to their own accounts, which means they can immediately access an account in the computer and enter the amount paid in.

13.9 Exercises on paying-in slips

1 You are the cashier for East African Trading PLC and on the 17 July 19. . you have the following sums to pay in: 7 × £50 notes; 13 × £20 notes; 27 × £10 notes; 13 × £5 notes; £121 in £1 coins; £15.50 in 50p coins; £3.80 in 20p coins; £3.70 other silver and £5.40 in bronze coins. You also have cheques as follows: £227.50 from

T. Cook & Son; £384.25 from D. Manlikova; £164.25 from D. Harare. Using a copy of the paying-in slip reproduced below enter the above items ready for paying in to the bank later in the day.

2 You are the cashier for Hardman Bros and on the 27 November 19. . you have the following sums to pay in: 4 × £50 notes; 7 × £20 notes; 13 × £10 notes; 85 × £5 notes; £87 in £1 coins; £41.50 in 50p coins; £14.20 in 20p coins; £1.40 in other silver and £3.20 in bronze coins. You also have cheques as follows: £175.50 from Dr A. Grogan and £235.50 from Menley Pharmaceuticals PLC. Using a copy of the paying-in slip reproduced below enter the above items ready for paying in to the bank later in the day.

3 You are the cashier for Eileen Deveraux PLC and on the 23 February 19. . you have the following sums to pay in: 11 × £50 notes; 275 × £20 notes; 314 × £10 notes; 426 × £5 notes; £117 in £1 coins; £83.50 in 50p coins; £17.20 in 20p coins; £8.50 in other silver and £3.35 in bronze coins. You also have cheques as follows: £176.25 from R. T. Jones; £238.45 from K. Al-Otaidi; £126.55 from Alpha Business Systems PLC and £18.75 from Vellaway Ltd.

Using a copy of the paying-in slip reproduced below enter the above items ready for paying in to the bank later in the day.

4 You are the cashier for C. Ahura Ltd and on the 2nd March 19. . you have the following sums to pay in 7 × £50 notes; 13 × £20 notes; 27 × £10 notes; 45 × £5 notes; £37 in £1 coins; £28.50 in 50p coins; £7.80 in 20p coins; £1.35 other silver and £3.25 in bronze coins. You also have cheques as follows: £72.75 from C. Nielson (Bergen) Ltd; £38.45 from T. North; £198.65 from A. Zimbabwe; £2026.50 from Universal Insurance PLC.

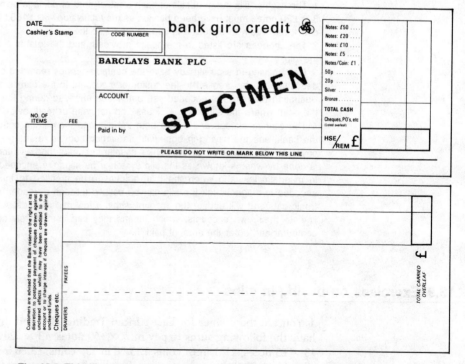

Fig. 13.4 This illustration may be reproduced for classroom purposes.

Using a copy of the paying-in slip reproduced opposite enter the above items ready for paying in to the bank later in the day.

13.10 Answers to self-assessment questions

1 The accounts in the Three Column Cash Book are the Cash Account and the Bank Account.

2 They are usually regarded as real accounts, because they are assets of the business. Certainly the Cash Account is real enough — you can actually touch the Cash. It might be argued that the Bank Account is a personal account, because the bank is actually a debtor of ours — it owes us back our money.

3 Discount allowed is one of the losses of the business — it is money you allow debtors to deduct from their accounts because they are settling their accounts within an agreed time limit. It appears on the debit side of the Cash Book.

4 Discount received is one of the profits of the business; money we are permitted to keep because we are paying promptly. It is found in the credit side of the Cash Book.

5 A contra entry is an entry which occurs in the Three Column Cash Book because, as there are two accounts in the book, it is possible to have a debit entry opposite (contra) the credit entry. Thus, if we take cash out of the tills and put it into the bank, Cash Account is credited (credit the giver) and Bank Account is debited (debit the receiver). Alternatively if we are short of cash in the office we could take cash out of the Bank Account and put it into the Cash Box, which would mean we must credit the Bank Account and debit the Cash Account, which is now receiving the money.

6 The balance will be on the credit side, because Tom owes the bank money, they are Tom's creditor.

14 Bank Reconciliation Statements

14.1 Introduction

The word 'reconcile' means 'to make friends again'. It frequently happens in business that two sets of figures which should agree, for some reason do not. When this happens we have to find out why. Is there an error somewhere in the book-keeping or can we explain the discrepancy in some sensible way? For example, if our Cash Book shows (in the Bank columns) that we have a balance of £520.50 at the bank, but when the bank statement arrives it shows a balance of only £485.00 we need to know why the two figures disagree. If we can show that the difference is due to some time lag in the system (for example we have paid in some cheques but they haven't yet been cleared by the bankers' clearing system) then we can reconcile the two figures and 'make them friends' again.

All banks have now adopted computerised systems which have speeded up the clearing process and changed the way in which bank statements are rendered to customers, but these changes are unlikely to affect the need for 'bank reconciliation statements' as described in the next few pages. In order to understand why reconciliation is necessary we must consider what happens in ordinary banking practice.

14.2 How banks keep accounts

When a customer opens a current account he or she is able to make and receive payments through the cheque system. The bank, for obvious reasons, does not undertake to correspond with the customer every time a transaction takes place. Some banks hardly ever write to their customers, except when an account is overdrawn. Similarly, the customer never writes to the bank to tell them he is making out a cheque. Just now and then, or perhaps monthly, the customer may ask for a bank statement, or the bank, feeling that a sufficiently large collection of paid cheques has accumulated on its files, will render a statement to the customer. At that moment the customer can check the account and reconcile the bank's statement with his/her own book-keeping records.

14.3 Why a bank statement usually differs from our Cash Book records

In practice it will rarely be the case that the bank's statement shows the same balance as our own Cash Book. The differences are nearly always due to a lack of knowledge of what the other person has been doing. For example, there may be:

1 differences arising from the bank's actions, about which we have not been notified. These include the payment of standing orders, the payment of direct debits and the collection of bank giro credits;

2 differences arising from the time-lag which is inevitable whenever cheques are sent in payment of debts, or are received and paid into the bank for clearing through the Bankers' Clearing House;

3 or errors, either by the bank or by ourselves. Such errors are unlikely to occur frequently, because the bank carries out careful checks on its entries, and we naturally do our best to avoid mistakes in our own book-keeping records. Inevitably though, mistakes occur from time to time.

The first two causes of difference need a little more explanation.

1 Lack of knowledge of what the bank has done

There are many occasions when the bank does not bother to inform us that it has taken money from, or has credited money to, our account. It sends us a statement at regular intervals, usually on a 'cyclical billing' basis. This means that about 4% of the bank's customers are handled every day. We might, for example receive our statement on the 25th of every month. Not until we receive this statement do we learn that the bank has taken certain actions. The most common items discovered on the bank statement are as follows:

(a) Debiting the account with bank charges, or interest on loans and overdrafts.

(b) Payment of standing orders and direct debits we have authorised in the past. We do not deduct these sums from the bank account until we receive the bank statement. Then we enter the items in our Cash Book on the date the statement arrives — even if they might have actually been paid earlier. These entries will bring our Cash Book into line with the Bank Statement.

(c) Receipt of sums by credit transfer. Numerous debtors use the credit-transfer system as a convenient method of paying sums directly into our bank account. The only problem is that until we receive our bank statement we usually have no idea that the debt has been settled. Such items will appear on the statement as a deposit increasing the balance. It is also possible that dividends or interest on gilt edged securities are paid in this way.

When such items are discovered on a bank statement, they must at once be entered on the Cash Book. Any receipts by credit transfer, either from customers or investments, should be entered on the debit side of the Bank Account (debit the receiver). Any deductions by the bank, either for bank charges or interest on loans should be entered in the Cash Book on the credit side of the Bank Account (credit the giver). Although a cheque has not been written out, the loss has been deducted from the bank account. Any standing orders or direct debits must be similarly entered on the credit side of the Bank Account, because it has given the money to the creditor.

2 Delays inevitable in the cheque system

Imagine that we send a cheque for £50.00 to the International Marine PLC, a company based in Aberdeen. Before posting the letter containing the cheque, we enter the item in the Cash Book. It will probably be at least two days before that letter arrives, and when it does arrive the Company may take a day to get to the bank and pay it in. There will then be a further delay while the cheque is passed through the bank's head office in London, or the Bankers' Clearing House if two different banks are involved. During this time lag, our Cash Book will show that we have deducted the cheque from our available funds, but the bank will think that we still have this money. Sometimes, when a creditor puts a cheque in his pocket and forgets to pay it in, several months may pass by before the bank statement and our Bank Account agree on this point. Neither of them is wrong, and it would be a mistake to 'correct' them or take any action — we must simply wait for International Marine PLC to put the matter right by paying the cheque into their account. Such a situation would be made clear in the Bank Reconciliation Statement, which as its name applies, is a written statement explaining a difference between the two records.

14.4 Drawing-up a Bank Reconciliation Statement

Everyone who has a Bank Account should do a bank reconciliation once a month. They are not very easy to do, and if you can master this piece of book-keeping it is quite a useful point to make in job interviews. Study the exercise in this section and then do several of the examples which follow and you will soon get the idea.

First, here is Kay Thorndike's Bank Account from her Cash Book for the month of April. She goes to the bank on 30 April with the paying-in-slip she has made out for £231.36 and at the same time collects a bank statement they have prepared for her. This is shown on the page opposite so you can compare the two.

Kay Thorndike's Cash Book (Bank columns only)

19. .			£	19. .			£
Apr 1	Balance	b/d	727.25	Apr 3	M. Stephens	L27	47.25
5	Cash	c	394.16	7	P. Shah	L39	148.56
12	Cash	c	521.18	15	Major		
14	Cash	c	286.50		Products		
19	Cash	c	381.75		PLC	L51	272.25
26	Cash	c	686.79	25	R. Layston	L29	1423.60
30	Cash	c	231.36	29	M. Weiskop	L44	87.60
				30	Balance	c/d	1249.73
			£3228.99				£3 228.99
19. .			£				
Apr 30	Balance	b/d	1 249.73				

Fig. 14.1 A Cash Book (Bank Columns only)

The Bank Statement is as shown below:

Kay Thorndike — Bank Statement in account with Helpful Bank PLC

Date	Details	Dr	Cr	Balance
		£	£	£
1.4.19..	Bal. c/fwd			727.25Cr
3.4.19..	107524	47.25		680.00
5.4.19..	Sundries		394.16	1074.16
12.4.19..	Sundries		521.18	1595.34
14.4.19..	S/O Biggs and Co.	248.60		1346.74
14.4.19..	Sundries		286.50	1633.24
15.4.19..	107526	272.25		1360.99
19.4.19..	Sundries		381.75	1742.74
26.4.19..	Sundries		686.79	2429.53
29.4.19..	107528	1423.60		1005.93
30.4.19..	Charges	7.21		998.72
30.4.19..	Industrial Investors (bank giro transfer)		27.32	1026.04

Fig. 14.2 The bank statement

Notes

1 Very important — note that the Cash Book and the Bank Statement appear to be opposite ways around. The opening balance is the same: £727.25, but in the Cash Book it is on the debit side and in the bank statement it is a credit entry. The reason is that the Bank Statement is kept from the Bank's point of view. When you have money in the bank you are a creditor of the bank, not a debtor. In your own book the same money is recorded as an asset (always debit the asset account). Similarly money going out of the Cash Book is a credit entry in the Cash Book as you give the money away. From the bank's point of view as it obeys your order to pay money to the named payee it owes you less money — a debit entry on your account at the bank.

2 Comparing the two accounts, we notice the following points:

(a) The starting point is the same: £727.25.

(b) On the debit side of the Cash Book all the entries have been made on the Bank Statement except the last one. This was only paid in this morning, £231.36 and has not yet had time to be cleared through the Bankers' Clearing House. It is a time-lag item.

(c) On the credit side of the Cash Book only three of the credit items (cheques paid out) have actually been recorded by the bank as paid. These are £47.25, £272.25 and £1423.60. The other cheques for P. Shah and M. Weiskop have not been paid in by them, and the bank thinks we still have the money. These are also time-lag items.

(d) On the debit side of the statement a standing order for £248.60 to Biggs & Co., has not been recorded on the Cash Book, and the bank has also taken charges of £7.21.

(e) On the credit side of the statement £27.32 received as a dividend from Industrial Investors has been received by the bank but has not been entered on the Cash Book.

We can see that the final balance on the Cash Book is a debit of £1249.73, whereas on the Bank Statement it is a credit balance of £1026.04. How shall we reconcile the two? The rules are:

1 Bring the Cash Book up-to-date, now that we know what the bank has been doing.

2 There will still be some items we cannot clear up, because they are time-lag items, caused by delays in the clearing house, or by debtors failing to pay in cheques. These have to be explained in a Bank Reconciliation Statement.

Carrying (1) out first, we have:

Kay Thorndike's Cash Book (Bank columns only)

19..			£	19..			£
Apr 30	Balance	b/d	1249.73	Apr 30	Biggs & Co. (standing		
31	Dividend				order)	L46	248.60
	received	L53	27.32	30	Bank charges	L52	7.21
				30	Balance	c/d	1021.24
			£1277.05				£1277.05
19..			£				
May 1	Balance	b/d	1021.24				

Now we see the difference between the two accounts is only a few pounds; the balance is £1021.24 in the Cash Book and £1026.04 in the Bank Statement. However to reconcile the two we have to write out a reconciliation statement as shown below.

Bank Reconciliation Statement as at 30 April 19..

		£
Balance as per Cash Book after updating	=	1021.24

Add back the cheques not yet presented (since the bank thinks we still have this money)

	£	
P. Shah	148.56	
M. Weiskop	87.60	
		236.16
		1257.40

Deduct cheques etc., paid in but not yet cleared (since the Bank did not know when the statement was issued that this money was about to be paid in ⟶ 231.36

Balance as per Bank Statement £1026.04

Notes

1 It doesn't really matter where we start from but it is easiest to start from the revised Cash Book balance.

2 Our line of reasoning now has to explain why the bank figure is different. If you think in each case 'Now what does the bank think about this time-lag item?' you will get to the right answer. The bank doesn't know we have paid out two cheques — it thinks we still have this money. We therefore add it back. The bank also does not know that money was paid in this morning. Therefore we deduct it because the bank doesn't know about this deposit.

3 The final total comes to the correct 'Bank Statement' figure, so we have reconciled the two sets of figures.

14.5 Exercises on Bank Reconciliation Statements

1 Here is Alan Ahlberg's Cash Book (Bank columns only) for March 19. . .

Cash Book (Bank columns only)

19. .			£	19. .			£
March 1	Balance	b/d	387.56	March 7	R. Frost	L14	127.62
4	T. Jameson	L27	56.42	14	Wages	L19	256.50
14	Cash takings	L37	1742.50	27	M. Larch	L32	275.60
25	Cash takings	L37	1675.25	29	T. Lodge	L35	362.50
				31	Balance	c/d	2839.51
			£3861.73				£3861.73
19. .			£				
March 31	Balance	b/d	2839.51				

Here is his bank statement for the month ending 31 March 19. . .

Bank Statement (A. Ahlberg)

Date	Details	Dr	Cr	Balance
		£	£	£
1.3.19. .	Balance			387.56Cr
4.3.19. .	Sundries		56.42	443.98
11.3.19. .	Cheque	127.62		316.36
12.3.19. .	Bank interest	12.98		303.38
14.3.19. .	Sundries		1742.50	2045.88
14.3.19. .	Cheque	256.50		1789.38
25.3.19. .	Sundries		1675.25	3464.63
27.3.19. .	Charges	7.56		3457.07

Check the statement against the Cash Book; make such adjustments as are necessary to the Cash Book to take account of banking activities of which the cashier was not aware, and then reconcile the revised Cash Book with the Bank Statement.

2 Here is J. M. Chara's Cash Book (Bank columns only) for the last week in March.

Cash Book (Bank columns only)

19. .			£	19. .			£
March 25	Balance	b/d	423.78	March 26	R. Ahura	L5	38.25
27	Cash	c	490.28	27	A. Ajakaiye	L7	44.05
29	Cash	c	589.94	29	B. Logan	L12	170.62
				31	Drawings	L21	200.00
				31	Balance	c/d	1051.08
			£1504.00				£1504.00
19. .			£				
March 31	Balance	b/d	1051.08				

His bank statement at 31 March reads as follows:

Date	Details	Dr	Cr	Balance
March		£	£	£
26	Balance			505.50
	Cheque	81.72		423.78
27	Sundries		490.28	914.06
28	Cheque	38.25		875.81
29	Cheque	170.62		705.19
	Sundries		584.94	1290.13
30	Direct Debit (Rates)	89.95		1200.18

Correct the Cash Book as necessary and then draw up a Bank Reconciliation Statement as at 31 March 19. . reconciling the new Cash Book balance with the Bank Statement. The error on the 29th of £5 is found to be a Cash Book error.

Note
Although the starting positions are different they are made right by the first cheque cleared on the Bank Statement.

3 Here are the entries made in K. Grieve's Cash Book for the third week in June.

Cash Book (Bank columns only)

19. .		£	19. .		£
June 16	Balance	3784.95	June 17	A. Brown	236.50
17	Cash	485.00	19	B. Winter	494.48
19	Cash	585.45	21	M. Lee	371.60
20	Cash	1462.35	21	Drawings	220.00

His bank statement arrives on 21 June, and is as follows:

Date	Details	Dr	Cr	Balance
June		£	£	£
16	Balance			3784.95
17	Sundries		485.00	4269.95
17	Cheque	236.50		4033.45
21	Cheque	494.48		3538.97
21	Sundries		585.45	4124.42
	Cheque	220.00		3904.42
	Direct debit (rates)	196.50		3707.92

(a) What should K. Grieve do about the direct debit for rates? Do this now and balance off the Cash Book.

(b) Draw up a Bank Reconciliation Statement, to reconcile the revised Cash Book with the Bank Statement.

4 T. Nash's Bank Statement reads as follows for March 19. .:

Date	Details	Dr £	Cr £	Balance £
1.3.19. .	Balance C/fwd			725.62Cr
3.3.19. .	Cheque	37.52		688.10
5.3.19. .	Sundries		249.62	937.72
12.3.19. .	Cheque	594.62		343.10
14.3.19. .	Sundries		581.14	924.24
14.3.19. .	Cheque	76.81		847.43
15.3.19. .	Sundries		672.25	1519.68
19.3.19. .	Sundries		773.25	2292.93
26.3.19. .	Cheque	542.65		1750.28
29.3.19. .	Sundries		676.41	2426.69
30.3.19. .	Charges	14.21		2412.48
30.3.19. .	Bank of England (transfer)		45.50	2457.98

On 31 March his bank balance according to his Cash Book was £3305.84. Checking through the month's records he finds the following differences between the Bank Statement and his Cash Book records.

The Bank charges he did not know about, and decides to enter them in the Cash Book straight away.

The Bank of England transfer (dividend on Government Stock he holds) he also did not know about. He decides to enter this receipt in his Cash Book at once.

The £542.65 cheque paid out on 26 March was paid to G. T. Glossop Ltd, for repair work. He had entirely forgotten to enter this in his Cash Book. To take this entry into account he entered it on 31 March in his Cash Book.

On 31 March he had paid in £436.50 which did not as yet appear on the Bank Statement.

Finally the payment into the bank on 19 March was recorded in error in his Cash Book as £673.25. This error he also decides to put right by putting an extra £100 transfer to the Bank in his Cash Book.

Starting with the balance on his Cash Book of £3305.84 correct the Cash Book with the entries outlined above and then go on to draw up a Bank Reconciliation Statement as at 31 march 19. .

5 The following statement was received from the bank indicating Lee Sim Huat's position during January.

Bank Statement as at 31 January 19. .

Date Jan.	Details	Dr £	Cr £	Balance £
1	Balance			1421.55
3	Sundries		880.00	2301.55
5	Direct Debit	136.72		2164.83
9	Bank giro credit (Goh)		256.00	2420.83
10	Cheque	86.42		2334.41
13	Cheque	130.50		2203.91
17	Sundries		975.00	3178.91
20	Standing Order	178.58		3000.33
22	Cheque	236.20		2764.13
25	Cheque	78.44		2685.69
29	Cheque	128.32		2557.37
30	Sundries		886.76	3444.13

On 31 January Lee's Cash Book showed a balance of £3117.41.

Comparing these items with his Cash Book Lee finds that he has to enter both the direct debit and the standing order in his Cash Book and he was also not aware that Goh had transferred £256 to his account. He decides to make these entries in his Cash Book straight away and then to reconcile his revised Bank Balance with his Bank Statement. Two cheques, sent to Industrial Services Ltd (£236.52) and Electronics Ltd (£149.50), had not yet been presented for payment by these firms. Do the necessary entries and draw up the Bank Reconciliation Statement.

14.6 Self-assessment questions

1 Why is a bank reconciliation statement necessary?
2 What sort of things might the bank do without notifying the customer?
3 What sort of time lags develop in the system?
4 What is the best procedure for doing a bank reconciliation statement?

14.7 Answers to self-assessment questions

1 Because the balance at any given time on our Cash Book is rarely the same as the balance shown on the Bank Statement. This is because of time lags in the system, and also because both parties (the customer and the bank) do things without consulting the other, expecting to sort them out later when the statement is rendered to the customer by the Bank.

2 The bank might: (a) pay standing orders; (b) pay direct debits; (c) charge interest or bank charges; (d) accept credit transfers (bank giro transfers) which increase the balance owing to the customer.

3 The most likely time lags are: (a) cheques sent to a creditor may not be paid in by the creditor straight away, so the bank will not know they have actually been sent out; (b) lodgments paid in by the customer may take a few days to clear through the Banker's Clearing House.

4 (a) Compare the two sorts of figures and note any points of disagreement on a scrap of paper.

(b) Get the Cash Book up-to-date by entering any entries the bank has made which have not yet been recorded in the Cash Book.

(c) Now reconcile the revised Cash Book balance with the Bank Statement by taking into account those items which are not wrong, but are different because of the time lags.

(d) Do a fair copy of the Bank Reconciliation Statement and file it away as evidence of the correctness of our records.

15 Keeping account of petty cash

15.1 The work of the petty cashier

Most large firms settle their main debts by cheque and do not pay for very many items in cash. Where they do — for example postage stamps may be purchased in cash, or small items such as string, sealing wax, etc., may be obtained from local shops — it is usual to appoint a petty cashier who will be given a small float of money to make such purchases. The sum allotted is called the **petty cash imprest** and the petty cash book is said to be kept on the **imprest system**.

The advantages of the imprest system are as follows:

1 The chief cashier need not be bothered for trifling sums of money, which can always be obtained from the petty cashier.

2 The sum impressed for this purpose is not large — rarely more than £100 per week — and does not represent much of a temptation to either the petty cashier or other members of staff. Even so, police records show that 90% of office thefts are thefts of petty cash, so the petty cashier must keep proper records and insist on having bills or other **petty cash vouchers** to vouch for the honesty of the person spending the money.

3 The keeping of a petty cash book is good training for young employees.

4 The analysis system used reduces the number of entries to be made in the ledger. This is explained in the notes to Fig. 15.1. The layout of the petty cash book is explained in Fig. 15.1 (see page 130).

15.2 Petty cash vouchers

Every item of expense should be authorised by a petty cash voucher. A voucher is a piece of paper which proves that the money was actually spent. Thus if I travel on a bus and receive a ticket the ticket becomes a petty cash voucher. If I park in a multi-storey car park for my firm, the cashier at the pay barrier will give me a receipt if I ask for one, and this becomes the petty cash voucher. Any shopkeeper will give me a bill for my purchases, or at least a slip from the cash register to prove that I paid the sum shown. Where a petty cash voucher cannot be obtained from outside the business — for example a gratuity given to a driver of a delivery vehicle is not usually acknowledged by a receipt — an internal petty cash voucher should be made out by the petty cashier, which can be authorised by the manager who approved the gratuity. An example is shown in Fig. 15.3.

Debit side £ p	Date	Details	PCV	Total £ p	Postage £ p	Travelling Expenses £ p	Cleaning £ p	Sundry Expenses £ p	Stationery £ p	£ p	F	Ledger A/cs £ p
	19..											PCB11
100 00	July 17	Imprest	CB17									
	17	Postage	1	2 75	2 75							
	17	Travelling expenses	2	3 60		3 60						
	18	Postage	3	1 46	1 46							
	18	String	4	0 75				0 75				
	19	Envelopes	5	8 85					8 85			
2 80	19	Private telephone call	L27									
	19	T. Jones	6	17 42							L7	17 42
	20	Postage	7	1 66	1 66							
	20	Busfares	8	0 85		0 85						
	20	Refreshments	9	3 60				3 60				
	21	R. Parker	10	13 85							L25	13 85
	21	Cleaner's wages	11	27 50			27 50					
	22	Note paper	12	14 65					14 65			
	22	Total		96 94	5 87	4 45	27 50	4 35	23 50			31 27
	22	Balance in hand		5 86	L17	L21	L35	L39	L56			
£102 80			c/d £	102 80								
5 86	July 23	Balance in hand	b/d									
94 14	24	Cash restored	CB23									

Fig. 15.1 The Petty Cash book

Notes

The layout and completion of the Petty Cash Book shown above may be explained as follows:

1 The page is divided into two 'halves', but the left hand side (the debit side) is very much smaller than the right-hand side (the credit side) which has extra analysis columns. The book is debited (entered on the debit side) whenever cash is received by the petty cashier. It is credited whenever cash is paid away by the petty cashier.

2 The 'Details' column is used to explain exactly what has happened on each entry. If it is an entry affecting the debit side (cash received) the figures will be entered on the debit side of the book. If it is an entry affecting the credit side (cash paid away) the figures will be entered on the credit side and analysed as explained in 3.

3 Each credit entry for cash paid is entered in the 'Total' column but is also carried into one of the analysis columns. These collect together similar items, like 'postage' or 'sundry expenses' but where items must be kept separate they are written in the last column, called 'Ledger A/cs'. Each item in this last column is posted separately to the correct ledger account, (in this case the accounts of T. Jones and R. Parker, two creditors) and the folio number (page number) is written in the column headed F.

4 At the end of the week the book is totalled as shown, and balanced off. The remaining balance is brought down to the debit side. The analysis totals should cross-total to agree with the total of the 'Total' column. The book is then taken to the chief cashier to be checked. The cashier will then restore the money spent to make the imprest £100 again. As £2.80 was received this week for a private telephone call the cashier only needs to restore £2.80 less than the amount spent.

5 The Petty Cash Book is now posted to the Ledger, and the folio numbers are written in, either below the analysis columns or in the special folio column. The money received for private telephone calls will be posted to the credit side of the Telephone Expenses Account and reduces the total expense of the telephone. The Ledger entries are shown in Fig. 15.2.

6 The petty cash vouchers, which authorised the payments made are arranged in order, numbered, and the PVC numbers are entered in the columns provided. The petty cashier is then ready for a further week's work. There will be no petty cash voucher of course for items appearing on the debit side, which are received by the petty cashier. Instead of a petty cash voucher number the folio member of the account where the double entry can be found will be inserted in the PCV column.

Postage A/c   L17

19..			£	
July	Petty Cash	PCB11	5.87

Travelling Expenses A/c   L21

19..			£	
July 23	Petty Cash	PCB11	4.45

Cleaning Expenses A/c   L35

19..			£	
July 23	Petty Cash	PCB11	27.50

Sundry Expenses A/c   L39

19..			£	
July 23	Petty Cash	PCB11	4.35

Stationery A/c   L56

19..			£	
July 23	Petty Cash	PCB11	23.50

T. Jones A/c   L7

19..			£	19..			£
July 23	Petty Cash	PCB11	17.42	June 16	Purchases	PDB17	17.42

R. Parker A/c   L26

19..			£	19..			£
July 23	Petty Cash	PCB11	13.85	June 19	Purchases	PDB19	13.85

L27   Telephone Expenses A/c

19..			£	19..			£
				July 23	Petty Cash	PCB11	2.80

Fig. 15.2 Posting the Petty Cash Book

Notes
1 The items on the credit side of the Petty Cash Book (which is really the Petty Cash Account) are posted over to the debit of the various loss accounts.
2 In the case of the two creditors whose accounts are being settled in this way the amounts paid are debited to their personal accounts to extinguish the sums owed.
3 In the case of the telephone money collected from a member of staff this is brought over to the credit side of the Telephone Expenses Account to reduce the losses by telephone expenses for the year.

Petty Cash Voucher		
Name: G. Smith	Yard Foreman	Date: 21 Aug. 19..
Required For:		Amount
Gratuity to delivery driver (late delivery) of goods required for Australian contract)		£1.00
TOTAL		£1.00
Signed: *G.Smith.*	Approved *R.T.Perkins*	Folio

Fig. 15.3 An internal petty cash voucher

15.3 Exercises: the Petty Cash Book

(*Note: Paper for petty cash exercises* It is possible to buy petty cash paper from a stationer, but in examinations one often has to rule up paper. It is therefore best to practise ruling up a few sheets, even though this is rather laborious. For the purpose of these exercises copy the sheet given on p. 134.)

1 Using the special petty cash paper photocopied from page 134 head up five columns: Sundry Expenses, Fares, Stationery, Postage and Ledger Accounts. Enter the following items:

19. .

Jan 1 Drew imprest £80.00 from the chief cashier; paid for envelopes £4.56; postage stamps £1.35; fares £2.50; collected from staff for private telephone calls £9.85.
   2 Paid for envelopes £8.25; paid M. Lewis, a creditor £13.85.
   3 Paid fares £4.75; cleaning materials £4.28.
   4 Paid stationery £10.33; paid R. Armstrong, a creditor £7.35.
   5 Paid for cleaning materials £1.25; paid fares £3.25.
   6 Paid for ball of string 60 pence.
   7 Paid for postage stamps £5.80.

Balance off the Petty Cash Book and restore the imprest.

2 Using paper for a Petty Cash Book that will record expenditure under the headings: Postage, Stationery, Travelling, Cleaning Expenses, General Expenses and Ledger Accounts, enter the following transactions:

19. .

July 21 Cash in hand £80.00.
   22 Paid postage £5.50; cleaning expenses £7.50; R. Tyler paid us in cash £7.80; paid for office refreshment supplies £8.25.
   23 Paid for typewriter paper £8.00; paid railway fares £4.25.
   24 Paid for postage £4.65; paid T. Rawlinson £3.25.
   25 Paid for postage stamps £2.30; paid bus fares £1.60.
   26 Paid for cleaning office windows £8.50; paid for postage on registered letters £2.20; paid T. Jarman £13.75.

Balance off the Petty Cash Book and restore the imprest.

3 W. Gardner runs his office petty cash on the Imprest System. He has a book with six columns: Postage, Travelling Expenses, Stationery, Cleaning, Sundry Expenses, and a column for Ledger Accounts. Enter the following items, balancing the book at the end of the week, and restoring the imprest:

19. .

Mar 25 Drew petty cash imprest £100; bought stamps £15.50.
     26 Paid postage £1.25; paid cleaner £18.75.
     27 Paid for string £0.75; fares £1.45; postage £4.36.
     28 Paid A. Grover £14.35 for goods supplied last month.
     29 Paid for cleaning materials £4.20; sundry expenses 84 p; postage £1.86; headed notepaper £15.60; tip to carrier £1.00.
     30 Paid £14.25 to L. Robbins; member of staff paid £4.95 for private telephone calls; paid travelling expenses £1.30.

4 A Petty Cash Book is kept on the imprest system, the amount of the imprest being £80.00. It has six analysis columns: Postage, Stationery, Cleaning Expenses, Travelling Expenses, Office Expenses, and a column for Ledger Accounts. Enter the following transactions:

19. .

Jan 4 Petty cash in hand £1.50; received cash to make up the imprest; bought stamps £2.25.
    7 Paid railway fares £12.80; bus fares 64 pence.
    8 Paid postage on small parcels £8.25; paid railway fares £4.40; bought cleaning materials £5.80; R. Johnson paid us £7.80 for goods supplied last month.
   10 Paid for repairs to typewriters £15.85, and headed notepaper £14.80.
   11 Paid postage £2.35; paid for stationery £8.60; paid R. Mason £7.25.

Balance the Petty Cash Book as on 11 January and bring down the balance, ready for checking by the cashier.

5 An office keeps a Petty Cash Book on the imprest system. It has five analysis columns for Postage, Travelling, Stationery, General Expenses and Ledger Accounts. Rule special petty cash paper and record the following week's transactions, inserting appropriate folio numbers and petty cash voucher numbers:

19. .

Jan 1 Drew imprest of £100 from cashier; paid postage £12.50; paid for office stationery £4.75.
    2 Paid fares £2.36; paid for sellotape £1; collected from staff for private telephone calls £7.35.
    3 Paid for cleaning materials £4.50; paid R. Long's account £7.85; paid postage £2.36.
    4 Paid postage £2.22; paid M. Lloyd's account £12.28.
    5 Paid cleaner's wages £25; paid fares £1.25; paid gratuity to carrier £1.00.

Rule off the book, bring down the balance in hand, and restore the imprest to £100.

Debit side	Credit side		PCV	Total											PCB ——		Ledger A/cs	
£	p	Date	Details	£	p	£	p	£	p	£	p	£	p	£	p	F	£	p

Fig. 15.4

This table may be reproduced for classroom use if required

16 Capital expenditure and revenue expenditure

16.1 Types of expenditure

We know that in any business there are many payments to be made. When we start up in business we need premises, machinery, fixtures and fittings, furniture, typewriters and many other things. As soon as we are ready to start trading, whether it is manufacturing, buying and selling or providing services of one sort or another we need other items, such as raw materials, goods for re-sale, stationery and forms for various purposes; account books, telephone directories, employees of various sorts, and so on. All these expenditures have to be recorded in our books, the Cash Book and the Petty Cash Book, the Journal and the other day books, and in the end they will finish up as part of our calculations for working out the profit (or loss) of the business.

How shall we know where everything goes in the book-keeping system if there are so many payments for so many items? The answer is very simple. All we need to do is to decide whether the expenses we are considering are capital expenses or revenue expenses. We must start by defining these terms:

Capital expenses

These are expenses on items which last a long while and are to be used in the business year after year. They are not just of use for a few hours (like the postage stamp we stick on a letter which, once used, only lasts a few days and then is thrown into someone's waste paper basket). They give us service year after year and are what are known as assets of the business. So premises, motor vehicles, machinery, furniture, typewriters, computers, etc., are all capital expenditure. They help us to earn whatever profits we manage to make by supplying us with a business framework within which all our activities are performed. A full definition of capital expenditure is therefore:

> **Capital expenditure is expenditure on fixed assets, which last longer than a year, and permanently increase the profit-making capacity of the business.**

Revenue expenses

By contrast revenue expenses do not last very long, and only bring us something we can use for a short time in the business. Like the postage stamp referred to earlier, they are here today and gone tomorrow. To take another example, light and heating only last a very short time; today's electric light will not illuminate the room tomorrow, and today's heat will disappear overnight. A packet of typing paper may last a week or two; the battery in a calculator soon goes flat; the office boy's wages pay for only one week's work and even the managing director's salary only buys his or her services for one month. In fact the dividing line between capital expenditure and revenue expenditure is one year. If a thing lasts longer than a year it will be capital expenditure, but if it is used in the business and lasts less than a year it is revenue expenditure. So the rent we pay is a revenue expense; the stocks we buy to sell again are a revenue expense, for we certainly hope that they will be sold before the end of the year; the petrol we use in the firm's vehicles is a revenue expense because it only lasts a few days, and so on.

We can distinguish three main types of revenue expenses; consumable items; services supplied to us for use in the business and purchases (goods for re-sale). A few examples of each are:

Consumables: postage, advertising materials, stationery, fuel, lubricants, cleaning materials.

Services: light, heat, water, telephone expenses, printing, rent, rates.

Goods for re-sale: these vary with every trade, for example groceries for a grocer, meat for a butcher, but also raw materials for a manufacturer, components for an assembly plant, materials worked into a finished job such as paving stones, cement, ornamental brickwork and plants for a landscape gardener and so on.

A full definition of revenue expenditure is therefore:

> **Revenue expenditure is expenditure on goods and services which are essential to the conduct of the business but do not last a long time (less than a year) and therefore only temporarily increase the profit-making capacity of the business.**

16.2 Exercises on capital and revenue expenditure

1 Alan Gash is about to set up a pizza parlour in the local High Street, selling snacks, cool drinks, ice creams and pizzas. In the first month he buys many items, but only ten of them are listed below. Copy them out and write against each one either *Cap* if you think it is capital expenditure or *Rev* if you think it is revenue expenditure.

(a) an electric oven
(b) flour of various kinds
(c) cooking utensils
(d) anchovies
(e) twelve flavours of ice cream

(f) tomatoes
(g) cutlery for the restaurant
(h) frankfurter sausages
(i) a motor van for deliveries
(j) coffee

2 Besides the items listed above his wife, Jean Gash, who is the book-keeper, pays out for the following items. Write down the letters (a)–(f) on a sheet of paper and against them write *Cap* or *Rev* if you think the item listed was capital expenditure or revenue expenditure:

(a) £37 000 for the premises they are going to occupy.

(b) £160 rates for the six monthly period ahead.

(c) £64 for an opening announcement in the local paper.

(d) £1260 for a computerised system to relay orders from the restaurant to the kitchen. This item has a three year guarantee.

(e) £84 for coloured menus printed by a local printer.

(f) £360 for glassware and crockery for the restaurant.

3 Write down five items of capital expenditure for a garage business and five items of revenue expenditure for a public relations consultant who advises a manufacturer about complaints from customers.

4 The Ixhampton Zoological Gardens purchased the following 20 items last year. Write them down and against each state whether you consider the item to be capital expenditure or revenue expenditure.

(a) a lioness	(b) tickets for the entrance office
(c) goods for the zoo shop	(d) a dolphinarium
(e) a land rover	(f) ice cream for re-sale
(g) a tranquilising dart gun	(h) meat
(i) postage stamps	(j) fruit and vegetables
(k) a till for the snack bar	(l) medicines
(m) keeper's uniforms	(n) bamboo shoots for the panda
(o) cutlery for the restaurant	(p) food for the kitchens
(q) fish for the aquarium	(r) a dustcart
(s) straw	(t) a penguin pool

16.3 What happens to capital expenditure?

As we have seen capital expenditure is expenditure on buying assets of the business, premises, machinery, office equipment, etc. We already know that when we purchase an asset of this sort the double entry requires a Journal entry, and the rules are:

> **Always debit the Asset Account, Premises Account, Motor Vehicles Account or whatever asset it is.**

> **Always credit the Cash Account if we pay cash, or the Bank Account if we pay by cheque or the creditor if we are not going to pay until later.**

Since the assets are not used up in less than a year they are not expenses of the business that can be written off the profits in the Trading Account or Profit and Loss Account at the end of the year. They will appear on the Balance Sheet of the business, not in the revenue accounts (the Trading Account and the Profit and Loss Account). The only thing that might appear in the revenue accounts would be depreciation of any assets that have reduced in value in the year due to fair wear and tear. Depreciation is fully explained in Chapter 17.

So the answer to the question 'What happens to capital expenditure?' is this:

> **Capital expenditure is debited in the appropriate asset account as one of the assets of the business and finishes up on the**

Balance Sheet of the business as one of the assets on the assets side. However, we may have it appearing at the end of the year at slightly less than its cost price, because we have depreciated it for fair wear and tear.

16.4 What happens to revenue expenditure?

When we pay out cash, or cheques for revenue expenditure, such as heat, light, petrol and oil, stationery, advertising, etc., etc., these items are of course entered on the credit side of the Cash Book or the Petty Cash Book as we pay out the money or the credit side of the creditor's account if we are going to pay later. Then they are debited in the appropriate expense account as expenses of the business, say Rent Account, or Petrol and Oil Account, or Cleaning Expenses Account, or Postage Account.

All these items are losses of the business and appear in the Profit and Loss Account as losses to be written off the profits.

When we pay out cash etc. for goods for re-sale these are not quite losses of the business in the ordinary sense of the word 'loss', but they are the expenses incurred in trading — we have to purchase goods before we can sell them again. So this type of revenue expense is a purchase of the business which is debited in the Purchases Account, and is carried into the Trading Account at the end of the year when we work out our gross profit on trading.

So the answer to the question 'What happens to revenue expenditure?' is:

Revenue expenditure is debited in one or other of the loss accounts of the business, either the Purchases Account or one of the many expense accounts, and finishes up in the Trading Account or the Profit and Loss Account when we work out the profits at the end of the year.

16.5 Borderline cases — capital or revenue

There are many situations in which we spend money and it is difficult to tell whether the expenditure is capital expenditure or revenue expenditure. For example, if we redecorate the premises every three years is the money we spend on redecoration capital expenditure or revenue expenditure? It will last more than a year, but it hasn't really given us a new asset — all that it has done is make sure the premises don't deteriorate and get into a bad state of repair. Another example would be where we buy a new machine which requires considerable expenditure apart from the cost of the machine, to install it and provide a proper working environment. Thus a machine may need to be cemented into position, linked up to raw material supplies by a belt or a mechanical feeding mechanism and after manufacture may need similar devices to get the finished product away to distribution channels, etc. When we pay staff wages to do the erection work and pay for materials are these expenses revenue expenses or capital expenses? These sort of problems affect book-keeping in two ways:

1 If we do not charge an expense to the Profit and Loss Account when we are working out the profits we shall *overstate the profits* for the year. On the other hand if we charge too much expenses to the Profit and Loss Account we shall *understate the profits*. There is a strict rule that we must prepare the final accounts of the business (in which we work out the profits or losses for the year) to give a 'true and fair view' of the affairs of the business. If we overstate the profits we shall pay more tax than we need to (which is rather silly); if we understate the profits we shall not only give a wrong view of our business but we shall defraud the tax inspector of some tax that the Government is entitled to. This can lead to fines or imprisonment.

2 The other way book-keeping is affected is in the Balance Sheet of the business. We shall soon see (see Chapter 22) that when we prepare the final accounts on the last day of the financial year there remain certain items that go on from one year to the next. These are put into a sheet called a Balance Sheet. For example, the premises, machinery, etc., go on to next year. If these have not been treated properly, according to the rules of capital and revenue expenditure, the Balance Sheet will not be correct. For example, if our Motor Vehicles are valued at £4000 but they are really only worth £3000 because of 'fair wear and tear' during the year we shall have a dishonest Balance Sheet. To put this right we must **depreciate** the motor vehicles by £1000, that is write off £1000 in the Profit and Loss Account for the loss suffered in the year. The aim is to get the final accounts of the business carrying the true loss — not a penny more and not a penny less.

16.6 Dealing with borderline cases

1 *Capitalisation of revenue expenses* Consider the following cases:

EXAMPLE 16.1

On 14 July Household Supplies Ltd decide to build an extension to their warehouse premises. The cost of the builder's work and materials is to be £8000 but the services of their own warehouse staff and electrician will be used. This eventually proves to cost £3200 for labour and £1400 for materials and fittings used from stock. The builder is paid by cheque on the day the work is completed, 31 July 19. . .

Since this is a rather unusual piece of book-keeping we shall have to do a Journal entry. Consider what has happened:

1 The premises have increased in value by £12 600 — debit the Premises Account.

2 The Bank Account has given the builder £8000 — credit the Bank Account.

Where has the other £4600 come from? It has partly come from the wages paid to our own people, which will have been debited in the Wages Account when they were paid over the last few weeks. The rest has come from the Purchases Account, materials and fittings we purchased to sell again, but instead of selling them we have used them on the extension. So here we have two revenue expenses, which are not really going to last only a short time; they have been turned into an asset — premises — that will last for years. We usually reckon premises to last 40 years.

Clearly we have to capitalise these revenue expenses because they are now going to last longer than one year.

Here are the entries. First, the Journal entry.

	Journal Proper		£ p	£ p
19 . .	Premises A/c	Dr	12 600.00	
July 31	Bank A/c			8000.00
	Wages A/c			3200.00
	Purchases A/c			1400.00
	Being 'capitalisation' of revenue expenditure on building an extension to the warehouse			

J27

Fig. 16.1 The capitalisation of revenue expenses

When posted to the Ledger the accounts will be as shown in Fig. 16.2 — but note that the figures paid out earlier for wages and purchases have been shown on the debit side of Wages Account and Purchases Account. This enables you to see how the capitalisation of revenue expenditure reduces the actual losses on wages and purchases, since these have not been expended in the usual way, but turned into a capital asset, premises. Balances have also been inserted on the Premises Account and the Bank Account.

Premises A/c   L1

19 . .			£	
Jan 1	Balance	b/d	49 000.00	
July 31	Bank, wages, etc.	J27	12 600.00	

Cash Book (Bank A/c only)   CB5

19 . .			£	19 . .			£
July 31	Balance	b/d	27 256.00	July 31	Premises	J27	8 000.00

Wages A/c

19 . . Jan–July	Cash and Bank	27 354.00	19 . . July 31	Premises	J27	3 200.00

Purchases A/c

19 . . Jan–July	Cash and Bank	38 254.75	19 . . July 31	Premises	J27	1 400.00

Fig. 16.2 Posting the Journal entry to the Ledger

Notes

The final results of these entries are:

1 The premises have increased from £49 000 to £61 600.
2 The Bank gave £8000 for the new premises.
3 The Wages Account (losses) were reduced because £3200 of the wages were not 'lost' but turned into premises.
4 Similarly the Purchases Account (another loss) was reduced by £1400 because this amount of the items purchased were changed into premises and not lost during the present year.

EXAMPLE 16.2

Ellen Brown redecorates her boutique at a total cost of £582. This does not represent any real improvement in the value of the property, but as she redecorates every three years she decides to write off one third of it only as 'repairs and redecorations' for the current year. The other two thirds will be capitalised in a Redecorations in Suspense Account, and will be written off over the next two years. Show the Journal entry and the postings to the Ledger for this entry. The £582 was paid by cheque on 27 November 19. . .

Think carefully what has happened. Bank Account has given £582 for repairs and redecorations. Credit Bank Account. What account has received this money? Really it is Repairs and Redecorations Account, which is one of the expenses of the business, and this expense would normally be written off the profits at the end of the year. As the benefit will last for several years we shall capitalise two thirds of it in what is called a Suspense Account. A Suspense Account is a name used for any account where money values are recorded temporarily while we are sorting out some little difficulty. In this case the 'little difficulty' is that we want to capitalise two thirds of this revenue expenditure to spread the redecorations over three years, and not makes this year carry the whole cost of redecorations. The Journal entry is shown in Fig. 16.3.

19 . .					J21
Nov 27	Repairs and redecoration A/c Dr	L27	194.00		
	Redecoration in Suspense A/c Dr	L28	388.00		
	Bank A/c	CB5			582.00
	Being redecorations, to be				
	written off over three years, with				
	two thirds going into the				
	Suspense Account				

Fig. 16.3 Capitalising some of a revenue expense

Notes

1 When posted to the Ledger the £194.00 will be a revenue expense, one of the losses of the business in a nominal account.
2 The £388.00 will be a temporary asset of the business — because we have turned this part of the revenue expense into a capital asset for the next two years. Half will be written off next year and half a year later.

16.7 Losses that never become expenses

There are some losses that never become expenses and never need to be written off the profits of the business. These are stock losses, which may be caused by various types of theft, or by inherent vice of the goods themselves.

There are many ways goods can be stolen; by the staff, by shoplifting (theft by customers) and by passing out (staff giving the goods to relatives and friends). All these forms of theft are viewed seriously. Never get involved in them; the punishments are severe and the loss of one's good name is even more serious. 'Passing out' requires collusion between the staff and outsiders and is therefore in law a conspiracy, which is punished more severely than theft by an individual.

Inherent vice of the goods is some defect in the very nature of the goods. Strawberries rot; pears go bad; fish go bad; powders blow away; petrol evaporates; sugar may get tainted by other products like paraffin oil or creosote; crockery gets broken. Many of these things finish up in the dustbin. They are losses of the business but we don't need to do any book-keeping for these losses. Why not?

The answer is that when we work out our profits at the end of the trading period one of the things we have to do is count stock. If we count the stock, all the goods thrown into the dustbin will not be available to count. So the stock value as counted will automatically take into account all these losses and we need do no entries for them at all. Often an employer will say to you 'I remember we lost a great deal of fruit in that hot week in August, when it all went bad very quickly. You don't seem to have written it off at all'. You will reply that there is no need to write it off the profits — the low stock figure took account of it, and deducted it from the profits.

16.8 Self-assessment questions

1 Name five assets for a firm that builds motorways.
2 Name five assets for a firm that makes bedroom furniture.
3 Name five revenue expenses for an architect.
4 Name five revenue expenses for a garage.
5 A garden centre repaints the lines on its car park every two years. The cost this year is £480. How should this be treated in the books? (The date is 1 July 19. . , and the financial year ends on 31 December each year.)

16.9 Exercises on capital and revenue expenditure

1 Write down the letters (a)–(j) on a sheet of paper. Against each letter write CE or RE according to whether the ten items below are capital expenditure or revenue expenditure for a garage business:

(a) wages of mechanics
(b) wages of manager
(c) a new breakdown truck
(d) cars for re-sale
(e) 20 000 litres of petrol
(f) a tool kit for trainee mechanics
(g) a car-wash installation
(h) a new lighting installation for the forecourt
(i) a new hose pipe for the air machine
(j) oil for re-sale.

2 Farmer Giles pays out cheques for the following in the month of July. Which would you describe as capital expenditure (CE) and which as revenue expenditure (RE)? Write (a)–(j) on a piece of paper and indicate with the letters which you consider to be capital expenditure and which revenue expenditure:

(a) purchase of a tractor
(b) purchase of fertiliser for autumn sowing period
(c) purchase of a bull at the local cattle market
(d) payment for rates
(e) payment for repairs to barn door
(f) purchase of vitamin supplement for cattle food
(g) purchase of a baling machine
(h) wages for the month
(i) purchase of a flock of sheep
(j) purchase of dipping material for sheep dipping.

3 (a) What is the difference between capital expenditure and revenue expenditure?
(b) A printer instals a new press for £30 000. It also costs £480 for delivery, £2000 building alterations which represent an improvement in the works and £500 for his own labour to assist in the rebuilding. Show the Journal entry for the purchase of this new machine. The press, delivery and building work are paid for by cheque.

4 A department store has alterations and redecorations done by a local builder, to a total cost of £34 000. £24 000 represents an improvement in the premises which is to be capitalised. The other £10 000 is to be spread over four years, with this year carrying the first quarter of the cost. The builder was paid by cheque. Show the Journal entry.

5 Lake Holidays PLC buys the following items. A pleasure boat £26 000; a 'mountain goat' vehicle for taking climbers up into the hills £12 600; tenting, etc., £1600 and site works valued at £4800. Half of this last item is an improvement in the site, the rest is repairs to be borne in two parts, half this year, half next year. Do the Journal entry if all payments are made by cheque to a single contractor.

16.10 Answers to self-assessment questions

(These are only suggestions — you may have thought of others)
1 Bulldozers, lorries, cranes, portakabins and pneumatic drills.
2 Planing machines, polishing machines, delivery vehicles, small tools and premises.
3 Wages, rates, copying machines, drawing paper and postage.
4 Petrol for re-sale, lighting, cleaning services, rates, wages.
5 Half of the present year is left, so this should carry one quarter of the cost = £120. Put £360 in a Suspense Account. Next year write off a full year (£240) and that leaves £120 to be written off in the third year — by which time the lines will want painting again.

17 Depreciation

17.1 Depreciation and revenue expenditure

We saw in Chapter 16 that all the expenses of running a business are called revenue expenditure and are allowed to be deducted from the receipts of the business at the end of the financial year when we are trying to work out the profits for the year. There is one type of expense that is rather different from ordinary expenses like rent, rates, light, heat, etc, but which must still be taken into account when we work out the profits of the business. It is depreciation. Depreciation is the loss in value suffered by the assets of a business as a result of their use during the course of the year. It is often called 'fair wear and tear'. For example if we buy a new van on 1 January for £4000 and use it for a full year it will not be worth £4000 at the end of the year. Everyone knows how quickly motor vehicles depreciate in value and by the end of the year it is quite likely that if we traded the van in and purchased a new one we would not get much more than £2500 as the trade-in value; possibly even less. Where has the missing £1500 gone? It has obviously been 'fair wear and tear' during the year, one of the expenses of the business during the current year. We should really treat this as a revenue expense, one of the losses of the business, and write it off the profits when we work them out at the end of the financial year.

There is another point here which is very important, and which we can adjust at the same time as we deal with the depreciation of the motor vehicle. When we purchase an asset such as the motor vehicle referred to we bring the asset onto the books by debiting the asset account. Thus the double entry for the purchase of a van for £4000 by cheque would be:

(a) debit Motor Vehicles Account with £4000.00 (it has received value)
(b) credit Bank Account (in the Cash Book) with £4000.00 (it has given value)

After this double entry had been made the Motor Vehicles Account would look like this:

		Motor Vehicles A/c		L21
19. .			£	
Jan 1	Bank	CB7	4000.00	

Fig. 17.1 An asset account

Now, by the end of the year the value of this vehicle has fallen as a result of depreciation, to £2500.00. Therefore unless we do something about it we have the asset on the books at an out-of-date value; it has ceased to be worth £4000.00 and is now only worth £2500.

Fortunately, as we shall see, we can write down the value of the vehicle on the books at the same time as we take notice of the depreciation. Before we do the depreciation entry we must just say a word about the Depreciation Account.

17.2 The Depreciation Account

The Depreciation Account is an account where we collect together all the various losses suffered by a business as a result of fair wear and tear of motor vehicles, plant and machinery, furniture and fittings etc. Of course the eventual aim is to write these losses off the profits at the end of the year, but until the end of the financial year arrives it is convenient to have an account where we can collect the various losses together. Therefore the rule in depreciating any item is to work out what the fall in value will be and reduce the book value of the asset by this amount, taking the loss to the Depreciation Account. Later, when all the depreciation has been collected together we shall make a single entry transferring all the losses to the Profit and Loss Account, which is one of the final accounts of the business — where we work out the final profits for the year.

Using our example from Fig. 17.1 where a motor van has depreciated by £1500.00, the actual double entry will be as shown in Figs. 17.2 and 17.3. Depreciation entries are best made by doing a Journal entry, and then posting the Journal entry to the Ledger, as shown in this example.

19..					J.12
Dec. 31	Depreciation A/c	Dr	L37	1500.00	
	Motor Vehicles A/c		L21		1500.00
	Being depreciation of motor				
	vehicles for the year at this date				

Fig. 17.2 A Journal entry for depreciation

Motor Vehicles A/c L21

19..			£	19..			£
Jan. 1	Bank	CB7	4000.00	Dec. 31	Depreciation	J12	1500.00

Depreciation A/c L37

19..		£	
Dec. 31	Motor vehicles J12	1500.00	

Fig. 17.3 The depreciation entries

Notes
1 The posting of the Journal entry reduces the value of the motor vehicles on the books from £4000 to £2500.
2 At the same time it brings the loss due to fair wear and tear onto the books as £1500 in the Depreciation Account. This will be written off the profits in the Profit and Loss Account later, as explained in Chapter 21.

Just before we leave the Depreciation Account consider what it will finally look like on the last day of the year. This is shown in Fig. 17.4.

Depreciation A/c					L37
19. .		£	19. .		£
Dec. 31 Motor			Dec. 31 Profit & Loss		
Vehicles	J12	1500.00	A/c	J19	3470.00
31 Machinery	J13	1200.00			
31 Fixtures and					
Fittings	J13	320.00			
31 Tools, jigs and					
dyes	J14	325.00			
31 Gardening					
equipment	J14	125.00			
		£3470.00			£3470.00

Fig. 17.4 The Depreciation Account written off to Profit and Loss Account

Notes
1 The various amounts of depreciation have been collected together in the Depreciation Account.
2 They have then been transferred in a single entry to the Profit and Loss Account, where they will reduce the profit made (because of these losses by fair wear and tear).

17.3 Depreciation by the straight-line (equal instalment) method

In the simple example used in Figs. 17.1–17.3 we knew how much the motor van had depreciated because we asked a garage for a trade-in value for the vehicle. This is easy enough to do for a motor vehicle, but with most other assets there is no ready market for second hand items. In that case we have to use one of the general methods of depreciation which are available. There are about ten different methods but for our purposes we will deal with only three. The first of these is called the straight-line method; sometimes called the equal instalment method because it results in the same amount of depreciation being written off the asset each year. There is a simple formula for working out what amount should be written off each year. It is:

$$\text{Amount of annual depreciation} = \frac{\text{original cost} - \text{residual value}}{\text{lifetime of asset}}$$

Suppose we expect a machine which cost £14000 to last ten years and then to be worth £2000 when sold at the end of its useful life. This is called its **residual value**.

The calculation is

$$\text{Amount of annual depreciation} = \frac{£14\,000 - £2000}{10}$$

$$= \frac{£12\,000}{10} = £1200 \text{ per annum}$$

Each year we shall debit Depreciation Account with £1200 which will be written off the profits for the year, and we shall credit the Machinery Account with £1200. The Machinery Account will be as shown in Fig. 17.5.

Machinery A/c L73

Year 1			£	Year 1			£
Jan 1	Bank	CB7	14 000.00	Dec 31	Depreciation	J5	1 200.00
				31	Balance	c/d	12 800.00
			£14 000.00				£14 000.00
Year 2			£	Year 2			£
Jan 1	Balance	b/d	12 800.00	Dec 31	Depreciation	J17	1 200.00
				31	Balance	c/d	11 600.00
			£12 800.00				£12 800.00
Year 3			£				
Jan 1	Balance	b/d	11 600.00				

and so on until Year 10

Year 10			£	Year 10			£
Jan 1	Balance	b/d	3 200.00	Dec 31	Depreciation	J26	1 200.00
				31	Balance	c/d	2 000.00
			£3 200.00				£3 200.00
Year 11			£				
Jan 1	Balance	b/d	2 000.00				

Fig. 17.5 How an asset account declines in value over the years

Notes
1 The amount written off each year is the same — hence the name 'equal instalment method'.
2 By the end of the lifetime, in this case ten years, the asset is reduced on the books to its residual value (sometimes called the **scrap value**). If the asset continues to be used it will stay on the books at this value, until finally disposed of. What happens then is explained later (see Chapter 19).

17.4 Exercises on the straight-line method

1 Croker Engineering Ltd purchase a machine for £74 000 on 1 January 19. . . Its estimated life is five years and its residual value is estimated at £14 000. Show the Journal entry for depreciation in Year 1 by the straight line method and the postings to the ledger on 31 December of Year 1.

2 On 1 January 19. . Antoinette Duray buys 12 sewing machines for her fashion workshop at a total cost of £3600. They are expected to last four years and to have a second hand value at the end of that time of £1400. Show:

(a) the calculation for the annual depreciation charge by the straight line method.
(b) the Sewing Machines Account for the four year period bringing out the final value on 1 January Year 5.

3 U. Eyo has a road repair business in Zimbabwe. He buys a bulldozer on 1 July 19. . for £36 500, which he believes will last ten years in service and then have a residual value of £4500. Show:
(a) the Journal entry for depreciation to 31 December (Year 1). (Be careful — it is only half a year).
(b) the Heavy Machinery Account for the Years 1, 2 and 3 bringing out clearly the value on 1 January Year 4.

4 Heavy Haulage PLC buys a motor vehicle for £34 000 on 1 April 19. . . The life of the vehicle is expected to be five years, with a residual value of £2800. Calculate the annual depreciation charge and show the Motor Vehicle Account for the depreciation to 31 December Year 1 and for Year 2 and Year 3 following.

17.5 Depreciation by the diminishing balance method

There is one disadvantage about the straight-line method of depreciation already described. Some assets require maintenance and repairs from time to time, and generally speaking these become more necessary as the item gets older. Thus a motor vehicle requires few repairs in its first two years, but after that breakdowns become more common and repair bills rise. It follows that equal instalments for depreciation and larger repair bills mean that year by year the charge for the asset increases. For example:

	Year 1	Year 2	Year 3	Year 4	Year 5
	£	£	£	£	£
Depreciation	1200	1200	1200	1200	1200
Repairs etc	—	160	240	386	540
Total	£1200	£1360	£1440	£1586	£1740

If we can devise a system that charges more for depreciation in the early years, when repair bills are low, and less in later years when repair bills rise, we shall even out the charges.

This is what the **diminishing balance method** does. It charges a fixed percentage rate (say 25%) on the diminishing balance year by year. The asset would therefore decrease in value as shown in Fig. 17.6 (calculations to the nearest £1).

Heavy Motor Vehicles A/c								L29
19. .	(Year 1)		£	19. .	(Year 1)			£
Jan 1	Bank	CB7	34 000.00	Dec 31	Depreciation	J5		8 500.00
				31	Balance	c/d		25 500.00
			£34 000.00					£34 000.00
19. .	(Year 2)		£	19. .	(Year 2)			£
Jan 1	Balance	b/d	25 500.00	Dec 31	Depreciation	J27		6 375.00
				31	Balance	c/d		19 125.00
			£25 500.00					£25 500.00
19. .	(Year 3)		£	19. .	(Year 3)			£
Jan 1	Balance	b/d	19 125.00	Dec 31	Depreciation	J42		4 781.00
				31	Balance	c/d		14 344.00
			£19 125.00					£19 125.00
19. .	(Year 4)		£	19. .	(Year 4)			£
Jan 1	Balance	b/d	14 344.00	Dec 31	Depreciation	J55		3 586.00
				31	Balance	c/d		10 758.00
			£14 344.00					£14 344.00
19. .	(Year 5)		£					
Jan 1	Balance	b/d	10 758.00					

Fig. 17.6 Depreciation by the diminishing balance method

Notes
1 The amount charged for depreciation is falling year by year as the balance diminishes.
2 However, as the repair bills will be increasing the total cost of the vehicle charged to Profit and Loss Account will be fairly steady year by year.

17.6 Depreciation by the revaluation method

Some assets do not depreciate steadily over a lifetime but vary in value from year to year. Thus a farmer's herds or flocks cannot be said to suffer from fair wear and tear. They might fall in value if disease hits the herd, but hopefully in most years they would increase in value as more animals were born. When an asset increases in value this is called **appreciation** (the opposite of depreciation) but this is dealt with in a later chapter.

Another asset which varies in this way is Loose Tools Account. These are the kind of tools made by toolmakers (a skilled engineering trade) in which, for example, steel press plates are made to stamp out plastic or soft metal articles. Some of these tools cost thousands of pounds, the surfaces being polished to a mirror finish so that when pressed out the plastic article is perfectly smooth and shiny. Since such tools might be kept for many years and new ones are made every year the stock of such tools is liable to rise and the value of the asset in total may increase.

Such assets are usually revalued each year, often by an outside valuer (rather than by someone within the firm or company). If the value is found to have increased over the year the extra value will be taken on to the books as a profit for the year, while if the value has fallen the decrease will be taken on to the books as a loss. Because of the difficulty of treating such losses as depreciation it will often be best to take the gain or loss direct to the Profit and Loss Account.

Figures 17.7 and 17.8 show one case of the changes in value on this type of account. A firm which had loose tools valued at £27 256.00 on 1 January 19. . makes a great many new ones as the year progresses. On 31 December the stock of loose tools is valued at £38 998. Find the increase in value and take it into account, with a Journal entry posted to the Ledger.

19 . .					J49
Dec 31	Loose Tools A/c Dr	L68	11 742.00		
	Profit and Loss A/c	L171		11 742.00	
	Being increase in value of loose				
	tools as a result of this year's				
	toolmaking activities				

Fig. 17.7 A Journal entry for appreciation in value

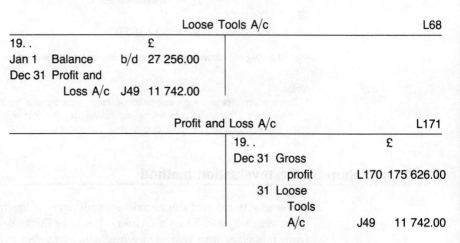

Loose Tools A/c			L68
19. .	£		
Jan 1 Balance b/d 27 256.00			
Dec 31 Profit and			
Loss A/c J49 11 742.00			

	Profit and Loss A/c		L171
	19. .		£
	Dec 31 Gross		
	profit	L170	175 626.00
	31 Loose		
	Tools		
	A/c	J49	11 742.00

Fig. 17.8 Increasing the value of loose tools on the books of a business

17.7 'Provision for Depreciation' Accounts

Company legislation in the UK calls for assets to be shown on the Balance Sheet at cost price, less the total depreciation to date, and this has led to a new way of keeping track of depreciation, not only by companies but by sole traders and partnerships as well. You can understand this most easily if you consider an earlier figure, Fig. 17.5, for a moment (see page 147). In this figure we have the original cost of the machinery on the left hand side and the depreciation deducted from it on the right hand side. The balance carried down at the end of the year shows the reduced value of the asset on the books at the start of Year 2. Over the years we might lose track of what the original cost of the Machinery was, and we might therefore find it difficult to comply with the Companies Act, 1985.

We can overcome the difficulty if we leave the asset alone on the books, so that it stays at its original value, and instead build up the depreciation in a Provision for Depreciation on Machinery Account. The two accounts would then appear as shown in Fig. 17.9.

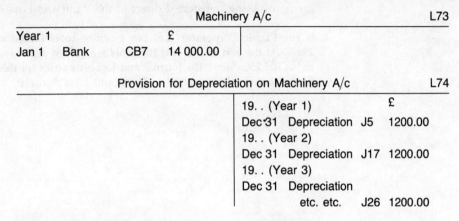

Fig. 17.9 *Keeping an asset on the book at the original cost*

Notes

1 Although the asset is being kept on the books at the original cost price it is of course being depreciated year by year.

2 The actual value of the asset at any given moment is found by deducting the depreciation to date from the original cost. Thus at the end of Year 3 the asset above is valued at £14 000.00 − £3 600.00 = £10 400.00.

17.8 More depreciation exercises

1 Thompson Bros buy machinery for £20 000 on 1 January 19. . . They decide to depreciate it at the rate of 25% of the diminishing balance year by year. Show the Machinery Account for the first three years (calculations to the nearest £1).

2 Marshall & Co buy an aeroplane for £56 500 on 1 July 19. . . They decide to depreciate it by 20% per annum on the diminishing balance method. This is carried out on the 31 December every year. Show the Aeroplane Account for the first three years.

3 The Somalia Desert Corporation buys water storage tankers to a total value of £176 000. These are to be kept on the books at cost price, but the depreciation is to be kept in a Provision for Depreciation Account. Depreciation is by the straight line method given a lifetime of ten years and a residual value for the vehicles of £26 000. Show the Water Tankers Account and the Provision for Depreciation Account for Years 1 and 2.

4 Far East Fuels PLC buys a supertanker on 1 July 19. . valued at £58 600 000. Depreciation at 20% *per annum* is written off each year on the diminishing balance method but the asset is not written down in value; instead the depreciation is accumulated in a Provision for Depreciation on Tankers Account. Show the Supertankers Account and the Provision for Depreciation Account for the first three years. What is the value of the supertanker at the end of Year 3?

5 Farmer Hendrikson has a herd of cattle on his books valued at £81 540 on 1 January 19. . . On 31 December the herd is revalued at £76 240. Show the Journal and Ledger entries for depreciation in the value of the herd at the 31 December, the figure being transferred direct to the Profit and Loss Account.

6 The Plastic Corporation Ltd has machine tools valued at £84 000 on 1 January 19. . . At the end of the year the tools are valued again and the valuation arrived at is £108 250. Show the Journal and Ledger entries for this increase in value, the figures being taken straight to Profit and Loss Account.

18 Understanding the Trial Balance

18.1 The two uses of the Trial Balance

We have already seen that a Trial Balance is a way of checking-up on the double entry book-keeping we have been doing. If the Trial Balance balances, and the total of the debit balances on the accounts comes to the same as the total of the accounts that have credit balances we can say *prima facie* (at a first glance) that the book-keeping has been carefully done. We have to say *prima facie* because there are five errors we could have made that will not show up on the Trial Balance. These are explained later.

So the first use of a Trial Balance is to tell whether the book-keeping has been properly done. If it has not we must find the mistake, or mistakes. The second use of a Trial Balance is as a starting point for working out the profits of the business. This is a very important function of the Trial Balance because working out whether we have made a profit is the whole point of keeping books. The Trial Balance leads us into what are called the **final accounts** of the business. There are two of these in most businesses, the **Trading Account** and the **Profit and Loss Account**, though they are sometimes run into one another and called a **Trading and Profit and Loss Account**. We will ignore this idea for the present. One further point is that where a business is a manufacturing business it is usual to have three final accounts, because before we can start trading we have to manufacture the things we are going to sell and therefore we need a **Manufacturing Account**, followed by a Trading Account and a Profit and Loss Account.

Finally when we have prepared the final accounts we have a few items on our Trial Balance which have not been used. These items are set out in a **Balance Sheet** of the business, and form the final part of a set of 'final accounts'.

18.2 Analysing the Trial Balance

It is easy to understand how the profits of a business are worked out if we have a really clear idea of the Trial Balance from which the profits are determined. The Trial Balance shown in Fig. 18.1 will be used as the basis for preparing a set of final accounts over the course of the next four chapters. Notice though, that there is one figure which we need which is outside the Trial Balance and has to be found separately. This is the Closing Stock, which is found by stock-taking, as explained below.

Study Fig. 18.1 and the notes opposite it now (see pages 154–5).

Trial Balance of K. Marshall's books as at 31 December 19. .

	Dr £	Cr £
Land and Buildings A/c	34 500	
Plant and Machinery A/c	14 800	
Furniture and Fittings A/c	8 650	
Motor Vehicles A/c	12 420	
Capital (K. Marshall) A/c		107 990
Purchases A/c	37 900	
Sales A/c		98 260
Purchases Returns A/c		155
Sales Returns A/c	1 260	
Carriage In A/c	855	
Carriage Out A/c	1 750	
Rent and Rates A/c	950	
Light and Heat A/c	684	
Insurance A/c	560	
Warehouse Wages A/c	13 250	
Stock A/c (opening stock)	6 985	
Commission Received A/c		758
Rent Received A/c		1 000
Salaries A/c	21 460	
Advertising A/c	1 790	
Bad Debts A/c	864	
Sundry Debtors A/cs (total)	17 250	
Sundry Creditors A/cs (total)		8 265
Cash A/c	1 740	
Bank A/c	38 640	
Drawings A/c	9 500	
Discount Allowed A/c	280	
Discount Received A/c		790
Postage A/c	455	
Travelling Expenses A/c	675	
Mortgage A/c		10 000
	£227 218	£227 218

At stock-taking the value of the stock in hand was found to be £9 762.

Fig. 18.1 A Trial Balance of the Ledger on the last day of the financial year

Notes
1 To understand the Trial Balance we have to analyse the various parts of it to see how it is built up. If we do this we find the following pattern:

Debit side	**Credit side**
Several asset accounts:	*Several liabilities:*
Land and Buildings A/c	Capital (K. Marshall) A/c
Plant and Machinery A/c	Sundry Creditors A/c
Furniture and Fittings A/c	Mortgage A/c

cont'd

Debit side	**Credit side**
Several asset accounts:	*Several liabilities:*
Motor Vehicles A/c	
Sundry Debtors A/c	
Cash A/c	
Bank A/c	
Three accounts to do with basic trading:	*Two accounts to do with basic trading:*
Purchases A/c	Sales A/c
Sales Returns A/c	Purchases Returns A/c
Opening Stock A/c	
Several loss (expense) accounts:	*Several profit (income) accounts:*
Carriage In A/c	Commission Received A/c
Carriage Out A/c	Rent Received A/c
Rent and Rates A/c	Discount Received A/c
Light and Heat A/c	
Insurance A/c	
Warehouse Wages A/c	
Salaries A/c	
Advertising A/c	
Bad Debts A/c	
Discount Allowed A/c	
Postage A/c	
Travelling Expenses A/c	
One special account:	
Drawings A/c	

2 The five accounts to do with basic trading will be used to prepare the Trading Account but also the Closing Stock figure found in stock-taking (£9762) will be used as well. This gives us a Trading Profit, called 'Gross Profit'.

3 The loss and profits accounts will be used in the Profit and Loss Account to work out the profits of the business. Of course, the profit made on trading is also used in this account.

4 The remaining items, the assets and liabilities, will be used to to produce a Balance Sheet of the business to start the next trading year.

5 The Drawings Account is the account where the proprietor draws out money to live on during the year. This is really profit that he/she hopes to have made in the year and is sometimes called 'Drawings in expectation of profits made'. It is deducted from the profits at the very end of the year—on the Balance Sheet, as explained in Chapter 22.

18.3 Extracting a Trial Balance from the accounts

The Trial Balance is the first section of the final accounts of any business. Once we know how to extract a Trial Balance of the accounts and how to prepare from it a Trading Account, Profit and Loss Account and Balance Sheet, we know all the basic things about Accounting. Everything else that follows is only a development of the basic principles of accounts — for example we might need to prepare the accounts of a partnership, or a limited company instead of a sole trader, but there is nothing difficult about any of these things — they are just variations on a basic theme which we will already have learned by the time we complete Chapter 22 of this book.

This is therefore a good place to revise our ideas of what we have learned up to now, and to carry the ideas one final stage — to the final accounts of a sole trader enterprise.

We now know:

1 That every transaction in business starts with an original document,

which may be an invoice, a credit note, a debit note, a statement, a cheque, a receipt or a petty cash voucher.

2 That these documents are entered in books of original entry before being posted to the ledger. The book of original entry may be either a Purchases Day Book, a Sales Day Book, a Purchases Returns Book, a Sales Returns Book or for the more unusual transactions such as the purchase of assets, the sale of worn-out assets, depreciation, bad debts, etc., it may be the Journal Proper.

3 Some original entries do also go in the Cash Book and the Petty Cash Book which are therefore a bit unusual since they are really part of the Ledger — they contain accounts, the Cash Account, the Bank Account and the Petty Cash Account. These two books are therefore both books of original entry and parts of the Ledger.

4 All the entries in books of original entry are posted to the ledger, so that a proper double entry is done, with the debit entries exactly equalling the credit entries made.

5 Periodically (at least once a month) a Trial Balance is extracted from the Ledger. This means that every account is looked at, and if necessary balanced off. Running-balance accounts will of course already be balanced off to show the running balance. Accounts kept in traditional style may need tidying up by balancing off. Consider the examples shown in Figs. 18.2, 18.3 and 18.4.

M. Nicholls A/c				L71
19. .			£	
July 17	Sales	SDB5	138.56	

Fig. 18.2 An account which needs no attention

Notes
1 This is a debtor's account, the debtor is owing us £138.56.
2 It is perfectly clear how much is owing, since there is only one item on the account and therefore the account does not need tidying up by balancing off. We can take the figure of £138.56 straight to the Trial Balance in the debit column.
3 In practice it is usual on a Trial Balance to put all the debtors together as a total figure of 'Sundry Debtors'. Many businesses have thousands of debtors, and some have as many as ten million debtors.

M. Abdullah A/c				L79
19. .			£	
July 5	Sales	SDB5	148.56	
17	Sales	SDB11	426.38	
26	Sales	SDB14	371.79	

Fig. 18.3 An account with several items

Notes
1 In this account there are several items, all on the debit side.
2 Abdullah is a debtor and the total debt is £946.73.
3 There is little point in balancing this account off, all we need to do is to pencil in on the edge of the page the total figure which is to be extracted and entered on the Trial Balance in the debit column.

19. .			£	19. .		£
July 1	Balance	b/d	366.84	July 23	Bank	348.50
4	Sales	SDB4	275.64	23	Discount allowed	18.34
30	Sales	SDB16	325.86	27	Sales Returns	14.56

G. Bench A/c   L84

Fig. 18.4 An account which does need tidying up

Notes
1 Here the account has several items on each side and it is not at all easy to tell what the true position on the account is.
2 To simplify it we must balance the account off, and bring down the balance. This will give us the figure we need to extract to the Trial Balance.
3 We know how to balance off such an account. Copy it out onto a sheet of ledger paper and balance it off, bringing down the balance. You will find that Bench is a debtor for £586.94, and this figure would be taken to the debit column of the Trial Balance.

6 If we have used some simplified system of book-keeping such as simultaneous records or computerised accounting, we may not have the actual books referred to in 1–5 above, but we will have some substitute for them, either loose leaf pages produced in the simultaneous records systems or a print-out of various sorts from the computer.

7 Now, all we have to do is to go to each ledger account, tidy it up if necessary and bring the balance down, either a debit balance or a credit balance. These debit and credit balances are then listed to give us the Trial Balance of the books. Remember:

Debit Column
(a) All the assets
(b) All the losses
(c) Three trading items
   (i) Opening Stock
   (ii) Purchases
   (iii) Sales Returns
(d) The Drawings Account

Credit Column
(a) All the liabilities (including Capital Account)
(b) All the profits
(c) Two trading items
   (i) Sales
   (ii) Purchases Returns

8 Note that Trial Balances are prepared each month, but for final accounts purposes the Trial Balance we are interested in is the one that is taken out at the end of the financial year. The financial year can end wherever the trader thinks is best, but for most businesses it is usually either:
   (a) at the end of the calendar year, ie as at 31 December, or
   (b) at the end of the tax year, which is usually taken as 31 March, or
   (c) on the anniversary of the day the trader set up in business whenever that might occur. The Trial Balance should always be headed with the name of the business, and give the date it was extracted, as shown in Fig. 18.1.

You should now try some of the exercises on extracting Trial Balances given in Section 18.4 below. Simply arrange them into two columns using the guidelines given above and if you have everything in the correct column the totals of the debit and credit columns should come to the same figure.

18.4 Exercises on the Trial Balance

In the exercises which follow you are given the balances as extracted from the accounts of various traders. Using your judgment about the column in which the balances should go, draw up the Trial Balance in each case.

1 Books of R. Patel as at 31 December, 19. . . The balances on the accounts are: Capital (R. Patel) £4950.00; Cash £127.25; Bank £3378.00; Purchases £24 405.00; Creditors £3269.40; Sales £60 018.80; Debtors £5109.25; Rent £2120.00; Wages £11 278.25; Insurance £386.00; Discount Allowed £142.00; Discount Received £160.60; Opening Stock £2000.00; Drawings £7200.00; Motor Vehicles £12 500.00; Commission Received £460.75; Sales Returns £518.80; Purchases Returns £305.00.

2 Books of Lee Kiang as at 31 March 19. . . The balances are:
Cash £168.50; Bank £3256.75; Purchases £17 295.65; Sales £48 326.50; Debtors £1428.59; Creditors £3035.90; Machinery £11 428.00; Motor Vehicles £6350.00; Opening Stock £3481.60; Capital £12 305.85; Drawings £5750.00; Postage £324.60; Telephone Expenses £427.50; Discount Allowed £137.50; Discount Received £426.25; Salaries £12 490.00; Rent £780.00; Sales Returns £1326.50; Purchases Returns £550.60.

3 Books of M. Finch as at 31 March 19. . . The balances are:
Cash £396.30; Bank £4035.00; Premises £36 000.00; Machinery £7250.00; Motor Vehicles £12 000.00; Debtors £2045.00; Creditors £4360.00; Stock at start of year £5850.60; Purchases £41 055.50; Sales £95 210.00; Purchases Returns £255.50; Sales Returns £610.00; Capital £16 125.60; Mortgage on Premises £15 000.00; Rates £600.00; Light and Heat £428.70; Salaries £11 320.00; Rent Received £580.00; Commission Received £210.00; Advertising £760.00; Motor Expenses £2140.00; Drawings £7250.00.

4 Books of R. Wylie as at 31 December 19. . . The balances are: Premises £44 000.00; Plant and Machinery £28 500.00; Furniture and Fittings £3530.00; Motor Vehicles £6800.00; Opening Stock £5980.00; Debtors £2310.00; Creditors £5650.00; Bank £2742.00; Cash £368.00; Bank Loan £15 000.00; Capital £55 773.00; Drawings £6250.00; Purchases £33 710.00; Sales £84 265.00; Purchases Returns £310.00; Sales Returns £1265.00; General Expenses £9565.00; Rent Received £1200.00; Discount Allowed £248.00; Discount Received £365.00; Wages £17 295.00.

5 Books of G. Haji as at 31 March 19. . . The balances are:
Capital £5956.00; Office Equipment £2360.00; Motor Vehicles £7250.00; Cash £501.40; Bank £12 405.60; Purchases £32 175.00; Purchases Returns £175.00; Sales Returns £1495.00; Sales £73 511.60; Motor Expenses £1382.60; Wages £12 926.00; Rent £2120.00; Drawings £6445.00; Debtors £2779.00; Creditors £5600.60; Discount Received £190.00; Discount Allowed £177.00; Opening Stock £6845.00; Bank Loan £5000.00; Postage £320.00; Telephone Expenses £426.60; Repairs £825.00.

6 Books of R. Maples as at 31 March 19. . . The balances are:
Furniture and Fittings £5215.00; Motor Vehicles £14 960.00; Office Machinery £7325.00; Opening Stock £14 965.00; Debtors £4216.00; Creditors £3384.00; Bank £14 295.00; Cash £1238.00; Capital £19 289.00; Drawings £8570.00; Sales £99 525.00; Purchases £33 216.00; Sales Returns £125.00; Purchases Returns £116.00; Wages £14 985.00; Salaries £7265.00; Light and Heat £835.00; Rent

£2400.00; Electricity £462.00; Advertising £1736.00; Commission Received £840.00; Discount Allowed £116.00; Discount Received £184.00; Bank Loan £10 000.00; Bad Debts £72.00; Travelling Expenses £196.00; Motor Vehicles Expenses £1146.00.

18.5 Self-assessment questions

1 What are the two reasons for taking out a Trial Balance?
2 How does a Trial Balance start?
3 What is a Trial Balance really?
4 Why should a Trial Balance always balance, with the total of the debit column equalling the total of the credit column?
5 List the types of balances that come on the debit side of a Trial Balance.
6 List the sort of balances that come on the credit side of a Trial Balance.

18.6 Answers to self-assessment questions

1 The two reasons are (a) to check whether a proper double entry has been done in the basic accounting records and that the books do in fact balance properly and (b) to give a starting point for the final accounts of the business so that the profits can be determined and the proprietor can be given the rewards to which he/she is entitled.
2 A Trial Balance always starts with the name of the business and a heading 'Trial Balance as at . . . .' (with the dated inserted to show when the Trial Balance was extracted). For example:

G. Kaufman & Sons
Trial Balance as at 31 December, 19 . . .

3 A Trial Balance is a list of the balances on every account in the Ledger of a business, arranged in two columns, with debit balances in the debit column and credit balances in the credit column. Since the ledger in some businesses is split into several parts, for example a Debtors Ledger, a Creditors Ledger, a General Ledger and sometimes a Private Ledger it is important that none of these are forgotten. We must also remember that there are three accounts which are outside the Ledger anyway — the Cash Account and Bank Account in the Cash Book and the Petty Cash Account in the Petty Cash Book.
4 A Trial Balance should always agree because all the entries are made as double entries, with one account receiving goods, services or money and another account giving goods, services or money.
5 On the debit side we have all the assets, all the losses of the business, three trading items (Opening Stock, Purchases and Sales Returns) and one special account, the drawings of the proprietor.
6 On the credit side we have all the liabilities of the business, (including one special liability, the Capital Account, which is owed back to the proprietor). We also have all the profits of the business, such as Commission Received and Rent Received and two trading items, the Sales Account and the Purchases Returns Account.

19 Some special double entries

19.1 A list of special problems

Many items are routine items, and occur every day — perhaps hundreds of times a day. In particular the purchase and sale of goods, returns inwards and outwards, receipts and payments of money and petty cash expenditures are everyday transactions.

By contrast some events are relatively rare, such as depreciation entries dealt with in Chapter 16, which only occur once a year. Other similar problems are:

(a) bad debts
(b) a bad debt recovered
(c) dishonoured cheques
(d) the sale of unwanted assets
(e) loan arrangements
(f) the correction of errors.

Each of these is fairly simply explained, but the secret in solving all such problems is to think clearly in terms of double entries.

19.2 Thinking in double entries

In every difficult situation that occurs in real life we must decide what to do on the basis of the principles we have studied on our book-keeping course. We cannot expect a text-book to deal with every problem, and we must make up our own minds what to do. We are considerably helped if we really understand the Trial Balance (see Chapter 18) because that taught us that there are four kinds of entries that finish up as debit entries and three kinds that finish up as credit entries. These were:

Debit entries	Credit entries
1 Assets	1 Liabilities
2 Losses	2 Profits
3 Three Trading items	3 Two Trading items
4 Drawings	

Every time we have a problem we should ask ourselves which of these seven items is involved. Since trading items (buying and selling) are routine items, and 'drawings' is a special case (the owner drawing out the profits) it means that only four items really need worry us. Is our problem connected with an asset of the business, a liability of the business, a loss or a profit? When we have decided which it is, we then shall be able to see which account needs to be debited because it has received value, and which account needs to be credited because it has given value. If we think in double-entries as we deal with each of these special problems we shall gradually gain confidence in dealing with them.

19.3 Bad debts

A debtor is a person who owes us money. A bad debtor is a person who owes us money and can't pay (or perhaps *won't* pay). In this situation what are we to do? We can choose:

1 recognise that the situation is hopeless and there is no way we can ever get our money back,

2 come to some arrangement whereby we agree to accept less than the full amount and thus get some of our money back,

3 put them under pressure, by taking legal action in the courts and thus persuade them to pay us (even if it means someone else does not get paid),

4 put them out of business, so that they are declared bankrupt. This is sometimes the kindest thing, and stops other people suffering in the same way as we are suffering.

Thinking in double entries, what does each of these mean?

Case A We are going to suffer the loss. Suppose it is £500. We have a bad debtor on our books for £500. The account is shown in Fig. 19.1.

A. Rottenpayer				L42
19. .			£	
July 27	Sales	SDB41	500.00	

Fig. 19.1 A bad debtor's account

If the debtor is in a bad situation through no real fault of his/her own (perhaps the breadwinner of the family has died) and we decide to take the loss, then the £500 has to be debited to the loss account — the Bad Debts Account. If we debit the Bad Debts Account, which Account shall we credit? Clearly the debtor's account must be cleared from the books. We don't want a bad debt staying on our books forever. If we credit the account above it will clear the account, even though it has been cleared

19 . .				J.17	
Oct 5	Bad Debts A/c	Dr	L37	500.00	
	A. Rottenpayer		L42		500.00
	Being bad debt written off at this date. Debtor died in tragic circumstances				

Fig. 19.2 Journal entry for writing off a bad debt

in an unsatisfactory way. The book of original entry will be the Journal Proper (the Journal) and when posted into the Ledger the asset (A. Rottenpayer's debt) will be replaced by a loss in Bad Debts Account. This will be written off the profits at the end of the year. The journal entry is shown in Fig. 19.2 and the postings to the ledger in Fig. 19.3.

Bad Debts A/c							L37
19. .		£					
Oct 5	A. Rottenpayer	J17	500.00				

A. Rottenpayer A/c							L41
19. .			£	19. .			£
July 27	Sales	SDB41	500.00	Oct 5	Bad Debts	J17	500.00

Fig. 19.3 Posting the Journal entry to the Ledger

Case B If the debtor comes to an arrangement to repay some part of the debt (which is called in law 'a composition with the creditors') the amount paid (say 50 pence in the £1) will be received in part settlement and taken into the Cash Book in the usual way. This will leave only the balance of £250 to be written off as a bad debt. The entry would be similar to Fig. 19.3 but only half the amount would be a bad debt.

Case C If we put the debtor under pressure because he/she is the type of person who clearly could pay, but in fact will not do so, we take out a summons against the person concerned. When we sue someone in this way we serve them with a notice of what is being claimed, and summon them to court to show why we should not have the justice we are demanding. We also claim the costs of the action. Many debtors will pay up rather than face a court action, in which case the debt is cleared, and the only expense we must meet is the small amount of legal charges incurred (which cannot be obtained unless the court hears the case).

Case D If we decide to pursue the debtor with the intention of driving him/her out of business the legal proceedings are held under the Insolvency Act 1986. The result as far as the book-keeping is concerned is that some final payment will be received. It is usually expressed as 'so many

19. .					J.19
Oct 27	Bank A/c	Dr	CB19	185.00	
	Bad Debts A/c	Dr	L37	315.00	
	A. Rottenpayer		L42		500.00
	Being cheque received from insolvency practitioner in the bankruptcy of A. Rottenpayer at this date				

Fig. 19.4 Journal entry for the final settlement in bankruptcy

pence in the £1'. For example, suppose the sale of the bankrupt's property realises enough to pay all the creditors 37 pence in the £1. We should then receive a cheque from the insolvency practitioner appointed by the court to settle the bankrupt's affairs. This cheque will be for 500 × 37 pence = £185. The balance will then be a bad debt of £315.

The Journal entry and ledger postings will be as shown in Figs. 19.4 and 19.5.

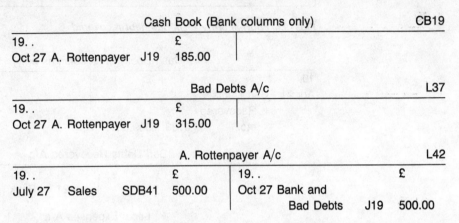

Cash Book (Bank columns only)			CB19
19. .		£	
Oct 27 A. Rottenpayer	J19	185.00	

Bad Debts A/c			L37
19. .		£	
Oct 27 A. Rottenpayer	J19	315.00	

A. Rottenpayer A/c				L42
19. .		£	19. .	£
July 27 Sales SDB41	500.00		Oct 27 Bank and	
			Bad Debts J19	500.00

Fig. 19.5 Posting the Journal entry for a bankruptcy case

19.4 Bad debts recovered

Sometimes bad debts are recovered, often many years later. Although a bankrupt can obtain a discharge from bankruptcy within two to three years of the bankruptcy with the Court's permission, and after that is officially free from debt, many debtors work to redeem their good names. Suppose one day we receive a cheque for £539.60 from A. Rottenpayer, with a note saying that it consists of the £315 owed from the debt, plus £65 legal costs, and £159.60 interest on these amounts. Clearly we need not open up A. Rottenpayer's account again, for it has been written off several years ago. What we have to think about is the best way to do a double entry for this £539.60 which has been received on the Cash Book and debited in the Bank Account. We reason as follows:

1 Some years ago this £315.00 bad debt was a loss of the business. Clearly, when we recover the money it is an unexpected profit of the business, which we must credit in a profit account. We call this account the Bad Debts Recovered Account and credit it with £315.

2 The debtor has also repaid us legal expenses of £65. If we credit this to Legal Expenses Account it will reduce our legal expenses for this year by £65.

3 A. Rottenpayer has also given us £159.60 interest and this is obviously a profit which we should credit in Interest Received Account. So the full double entry is as shown in Fig. 19.6 and the ledger entries will be as shown in Fig. 19.7.

19..					J133
April 21	Bank A/c	Dr	CB29	539.60	
	Bad Debts Recovered A/c		L68		315.00
	Legal Expenses A/c		L69		65.00
	Interest Received A/c		L77		159.60
	Being a bad debt recovered				
	from A. Rottenpayer at this date.				

Fig. 19.6 Journal entry for a bad debt recovered

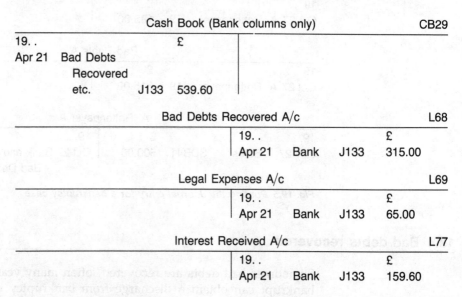

Cash Book (Bank columns only)   CB29

19..		£			
Apr 21	Bad Debts Recovered etc.	J133 539.60			

Bad Debts Recovered A/c   L68

				19..		£
				Apr 21	Bank J133	315.00

Legal Expenses A/c   L69

				19..		£
				Apr 21	Bank J133	65.00

Interest Received A/c   L77

				19..		£
				Apr 21	Bank J133	159.60

Fig. 19.7 Posting the Journal entry for a bad debt recovered

19.5 Exercises on bad debts

1 On 19 January R. Brown hears that a debtor P. Jones who owes him £150 has died in heroic circumstances rescuing a drowning child. He decides to write off the debt as a gesture of sympathy to Jones' widow. Do the Journal entry and post it to the ledger.

2 R. Mayotte is your debtor for £1800. You hear he is in financial difficulty and attend a creditors meeting at which Mayotte's solicitor explains that Mayotte is prepared to pay 50 pence in the £1. The creditors agree to accept this composition. Do the Journal entry when the solicitor's cheque for £900 arrives. Post it to the ledger and the Cash Book.

3 St Kildas Airlines Ltd is in financial difficulties and owes you £850. The final settlement is for 35 pence in the £1. Show the Journal entry and post it to the ledger and Cash Book.

4 R. Kellaway sends you a cheque for £320, together with a letter explaining that it represents a bad debt from four years previously, of which £210 is the actual debt, £25 is legal expenses and the rest is interest. Do the Journal entry and post it to the ledger accounts and Cash Book.

5 M. Shore, a bad debtor of yours from some years ago, sends a cheque for £718.52. It* is made up of the original debt of £420 + £86 legal expenses and interest of £212.52. Do the Journal entry and post it to the ledger accounts and Cash Book.

19.6 Dishonoured cheques

A cheque is an order to a banker to pay money to the named person on the cheque, but the banker does not have to obey the order if there are insufficient funds to cover the cheque. Such a cheque is returned to the person who paid it in with the words 'refer to drawer' written on it. This invites the person who paid it in to approach the person who drew the cheque and ask for an explanation of the matter. It is an offence to pass bad cheques, as well as a serious breach of good faith between business acquaintances. A good explanation may be available, but whether it is or not the book-keeping entry for the disappointed payee is the same: *restore the debt to the debtor*. The debtor's account has been cleared, or a least reduced, when the cheque was received. It would have been debited in the Bank Account; this debit being posted over to the credit side of the customer's account.

Now the procedure must be reversed. We restore the debt to the debtor by debiting his/her account, and credit the Bank Account in the Cash Book to remove the money from the account since the paying banker has refused to honour the cheque for us. Consider the following example.

EXAMPLE

Kerbside Motors has paid by cheque for a second-hand vehicle sold to them for £760, but this has been returned marked 'Refer to drawer' on 31 January, 19. . . Restore the debt to the debtor while an explanation is sought from Kerbside Motors. The Journal entry and the postings to the Ledger and Cash Book are as follows:

19 . . Jan 31	Kerbride Motors Bank A/c Being cheque dishonoured at this date	Dr	L49 CB29	760.00	J27 760.00

Fig. 19.8 Journal entry for a dishonoured cheque

Kerbside Motors   L49

19 . .			£	19 . .			£
Jan 1	Balance	b/d	760.00	Jan 27	Bank	CB27	760.00
Jan 31	Bank	J27	760.00				

Cash Book (Bank columns Only)

19 . .			£	19 . .			£
Jan 31	Balance	b/d	3418.75	Jan 31	Kerbside Motors	J27	760.00

Fig. 19.9 Posting the Journal entry for a dishonoured cheque

19.7 The sale of unwanted assets

When an asset reaches the end of its useful life, or is surplus to requirements for any reason, it is usual to sell it off at the best price obtainable. By this time, because of depreciation, it will be valued on the books at some residual value. Suppose a motor vehicle is now valued on the books at only £850. When we dispose of it on 31 December 19. . there are three possibilities:

1 We may sell it for exactly £850. This is a bit unlikely; it would mean we had guessed the depreciation exactly right all those years ago.

2 We may sell it for less than £850, in which case there will be a 'loss on sale of motor vehicle' to take into account.

3 We may sell it for more than £850, in which case there will be a 'profit on sale of motor vehicle' to take into account.

It would be usual to do a Journal entry for this transaction, debiting either Cash Account (if we sold for cash) or Bank Account (if we were

19 . .					J37
Dec 31	Bank A/c Dr	CB27	850.000		
	Motor Vehicles A/c	L152		850.00	
	Being sale of motor vehicle at its book value — Case (a)				
19 . .					
Dec 31	Bank A/c Dr	CB27	425.00		
	Loss on Sale of Motor Vehicle				
	A/c	L190	425.00		
	Motor Vehicles A/c	L152		850.00	
	Being sale of motor vehicle at less than its book value — Case (b)				
19 . .					
Dec 31	Bank A/c Dr	CB27	1000.00		
	Motor Vehicles A/c	L152		850.00	
	Profit on Sale of				
	Motor Vehicle A/c	L191		150.00	
	Being sale of motor vehicle at more than its book value — Case (c)				

Fig. 19.10 Three different ways of disposing of a motor vehicle

Notes
1 In each case the book value is written off to clear the old vehicle from the books completely.
2 The cheque received is debited to the Bank Account in each case.
3 If there is any difference the balance is taken to a nominal account either a loss account or a profit account, and this will be taken into the Profit and Loss Account at the end of the financial year.

paid by cheque). If the purchaser agreed to pay later we would debit an account in his/her name, as debtor for the amount agreed.

Which account would be credited? Clearly we have to remove the present book value from the Motor Vehicles Account, which must therefore be credited with £850. The various alternative Journal entries are shown in Fig. 19.10, assuming payment by cheque. When posted to the Cash Book and the Ledger they would clear the old vehicle from the books and take account of any loss or profit on sale. Remember, the rule is:

> **always credit the asset account with the book value of the asset, to remove it from the books**.

19.8 Loan arrangements

When a loan is arranged from a bank or finance house the terms of the loan may vary as far as interest is concerned. Sometimes the loan is simply made available to the customer by putting the money into the customer's Current Account. Interest is added at a later date at regular intervals. With other loans the interest is added at a flat rate, say 10%, for the number of years the loan has to run. Thus a loan of £5000, repayable over three years at a flat rate of 10% per annum would have interest added as follows:

$$£5000 \times \frac{10}{100} \times 3 = £1500$$

This means the £5000 would be loaned to the borrower, but £6500 would be repaid over the three years. Note that in fact the true rate of interest would be much more than the flat rate of 10%, but this need not concern us here (see *Discover Business and Commerce*, also published by Pitman, for a full explanation).

To record either of these loans we need a simple Journal entry, posted to the accounts as shown in Figs. 19.11, 19.12, 19.13 and 19.14, supposing in each case a loan of £5000 made on 1 Jan 19. ., in one of which interest will be added in due course, while in the other case it is added on a flat rate basis as explained above.

19 . .				J35
Jan 1	Bank A/c Dr	CB37	5000.00	
	Bank Loan A/c (Helpful Bank			
	PLC)	L69		5000.00
	Being loan arranged at this date.			

Fig. 19.11 A Journal entry for a bank loan

Cash Book (Bank columns only)   CB37

19..			£
Jan 1	Bank Loan		
	A/c	J35	5000.00

Bank Loan A/c (Helpful Bank PLC)   L69

			19..		£
			Jan 1	Bank J35	5000.00

Fig. 19.12 Posting the Journal entry for a bank loan

19..					J37
Jan 1	Bank A/c	Dr	CB37	5000.00	
	Interest Paid A/c	Dr	L73	1500.00	
	Loan A/c (Helpful Finance				
	Ltd)		L74		6500.00
	Being loan at a flat rate of				
	interest (10%) for 3 years				
	arranged at this date.				

Fig. 19.13 Journal entry for a loan at a flat rate of interest

Cash Book (Bank columns only)   CB37

19..			£
Jan 1	Loan A/c	J37	5000.00

Interest Paid A/c   L73

19..			£
Jan 1	Loan A/c	J37	1500.00

Loan A/c (Helpful Finance Ltd)   L74

		19..		£
		Jan 1	Bank and	
			Interest	
			Paid A/c J37	6500.00

Fig. 19.14 Posting the Journal entry for a finance house loan

19.9 Exercises on the sale of assets and the arrangement of loans

1 Toni's Snack Bar has kitchen equipment valued on its books at £350. Toni decides to sell it for £120 as part of an improvement to the premises. Show the Journal entry for the sale, which is settled in cash on 11 July, 19. . .

2 K. F. Tong disposes of printing machinery valued on the books at £18 000 for £23 600. Settlement is by cheque made out on delivery of the presses to the purchaser on 4 May 19. . . . Show the Journal entry for this transaction.

3 Watkins Road Haulage sells a motor vehicle which is surplus to requirements for £1550, the payment to be made partly by cheque (£1000) and the balance by the supply of workshop equipment worth £550. The book value of the vehicle was £2000 on Watkins Motor Vehicle Account. Do the Journal entry for this transaction, which took place on 17 October 19. . .

4 S. K. Zaidi has a power launch valued on his books at £5600. He sells it on credit to Zakaria Security Co., for £5800. Show the Journal entry for this transaction, which took place on 1 January, 19. . .

5 Helpful Bank PLC makes a loan to K. Skaife of £4000, on 14 June 19. . . No interest was charged on this loan at the date of arrangement. Show the Journal entry in K. Skaife's books.

6 Spiro Products Ltd arrange to borrow £15 000 from Union Finance Ltd, at a flat rate of 10% for three years, to be added to the loan on the starting date, 22 March 19. . . Their cheque for £15 000 is received on this date. Show the Journal entry and the postings to the Ledger and Cash Book.

7 Tasman Exports Ltd arrange to borrow £25 000 from Commercial Bankers Corporation at a flat rate of 8% payable over five years. This interest is to be added to the loan on the commencement date. Their cheque for £25 000 was collected on 17 November 19. . .

8 A cheque from a debtor, T. Smith for £49.50 was received on 29 December 19. . and entered in the Cash Book in the normal way, but it was returned marked 'refer to drawer' on 31 December 19. . . Restore the debt to the debtor with a Journal entry, posted to the Ledger.

19.10 Errors in book-keeping

Errors may occur at any time in book-keeping and when they do occur we must of course correct them. Generally speaking we discover errors when we do a Trial Balance, because that is the whole purpose of doing a Trial Balance, to find out whether the book-keeping has been properly done. If it has not then the Trial Balance will not balance and we must discover why, and correct the error. However, there are five kinds of errors which do not show up in a Trial Balance, for reasons that will be explained in this section, so that when we take out a Trial Balance we still cannot be absolutely sure that our book-keeping is perfect. A Trial Balance is therefore said to be *prima facie* evidence of the correctness of the book-keeping. *Prima facie* means 'at first sight'.

The five classes of error that do not show up on a Trial Balance are as follows:

1 original errors
2 errors of omission
3 errors of commission
4 errors of principle
5 compensating errors

1 *Original errors* If an original document is incorrect the book-keeping entries from that document will be incorrect too. Similarly if we copy the figures from a correct document wrongly — so that goods purchased to the value of £500 are entered as £5000, for example — this error will be debited to Purchases Account and credited to the supplier's account at £5000. The Trial Balance will agree, but it is wrong in two places.

2 *Errors of omission* Sometimes a document is mislaid before it is even entered into the books and in these circumstances the entry will not reach either the debit side or the credit side of an account. The Trial Balance balances, but in fact has two errors on it.

3 *Errors of Commission* The word 'commission' means 'power to take action'. An error of commission is one where the action taken is incorrect. For example, if a debtor P. Humboldt, settles his account for £250, but in fact the entry on the credit side of the debtor's account is made by mistake in R. Humboldt's Account, the Trial Balance will agree, but P. Humboldt will appear to be still a debtor, while R. Humboldt's debt will have been reduced by £250 although he has not paid anything.

4 *Errors of principle* We know that capital expenditure should never be confused with revenue expenditure because they are treated differently in the final accounts of a business. It is a common mistake when purchasing assets to treat them as ordinary purchases and include them in Purchases Account. Later we shall see that this has a serious effect on the profits of the business. This is called an error of principle. The Trial Balance agrees, but the 'assets' figure is too small and the 'purchases' figure is too large.

5 *Compensating errors* Sometimes two errors, one in the debit column and one in the credit column, compensate for one another and consequently neither error is discovered. This particularly applies to errors in addition and subtraction, where a book-keeper who is weak at arithmetic may make errors in more than one place, which compensate for one another.

19.11 The correction of errors

Since errors can occur in many different ways the correction of errors depends upon clear reasoning. We have to find what the error is, compare it with what the true situation should be and then take steps to eliminate the wrong action and carry out the correct one. You have to think hard about the problem, and put it right. A few examples are given below.

EXAMPLE 19.1

J. McMahon sends a cheque for £42 to settle his debt of £44.21, the balance being discount allowed. In making the entry we posted the entry to Mr T. McMahon's Account. Correct the error.

Solution: Clearly J. McMahon's Account should be clear, but it still says that he owes £44.21, because the credit entry that would have cleared it has gone into T. McMahon's Account. To correct the error we must debit T. McMahon to restore his account to the correct position and credit J. McMahon's Account. The Journal entry will be as shown in Fig. 19.15, assuming the entry was made on 22 July 19. . .

19 . .					J44
July 22	T. McMahon	Dr	L27	44.21	
	J. McMahon		L63		44.21
	Being correction of an error in				
	which T. McMahon was credited				
	in error with an entry intended				
	for J. McMahon.				

Fig. 19.15 Correcting an error of commission

Notes
1 When the debit entry is posted to T. McMahon's account it will correct the wrong credit entry on his account, restoring it to its original position.
2 When the credit entry is posted to J. McMahon's account it will clear the account recognising that he has paid in full.

EXAMPLE 19.2

The purchase of a motor lorry for £18 250 has been entered in the Purchases Account instead of in Motor Vehicles Account in the books of T. Shah. Correct this entry with a Journal entry dated 15 August, 19. . .

Solution: This is an error of principle. The purchase of an asset has been treated as ordinary purchases and debited in Purchases Account. We must credit Purchases Account to remove the £18 250, and debit it instead in Motor Vehicles Account. The Journal entry will be as shown in Fig. 19.16.

19 . .					J45
Aug 15	Motor Vehicles A/c	Dr	L72	18 250.00	
	Purchases A/c		L38		18 250.00
	Being correction of an error of				
	principle in which the purchase				
	of an asset was treated as a				
	purchase of goods for resale.				

Fig. 19.16 Correcting an error of principle

EXAMPLE 19.3

The Sales Day Book has been undercast by £10. The word 'casting' means 'adding-up' and if we make a slip in the addition of a book like the Sales Day Book it leads to a single-sided error — in other words an error that cannot be put right with a double-entry. Imagine that 500 invoices have been made out in a particular month, and entered into the Sales Day Book. All these 500 accounts have then been posted with the correct figure and all on the debit side, so there is no error on the debit side. The book has then been totalled and a £10 error has been made. The book totals £23 051.95 but in fact because of the error it only reads £23 041.95. When this is credited to Sales Account there is a £10 error on the books. The Trial Balance will not agree. When we discover the mistake it is only necessary to do a single sided Journal entry. It is shown in Fig. 19.17, dated 31 May 19. . .

19 . . May 31	(No debit entry) Sales Account Being single sided entry necessary to correct error in casting the Sales Day Book.	L67	— —	J45 10.00

Fig. 19.17 A single sided Journal entry to correct an error

Notes
1 Since there is no debit entry it is usual to indicate that this is so.
2 When posted to the Sales Account the £10 error will be corrected.
3 A less formal way to do this correction would be to go to the Sales Account and just correct it by crediting £10 on it, but this would mean there was no real explanation of the problem in the books. The narration in the Journal entry is the official explanation for the entry.

19.12 Suspense Accounts and the correction of errors

When a Trial Balance does not agree, but we are unable to find the error, we may decide to put the outstanding balance in a Suspense Account. As its name implies this is an account which is in suspense, waiting for a decision to be made about it. Sooner or later the error will be sorted out, because someone will complain about something. Thus if we have forgotten to credit a creditor with an amount, we shall receive a statement at the end of the month saying — 'Please pay us this amount which is now due'. When we check the account to make sure we do actually owe the creditor the sum claimed we shall find there is no balance outstanding on the account. Checking back to see if we have ever received an invoice for this amount we shall find we did receive one, and it has been entered in the Purchases Day Book, but it has never been credited to the account of the creditor. Sooner or later every error turns up.

A Suspense Account can have a balance on either side, whatever is necessary to make the Trial Balance balance. Suppose a Trial Balance has totals as shown below:

£217 256.25	217 386.25

The difference is £130. To make the Trial Balance agree, we must put the £130 on the debit side of the Suspense A/c as shown in Fig. 19.18.

Suspense A/c		L137
19 . . Dec 31 Difference on books	£ 130.00	

Fig. 19.18 A debit balance on the Suspense Account

When this comes in at the end of the Trial Balance we shall have both sides of the Trial Balance coming to the same figure. We can now proceed with our normal work, but the Suspense Account is a constant reminder to us that there are some undiscovered errors on the books somewhere.

Consider the following errors, which are subsequently revealed.

List of errors discovered on the dates shown

1 A debtor, P. Tomlinson, was sent goods for £532.00 last month, but no entry to debit his account was made (5 January 19. .).

2 Bank charges of £15.60 were entered in the Bank Account but never debited in Bank Charges Account (8 January, 19. .).

3 The Sales Account has been undercast by £200 (10 January 19. .).

4 A motor van, valued on the books at £217.60, and sold to an employee at book value, was not written off the Motor Vehicle A/c even though the employee had paid by cheque and the cheque had been entered in the Bank Account (25 January 19. .).

We can see how each of these errors can be put right, and what it will do to the Suspense Account:

1 We have to debit P. Tomlinson's Account and as we do so we must credit Suspense Account (since all these errors are partly to blame for the Suspense Account coming into existence).

2 Bank Charges Account has to be debited, and of course this means a credit in the Suspense Account again.

3 The Sales Account is always credited with the sales. As it has been undercast we need a further £200 on the credit side of the Sales Account. This means a double entry on the debit side of the Suspense Account.

4 Finally we have to write the motor vehicle off the Motor Vehicle Account, so we credit Motor Vehicle Account with £217.60. This means a debit entry in the Suspense Account, and this last entry clears the Suspense Account altogether.

The Journal entries are shown in Fig. 19.19 and the Ledger entries in Fig. 19.20.

19 . .					J37
Jan 5	P. Tomlinson A/c Dr	L16	532.00		
	Suspense A/c	L121			532.00
	Being sales to P. Tomlinson not debited to his account				
8	Bank charges A/c Dr	L29	15.60		
	Suspense A/c	L121			15.60
	Being bank charges deducted from Bank Account but not posted to the expense account				
10	Suspense A/c Dr	L121	200.00		
	Sales A/c	L36			200.00
	Being undercasting of Sales Day Book corrected at this date				
25	Suspense A/c Dr	L121	217.60		
	Motor Vehicles A/c	L74			217.60
	Being writing-off of a motor vehicle sold at book valve to an employee.				

Fig. 19.19 A series of Journal entries to correct errors

Suspense A/c							L121
19..			£	19..			£
Dec 31	Difference			Jan 5	P. Tomlinson	J37	532.00
	on books	J36	130.00	8	Bank charges	J37	15.60
Jan 10	Sales	J37	200.00				
25	Motor						
	Vehicles	J37	217.60				
			£547.60				£547.60

	P. Tomlinson A/c			L16
19..			£	
Jan 5	Suspense	J37	532.00	

	Bank Charges A/c			L29
19..			£	
Jan 5	Suspense	J37	15.60	

	Sales A/c				L36
		19..			£
		Jan 10	Suspense	J37	200.00

	Motor Vehicles A/c				L74
		19..			£
		Jan 25	Suspense	J37	217.60

Fig. 19.20 How the Suspense Account is finally cleared

19.13 Self-assessment questions

1 What sort of errors are likely to be made in book-keeping?
2 What is an error of omission?
3 What is an error of commission?
4 What sort of an error would it be if furniture purchased for use in the business as an asset, Office Furniture, was debited in Purchases Account?
5 What is a Suspense Account?

19.14 Exercises on the correction of errors

1 Eastern Chemicals Ltd were sold goods valued at £642.00 by P. Taylor Ltd on 5 January 19. . , but these were posted to the account of another debtor Eastern Chemists Ltd. The error was discovered on 11 January. Do the Journal entry to correct this error and post it to the Ledger.

2 Goods returned to a supplier T. Edmunds and valued at £84.50 were posted incorrectly to the account of another creditor T. Edwards. The error was discovered on 4 May 19. . . Do the Journal entry to correct this error and post it to the Ledger.

3 A motor vehicle purchased by the Hatterly Municipal College for £4950 on 4 January 19. . , has been debited to Furniture and Fittings Account instead of Motor Vehicles Account. Do the Journal entry to correct this error and post it to the Ledger.

4 Horizon Computers purchased goods for re-sale valued at £1756.00, on 12 July 19. . . On 17 July it was found that these items had been posted to Computers Account (an asset account) instead of being treated as ordinary goods for re-sale. Do the Journal entry to correct the error and post it to the Ledger.

5 A motor lorry purchased on credit by Thomas Sharpe and Co., from Heavy-motors Ltd actually cost £18 560. The invoice was entered correctly in the Journal as the purchase of an asset, but when actually posting the new vehicle to the Motor Vehicles Account the book-keeper entered it as £18 650. What correction is required to put the books right on the day the error was discovered 6 July 19. . ? Do the Journal entry.

6 Abdul Kadar's Trial Balance failed to agree on the last day of the financial year (31 March 19. .), the debit side being larger by £90. He opens a Suspense Account with the necessary balance. On 19 April 19. . he discovers that the error was due to a mis-posting by which furniture purchased on credit from Millers Ltd, for £650 had been credited to their account at £560. Do the Journal entry to clear the Suspense Account and correct the error.

7 A Trial Balance fails to agree by £721.70 and no error being located a Suspense Account is opened with a debit balance for this sum on 31 December 19. . . During January the following mistakes are discovered:
(a) A dividend from an investment had been correctly entered in the Cash Book as £121.40, but no posting to the Interest Received Account had been made for this amount.
(b) £1000 repaid on a loan from a finance house had been credited in the Cash Book, but not posted to the debit side of Loan Account.
(c) A credit note sent to a debtor R. Higgs for £156.90 for goods returned had been entered in the Sales Returns Book but not posted to the debtor's ledger account.
   Do the Journal entries to correct these errors and clear the Suspense Account. Show the Suspense Account with the opening balance and the entries which clear it.

8 On 31 December 19. . the Trial Balance of Garden Landscapes Ltd failed to agree, the credit side being £425.50 greater than the debit side. The chief clerk could not find any errors, and opened a Suspense Account. Later the following errors were found:
(a) A cheque paid out to S. Iskander for £90.00 had been entered as £9 only when posted to her account.
(b) A cheque for £42.50 posted to Anne Archer's account on the debit side should really have been posted to A. N. Archer's account. (Careful — does it affect the Suspense Account or not?)
(c) Bank charges of £5.50 have been debited in Bank Charges Account but have not been credited in the Bank Account although the bank deducted them on the bank statement.
(d) Goods valued at £350.00 returned to a supplier T. Heron & Co., have been entered in the Sales Returns Book but have not been debited in the supplier's account.

Do the Journal entries for these items and show the Suspense Account after all postings have been done.

19.15 Answers to self-assessment questions

1 Every type of error can be made, which makes it difficult to learn how to correct them. The main thing is to use common sense — decide what the error is and what should really have been done. Then take action to correct the error.

2 An error of omission is where something is left out altogether (for example where an invoice is mislaid and no entry is made for it).

3 An error of commission is where something is done wrongly — for example where goods sold to Kay Shore are debited to K. Shah's account by mistake.

4 This error would be an error of principle. Expenditure on an asset is capital expenditure not revenue expenditure and it must be debited in an asset account, not in an expense account.

5 A Suspense Account is an account which is opened when a Trial Balance fails to agree and we cannot locate the error. We give the Suspense Account either a debit balance or a credit balance, according to what is needed. This makes the Trial Balance agree, but of course, sooner or later the error or errors will be discovered and they can then be corrected. As this is done the balance on the Suspense Account will be removed.

20 Finding the profits of a business — 1 the Trading Account

20.1 The Final Accounts of a business

There are three main types of businesses, manufacturing businesses, trading businesses and service businesses which offer services to the public and are not actually engaged in either manufacturing or trade. Some of these services are offered by skilled tradesmen, such as plumbers, electricians, carpenters, etc while others are professional services, offered by doctors, dentists, accountants, lawyers, etc. It makes a difference in that professional people dislike the use of the word 'profit' when applied to their professional services. A doctor would not say 'I made £500 profit on Mrs Smith's pneumonia case'.

The final accounts of any business are the accounts in which we work out the profits of the business at the end of the financial year. To suit the various types of business mentioned above we have various sets of final accounts which may be listed as follows:

Manufacturing businesses	Trading businesses	Service businesses Skilled trades	Professional
a **Manufacturing Account**	a **Trading Account**	a **Profit and Loss Account**	an **Income and Expenditure Account**
followed by a **Trading Account**	followed by a **Profit and Loss Account**	followed by a **Balance Sheet**	followed by a **Balance Sheet**
followed by a **Profit and Loss Account**	followed by a **Balance Sheet**		
followed by a **Balance Sheet**			

Note

Because professional people object to the term 'profit', their Profit and Loss Accounts are called Income and Expenditure Accounts. It is easiest to learn how to deal with final accounts by starting with the commonest type of business — the trading business. This means we must start with the Trading Account.

20.2 The Trading Account 1 — Purchases and Sales

If I buy something for £5 and sell it for £8 I have made a profit of £3, because profit is the difference between the purchase price and the selling price. In business we collect all our purchases together in the Purchases Account and all our sales in the Sales Account. Therefore the profit will be the difference between our 'Purchases' figure and our 'Sales' figure.

In this chapter and the next two chapters we shall be using the Trial Balance given in Fig. 18.1 (see page 154). For simplicity we will build up the Trading Account gradually. The two sets of figures given in Fig. 18.1 are Purchases Account £37 900 and Sales Account £98 260. Set down in the Trading Account these would give us a profit of £60 360, as shown in Fig. 20.1.

K. Marshall

Trading Account for year ending 31 December 19. .					L127
19. .		£	19. .		£
Dec 31	Purchases	37 900.00	Dec 31	Sales	98 260.00
	Gross Profit (to P&L A/c)	60 360.00			
		37 900.00 *(rule)*			
		£98 260.00			£98 260.00

Fig. 20.1 Starting the Trading Account

Notes

1 The Trading Account always starts with the name of the firm concerned and the phrase for year ended . . . etc (or if prepared more frequently than once a year it may say 'quarter' or 'month' ended etc).

2 The profit discovered in the Trading Account is called the Gross Profit. The word means 'fat' profit, because it has not yet had deducted from it the many expenses of the business.

3 The gross profit will be transferred to the Profit and Loss Account and the expenses (losses) will be deducted there.

4 Actually we cannot transfer the Purchases and Sales figures in this way unless we do a proper double entry, transferring the figures out of the Purchases Account into the Trading Account, and out of the Sales Account into the Trading Account. This is called a Closing Entry and is explained below.

5 Finally, we can see that this Gross Profit figure is not very satisfactory because we have on our Trial Balance both Sales Returns of £1260 and Purchases Returns of £155. These need to be taken into account.

20.3 Closing Journal entries and Final Accounts

Whenever we transfer figures on a Trial Balance into one of the final accounts such as the Trading Account, what we are really doing is a double entry which will close the nominal account (the account where the money is recorded in name only) — leaving it ready to start a new financial year. In the process the figure for Purchases or Sales, as the case may be, will be brought into the Trading Account and used to work out the profits of the business. The closing entry in every case is a Journal entry similar to those shown in Fig. 20.2, and posted into the Ledger to close off the Purchases Account and the Sales Account, and open up the Trading Account.

19 . .					J17
Dec 31	Trading A/c Dr	L127	37 900.00		
	Purchases A/c	L29			37 900.00
	Being purchases for the year transferred to Trading Account at this date				
31	Sales A/c Dr	L30	98 260.00		
	Trading A/c	L127			98 260.00
	Being sales for the year transferred to Trading Account at this date				

Fig. 20.2 Closing the Purchases Account and Sales Account

		Purchases A/c			L29
19 . .		£	19 . .		£
Jan 31	Sundry		Dec 31 Trading A/c J17		37 900.00
	creditors DB12	2 729.50			
Feb 28	etc. until 31				
	December				
	19 . .	35 170.50			
		£37 900.00			£37 900.00

		Sales A/c			L30
19 . .		£	19 . .		£
Dec 31	Trading A/c J17	98 260.00	Jan 31	SDB17	7 964.50
			Feb 28	SDB24	11 427.50
			etc.	until 31	
				December	
			19 . .	etc.	78 868.00
		£98 260.00			£98 260.00

Fig. 20.3 The nominal accounts closed off and cleared of any balance

20.4 The Trading Account 2 — Returns inwards and outwards

The Trial Balance on Fig. 18.1 had five trading items of which three were on the debit side, Purchases, Sales Returns and Opening Stock, and two had credit balances, Sales and Purchases Returns. There was also a Closing Stock figure of £9762 found by stock-taking on the last day of the year. Two of these accounts have already been cleared into the Trading Account and we must now deal with all the rest. First we must deal with

19 . .					J17
Dec 31	Trading A/c Dr	L127	1260.00	
	Sales Returns A/c	L31		1260.00
	Being transfer of Sales			
	Returns to Trading Account at			
	this date.			
31	Purchases Returns A/c Dr	L32	155.00	
	Trading A/c	L127		155.00
	Being transfer of Purchases			
	Returns to Trading Account at			
	this date			

Fig. 20.4 Clearing the Returns Accounts to Trading Account

Sales Returns (Returns In) and Purchases Returns (Returns Out). To clear these accounts we need Journal entries as shown in Fig. 20.4.

However at this point we have to learn something special about final accounts. Since these accounts are the last accounts of the year, in which the results of the business are displayed for the benefit of the proprietor, the Inland Revenue Department and anyone else who is interested, we do adjust our layout and our double entries to give a better presentation than ordinary double entry would allow.

For example, the Sales figure of £98 260 is to be transferred to the credit side of the Trading Account as in Fig. 20.1. The Sales Returns figure, according to the Journal entry in Fig. 20.4 is to be debited in the Trading Account, if we stick to strict double-entry. However it will be a better presentation if we do not put Sales Returns on the debit side of Trading Account, but instead deduct it from the Sales on the credit side. This is still a correct double-entry, because to deduct something on the credit side is the same as adding it to the debit side. The same thing applies to the Purchases Returns; instead of transferring it to the credit side of the Trading Account we deduct it from Purchases on the debit side. This clears these two accounts from the Trial Balance, and gives us a Trading Account in the form shown in Fig. 20.5.

K. Marshall
Trading Account for year ended 31 December 19. .

19 . .		£	19 . .		£
Dec 31	Purchases	37 900.00	Dec 31	Sales	98 260.00
	Less Purchases			*Less* Sales	
	Returns	155.00		Returns	1260.00
	Net purchases	37 745.00		Net turnover	97 000.00

Fig. 20.5 Good style to bring out net purchases and net turnover

Notes
1 Although the Trading Account is really just another account in the Ledger, we are more interested in good style and presentation than in strict double entry.
2 The style shown above is better because it brings out the true purchases and sales figures

for the year. The word 'net' means clear, or clean. We did not purchase £37 900 of goods because we returned £155.00 so that clear purchases were only £37 745.00. Similarly the clear sales were £97 000.00, not £98 260.00.

3 The clear sales figure is a very important figure, and is called in business the 'net turnover'. This figure is used when businesses are bought and sold — we have to pay more for a business with a large turnover than for one with a small turnover. You will often hear this figure quoted on television programmes about take-over bids. Always write 'Net turnover' on your Trading Account against this figure.

4 Since the date is given at the top of the Trading Account we usually leave out the dates on either side.

5 Of course this account has not been finished off because we are not quite ready to find the gross profit.

20.5 The Trading Account 3 — Taking stocks into account

Stocks also present a problem when drawing up a Trading Account. The Stock Account is a very special type of account. It only has three entries on the account at any time in the year. On the first day of the year it starts with the opening balance of stock in hand, as found at the stock-taking. Stock taking is explained more fully in Chapter 23. On the first day of the year the Stock Account is as shown in Fig. 20.6.

	Stock A/c		L15
19. .		£	
Jan 1	Balance b/d	6985.00	

Fig. 20.6 The Stock Account at the start of the year

Notes
1 The balance is the closing stock figure for last year as found at the stock-taking on the last day of the year. The best way to look at it is that it is what last year hands over to next year as an asset to begin the new year with. So for a few minutes, on the first day of the year, the Stock Account is an asset account, a real account, representing Stock on the shelves that can really be touched and handled, and it is worth £6985 in this case.

2 Now imagine that the first customer walks in and buys one item. Immediately the Stock Account is wrong — the stock is no longer worth £6985, because we have sold some of it. It becomes a nominal account, one where the money is there in name only, and by the end of the year it will all have been sold, and just becomes one more loss of the business, it has gone into the trading of the business.

3 When we buy more stock to sell again we do not put it in the Stock Account. Goods purchased for re-sale are called 'Purchases' and go in Purchases Account. The Stock Account stays the same all through the year, although the stock it represented has long ago been sold.

What happens on 31 December? We transfer this stock to the Trading Account, with a simple Journal Entry that clears the Stock Account and debits Trading Account. The Stock Account then looks as shown in Fig. 20.7. The Trading Account is shown in Fig. 20.10 later.

	Stock A/c				L15
19. .		£	19. .		£
Jan 1	Balance b/d	6985.00	Dec 31	Trading A/c J17	6985.00

Fig. 20.7 The opening stock cleared into the Trading Account

19 . .					J17
Dec 31	Stock A/c Dr	L15	9762.00		
	Trading A/c	L127		9762.00	
	Being closing stock at the end of the year found on stock taking on 31 Dec. 19. .				

Fig. 20.8 Entering the closing stock at the end of the year

Having cleared the old stock of £ the account (it was sold long ago), we now bring on the stock at the end of the year. This has been found, by doing the stock-taking, to be £9762.00. This is another simple Journal entry, debit the Stock Account and credit the Trading Account, as shown in Fig. 20.8.

When posted to the Stock Account it looks as shown in Fig. 20.9 and as this is the end of the financial year we balance the account off and bring down the balance. This balance is of course the opening stock for next year, and is once again an asset account for a few hours until the first customer arrives on the first day of the new trading year.

Stock A/c   L15

19. .			£	19. .			£
Jan 1	Balance	b/d	6 985.00	Dec 31	Trading A/c	J17	6 985.00
Dec 31	Trading A/c	J17	9 762.00	Dec 31	Balance	c/d	9 762.00
			£16 747.00				£16 747.00
19. .			£				
Jan 1	Balance	b/d	9 762.00				

Fig. 20.9 The Stock Account closed and re-opened for the next year

When we post the closing stock to the Trading Account we should of course credit the Trading Account, as shown in the Journal entry in Fig. 20.8. In fact we don't. Instead we deduct it from the debit side to bring out another very important figure, the **cost of stock sold**. This is illustrated in Fig. 20.10. Once again, deducting a figure from the debit side has the same effect as adding it to the credit side.

K. Marshall
Trading Account for year ended 31 December 19. .

	£		£
Opening Stock	6 985	Sales	98 260
Purchases	37 900	*Less* Sales Returns	1 260
Less Purchases Returns	155	Net turnover	97 000
Net purchases	37 745		
Total stock available	44 730		
Less Closing Stock	9 762		
Cost of stock sold	34 968		

Fig. 20.10 A Trading Account which includes the stock figures

Notes

1 On the debit side it is important to follow what has actually been done. We started off the year with some opening stock. We then purchased a lot of items, but returned a few of them, so the net purchases was £37 745. These items were put on the shelves with the opening stock, giving us a figure of £44 730 as the total stock available. Now as the closing stock was left on the shelves on the last day of the financial year we did not sell it, and it has to be handed on to the next year as the opening stock for the new year. What we want to know is this: What did the things we sold in the year cost us. If we deduct the closing stock from the total stock available we get the cost of the stock sold. This was £34 968.

2 What did we sell them for? The answer is £97 000. It looks as though we made a large gross profit. However we still have a few little points to worry about, because there are certain expenses we need to take into the Trading Account.

20.6 The Trading Account 4 — Carriage In and other expenses

Although most of the expenses of a business (the overhead expenses) are written off in the Profit and Loss Account there are a few expenses that are dealt with in the Trading Account, while for manufacturing businesses the factory expenses are dealt with in the Manufacturing Account (see Chapter 29). To complete our Trading Account we must therefore deal with the trading expenses.

'Carriage In' and 'Customs Duty on Imported Purchases'

These two expenses are rather special in that they are really an increase in the cost of the purchases we make. As such they should really be added to the Purchases figure in the Trading Account. The 'Carriage In' listed on the Trial Balance was £855, and this account should be cleared off by crediting it and debiting the £855 in the Trading Account, as shown in Fig. 20.11. Note that Carriage Out Account is carriage on sales, not on purchases, and therefore goes in the Profit and Loss Account with other selling expenses like advertising, transport expenses, etc.

Besides these two special cases of expenses that go in the Trading Account and not the Profit and Loss Account, it is also usual to include certain expenses in the Trading Account if they relate particularly to trading, as distinct from overhead expenses which go in the Profit and Loss Account. The commonest of these would be warehouse wages and warehouse expenses. These are added to the 'cost of stock sold', as shown in Fig. 20.11 and thus give us a new figure 'cost of sales'. This enables us to work out the gross profit, which is the difference between the net turnover of the business (the total sales made) and the cost of those sales. Study Fig. 20.11 carefully at this point.

K. Marshall
Trading Account for year ended 31 December 19. .

	£			£
Opening Stock		6 985	Sales	98 260
Purchases	37 900		*Less* Sales Returns	1 260
Add Carriage In	855		Net turnover	97 000
	38 755			
Less Purchases				
Returns	155			
Net Purchases		38 600		
Total Stock available		45 585		
Less Closing Stock		9 762		
Cost of stock sold		35 823		
Warehouse Wages		13 250		
Cost of sales		49 073		
Gross Profit (to P/L A/c)		47 927		
		£97 000		£97 000

Fig. 20.11 A Trading Account in good style

Notes
1 The calculations for the net purchases are carried out in an indented section of the display to clarify the figures.
2 The cost of stock sold, and the cost of sales, are important sub-totals which are used later in certain business ratios which help us control a business by following trends in business activity.
3 On the credit side the calculation of the net turnover is a simple procedure, which brings out this very important figure which is also used in several control ratios, which are explained later.
4 The gross profit figure is labelled — to Profit and Loss Account.

20.7 Self-assessment questions

1 What is a Trading Account?
2 What is the gross profit?
3 How do we find the gross profit?
4 Why is net turnover an important term?
5 How do we find the 'closing stock' figure?
6 What is meant by a Trading Account in good style?
7 What happens to the gross profit once we have found it on the Trading Account?

20.8 Exercises on Trading Accounts

In the following exercises you should not be too concerned to have the Trading Account in the traditional form as it would appear in an ordinary ledger account. Instead use the style shown in Fig. 20.11 to give room for indenting the purchases calculations where necessary. The exercises are graded, the later ones having more detail than the earlier ones. In each case the final figure will be the gross profit, which should be labelled (To P/L A/c) — to Profit and Loss Account.

1 Here are the basic figures for M. Shute's Trading Account. Draw up the Trading Account and find the gross profit for the year ended 31 December 19. . .
Opening Stock £3274.50; Purchases £15 956.00; Purchases Returns £956.00; Sales £67 245.90; Sales Returns £1245.90; Closing Stock £4842.50.

2 Figures extracted from K. Lawal's Trial Balance to prepare his Trading Account are as follows:
Opening Stock £4000; Sales £120 037.60; Sales Returns £1037.60; Purchases £48 910.00; Purchases Returns £610.00; Closing Stock £9236.00. Draw up Lawal's Trading Account and find the gross profit for the year ended 31 March 19. . .

3 Draw up R. Phillipson's Trading Account and find the gross profit for the year ended 31 December 19. . given that the following figures are available from her Trial Balance and stock-taking activities:
Opening Stock £10 444.80; Purchases £51 886.95; Carriage In £842.60; Customs Duty on Imports £825.00; Purchases Returns £1651.80; Sales £144 979.50; Sales Returns £3979.50; Closing Stock £27 264.50.

4 Draw up M. Ankor's Trading Account and find the gross profit for the year ended 31 December 19. . given that the following figures are available from his Trial Balance and stock-taking activities:
Opening Stock £9759.25; Purchases £41 895.60; Carriage In £725.40; Customs Duty on Imports £732.50; Purchases Returns £1795.40; Sales £173 250.50; Sales Returns £1250.50; Closing Stock £8856.42.

5 Draw up the Trading Account of M. Stevenson and find her gross profit for the year ended 31 December 19. . from the following figures:
Opening Stock £7250.00; Purchases £41 264.50; Carriage In £187.50; Sales £99 256.50; Sales Returns £875.40; Purchases Returns £1 842.50; Closing Stock £5995.65; Warehouse wages £17 244.60; Warehouse Expenses £1742.45.

6 Draw up a Trading Account and find the gross profit of M. Tully for the quarter year ended 30 September 19. . given the following figures:
Opening Stock £5980; Purchases £11 270; Purchases Returns £1840; Carriage In £726; Customs Duty on Imports £186; Sales £44 163; Sales Returns £163; Closing Stock £4995; Warehouse Wages £11 256.

7 Choosing such figures as you think are relevant from the list below draw up the Trial Balance of F. Dearborn and find his gross profit for the year ended 31 December 19. . .
Opening Stock £5980; Debtors £2310; Purchases £33 710; Sales £84 265; Creditors £5650; Purchases Returns £310; Sales Returns £1265; General Expenses £9565; Warehouse Expenses £14 725; Closing Stock £6260; Carriage In £550; Carriage Out £780; Motor Vehicles £24 000; Mortgage £15 000.

8 Choosing such figures as you think are relevant from the list below draw up the Trial Balance of T. Honeywell and find her gross profit for the year ended 31 March 19. . .

Opening Stock £6265; Premises £44 000; Purchases £42 656; Sales £118 256; Drawings £6250; Purchases Returns £656; Sales Returns £1845; Rent £4800; Warehouse expenses £5265; Warehouse Wages £11 275; Closing Stock £7150; Carriage In £726; Travelling Expenses £1756; Capital £32 000.

20.9 Answers to self-assessment questions

1 A Trading Account is the account where we work out the gross profit of a business.

2 It is the over-all profit on trading, before the overhead expenses are deducted.

3 It is the difference between the sales figure (the net turnover) and the cost of those sales.

4 Net turnover is used in buying and selling businesses, because profits can only be made when we turn-over (i.e. sell) our stocks, and the bigger the turnover the more likely it is that profits will be made. So we have to pay more for a business which has a big turnover.

5 By doing a stock-taking. We count the stock, value each item and calculate the total value of each type of stock and of all items together.

6 A Trading Account in good style is one where the strict principles of double entry have been adapted to bring out helpful figures, particularly the net turnover, the net purchases, the cost of stock sold and the cost of sales.

7 The gross profit is carried from the Trading Account to the credit side of the Profit and Loss Account where it starts off the account. Other profits of a non-trading nature are added to it and the expenses of the business are deducted to give a final clear profit — the net profit of the business.

21 Finding the profits of the business — The Profit and Loss Account

21.1 Finding the net profit

The word 'net' means clean (from the French word *nettoyer*: to clean out). Having found the gross profit in the Trading Account we now have to find the net profit by cleaning out of the Trial Balance all those losses and profits which are not directly part of the trading activities. These are either miscellaneous profits, such as Discount Received and Commission Received, or overheads (losses such as rent, rates, light, heat, etc.).

The idea of cleaning these items out of the Trial Balance is quite important, since every item that is taken into the Profit and Loss Account is going to disappear from the Trial Balance, as has already happened with those items used in the Trading Account. For example the Purchases Account, the Sales Account, the Purchases Returns Account and the Sales Returns Account, the Carriage In Account and the Warehouse Wages Account have all disappeared from the Trial Balance in Fig. 18.1. The Opening Stock £6985 has also disappeared, but has been replaced by the Closing Stock of £9762, so although there is still a balance on the Stock Account it is now a different figure. Finally, the gross profit found in the Trading Account has been transferred to the credit side of the Profit and Loss Account, so the Trading Account also is clear. The Trial Balance in Fig. 18.1 has therefore become a slimmer 'Revised Trial Balance' shown in Fig. 21.1 — a great many items have been cleared out if it already. Study Fig. 21.1 on the following page, and think about which items are now likely to be cleared out of the revised Trial Balance as we draw up the Profit and Loss Account.

21.2 Closing entries for the losses and profits

We now have to clear all the losses (overhead expenses) and any profit items, in this case Commission Received Account, Rent Received Account and Discount Received Account into the Profit and Loss Account. As with the trading items this means a closing Journal entry to close the account and transfer the figure in each case into the Profit and Loss Account. The Journal entry will be as shown in Fig. 21.2 where one of the losses, Carriage Out Account, and one of the profits, Commission Received Account have been illustrated. When posted to the respective Ledger accounts we can see how the Profit and Loss Account is built up (Fig. 21.3). The complete Profit and Loss Account is then shown in Fig. 21.4.

K. Marshall

Revised Trial Balance as at 31 December 19. . .

	Dr £	Cr £
Land and Buildings A/c	34 500	
Plant and Machinery A/c	14 800	
Furniture and Fittings A/c	8 650	
Motor Vehicles A/c	12 420	
Capital (K. Marshall) A/c		107 990
Carriage Out A/c	1 750	
Rent and Rates A/c	950	
Light and Heat A/c	684	
Insurance A/c	560	
Stock A/c (Closing Stock)	9 762	
Commission Received A/c		758
Rent Received A/c		1 000
Salaries A/c	21 460	
Advertising A/c	1 790	
Bad Debts A/c	864	
Sundry Debtors A/cs (total)	17 250	
Sundry Creditors A/cs (total)		8 265
Cash A/c	1 740	
Bank A/c	38 640	
Drawings A/c	9 500	
Discount Allowed A/c	280	
Discount Received A/c		790
Postage A/c	455	
Travelling Expenses A/c	675	
Mortgage A/c		100 000
Profit and Loss A/c		47 927
	£176 730	176 730

Fig. 21.1 The Revised Trial Balance

Notes
1 The only trading item left on this Trial Balance is the closing stock figure, £9762.
2 The other change is that the Profit and Loss Account has been opened up with the gross profit of £47 927.

19 . .					
Dec 31	Profit and Loss A/c Dr		L134	1750.00	
	Carriage Out A/c		L94		1750.00
	Being total of carriage				
	outwards for the year written				
	off to Profit and Loss Account				
31	Commission Received A/c Dr		L95	758.00	
	Profit and Loss A/c		L134		758.00
	Being total commission				
	received during the year taken				
	in as profit to the Profit and				
	Loss Account				

Fig. 21.2 Closing entries for the losses and profits

Carriage Out A/c   L94

19. .			£	19. .			£
Jan–	Sundry			Dec 31	Profit and		
Dec	Payments	CB?	1 750.00		Loss	L134	1 750.00

Commission Received A/c   L95

19. .			£	19. .			£
Dec 31	Profit and			Jan–	Sundry		
	Loss	L134	758.00	Dec	receipts	CB?	758.00

Profit and Loss A/c for year ending 31 December 19. .   L134

19. .			£	19. .			£
	Carriage Out	L94	1 750.00		Gross Profit	L133	47 927.00
					Commission		
					Rec'd	L 95	758.00

Fig. 21.3 The Ledger entries for these closing Journal entries

Notes
1 The Carriage Out Account and the Commission Received Account have both been written off by the closing entry. They cease to have a balance on them, and consequently will disappear from the Trial Balance.
2 Similarly all other losses and profits will be cleared from the books and into the Profit and Loss Account.
3 The Profit and Loss Account starts with the gross profit on the credit side, all other profits are added to it on the credit side and all losses are found on the debit side where they are subtracted from the profit. The final profit, the net profit, is then found as shown in Fig. 21.4.

K. Marshall
Profit and Loss Account for year ended 31 December 19. .

	£		£
Carriage Out	1 750	Gross profit	47 927
Rent and Rates	950	Commission Received	758
Light and Heat	684	Rent Received	1 000
Insurance	560	Discount Received	790
Salaries	21 460		50 475
Advertising	1 790		
Bad Debts	864		
Discount Allowed	280		
Postage	455		
Travelling Expenses	675		
	29 468		
Net Profit (to Capital A/c)	21 007		
	£50 475		£50 475

Fig. 21.4 The Profit and Loss Account

Notes
1 It is easier to work out the gross profit if we put in sub-totals as shown on the debit side (the total losses) and the credit side (the total profits).
2 When the total losses are deducted from the total profits we are left with the clear profit, the net profit.
3 This net profit belongs to the owner of the business and is transferred to the Capital A/c as shown in Fig. 21.5.

Capital A/c   L7

19. .			£
Jan 1	Opening capital	J1	107 990
Dec 31	Net profit		21 007

Fig. 21.5 Transferring the net profit to the proprietor's Capital Account

21.3 Self-assessment questions

1 What is the Profit and Loss Account?
2 What does net profit mean?
3 What does the Profit and Loss Account start with?
4 Name five common losses (expenses) of the business.
5 Name three common profits of the business besides the gross profit.
6 Who is entitled to the profits of the business?
7 What do professional people call the Profit and Loss Account?

21.4 Exercises in finding the net profit

You should now try some of the exercises below. The first four only require you to produce a Profit and Loss Account. The last two require you to produce both a Trading Account and a Profit and Loss Account.

1 The following figures for expenses and receipts appear in the books of George Vyner for the year ended 31 December 19. . . Draw up the Profit and Loss Account and thus find the net profit for the year.

Gross profit £43 286.50; Rent £2 200.00; Rates £876.50; motor expenses £426.56; discount allowed £154.62; discount received £320.80; bad debts £45.50; advertising £725.50: repairs and renewals £184.60; salaries £21 246.50; commission received £4 614.25.

2 The following figures for expenses and receipts appear in the books of T. Calthorpe and Sons for the year ended 31 March 19. . . Draw up the Profit and Loss Account and thus find the net profit for the year.

Gross profit £67 246.54; rent £1 850.50; light and heat £624.50; motor expenses £824.74; telephone expenses £736.50; advertising £1 058.55; office salaries £18 164.27; postage £178.54; rent received from sub-tenant £640.

3 From the following figures calculate the net profit of T. Boake in the form of a Profit and Loss Account, for the year ended 31 December 19. . .

	£		£
Gross Profit	56 284	Rent and Rates	3 425
Rent Received	2 164	Light and Heat	875
Commission Received	1 725	Carriage Out	1 024
Bad Debt Recovered	186	Motor Expenses	1 865
Discount Received	172	Travelling	138
Discount Allowed	325	Sundry Expenses	185
		Salaries	18 264

4 From the following figures calculate the net profit of Kenya Fashions (Baragoi) Ltd, in the form of a Profit and Loss Account for the year ending 31 December 19. . .

	£		£
Gross Profit	62 756	Insurance	845
Commission Received	32 780	Advertising	2 238
Discount Received	1 546	Wages and Salaries	27 568
Discount Allowed	2 725	Telephone Expenses	1 687
Repairs and Redecorations	11 865	Travellers' Salaries	8 856
Rent	2 000	Travellers' Expenses	8 859
Lighting	1 500	Sundry Expenses	184

5 Using the following sets of figures prepare first the Trading Account and then the Profit and Loss Account of Tina Price's business, to bring out the net profit for the year ending 31 December 19. . .

Opening stock £2400; Purchases £42 280; Purchases Returns £280; Sales £84 600; Sales Returns £600; Carriage In £560; Closing Stock £3900; Commission Received £700; rent and rates £1364; light and heat £840; postage £372; packing materials £248; motor expenses £744; telephone £570; wages £16 950.

6 Using the following sets of figures for Isaac Adeleye's business draw up a Trading Account and then a Profit and Loss Account to bring out the net profit for the year ending 31 March 19. . .

Opening stock £6750; Purchases £138 850; Purchases Returns £1100; Sales £263 900; Closing Stock £9250; Sales Returns £2900; Carriage In £826; light and heat £2500; travelling £250; cleaning expenses £1850; repairs £830; advertising £3750; bank charges £285; salaries £27 295.

21.5 Combining the Trading Account and Profit and Loss Account

Some accountants combine these accounts and simply talk of a Trading and Profit and Loss Account. It is an artificial combination really, since all it amounts to is a single heading for the two accounts, which then run on into one another, as shown in Fig. 21.6.

K. Marshall
Trading and Profit and Loss Account for year ending 31 December 19. . .

	£			£
Opening Stock		6 985	Sales	98 260
Purchases	37 900		Less Sales Returns	1 260
Add Carriage In	855		Net turnover	97 000
	38 755			
Less Purchases Returns	155			
		38 600		
Total stock available		45 585		
Less Closing Stock		9 762		
Cost of stock sold		35 823		
Warehouse Wages		13 250		
Cost of Sales		49 073		
Gross Profit	c/d	47 927		
		£97 000		£97 000
Carriage Out		1 750	Gross Profit b/d	47 927
Rent and Rates		950	Commission Received	758
Light and Heat		684	Rent Received	1 000
Insurance		560	Discount Received	790
Salaries		21 460		50 475
Advertising		1 790		
Bad Debts		864		
Discount Allowed		280		
Postage		455		
Travelling Expenses		675		
		29 468		
Net Profit (to Capital A/c)		21 007		
		£50 475		£50 475

Fig. 21.6 Combining the Final Accounts into a single account

21.6 Exercises on the Trading and Profit and Loss Account

1 From the figures given below prepare the Trading and Profit and Loss Account of M. Tyler for the year ending 31 December 19. . .
Opening Stock £4295; Purchases £24 284; Purchases Returns £184; Sales £69 285;

Sales Returns £1285; Closing Stock £5156; Rent Received £1450; Carriage Outwards £860; Postage £425; Telephones £1625; Sundry Expenses £4894; Motor Expenses £1650; Salaries £17 265.

2 From the figures given below prepare the Trading and Profit and Loss Account of the Bombay Restaurant for the year ending 31 December 19. . .

Opening Stock £1275; Purchases £25 462; Purchases Returned £162; Sales £135 495; Sales Returns £84; Closing Stock £1895; Advertising Income £2850; Advertising Expenditure £7659; Telephone Expenses £625; Postage £88; Wages £39 286 (Profit and Loss Account); Motor Expenses £1245; Rent £4256; Rates £6752; Repairs £3358.

3 From the figures given below prepare the Trading and Profit and Loss Account of Oakpride Furnishing for the year ending 31 March 19. . .

	£
Opening Stock	14 248
Closing Stock	19 510
Purchases	36 756
Purchases Returns	656
Carriage In	1 900
Sales	126 420
Sales Returns	3 420
Warehouse Wages	18 746
Warehouse Expenses	4 950
Light and Heat	3 636
Rates	4 850
Repairs	1 862
Office Salaries	27 956
Bad Debts	385
Insurance	1 214
Commission Received	865
Commission Paid	1 240
Discount Allowed	826
Discount Received	1 042
Advertising	7 678

21.7 Answers to self-assessment questions

1 The Profit and Loss Account is the account where we find out the net profit of the business, by deducting all the losses of the business from the profits made.
2 Net profit means clean profit.
3 The Profit and Loss Account starts with the Gross Profit.
4 Five common losses are rent, rates, lighting expenses, salaries and motor vehicle expenses.
5 Common profits are rent received, discount received and commission received.
6 The profits of the business belong to the proprietor if it is a sole trader business. For partnerships profits must be shared between the partners and for limited companies the shareholders must receive a share of the profits.
7 Professional people call the Profit and Loss Account the Income and Expenditure Account.

22 Finding the profits of the business — 3 The Balance Sheet

22.1 The residue of the Trial Balance

Once the Trading Account and the Profit and Loss Account have been prepared, the trading items, the profits and the various losses have all been cleared from the Trial Balance. We are left with a residue of accounts all of which are assets and liabilities of the business. The best way to look at these accounts is to regard them as the items which the old year which has just come to an end is to hand to the new year which is just beginning. There are all the useful things, like premises, machinery, motor vehicles and cash in hand (the assets), and all the duties and responsibilities, such as the duty to pay the creditors, or to repay loans or mortgages, and also to repay the proprietor the capital contributed over the years, as well as any profits outstanding. We will now look at this residue of the Trial Balance.

K. Marshall
Residue of Trial Balance as at 31 December 19. .

	Dr £	Cr £
Land and Buildings A/c	34 500	
Plant and Machinery A/c	14 800	
Furniture and Fittings A/c	8 650	
Motor Vehicles A/c	12 420	
Capital (E. Marshall) A/c		128 997
Stock A/c (Closing Stock)	9 762	
Sundry Debtors A/cs (total)	17 250	
Sundry Creditors A/cs (total)		8 265
Cash A/c	1 740	
Bank A/c	38 640	
Drawings A/c	9 500	
Mortgage A/c		10 000
	£147 262	147 262

Fig. 22.1 The residue of the Trial Balance

Notes
1 All the figures are the same as in the original Trial Balance (see Fig. 18.1) except two, the Stock Account and the Capital Account.
2 The Stock Account has changed from the Opening Stock at the start of the year to the

Closing Stock at the end of the year, as explained in Chapter 20 (Fig. 20.9).

3 The Capital Account has changed from the original capital at the start of the year, £107 990, to a revised figure of £128 997, because the net profit of £21 007 from the Profit and Loss Account has been added to it.

4 The totals of the Trial Balance still balance, showing that no mistakes have been made in doing the Trading Account and the Profit and Loss Account.

22.2 Clearing the Drawings Account

The only account in Fig. 22.1 which is neither an asset nor a liability is the Drawings Account, which shows the total that the proprietor E. Marshall has drawn over the year for personal expenses. This is really some of the profit withdrawn (it is often called 'Drawings in expectation of profit made'). To clear the Drawings Account we must debit it to Capital Account, where it will reduce the amount owed to the proprietor because he has already drawn it out during the year. The Journal entry will be as shown in Fig. 22.2 and the postings to the Ledger as in Fig. 22.3.

19 . .				J39
Dec 31	Capital A/c Dr		9500.00	
	Drawings A/c			9500.00
	Being drawings for the year			
	transferred to capital account			
	to reduce the amount owed to			
	the proprietor.			

Fig. 22.2 Clearing the Drawings Account

Drawings A/c   L119

19 . . Jan–Dec		£	19 . .			£
Sundry drawings CB . .		9 500.00	Dec 31	Capital		9 500.00

Capital A/c   L7

19 . .			£	19 . .			£
Dec 31	Drawings	J39	9 500	Jan 1	Opening		
31	Balance	c/d	119 497		Capital	J1	107 990
				Dec 31	Net profit	L33	21 007
			£128 997				£128 997
				19 . .			£
				Jan 1	Balance	b/d	119 497

Fig. 22.3 Ledger entries to clear the Drawings Account

Notes
1 The left hand side of the Drawings Account should really show all the separate amounts drawn by the proprietor week by week over the year.

2 When this is all cleared off to Capital Account it leaves the Drawings Account clear ready for the next year's entries.

3 The Capital Account can now be balanced off ready to start a new year. The amount owing to the proprietor has risen because although profits were £21 007 he has only drawn £9 500 — the remaining £11 507 being left in the business and helping it to expand.

We are now ready to draw up a Balance Sheet.

22.3 Drawing up the Balance Sheet

A Balance Sheet is a list of the assets and liabilities of a business drawn up in such a way as to display the financial position of the firm or company clearly. This is usually done on the last day of the financial year to show the financial position at that moment, as the old year ends and the new year begins. We could therefore describe a Balance Sheet as a snapshot of the affairs of a business at a given moment in time, usually at the last moment of the financial year, although a Balance Sheet can be drawn up at any time.

In drawing up this list of assets and liabilities we can choose to some extent the method that we use, and over the years, in the UK particularly, we have adopted such a variety of methods that it seems rather confusing, especially to a beginner. To simplify things in this section we will learn the most common method used for small businesses, which is the **traditional style** in the **order of permanence**.

The traditional style

In this style the assets are displayed on the right hand side and the liabilities are displayed on the left hand side. Actually this isn't very sensible, because it is the opposite way to their arrangement in the Trial Balance. The reasons go back to the year 1536 when the Balance Sheet was first invented by Simon Stevin of Bruges, but they need not concern us here. Remember, in the traditional British style, liabilities on the left and assets on the right.

The order of permanence

In this style the most permanent assets are listed first and the most permanent liabilities are listed first. The least permanent assets are mentioned last, and so are the least permanent liabilities. In Fig. 22.4 the items still left in the Trial Balance of Fig. 22.1 are displayed as a Balance Sheet in traditional style, in the order of permanence. A Balance Sheet always begins with the name of the firm and a heading which reads 'Balance Sheet as at . . . .' giving the date on which it was drawn up, which is usually the last day of the financial year.

One further point is that it is usual to show on the Balance Sheet how the proprietor's Capital changed during the year, by showing the profit made, and the drawings. Study this Balance Sheet now, and the notes below it.

K. Marshall
Balance Sheet as at 31 December 19 . .

Capital	£	£	Fixed Assets		£
At start		107 990	Land and		
Add net profit	21 007		Buildings		34 500
Less Drawings	9 500		Plant and		
		11 507	Machinery		14 800
		119 497	Furniture and		
			Fittings		8 650
			Motor Vehicles		12 420
					70 370
Long-term Liabilities			Current Assets	£	
Mortgage		10 000	Stock at close	9 762	
			Sundry Debtors	17 250	
Current Liabilities			Bank	38 640	
Sundry Creditors		8 265	Cash	1 740	
					67 392
		£137 762			£137 762

Fig. 22.4 A Balance Sheet in traditional style, in the order of permanence

Notes

1 Fixed assets are assets that last a long time (certainly longer than one year) and therefore serve the business during their lifetime. They do not move on during this working life and so are said to be 'fixed'.

2 The most long lasting is Land and Buildings, while motor vehicles have a relatively short life and are therefore shown last in the order of permanence.

3 Current assets are assets which would normally be used in less than one year. For example stock will be sold in the next few weeks and replaced by further supplies. Debtors should normally pay within one month, and cash, and bank moneys are liquid assets. This means that they are in money form. Since the opposite of the order of permanence is the order of liquidity — in which the most liquid assets are placed first — we would expect these items to come last in the order of permanence.

4 On the liabilities side we may look on the liabilities as debts that we must pay sooner or later. Starting at the bottom we have the creditors — who are due to be paid within one month. Above them we have a sub-heading 'Long-term Liabilities'. These are liabilities that are not due to be paid for more than a year. The best examples are mortgages and bank loans. In this case we have a mortgage of £10 000, which may be repayable over many years; let us pretend in this case over 15 years. Therefore the liability is very long-term.

5 The Capital Account is of course the longest term liability of all, for the business only repays the proprietor on the day he/she ceases to trade, usually because of retirement. In the event of the proprietor's death the business becomes part of the estate and the capital is repaid to the beneficiaries under the will.

6 Note that the indented section of the Capital shows how the proprietor drew £9500 of the profits during the year, leaving £11 507 to be added to the capital. This is called 'ploughing back' profits into the business. Suppose the proprietor had enjoyed a richer lifestyle and had drawn out £30 000 drawings, when he only made profits of £21 007. This would have meant a negative figure of £8993, which would have reduced the capital to £98 997. Such a trader is said to be 'living off his capital' — never a wise thing to do.

22.4 Other styles of Balance Sheet

Balance Sheets in the order of liquidity

Besides the order of permanence it is possible to display the assets in the order of liquidity, as referred to in the notes to Fig. 22.4. In accounting the word 'liquid' means 'in cash form', so that 'cash in hand' and 'cash at the bank' are regarded as liquid assets (you only have to go to the bank and draw your money to have it in liquid form). Debtors are fairly liquid assets (they are due to pay us within one month in most cases). Stocks are not so liquid — you can force a debtor to pay you but you cannot force anyone to buy your stock. In the order of liquidity the assets and liabilities would simply be listed the opposite way round with Current Assets first — starting with cash — and Fixed Assets afterwards ending with the most illiquid asset, Land and Buildings Account. Similarly the liabilities would be displayed with the Current Liabilities first, followed by the Long-term Liabilities and finally the Capital Account.

Balance Sheets in non-traditional (European) style

The Trial Balance has assets on the left-hand side, and liabilities on the right-hand side, and there is no reason why this style should not be kept in the Balance Sheet. All European nations except Italy (which many years ago copied the UK traditional style) do their Balance Sheets in this more sensible form. Such a Balance Sheet is shown in Fig. 22.5 in the order of permanence. In view of current moves to harmonise accounting procedures within the European Community it could be that this more logical style will be adopted in the UK in the years ahead.

K. Marshall
Balance Sheet as at 31 December, 19 . .

Fixed Assets	£		Capital	£	£
Land & Buildings	34 500		At start		107 990
Plant & Machinery	14 800		Add net profit	21 007	
Furniture & Fittings	8 650		Less Drawings	9 500	
Motor Vehicles	12 420				11 507
	70 370				119 497
Current Assets	£		Long-term Liabilities		
Stock at close	9 762		Mortgage		10 000
Sundry Debtors	17 250				
Bank	38 640		Current Liabilities		
Cash	1 740		Sundry Creditors		8 265
	67 392				
	£137 762				£137 762

Fig. 22.5 A Balance Sheet in correct (European) style

Notes
1 In this style the assets appear on the left hand side and the liabilities on the right hand side, as they do in the Trial Balance.
2 This is the style used in most of the European Community countries and there is a strong case for adopting it in the UK since it is in fact more correct than the traditional UK style.

22.5 Self-assessment questions

1 What is a Balance Sheet?
2 What does the preparation of the Trading Account and the Profit and Loss Account do to the Trial Balance of the business?
3 How is the Balance Sheet headed?
4 What is the order of permanence?
5 What does 'liquid' mean in accounting?
6 What are fixed assets? Give four examples.
7 What are current assets? Give four examples.

22.6 Exercises on the preparation of Balance Sheets

You should now try the following exercises. The first four require you to produce a Balance Sheet only, question **5** requires you to produce a Profit and Loss Account and a Balance Sheet, while **6** and **7** require you to produce a full set of Final Accounts.

1 From the figures provided below draw up the Balance Sheet of R. Seagrave as at 31 December 19. . .
Premises £17 250; Plant and Machinery £7400; Furniture and Fittings £4400; Motor Vehicles £6135; Capital (R. Seagrave) £50 000; net profit £14 492; Stock at close £4800; Sundry Creditors £4058; Sundry Debtors £8625; Cash £870; Bank £19 320; Drawings £4750; Mortgage £5000.

2 From the following figures from her accounts draw up the Balance Sheet of Tanya Sillitoe as at 31 March 19 . . .
Premises £36 000; Furniture and Fittings £8500; Motor Vehicles £8200; Stock at end of year £5270; Debtors £4645; Bank £3600; Cash £272; Capital at start £40 000; Net profit for year £19 237; Drawings by T. Sillito £8500; Loan from A. Heller £11 500; Creditors £4250.

3 From the following figures taken from his accounts draw up the Balance Sheet of Isaac Olaleye as at 31 December 19. . .
Capital at start £55 260; Land and Buildings £40 500; Plant and Machinery £17 285; Creditors £3680; Debtors £2242; Cash in hand £827; Cash at Bank £2231; Stock at close of year £4315; Motor Vehicles £21 000; Net profit £23 770; Drawings (I. Olaleye) £10 560; Furniture and Fittings £7500; Mortgage £23 750.

4 From the following figures taken from the accounts of G. Franklin draw up his Balance Sheet as at 31 December 19. . . (*Note*: Be careful — the Drawings are greater than the profits; he is living on his capital.)
Premises £28 000; Furniture and Fittings £4250; Closing Stock £7385; Debtors £2100; Creditors £2450; Mortgage £15 300; Bank Loan £3755; Motor Vehicles £6550; Cash in hand £343; Cash at bank £5718; Net profit £17 250; Drawings £19 409; Capital at start of the year £35 000.

5 From the figures given below work out the Profit and Loss Account and Balance Sheet of E. Diane, on the 31 December 19 . . .

	Dr £	Cr £
Gross profit from Trading Account		61 301
Discount Received		420
Heat and Light	1 240	
Wages	17 265	
Discount Allowed	432	
Office Expenses	5 618	
Rates	2 200	
Carriage Out	1 130	
Telephone	846	
Premises	36 250	
Capital at start		55 500
Drawings	13 200	
Debtors and Creditors	2 120	1 850
Machinery	13 750	
Furniture and Fittings	4 250	
Stock	4 560	
Bank	15 620	
Cash in hand	160	
Insurance	430	
	£119 071	119 071

6 From the Trial Balance of R. Shah given below, prepare his Trading Account, Profit and Loss Account and Balance Sheet.

R. Shah
Trial Balance as at 31 December 19. . .

	Dr £	Cr £
Purchases and Sales	25 445	73 946
Returns In and Out	1 468	310
Opening Stock	4 250	
Carriage In	1 260	
Warehouse Expenses	4 745	
Discount Allowed and Received	212	1 170
Heat and Light	1 240	
Wages	17 625	
Office Expenses	4 316	
Rates	2 412	
Carriage Out	2 137	
Telephone Expenses	446	
Insurance	297	
Premises	36 250	
Machinery	18 750	
C/fwd	120 853	75 426

		£	£
	B/fwd	12 0853	75 426
Capital at 1 January 19. . .			58 912
Drawings		13 205	
Furniture and Fittings		2 580	
Motor Vehicles		4 600	
Debtors and Creditors		2 120	3 125
Bank		15 620	
Cash in hand		485	
Mortgage			15 000
Bank Loan			7 000
		£159 463	159 463

The value of the closing stock on 31 December was found to be £5 560.

7 From the Trial Balance of Frances Eve given below, prepare her Trading Account, Profit and Loss Account and Balance Sheet. The Closing Stock on 31 March 19. . was found on stock taking to be £4946.

Frances Eve
Trial Balance as at 31 March 19. . .

	Dr	Cr
	£	£
Opening Stock	3 854	
Purchases and Sales	37 814	117 205
Sales Returns and Purchases Returns	2 394	814
Warehouse Expenses	11 425	
Bad Debts Recovered		386
General Expenses	9 854	
Telephone	487	
Electricity	890	
Discount Allowed and Received	204	713
Rates	1 162	
Depreciation	1 260	
Motor Vehicle Expenses	920	
Interest paid	325	
Carriage Out	264	
Advertising	460	
Wages	15 320	
Capital at start		43 050
Drawings	15 250	
Bank Loan		4 500
Debtors and Creditors	1 800	1 875
Land and Buildings	46 000	
Furniture and Fittings	2 800	
Motor Vehicles	11 200	
Cash at Bank	4 350	
Cash in Hand	510	
	£168 543	168 543

22.7 Answers to self-assessment questions

1 A Balance Sheet is a snapshot of the affairs of a business at a given moment in time (usually at the last minute of the last day of the financial year). It is a list of the assets and liabilities of the business as at the date specified, after the Trading and Profit and Loss Accounts have been prepared.

2 Preparing the Trading and Profit and Loss Account clears the Trial Balance of all the losses and all the profits, leaving only the assets and liabilities, and one other account — the Drawings Account. We can therefore easily draw up a Balance Sheet of the business.

3 The Balance Sheet starts with the name of the firm, and a heading 'Balance Sheet as at . . . .' whatever the date may be.

4 The order of permanence is a method of displaying the items on a Balance Sheet with the most permanent items first and other less permanent items following, until the last item is the most liquid item, Cash in Hand.

5 In accounting liquid means 'in cash form'. An item that can be easily turned into cash (such as 'stock') is more liquid than an item like 'land and buildings' which has to be conveyed by a legal deed and cannot be transferred at once by a cash transaction.

6 Fixed assets are assets which last a long time (more than one year) and are used in the business over a considerable period to carry out profit-making activities. Examples are premises, machinery, furniture and motor vehicles.

7 Current assets are assets which are not intended to be kept for a long time without being converted to cash. Examples are stock, debtors, cash at the bank and certain types of investment held temporarily until cash is required (when they can quickly be sold to provide the firm with the funds it needs).

23 Stock Records

23.1 Keeping control of stock

We have seen that the value of stock in hand enters into the calculation of profits in the Trading Account, and that the opening stock value and the closing stock value have to be found by a process known as 'stock-taking'. We must now learn a bit more about stock, and how to keep control of it.

All stock is valuable and the pilfering of stock by (a) customers (b) shop staff (c) factory workers is widespread and estimated to cost firms millions of pounds every year. Watch your local paper and cut out a few cases of people charged with thefts of stock. Notice how heavy the fines are, and how often prison sentences are imposed. Add the cuttings to your accountancy file, to remind you how important honesty is in all employment situations.

We control stock with stock record cards of various sorts, bin cards, rack cards, tray cards, stock ledger cards, etc. These keep a running balance on each item of stock. An example is shown in Fig. 23.1.

Bin Card						
Description Bracket					**Bin number** 1302	
Max Stock 100					**Part number** A156	
Min Stock 20					**Re-order qty** 50	
Re-order level 40					**Unit of issue** 10	
Received			Issued			Balance
Date	Ref	Qty	Date	Ref	Qty	Qty
19. .			19. .			60
			17/4	R103	10	50
			29/4	R159	10	40
			5/5	R172	10	30
17/5	GRN72	50				80

Fig. 23.1 A bin card to keep control of stock

Notes
1 The opening balance is 60 units.
2 Items are issued against Requisitions (R103 etc.) and are deducted from the balance in hand.
3 Stock which is received is recorded from the Goods Received Note (GRN72) and is added to the balance in hand.
4 Details given at the top of the bin card show when to re-order, and how many units to reorder at a time, etc.

23.2 Stock-taking procedures

For ordinary routine stock control it is desirable to hold spot checks without warning. Spot checks should be done by different staff from the ordinary store-keepers. The aim is to detect stock shortages — are the units stated to be in stock on the bin card (80 in the illustration) actually present when the spot check is held. If not, what has caused the discrepancy? We may be unable to discover, but the questioning of staff will almost certainly reduce future stock losses so many managements believe such investigations are well worth while.

At the end of the year the stock-takings procedure is more difficult. We have to count the stock physically to ensure it is actually present, but we also have to value it so that we can work out the total value of the stock in hand at the end of the year. The procedure is as follows:

(a) Draw up stock sheets showing every item handled in the trading year.

(b) Count and record the number of units in stock of each item on the stock sheet.

(c) Make a note of any special points, such as damaged, shop-soiled or unfashionable items which are unlikely to fetch their full selling price when sold.

(d) Value the items which are in good condition *at their cost price*.

(e) Value damaged items *at cost price or their net realisable value if this is lower*.

Note The word 'net' implies 'after the costs of disposal have been deducted'. Thus if water-damaged furniture stock which had cost £380 was sold at auction for £150 and the auctioneer took 10% commission and charged £18.50 for transport charges the net realisable value would be:

$$
\begin{aligned}
\text{NRV} &= £150 - (£15 + £18.50) \\
&= £150 - £33.50 \\
&= £116.50
\end{aligned}
$$

(f) Value the stock of each item by taking the price per unit and multiplying it by the number of units, making adjustments for any damaged items to be priced at their net realisable value.

(g) Add up the value of all items to give the closing stock figure.

23.3 Exercises on bin cards etc.

1 A bin card for water pumps in a garage stores show that at 1 April 19. . the balance of pumps in hand was 18. Pumps were issued as follows:
4 April (R95) 3; 5 April (R99) 1; 8 April (R107) 2; 10 April (R119) 3; 23 April (126) 12. A further delivery of 10 pumps was received on 9 April (GRN75) and another delivery of 10 pumps was received on 29 April 19. . . Show the entries (in correct date order) on a bin card ruled as in Fig. 23.1 (a blank form which may be photocopied appears in Fig. 23.3).

2 A stock record card for stationery relates to A4 bond paper. The stock in hand on 1 January was 27 reams. Issues of five reams at a time were made on 7 (R14); 11 (R29); 19 (R37) and 26 January (R48). An issue of 10 reams was made on 27 January (R54). New supplies of 25 reams each were received on 4 January (GRN75) and 25 January (GRN91). Show the entries on a card as illustrated in Fig. 23.3.

3 A stock record card for Simplex Account books shows the following figures on 1 April 19. . . Copies in hand 420 on 1 April. Issues to branches made during April were as follows: 14 (R256) 120; 17 (R281) 150; 22 (R299) 40; 27 (R316) 50; 29 (R336) 50. Further supplies were received on 18 April (GRN272) 200 copies and 28 April (GRN284) 200 copies. Show the entries in correct date order on a card similar to Fig. 23.3.

4 A. Trader only has three lines of electronic goods. On 31 December 19. . these were counted as follows:

Item	Cost price	Stock in hand
Flexible disks 5¼ inch boxes of 10	£19.40	420 boxes
Roll top floppy disk storage files	£19.95	73
Coaxial connector kits	£85.00	19

Two of the storage files are shop-soiled and are to be offered at £10 each. One of the coaxial connector kits is damaged slightly and the sale price (£165) is to be reduced to £120.

What is the value of the stock, bearing in mind the rule that closing stock should be valued at cost, or net realisable value, whichever is the lower.

5 A furniture dealer has three chief lines. On 31 December 19. ., these were counted as follows:

Item	Cost price	Stock in hand
Pedestal desks	£120	34
Computer monitor tables	£ 84	25
Executive chairs	£236	19

One of the executive chairs is poorly finished and is offered at £200. Four of the monitor tables are in unfashionable colours. Two plum-coloured tables are to be sold at a selling price of £60 and two grey tables are to be offered at a selling price of £100, instead of £146. What is the value of the closing stock?.

23.4 Retail trade and stock-taking

In many retail outlets a special system of book-keeping operates which uses a different system of stock-taking. Students doing part-time jobs may meet this system and wonder what is happening. It consists of counting the items on the shelves and valuing them at selling price. Thus staff may be heard calling out '19 at 43 pence!', '11 at £1.22!', '37 at 95 pence!'. A member of the checking staff will be repeating these as he/she keys them in to a printing calculator which thus produces a huge list of stock items and adds them up to a grand total. This has nothing to do with stock-taking as described above.

The explanation is that retail outlets of this type are supplied with goods from Head Office and are never told the cost price; they are charged out to the branch at selling price. Suppose a branch has been sent goods valued at £20 000 at selling price. If the manager has been running the shop carefully, and charging the correct prices, whenever the Head Office decides to do a check the manager should either have the stock, or he should have the money for it, because if the stock is not present it must have been sold.

If our quick count up reveals that £5120 of stock is on the shelves then the manager should have paid in £14 880 to his local bank, or have it in the tills. It is a very good way to check on a branch, and its staff. Interesting as this is, it need not concern us in our book-keeping.

23.5 Stock-taking sales

Since the counting of stock is a long process and involves valuing stock at cost price or net realisable value, it is helpful if as many items of stock as possible, especially shop-soiled or less-than-fashionable items are disposed of before the end of the financial year. Most firms do this at stock-taking sales where prices are reduced drastically to clear as many items as possible. They may even arrange for a surplus dealer to buy up the unsold items (called 'cabbage' in the fashion trade) for disposal elsewhere, leaving the store with clear shelves for the new trading period and very little stock-taking to worry about.

23.6 Taking-stock at the end of the year

The financial year may end on any day of the week. Stock-taking is a time-consuming activity and difficult to do in mid-week when ordinary business activities are proceeding. It is therefore more convenient to do it at week-ends, either just before the end of the financial year or just after the year has ended. A simple calculation can then be done to work out the value of the closing stock on the actual last day of the year. Consider Example 23.1.

EXAMPLE 23.1

Brighter Fashions does its stock taking on the 29 December 19. . and finds the value of stock to be £7425 at that date. On 30 and 31 December the takings (at selling price) were £842 and £936 respectively. Goods were received on these two days worth £385 and £450 and returns from a customer of £24 (valued at selling price) were taken back into stock. Brighter Fashions always add 50% to cost price to find their selling prices. What was the value of the stock on 31 December?

The difficulty in this calculation is that we have to value stock at cost price whereas some of the figures are given at selling price.

This is a simple piece of business arithmetic, and is explained fully in *Business Calculations*, by the same author, and also published by Pitman. So long as we know the mark-up price the trader is adding on, we can work back to the cost price from the selling price by deducting the profit margin. The rule is

Mark-up		*Margin*
$\frac{1}{2}$ on the Cost Price	=	$\frac{1}{3}$ off the Selling Price
$\frac{1}{3}$ on the CP	=	$\frac{1}{4}$ off the SP
$\frac{1}{4}$ on the CP	=	$\frac{1}{5}$ off the SP
$\frac{1}{5}$ on the CP	=	$\frac{1}{6}$ off the SP

etc. .

Since Brighter Fashions adds on 50% ($\frac{1}{2}$) to its cost prices to get its selling prices the goods sold on 30 and 31 December must be reduced by $\frac{1}{3}$ ($\frac{1}{2}$ on the CP = $\frac{1}{3}$ off the SP) to find the cost price.

i.e. £843 selling price = £843 − ($\frac{1}{3}$ of £843) to find the cost price
                                              = £843 − £281
                                              = £562 at cost price

       £936 selling price = £936 − ($\frac{1}{3}$ of £936) £312
                                              = £624 at cost price

Similarly the returns of £24 taking back into stock would be valued at

$$£24 − £8 = £16$$

The final calculation is as follows:

	£	£
Stock value as counted on 29 December =		7425
Deduct (at cost price) goods sold before the end of the financial year	562	
	624	
		1186
		6239
	£	
Add goods received	385	
	450	
and returns at CP	16	
		851
Value of closing stock		£7090

Where the mark-up on cost does not work out to an easy fraction like $\frac{1}{2}$ or $\frac{1}{3}$ as shown in the table above the calculation of the margin is still a very easy calculation.

EXAMPLE 23.2 A retailer marks-up an article by 60% on cost price and sells it for £64. What was the margin on sell price? What did the article cost originally?

$$CP + 60\% = £64$$

If we regard the CP as 100% then:

$$100\% + 60\% = 160\%$$

Therefore the CP is $\frac{100}{160}$ of £64 and the margin is $\frac{60}{160}$

$$CP = \frac{10\emptyset}{16\emptyset} \times £6\!\!\!/4$$

= 10 × 4 (cancelling by 10 and 16)

= £40

Margin on selling price:

$$= \frac{6\emptyset}{16\emptyset} \times 1\emptyset\emptyset$$

$$= \frac{75}{2} \quad \text{(cancelling by 10, 2 and 4)}$$

$$= 37\tfrac{1}{2}\%$$

So we must deduct $37\frac{1}{2}\%$ from the selling price to find the Cost Price.

23.7 FIFO, LIFO and AVCO

One final point about stock is that in inflationary times, when prices are rising, it makes a difference to the profits we declare and to the value of closing stock if we vary the prices that we charge for the items when using them in production or for trading purposes. Consider the following example:

EXAMPLE 23.3

A. Marcos uses electric motors in his production processes. At the 1 January 19. . he has 18 motors in stock, all exactly alike, purchased as follows:

5 motors purchased at £16 each
3 motors purchased at £18.50 each
10 motors purchased at £25 each

During January he purchases 10 motors at £26.50 and uses 20 motors in production. What is the value of his closing stock at 31 January?

Of course we cannot tell, unless we know what his policy is for using motors, and for charging motors out to production. Almost certainly he will use the motors in strict rotation, so that deterioration cannot occur — using the old saying 'Worst first' or we could say 'oldest first'. It is only sensible to use the ones that have been in stock longest first. However, should we charge the customer a selling price based on a cost price of £16, or on £26.50 which is the present day replacement price? If we base the charge on the original cost (called FIFO = first in first out) we shall be carrying all the inflationary burden ourselves. If we base the charge on LIFO (last in first out) we shall charge the customer a price based on the current price, and pass on the inflationary charge to the customer. Some people work out the average cost of each item and charge the customer a cost based on AVCO (average cost). The disadvantage is that the average price has to be recalculated every time stock is received.

Suppose we have the following figures for a particular item of stock:

1 January 19. .	Balance in hand	200 items	at £4 each
5 January 19. .	Purchased	100 items	at £5.50 each
10 January 19. .	Issued	250 items	
19 January 19. .	Purchased	500 items	at £7.20 each
26 January 19. .	Issued	400 items	

If used on a FIFO basis the 250 items issued on 10 January would be charged at production cost as 200 items costing £4 and 50 items costing £5.50 = £800 + £275 = £1075.

On a LIFO basis the charge would be 100 items at £5.50 and 150 items at £4 = £550 + £600 = £1150.

On an AVCO basis the average cost would be:

$$\text{Average cost} = \frac{\text{total cost}}{\text{number of items}}$$

$$= \frac{£800 + £550}{300}$$

$$= \frac{£1350}{300}$$

$$= £4.50 \text{ each}$$

Therefore the 250 items would have been charged to production at £1125. At the same time the closing stocks would have been as follows on the 10th January:

FIFO	LIFO	AVCO
50 at £5.50	50 at £4	50 at £4.50
= £275	= £200	= £225

Clearly the method of charging used affects not only the price charged to the customer eventually but also the profit of the business.

We need not worry too much about FIFO, LIFO and AVCO at this level of our studies, but it is helpful to know these abbreviations which are sometimes mentioned in employment interviews, and other real-life situations. A typical FIFO Stock Ledger card is shown in Fig. 23.2. Students might like to work out what the figures would have been if LIFO or AVCO had been used.

					Stock Ledger Card				Charging System ....FIFO.........		
Description ....T junction...........				**Maximum Stock**				**Delivery time**			
Code No ....Xa 427...................				**Minimum Stock**				**Re-order point**			
Location ....27.13.3...................				**Supplier** ....UBJ Supplies........				**EOQ**			
Receipts				Issues					Balance		
Date	Ref.	Qty	Price £	Value £	Date	Ref.	Qty	Price £	Value £	Qty	Price £	Value £
19 . .					19 . .							
					Jan 1					200	4.00	800.00
Jan 5	GRN12	100	5.50	550.00						300	Various	1350.00
					Jan 10	R107	250	200 × 4.00 }1075.00 50 × 5.50		50	5.50	275.00
Jan 19	GRN27	500	7.20	3600.00						550	Various	3875.00
					Jan 26	R157	400	50 × 5.50 }2795.00 350 × 7.20		150	7.20	1080.00

Fig. 23.2   A FIFO stock ledger card

23.8 Insurance claims after fires and burglaries

Events such as fires and burglaries involve stock losses which may be covered by insurance. The problem often is to decide the value of the stock lost. It requires calculations based on such figures as are available on the books, provided they have not been destroyed in the fire, or stolen. It is usual to lock the books in a fire-proof safe at night, but this is sometimes not helpful if thieves steal the whole safe, as they frequently do. An example will illustrate the calculation:

EXAMPLE 23.4

Templars Ltd lose a considerable amount of stock in a fire on 24 January 19. . . Afterwards the following figures are built up from such records as are available.

	£
Opening Stock on 1 January 19. .	17 256
Purchases in the period 1–24 January	12 725 (cost price)
Sales in the same period	29 250 (selling price)
Sales returned in the same period	630 (selling price)
Stock available after the fire	1 214

Templars Ltd add 50% to cost price to fix their selling prices. What amount should be claimed for the missing stock?

The secret is to find the stock that should have been in hand on 24 January. Since only £1214 is available after the fire we can easily tell how much is missing and must be claimed on the insurance policy. The calculation is:

Opening Stock at 1 January	£17 256
Purchases added to stock from 1–24 January	12 725
	29 981
Less items sold at cost price	
= £29 250 − $\frac{1}{3}$ of £29 250	
= £29 250 − £9 750 =	19 500
	10 481
Add sales returns (at cost price)	
= £630 − $\frac{1}{3}$ of £630	
= £630 − £210 =	420
Total stock that should be available	10 901
Less stock left after fire	1 214
Amount to be claimed	£ 9 687

23.9 Self-assessment questions

1 What is a stock record card?
2 How might stock records be kept in a large organisation?
3 What is special about the Stock Account?
4 What is the opening stock?
5 List the activities at stock-taking.

23.10 Exercises on stock-taking

1 What is the basis on which stock is valued? A fashion house has four items in stock which cost £13.50 each and which it normally sells at £36 each. However, two of them have been damaged by sunlight, and are believed to be only saleable at £5 each. What should the total value of these four items be on the stock-list at stock-taking?

2 From the following information calculate the value of R. Patel's stock on 31 March 19. .:

	£
Stock at cost on 1 January 19. .	7 600
Purchases during quarter	33 000
Sales during quarter	48 000
Goods returned at selling price by a customer	600

Patel adds $33\frac{1}{3}\%$ to cost prices to find his selling price.

3 From the following information calculate the value of R. Bayford's stock on 31 July 19. .:

	£
Stock at cost on 1 July 19. .	4 240
Purchases during month	18 400
Sales during month	24 000
Goods returned at selling price by a customer	840
Goods returned by Bayford to a supplier	240

Bayford adds 50% to cost prices to find his selling prices.

4 Mumtaz and Kadar's financial year closed on Thursday 31 December 19. . . They took stock on Sunday 27 December and found the stock to be worth £18 256. In the next four days the following changes occurred:
(a) Takings for goods sold were £840, £720, £600 and £960 respectively.
(b) Supplier's delivered goods on Wednesday valued at cost £1656.
(c) Goods were sold on credit on Tuesday £400 and Thursday £640.
(d) A customer returned goods at £36 (selling price).
   They always add $33\frac{1}{3}\%$ to cost prices to get their selling prices. What was the value of the stock at 31 December, 19. .? Show your calculations.

5 Colby & Co.'s financial year ends on Tuesday 30 June. They do the stock-taking on Saturday 27 June and find the stock to be worth £32 850. During the remaining few days of June sales are as follows:

Monday	Cash sales £650; credit sales £320
Tuesday	Cash sales £850; credit sales £460
Monday	Purchases delivered by a supplier £1864
	Returns from a customer at selling price £186
Tuesday	Returns of some of the goods delivered yesterday (damaged in transit) £44

Colby & Co. always add 50% to cost prices to get their selling prices. What was the value of the stock on 30 June? Show your calculations.

6 New Arrival sell baby clothes, soft toys, etc., at six market towns, as a cooperative. The six cooperators do their stock-taking on Tuesday 4 January, as Tuesday is their only free day of the week. The total stock is valued at that date at £12 081.
   Some new stock was received on 2 January, worth £420 and sales on 1, 2 and 3 January were £426, £550 and £624 respectively. One of the cooperators had taken goods for her personal use at selling price worth £45 on 3 January. What was the value of the stock on 31 December, taking into account that they always add 25% to cost prices to find their selling prices.

7 Peter Farmer does his stock-taking after work has finished on 2nd January and finds the stock to be £5756. During the first two days of the new year sales had totalled £1347 and suppliers had supplied goods worth £586. A customer had returned goods sold to her for £45 and Farmer had taken items for his own use valued at £133 (selling price). One of the suppliers who had delivered goods in those days had taken away an unsatisfactory item supplied earlier valued at £36 (cost price). What was the true value of the stock at 31 December? (Show your calculations). Farmer always adds 25% to his cost prices to find his selling prices.

23.11 Answers to self-assessment questions

1 A stock record card is a card where we keep a record of the balance in hand of each type of stock we have. Any stock arriving is recorded on a goods received note which is added to the stock record and then passed to the Accounts Department. Any stock issued against a requisition is deducted from the stock record as it is issued.

2 In large organisations stock records are computerised, with bar codes being read by electronic pencils to catch the data required as stocks arrive and are issued.

3 It only has three entries each year, to record the opening and closing stocks at stock-taking time, when the Final Accounts of the business are being prepared.

4 Opening stock is the stock that last year hands on to next year as an asset to start the new year's business with. It is the same figure as last year's closing stock.

5 To do stock taking we must (a) Draw up stock sheets listing all types of stock held; (b) Count the actual stock in hand of each type; (c) Value it at cost price or net realisable value, whichever is lower; (d) Multiply this value by the number of items concerned; (e) Add up the total value to give a grand total.

Bin Card

Description			Bin number			
Max Stock			Part number			
Min Stock			Re-order qty			
Re-order level			Unit of issue			

Received			Issued			Balance
Date	Ref	Qty	Date	Ref	Qty	Qty
19. .			19. .			

Fig. 23.3 A bin card which may be copied for class use

Stock Ledger Card											

Description .... **Maximum Stock** .... **Charging System** ....
Code No .... **Minimum Stock** : .... **Delivery time** ....
Location .... **Supplier** .... **Re-order point** ....
                                                                                              EOQ ....

Receipts					Issued					Balance		
Date	Ref	Qty	Price	Value	Date	Ref	Qty	Price	Value	Qty	Price	Value
19. .					19. .							

Fig. 23.4 A stock ledger card which may be copied for class use

24 Adjustments in Final Accounts

24.1 What are adjustments?

Business activities go on all the time, but accounting periods end at a precise moment like midnight on 31 December, or midnight on 31 March. It follows that we sometimes have to adjust the accounts to ensure that we arrive at a correct profit figure for the year. For example if we sell goods on 27 December which are not paid for until 13 February should the profit on the transaction be taken into account for the year in which the sale was made, or in the year when the payment was actually received? We have to have rules about such matters, so that everyone knows what is the correct procedure. These are explained in detail as each problem area is described. The chief areas are:

- (a) payments in advance by the firm
- (b) payment in advance to the firm
- (c) payments due by the firm
- (d) payments due to the firm
- (e) bad debts and provisions for bad debts
- (f) goodwill
- (g) depreciation, appreciation and amortization of leases

The underlying principle on which such matters are decided is this. The book-keeper or accountant should prepare the accounts in such a way that every penny of profit that truly belongs to the accounting period under consideration is included in the profits, whether it has actually been received or not. Set against this profit should be every penny of expense incurred in earning the profit, even if that expense has not actually been paid yet. We shall see how these rules apply to the problem areas listed above. Before doing so it is worth mentioning that the Companies Act of 1985 requires auditors to certify that the accounts of a company do in fact give a 'true and fair view' of the profits of the company. Such a true and fair view must mean that they have checked the accounts to ensure that they comply with the fundamental principle outlined above. This principle is known as the 'matching principle' since the incomes and expenditures have been matched with one another. Another name is the 'accruals principle', since any items that have accrued due are taken into account, whether they are due to the business or due to be paid by the business.

24.2 Payments in advance by the firm

Some payments are always made in advance. For example insurance policies do not come into effect until the premium is paid, usually an annual premium. Similarly rates are usually paid in advance to local authorities. Suppose we take out a policy for Fire Insurance on 1 October 19. ., and the annual premium is £400. The cheque will be credited in the Bank Account and posted to the debit side of the Insurance Account. Here is the account.

Insurance Account			L29
19. .		£	
Oct 1 Bank	CB13	400.00	

Fig. 24.1 The Insurance Account

The financial year ends on 31 December 19. . . Should we carry this £400 to the Profit and Loss Account for the year ending 31 December 19. . . Clearly we should not, for some of this insurance cover will last into next year. We must not make this year's profits carry next year's expenses. We have to adjust the figures to get this years's expenses only in the accounts.

The cover used up in October, November and December (one quarter of a year) is one quarter of £400 = £100. Therefore the amount written off to Profit and Loss Account will be £100. A simple Journal entry would be done to debit Profit and Loss Account — a loss — and credit Insurance Account. This is shown in Fig. 24.2 — but please read carefully the notes under this figure.

Insurance Account						L29
19. .		£	19. .			£
Oct 1 Bank	CB13	400.00	Dec 31 Profit and Loss			
				A/c	J56	100.00
			31 Balance		c/d	300.00
		£400.00				£400.00
19. .		£				
Jan 1 Balance	b/d	300.00				

Profit and Loss Account			L133
19. .		£	
Dec 31 Insurance	J56	100.00	

Fig. 24.2 Clearing the insurance used to Profit and Loss Account

Notes
1 Only the correct amount of expense for the year in question has been written off the Profit and Loss Account.
2 This leaves a balance on the Insurance Account to be carried down to next year. Since that balance is being handed on from this year to next year it is one of the assets of the business.

As it will last less than one year (cover will be completely used up by 30 September) it is a current asset. This current asset will be the most liquid asset of all on the Balance Sheet — so liquid that we have already spent the money. This is shown in simple form in Fig. 24.3.

Balance Sheet as at 31 December 19. .

Fixed Assets		£
Current Assets	£	
Insurance in advance	300.00	

Fig. 24.3 A current asset — insurance in advance

24.3 Payments in advance to the firm

Imagine the insurance transaction mentioned earlier from the insurance company's point of view. They have been paid to provide cover for a full year and have received payment in advance. By 31 December they have covered one quarter of the year without any claim, so they can regard £100 of the premium as being earned. The other £300 is next year's receipts, not this years and must be carried forward. This time it will become not an asset, but a liability — the insurance company is liable to give cover to the assured for nine more months before a further premium can be called for. In fact special considerations enter into insurance accounts so we will not pursue this example any further. Instead let us consider a property company which collects rents from its tenants — many of them in advance. Suppose the total Rent Received in the year is £830 500. £384 650 of this is rent in advance, in other words the tenants who paid it are entitled to go on living in their flats and apartments for several more months before the next payment becomes due. The rest of the money, £445 850, has really been earned because the tenants have already enjoyed the accommodation to this extent. This money is therefore profit for the year, to be taken to the credit side of the Profit and Loss Account. The entries in the accounts when the Journal entry is posted would be as shown in Fig. 24.4.

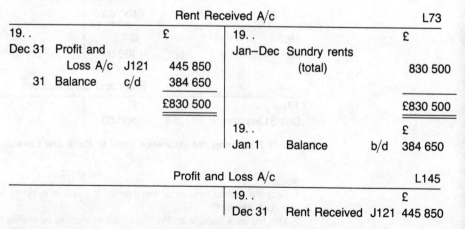

Fig. 24.4 Taking the Rent Received to the Profit and Loss Account

Notes

1 The part of the Rent Received which is actually earned in the present year is taken to the Profit and Loss Account as a profit.

2 The balance on the account is owed by the property company to the tenants — in other words they have not yet enjoyed the services they paid for — they are still entitled to live in their flats. The balance is therefore a liability to the tenants — the property company owes them accommodation in the months ahead. This would therefore appear on the Balance Sheet as a liability. As it will be settled in less than a year it is a current liability as shown in Fig. 24.5.

Balance Sheet as at 31 December 19. .

	£
Capital	
etc., etc.	
Long-term Liabilities	
etc., etc.	
Current Liabilities	£
Rent Rec'd in advance	384 650

Fig. 24.5 A current liability — Rent in Advance

24.4 Exercises on payments in advance

1 M. Nolan paid insurance as follows in 19. .:

1 January	£230 employer's liability insurance
1 April	£360 fire insurance
1 October	£240 freehold premises and contents insurance

In each case the premium gave a full year's cover. Show:

(a) How much of this insurance would be written to Profit and Loss Account on 31 December and;

(b) The entry for 'insurance in advance' on his Balance Sheet as at that date.

2 Rates in Newtown are payable on 1 April and 1 October in advance for the six monthly period commencing on those dates. W. Akram pays £386.50 on each occasion. Show the amount taken to Profit and Loss Account and the balance carried down and (b) the entry for this balance on the Balance Sheet as at 31 December, 19. . .

3 Industrial Properties Ltd, charge their tenants rent in advance, on a yearly basis. The three tenants pay as follows:

Industrial Brick Co. £136 000 on 1 April 19. .
Moto Caravan Park Ltd £85 000 on 1 July 19. .
Lilywhite's Garden Centre Ltd £66 000 on 1 August 19. .

Show the Rent Received Account for the year ended 31 December 19. . and the amount transferred to the Profit and Loss Account. Bring the Balance down and show how this balance would appear on the Balance Sheet as at that date.

4 The Helpful Bank PLC charges interest at a flat rate for the duration of the loan on all loans made. This interest is charged on the first day of the loan. In the year 19. . the total interest received was £17 246 045. Of this £7 256 056 was interest for the current year. The rest was in advance for the year's ahead. Show:

(a) the Interest Received Account for the year 19. ., the transfer of this year's interest to the Profit and Loss Account and the balance carried over to the new year.

(b) the entry for the Interest in Advance on the Balance Sheet as at 31 December 19. . .

24.5 Payments due by the firm

At the end of the year we often owe money for expenses. These are called **accrued expenses**, meaning expenses that have built-up and are due for payment. It is usually the case that these expenses are expenses of the current year, which should be included on the Profit and Loss Account as if they had actually been paid. For example, if we pay wages monthly on the last Friday of the month, the December payment might be made on the 26 December. There are really five more day's pay to include in the current year's wages, but they will not actually be paid until Friday 2 January. We must adjust the wages figure for the year to take account of this. Consider the following example:

EXAMPLE 24.1

Mary's Fashions pay wages on the last Friday in each month and the total wages paid in the year to 26 December 19. ., were £128 724. The wages for the last five days of the year are estimated at £1896. Show the Wages Account at the end of the year; the transfer to Profit and Loss Account and the Balance Sheet entry at 31 December 19. . . The entries are as follows:

Wages A/c   L19

19. .			£	19. .			£
Jan 1–				Dec 31	Profit and		
Dec 26	Sundry				Loss A/c	L175	130 620
	payments	CB?	128 724				
Dec 31	Balance		1 896				
		c/d	£130 620				£130 620
				19. .			£
				Jan 1	Balance	b/d	1 896

Profit and Loss A/c for year ending 31 December 19. .

			£
Wages		L19	130 620

Fig. 24.6 *Wages for the year taken to the Profit and Loss Account*

Balance Sheet as at 31 December 19. .

Capital	
Long-term liabilities	
Current liabilities	£
Wages due	1896

Fig. 24.7 *An accrued expense carries to next year as a liability*

Notes

1 It is useful to remind ourselves what has happened here. We want to arrange for this year to carry all the expenses it ought to carry. By taking the full figure for wages to the Profit and Loss Account we *do* make this year carry its full burden of wages.

2 As a result £1896 is carried down on the Wages Account as a liability.

3 On 2 January, when we pay the next week's wages (say £2500), the £2500 paid out of the Bank Account will be debited in the Wages Account. As £1896 has already been carried by the year that has just ended it will cancel out most of the £2500 and only £604 will need to be carried by next year's Profit and Loss Account.

24.6 Payments due to the firm

We now consider the opposite case to the one given in Section 24.5. Suppose a firm is due to receive rent from a sub-tenant of £150 in December, but the tenant is abroad and will not return until January. The Rent Received Account therefore shows that £1650 only has been received in the year (11 × £150) instead of £1800. We should credit the Profit and Loss Account with the full £1800 which means debiting the Rent Received Account with £1800. This leaves a balance on the account of £150, on the left hand side. This will be a temporary asset of the business; next year has to collect £150 from the sub-tenant which was really earned this year. This asset will appear on the Balance Sheet as 'rent due', a current asset. The position is illustrated in Figs. 24.8 and 24.9.

Profit and Loss A/c for year ending 31 December 19. .

	£			£
		Gross profit		27 824
		Rent Received		1 800

Rent Received A/c   L127

19. .			£	19. .			£
Dec 31	Profit &			Jan–Nov	Sundry		
	Loss A/c	L175	1800		receipts	CB?	1650
				Dec 31	Balance	c/d	150
			£1800				£1 800
			£				
Dec 31	Balance	b/d	150				

Fig. 24.8 Rent Received for the year taken to the Profit and Loss Account

Balance Sheet as at 31 December 19. .

Fixed Assets		
Current Assets		£
Rent due from sub-tenant		150

Fig. 24.9 The asset 'Rent Due' on the Balance Sheet

Note

The amount accrued due is really a special case of a debtor, and ideally should appear below debtors in the list of current assets. However, in agreement with the principal of materiality — see Chapter 25 — it could be merged with the other debtors and not shown separately.

24.7 Exercises: Payments in advance and accrued expenses

1 The books of T. Philips have the following balances on the accounts named at the end of the financial year, 31 December 19. . .

	£
Rent Received	2350
Rates	860
Insurance	720

Adjustments to these figures are required as follows:
(a) £50 rent is due from a sub-tenant.
(b) £215 of the rates is paid in advance for next year.
(c) £180 of the insurance is for cover to be provided in the new year.

Show (a) the ledger accounts concerned, including the transfer to the Profit and Loss Account and the balances brought down, and (b) the relevant entries on the Balance Sheet as at 31 December 19. . .

2 A. Garageowner allows the public who have cars to sell to display them on his forecourt in return for a commission of 10% on the sale price achieved. On 31 December 19. ., he has a total of £2385 on his Commission Received Account but three sums of commission of £85, £145 and £235 are due from customers. He feels confident all will pay in due course. Show the Commission Received Account for the end of the financial year, the transfer to Profit and Loss Account and the relevant entry on the Balance Sheet as at 31 December 19. . .

3 Yosemite Wholesaling Co., pays wages monthly on the 3rd day of the month, complete to the last day of the preceding month. On 31 December 19. . the eleven months' wages on its books total £130 600. The amount due for December and payable on 3 January is £11 966. Two thirds of the total wages are to go to Trading Account and one third to Profit and Loss Account.

Show the Wages Account at the end of the year and the relevant entry on The Balance Sheet as at 31 December 19. . .

4 On 31 December 19. . Joseph Chicoh had a Rent and Rates Account which had the following entries:

Rent paid:	1 January	£2400
	1 July	£2400
Rent from		
Sub-tenant	1 April	£800 ($\frac{1}{2}$ year to 30 Sept)
	1 October	£800 ($\frac{1}{2}$ year to 1 April)
Rates:	1 January	Balance in hand £246
	1 April	£1250 (Year to 31 March next)

Write up the account in correct date order, and show the amount carried to Profit and Loss Account for Rent and Rates for the year, and the Balance Sheet entry as at 31 December 19. . .

5 On the first day of January 19. . R. Chequeurs had a stock of advertising material worth £380 and owed a small advertising bill to a printer of £35. During the year advertising material, including the £35 owing, was paid for to the printers £1760 and a bill for £52 was outstanding. The stock at the end year was valued at £156. What was the amount charged to the Profit and Loss Account on 31 December for advertising materials used in the current year?

24.8 Final Accounts with adjustments

At the end of the year before the accountant prepares the Final Accounts it is necessary to decide whether there are any items that need adjustment. The figures for each adjustment that is considered necessary are calculated and the Trading Account, Profit and Loss Account and Balance Sheet are then prepared.

In examinations it is usual for the student to be given the details of any adjustments at the end of the Trial Balance, along with the Closing Stock figures. The student then shows these as an indentation on the accounts so it is clear what has been done. *Remember that as every adjustment affects not only the figures for the old year, but also what the old year hands on in the Balance Sheet to the new year, each adjustment will appear twice, once in the Final Accounts and once in the Balance Sheet.* An example is given below.

EXAMPLE 24.2

Here is the Trial Balance of G . Franklin. Some adjustments are given below the Trial Balance. Draw up the Trading Account, Profit and Loss Account and Balance Sheet of the business.

G. Franklin
Trial Balance as at 31 December 19. .

	Dr	Cr
	£	£
Purchases and Sales	21 425	67 192
Returns In and Out	215	130
Carriage In	125	
Opening Stock	5 335	
Commission Received		2 250
Rates	1 280	
Light and Heat	1 220	
Wages (Profit & Loss A/c)	17 572	
General Expenses	4 183	
Carriage Out	1 206	
Premises	48 000	
Motor Vehicles	4 250	
Fixtures and Fittings	4 850	
Debtors and Creditors	2 100	1 100
Drawings	13 000	
Cash in hand	43	
Cash at Bank	3 118	
Capital		57 250
	£127 922	127 922

Fig. 24.10 A Trial Balance with adjustments

Notes
1 Closing Stock was valued at £6385.
2 Rates included £180 for the quarter starting on 1 January next.
3 £185 wages for an employee visiting Paris on business have not been paid yet and are not included above.
4 An item of commission received (£180) has to be taken into account as Commission Due. The answer to this exercise is given in Fig. 24.11.

G. Franklin
Trading Account for year ending 31 December 19. .

	£		£
Opening Stock	5 335	Sales	67 192
Purchases	21 425	*Less* Returns	215
Add Carriage In	125	Net turnover	66 977
	21 550		
Less Returns	130		
Net Purchases	21 420		
Total Stock Available	26 755		
Less Closing Stock	6 385		
Cost of Stock Sold	20 370		
Gross Profit	46 607		
	£66 977		£66 977

Profit and Loss Account for year ending 31 December 19. .

	£		£
Rates	1 280	Gross profit	46 607
Less Amount in advance	180	Commission Received	2 250
	1 100	*Add* amount due	180
Light and Heat	1 220		2 430
Wages	17 572		49 037
Add Wages due	185		
	17 757		
General Expenses	4 183		
Carriage Out	1 206		
	25 466		
Net Profit	23 571		
	£49 037		£49 037

Balance Sheet as at 31 December 19. .

Capital		£	Fixed Assets		£
At start		57 250	Premises		48 000
Add Net Profit	23 571		Motor Vehicles		4 250
Less Drawings	13 000		Furniture and		
		10 571	Fittings		4 850
		67 821			57 100
Current Liabilities	£		Current Assets	£	
Creditors	1 100		Stock	6 385	
Wages due	185		Debtors	2 100	
		1 285	Commission due	180	
			Bank	3 118	
			Cash	43	
			Rates in advance	180	
					12 006
		£69 106			£69 106

Fig. 24.11 Final Accounts with adjustments

You should now try the following exercises which require the preparation of Final Accounts with adjustments.

24.9 Exercises: Final Accounts with adjustments

1 Here is the Trial Balance of Mohammed Jaffrey as at 31 March 19. . . . Draw up the Trading Account, Profit and Loss Account and Balance Sheet of the business taking into account the adjustments given below the Trial Balance.

	£	£
Premises	23 000	
Plant and Machinery	5 800	
Furniture and Fittings	3 600	
Motor Vehicles	12 750	
Opening Stock	13 250	
Purchases and Sales	34 729	95 616
Sales Returns and Purchases Returns	616	529
Carriage in	340	
Wages (Trading Account)	17 294	
Salaries (Profit and Loss Account)	13 816	
Discount Allowed	425	
Discount Received		784
Rent Received		2 300
Light and Heat	1 429	
Telephone Expenses	746	
C/fwd	127 795	99 229

		£	£
	B/fwd	127 795	99 229
Debtors and Creditors		1 384	2 165
Mortgage on Premises			15 000
Cash at Bank		3 385	
Cash in Hand		125	
Capital			30 395
Advertising		790	
Rates		1 456	
General Expenses		5 854	
Drawings		6 000	
		£146 789	146 789

Notes
1 Closing Stock was valued at £14 240 on 31 March 19. . .
2 Salaries are due to two employees on convalescence £726.
3 Rent of £100 is due from the sub-tenant.
4 Rates in advance come to £124.

2 Here is the Trial Balance of Young Alert as at 31 December 19. . . Draw up the Trading Account, Profit and Loss Account and Balance Sheet of the business taking into account the adjustments given below the Trial Balance.

	£	£
Premises	42 000	
Plant and Machinery	15 600	
Furniture and Fittings	5 850	
Motor Vehicles	12 260	
Opening Stock	7 146	
Purchases and Sales	43 854	129 265
Sales Returns and Purchases Returns	1 265	1 854
Bad Debts	265	
Wages (Trading Account)	12 250	
Salaries (Profit and Loss Account)	17 290	
Discount Allowed	426	
Discount Received		625
Rent Received		1 800
Light and Heat	725	
Telephone Expenses	842	
Debtors and Creditors	1 965	2 348
Mortgage on Premises		12 250
Cash at Bank	2 720	
Cash in Hand	134	
Capital		47 397
Advertising	792	
Rates	1 860	
General Expenses	4 295	
Drawings	24 000	
	£195 539	195 539

Notes

1 Closing Stock was valued at £14 258 on 31 December 19. . .

2 One of the debtors who owes £185 is believed to be unlikely to pay and this is to be included as another bad debt.

3 Rates paid in advance for next year amount to £260.

4 An advertising bill for £318 is to be taken into account.

3 Here is the Trial Balance of Peter Osborne as at 31 March 19. . . Draw up the Trading Account, Profit and Loss Account and Balance Sheet of the business taking into account the adjustments given below the Trial Balance.

	£	£
Premises	42 000	
Plant and Machinery	6 650	
Furniture and Fittings	7 250	
Motor Vehicles	8 680	
Opening Stock	14 244	
Purchases and Sales	39 285	107 256
Sales Returns and Purchases Returns	256	1 285
Carriage In	450	
Wages (Trading Account)	19 240	
Salaries (Profit and Loss Account)	16 246	
Discount Allowed	454	
Discount Received		625
Rent Received		2 420
Light and Heat	1 949	
Telephone Expenses	586	
Debtors and Creditors	1 275	3 250
Mortgage on Premises		20 500
Cash at Bank	4 925	
Cash in Hand	126	
Capital		49 584
Advertising	848	
Rates	1 200	
General Expenses	7 256	
Drawings	12 000	
	£184 920	184 920

Notes

1 Closing Stock was valued at £11 848 on 31 March 19. . .

2 Wages owing amounted to £1 260.

3 Rent Received included £20 for the next year.

4 A telephone bill for £214 has yet to be paid for the year to 31 March.

24.10 Bad debts and provisions for bad debts

When a debtor is quite unable to pay we know that we have to write the debt off by transferring it into Bad Debts Account. The end of the financial year is a good time to appraise the debts of the business and consider whether any of them are bad. Some of them might be partially bad, in that we still hope to get some of our money back. We might therefore consider writing a debt down to its true value, and transferring the rest of it to Bad Debts Account. Such an entry would be done by a simple Journal entry, and the account of the debtor would then appear as shown in Fig. 24.12.

19..			£	19..			£
Oct 15	Sales	SDB1	240.00	Dec 31	Bad Debts A/c	J25	120.00
				31	Balance	c/d	120.00
			£240.00				£240.00
19..			£				
Jan 1	Balance	b/d	120.00				

A. Slowpayer A/c   L29

Fig. 24.12 A debt that is partially bad

Notes
1 The advantages of writing a debt down in this way are the usual advantages of any adjustment; it makes this year carry the loss caused by the bad debt that has been incurred in the year as a result of dealing with A. Slowpayer.
2 It also leaves the debtors' figure on the Balance Sheet at a true value for the asset 'debtors'.
3 The disadvantage is that we might send the debtor a statement showing he owes us only half what he really does owe. We would probably therefore make a note on the account to ensure that the debtor was not given misleading information.

Having cleared off all the debts we know to be bad, or partially bad, there is one further thought for which we could make allowances. Suppose we have debtors of £4500. We don't know, but we can feel fairly certain, that some of these debtors will get into financial difficulties and finish up as bad debtors at some time in the year ahead. If we are to make this year carry its full burden of bad debts we ought to make it provide some funds for these losses which are going to occur in the years ahead. To do this we set up a Provision for Bad Debts Account. How much should be provided? It depends upon our sort of business, 10% of the debtors might be fair in one trade, 5% might be enough in another.

Normally we would debit the Bad Debts Account with a bad debt, (one of the losses of the business) and credit the debtor's account which is being written off. We can't do this because we don't know which of our present debtors will be the unlucky one, or the dishonest one who does not pay. Therefore the double entry is put as a credit item in the Provision for Bad Debts Account. This is shown in Fig. 24.13 and 24.14, using 10% of £4500 as the amount to be provided.

19..				J26
Dec 31	Bad Debts A/c	L74	450 00	
	Provision for Bad Debts A/c	L75		450 00
	Being 10% of outstanding debtors (£4500) provided for at this date.			

Fig. 24.13 Journal entry for bad debts that might occur

Bad Debts A/c   L74

19. .			£
July 29	B. Sharpe	J19	17.25
Oct 15	M. Smythe	J23	137.50
Dec 31	A. Slowpayer	J23	120.00
Dec 31	Provision for	J26	
	Bad Debts		450.00

Provision for Bad Debts A/c   L75

				19. .			£
				Dec 31	Bad Debts	J26	450.00

Fig. 24.14 Ledger entries for the provision for bad debts

Notes
1 In the Bad Debts Account the amount provided simply becomes one more bad debt, to be carried as a loss to the Profit and Loss Account. The total of £724.75 is made up of three bad debts which have actually taken place, worth £274.75 and £450 of bad debts we expect to lose at some time in the future.
2 What exactly is the balance of £450.00 in the Provision Account? It is some of the owner's profit kept back in the business in case bad debts are suffered in the months ahead. Clearly it is a liability, but to whom is it owed? It is owed to the owner of the business, because it is the owner's profit tucked away in a Provision Account.
3 How will this liability be shown on the Balance Sheet? The answer is that it is not shown on the liabilities side but is deducted from the debtors as shown in Fig. 24.15.

Balance Sheet as at 31 December 19. .
Fixed Assets
Current Assets

	£
Debtors	4500.00
Less Provision	450.00

4050.00

Fig. 24.15 Displaying the debtors and the provision made for bad debts

What happens next year with a Provision for Bad Debts?

Consider what happens once the new year has started. We have a Provision for Bad Debts Account of £450 — on the credit side of the account. Debtors begin to get into difficulties and we treat them in the usual way, writing the losses off to Bad Debts Account and closing the debtors' accounts so that no further trading with them can occur. At the end of the year let us suppose the bad debts total £720. This is enough to swallow up all the Provision for Bad Debts — but we would expect this because some of the bad debts will be for this year's bad debts, not just last year's bad debtors. Let us take an example and see what to do.

EXAMPLE 24.2 Amanda Walters has a Provision for Bad Debts of £450 on her books on 1 January 19. . . In the next year she has bad debts of £720 and a further debt of £130 from T. Cook has to be written off from her total debtors of £6150. She always provides 10% of outstanding debtors as a new provision at the end of the year. Show the

Bad Debts Account, the Provision for Bad Debts Account and the Profit and Loss
Account and Balance Sheet entries.

Calculations: (a) The bad debts will be £850 once T. Cook's debt has been
written off.

(b) This will leave her debtors of £6150 − £130 = £6020.

(c) The new provision required is 10% of £6020 = £602.

The best way to deal with the problem is to transfer the bad debts to the Provision
for Bad Debts Account, not the Profit and Loss Account. We can then see how much
we need to take to make the new provision. Follow the figures in the set of accounts
shown in Fig. 24.16.

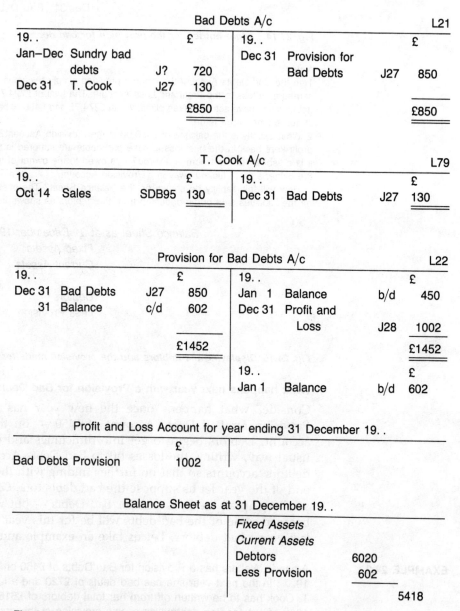

Bad Debts A/c   L21

19..			£	19..			£
Jan–Dec	Sundry bad debts	J?	720	Dec 31	Provision for Bad Debts	J27	850
Dec 31	T. Cook	J27	130				
			£850				£850

T. Cook A/c   L79

19..			£	19..			£
Oct 14	Sales	SDB95	130	Dec 31	Bad Debts	J27	130

Provision for Bad Debts A/c   L22

19..			£	19..			£
Dec 31	Bad Debts	J27	850	Jan 1	Balance	b/d	450
31	Balance	c/d	602	Dec 31	Profit and Loss	J28	1002
			£1452				£1452
				19..			£
				Jan 1	Balance	b/d	602

Profit and Loss Account for year ending 31 December 19..

	£	
Bad Debts Provision	1002	

Balance Sheet as at 31 December 19..

Fixed Assets			
Current Assets			
Debtors		6020	
Less Provision		602	
			5418

Fig. 24.16 Another year of bad debts

Notes

1 The tricky point here is how much to carry as a loss to the Profit and Loss Account. As you can see it was £1002. This was £400 of this year's bad debts (they came to £850 and the old provision was only £450) and £602 for the new provision (10% of £6020). £1002 in all.

2 This left a balance on the Provision Account of £602, as required.

3 This new provision is deducted from the Debtors on the Balance Sheet.

4 You might like to work out what would have been charged to Profit and Loss Account if bad debts had only totalled £320 instead of £850. (The answer is £472. Can you see why?)

24.11 Exercises on provisions for bad debts

1 M. Lark has debtors worth £2400 on 31 December, at the end of the financial year. One of these debts (T. Smith — £380 incurred on 1 June 19. .) is long overdue and is to be written off. A provision of 10% of the remaining debts is to be provided. Show:

(a) T. Smith's account after it is written off.

(b) The entry in the Journal for the Provision for Bad Debts and the Provision for Bad Debts Account itself after posting.

(c) The entry for debtors on the Balance Sheet prepared by M. Lark as part of his Final Accounts.

2 R. Prashad Ltd had debtors of £17 269 of which debts due from T. Green and B. Lee for £240 and £389 are deemed to be bad. The accountant decides to write off these two debts and to make a provision for bad debts of 10% of the remaining debtors. Show (a) The calculation of the amount to be provided. (b) The entry in the Journal for the Provision for Bad Debts and the Provision for Bad Debts Account after posting. (c) The Balance Sheet entry for debtors.

3 On 31 December 19. . Brian Scrivenor had debts on his books of £3248, and a Provision for Bad Debts from last year of £280. The debts include:

A. Jones	£120
B. Cameron	£ 28
Acme Trading	£160

Scrivenor believes Jones will only pay half the amount owing and the other two debts are bad. Earlier in the year he had already written off debts of £184. He decides to write off the three debts to the extent suggested above, and to make a Provision for Bad Debts of 10% of the remaining debts. Show (a) the Bad Debts Account; (b) the Provision for Bad Debts Account including the amount charged to Profit and Loss Account and (c) the Balance Sheet entry for debtors as at 31 December 19. . .

4 On 31 December W. Mathai has debts on her books of £5179 and a Provision for Bad Debts from last year of £420. £252 has already been written off during the year to Bad Debts Account and further bad debts seem to be:

R. Landseer	£142	(totally bad)
B. Jones	£ 66	(expected to yield 50% only)
MTC. Processes Ltd	£184	(totally bad)

Mathai decides to write these off to the extent shown and to provide a new provision of 10% of the outstanding debts. Show (a) the Bad Debts Account (b) the Provision for Bad Debts Account including the amount charged to Profit and Loss and (c) the Balance Sheet entry for debtors.

24.12 Goodwill

Goodwill is an intangible asset, that is an asset which you buy but which you cannot touch. When we buy a business we are often charged an extra sum for 'goodwill' — in other words we are charged for the good opinion local people have of the business, as a result of the hard work done by the present owner. Some of the profits we make in the future will be the result not of our hard work, but of the previous owner's hard work. One judge said 'Goodwill is based on the probability that the old customer will return for supplies to the old place.'

The value of goodwill is always a matter for negotiation, the new owner paying as little as possible and the old owner trying to get as much for goodwill as he can.

When the purchaser of a business pays for goodwill the amount paid is an asset of the business, debited in Goodwill Account like any other asset purchased. It is a fixed asset, and appears as the most fixed asset of all, but it is treated specially as we shall see. Fig. 24.17 shows such a Goodwill Account. Although we own this asset and it appears on our book, there is nothing to show for it — the goodwill exists in the minds of the old customers of the firm — we hope!

	Goodwill Account				L7
19. .		£			
Jan 1	Purchase of				
	Business	J1	2400		

Fig. 24.17 An intangible asset

Writing off Goodwill Account

Goodwill Account is a strange account. The people who owe us goodwill do not even know us — the goodwill is owed to the previous owner. Clearly the goodwill owed to us is absolutely zero. We therefore write Goodwill Account off as quickly as we can — usually over the first four years. There is a difficulty here. Since goodwill is a capital item, we are not allowed to depreciate it in the usual way, and charge depreciation to the Profit and Loss Account. We have to charge the depreciation to Capital Account — the amount written down has to come out of the owner's profits after tax, not before tax. For this reason we usually have to spread it over a few years. This is shown in Fig. 24.18, and a note explains a special point — the **paradox of goodwill**. A paradox is a statement that seems to be the very reverse of what is sensible.

			Goodwill A/c					L7
Year 1			£	Year 1				£
Jan 1	Purchase of			Dec 31	Capital	J17	600
	Business	J1	2400	31	Balance	c/d	1800
			£2400				£2400
Year 2			£	Year 2				£
Jan 1	Balance	c/d	1800	Dec 31	Capital	J35	600
				31	Balance	c/d	1200
			£1800				£1800

etc., etc. until Year 4

Year 4			£	Year 4				£
Jan 1	Balance	b/d	600	Dec 31	Capital	J56	600
			£600				£600

Fig. 24.18 Writing off goodwill

Notes
1 By the end of Year 4 the Goodwill Account is clear and disappears from the Balance Sheet.
2 The paradox of goodwill is that in the early years when goodwill is valued at most on the books no-one in the district really knows us and therefore really we have no goodwill at all. By the end of Year 4 many people know and like us, and consequently bear us plenty of goodwill, but by now goodwill on our books is valued at nothing. So the paradox of goodwill is that it is worth least when it is worth most on the books, and it is worth most when it is worth nothing on the books.

24.13 Depreciation, appreciation and amortization of leases

We have already learned (see Chapter 17) how to depreciate items on the books; an activity usually carried out at the end of the financial year when we are preparing the Final Accounts of the business. It is often the case that the adjustments in an examination include an instruction 'Depreciate Plant and Machinery by £2000'. This of course means that you must write off depreciation £2000 in the Profit and Loss Account. Like all adjustments it will affect the Balance Sheet as well, since it will reduce the value of the Plant and Machinery shown on the Trial Balance by £2000.

At this point we should say that most Balance Sheets (as far as fixed assets are concerned) are set out as shown below these days:

	At Cost	Less Depreciation to date	Value
Fixed Assets	£	£	£
Premises	54 000	—	54 000
Plant and Machinery	24 000	2000	22 000
Furn. and Fittings	7 600	1520	6 080
Motor Vehicles	12 500	5000	7 500
	98 100	8520	89 580

This has the advantage of showing how each asset has been depreciated and gives some idea how close it is to the end of its useful life. Notice that premises rarely depreciate in value, they tend to rise in value over the years. This is called appreciation.

Appreciation

When assets rise in value we don't usually take any notice of it unless we sell the asset, when of course we make a profit on the sale. However, there is one time when we should take the profit into account. That is when premises rise in value, and if a business is taken over there is some risk that the purchaser may make a profit he does not really deserve. This is most likely to happen with large companies, but if we take a simple example of a business that has assets worth £30 000 on the books, of which £20 000 is the premises purchased at that figure twenty years ago. They are now worth £65 000. If someone buys the business at the book value — plus goodwill of £5000 they will pay only £35 000 for a business which has premises that are alone worth £65 000.

Clearly this would not be sensible, and it is better to review the value of the premises from time to time and upgrade the value on the books. The change in value from £20 000 to £65 000 is a £45 000 profit, but this is a capital profit not a revenue profit. The asset is debited with £45 000 and the credit entry to balance it is not in the Profit and Loss Account but in the owner's Capital Account. The Journal entry is shown in Fig. 24.19 and the accounts are given in Fig. 24.20.

19 . .					J49
Dec 31	Premises A/c	Dr	L1	45 000.00	
	Capital A/c		L8		45 000.00
	Being appreciation of premises over the years.				

Fig. 24.19 *Taking account of rising property values*

Premises A/c						L1
19 . .			£			
Jan 1	Balance	b/d	20 000			
Dec 31	Capital	J49	45 000			

Capital A/c						L8
			19 . .			£
			Jan 1	Balance	b/d	37 285
			Dec 31	Premises	J49	45 000

Fig. 24.20 *Taking appreciation of premises into account*

Lease amortisation

There are two ways of owning property, freehold and leasehold. With freehold you own the land outright, for ever. With leasehold you own it for a period of time only — often 99 years — but it can be as short as one week. As the years pass the lease runs out and at the end of the lease the property has to be returned to the landlord. The value of the lease-hold property therefore 'wastes' as the years go by and it is usual to write off the value to recognise that some of its value has 'died' during the year. This is called amortisation of the lease. The French word 'mort' meaning 'death' gives us this word for the lease which gradually dies.

Thus, if Farmer Brown has a lease on a farm for 20 years, for which he paid £40 000, one twentieth of the value is used up every year and the lease would be depreciated (amortised) by £2000 per year. Debit Depreciation Account with £2000 (which will eventually be written off the Profit and Loss Account). Credit the Lease Account, which falls in value to £38 000.

	Depreciation A/c				L27
19. .		£			
Dec 31 Lease A/c		20 000			

		Lease A/c				L54
19. .			£	19. .			£
Jan 1 Balance	b/d	40 000	Dec 31 Amortisation of			
				Lease	L27	2 000
			31 Balance	c/d	38 000
		£40 000			£40 000
19. .		£			
Jan 1 Balance	38 000				

Fig. 24.21 Amortisation of a lease which has 20 years to run

24.14 More Exercises on adjustments in Final Accounts

1 What is goodwill? M. Murjani buys a small business on 1 January 19. ., and pays £2500 for goodwill. He decides to write off the goodwill over the first five years of the business. Show the Goodwill Account for the five years.

2 P. A. Munro buys a business for £35 000. For this he gets premises £25 000; Furniture and Fittings £2000; Motor Vehicles £3500 and Stock £1000. Do the Opening Journal entry, bringing out the amount paid for goodwill. He then asks your advice about the Goodwill Account, which he has heard is usually written off. Recommend to him what he should do.

3 Why do we sometimes appreciate Land and Building Account? What happens about the profit made when premises are increased in value in this way?

4 Electronics Ltd has a lease on a factory which is valued on the books at £45 000. It had 15 years to run at the start of the year. How much should be written off the lease on 31 December, 19. .?

5 On 1 January Smokestack Industries PLC has a lease on its books for a factory. The lease is valued at £38 500 and it has seven years to run.
(a) How much should be written off the lease at the end of the year?
(b) Show the Journal entry and the Lease Account for the year.

6 Here is the Trial Balance of Leone Ogbara as at 31 December 19. . . Draw up the Trading Account, Profit and Loss Account and Balance Sheet bearing in mind the adjustments given below the Trial Balance.

Leone Ogbara
Trial Balance as at 31 December 19. .

	Dr	Cr
Purchases	25 445	
Sales		123 946
Returns In	2 468	
Returns Out		310
Heat and Light	788	
Wages	24 250	
Discount Allowed	1 212	
Discount Received		1 170
Office Expenses	8 316	
Rates	2 412	
Telephone	2 146	
Insurance	1 097	
Opening Stock	3 000	
Carriage In	1 260	
Carriage Out	4 137	
Drawings	23 200	
Bank	15 620	
Cash in Hand	650	
Debtors	2 120	
Creditors		2 195
Premises	56 250	
Machinery	13 750	
Furniture and Fittings	2 500	
Mortgage on Premises		25 000
Capital		38 000
	£190 621	190 621

Notes
1 Closing Stock is valued at £8560.
2 Light and Heat and Wages are to be shared half to the warehouse (Trading Account) and half to the office (Profit and Loss Account).
3 The debtors include bad debts to the value of £320, and a provision for bad debts of 10% of the remaining debtors is to be made.
4 £400 of the rates is paid in advance for next year.
5 Depreciate Machinery by £3250 and Furniture and Fittings by £500.

7 Here is a Trial Balance of Helen Cartwright's pottery business as at 31 December 19. . . Prepare the Trading and Profit and Loss Account for the year ending 31 December 19. . and the Balance Sheet at that date. You are to take into account the adjustments given at the end of the Trial Balance.

	Dr	Cr
	£	£
Land Buildings A/c	44 500	
Plant and Machinery A/c	4 800	
Furniture and Fittings A/c	2 650	
Motor Vehicles A/c	12 425	
Capital (Helen Cartwright) A/c		67 990
Purchases A/c	43 900	
Sales A/c		108 260
Purchases Returns A/c		455
Sales Returns A/c	1 260	
Carriage In A/c	855	
Carriage Out A/c	1 750	
Rent and Rates A/c	945	
Light and Heat A/c	680	
Insurance A/c	564	
Warehouse Wages A/c	18 250	
Opening Stock A/c	6 485	
Commission Received A/c		15 758
Rent Received A/c		4 000
Salaries A/c	24 250	
Provision for Bad Debts A/c (1 January)		500
Bad Debts A/c	864	
Sundry Debtors A/cs (total)	2 250	
Sundry Creditors A/cs (total)		8 565
Cash A/c	1 740	
Bank A/c	18 640	
Drawings A/c	19 500	
Discount Allowed A/c	280	
Discount Received A/c		2 190
Postage A/c	555	
Travelling Expenses A/c	575	
	£207 718	207 718

Notes
1 At stock-taking the value of the stock in hand was found to be £8760.
2 The new provision for bad debts is to be 10% of the debtors.
3 Plant and Machinery is to be depreciated by 25%; furniture and fittings by 10% and Motor Vehicles by 20%.
4 The premises are to be up-valued to £50 000. The profit on this is to be treated as a capital gain, not a revenue profit.
5 Rates in advance amount to £145.

25 More concepts of accounting

25.1 A further list of concepts

In Chapter 6 we studied some of the basic concepts of accounting; the concept of business entity, the concept of stewardship and the concept of duality (i.e. double entry). Because we now know how to do the Final Accounts of a business, the Trading Account, Profit and Loss Account, and Balance Sheet we are ready to consider some other concepts which are important when reporting the state of affairs of any business at the end of any financial period. These further concepts may be listed as follows:

(a) The 'going-concern' concept
(b) The 'consistency' concept
(c) The 'objectivity' concept
(d) The 'prudence' concept
(e) The 'matching' concept, or 'accruals' concept
(f) The 'materiality' concept
(g) The 'stable-money' concept

Most of these concepts have already been considered, particularly in the chapter about adjustments in the final accounts (Chapter 24) but we must gather our thoughts together on them so that we really understand the principles which underlie the book-keeping and accounting we are doing.

25.2 The 'going-concern' concept

If a business is a 'going-concern' which has been operating over the past year and is to go on operating into the new year we are entitled to treat all its assets as being a part of a continuing business with a usefulness which will continue for the conceivable future. Our attitude might be entirely different if we knew that the business was to close down next week, or in the next few months. Similarly any supplier of goods to a business may be perfectly happy to wait for any money due according to the usual terms of business, if further orders are expected in the months ahead. If the word gets around that the business is to close the supplier's attitude will change and he/she will start to worry about payment for the goods already supplied. It is a principle of accounting that the final accounts will be regarded as the accounts of a 'going-concern', and if there is any suggestion that the business will close in the near future the accountant must say so in any report he makes to interested parties, and must value the assets in a different way. For instance a cement manufacturer may have cement-making plant worth £1 million, but if the works closes the value will fall to almost nothing, or at best to its scrap value, for there are very few uses to which such plant can be put by anyone else.

The phrase 'a gone concern' is sometimes used for a business which has ceased to trade, to distinguish it from a going-concern which will continue for the forseeable future.

The going-concern concept therefore holds that an accountant must always enquire from his client whether the business whose final accounts are to be prepared is continuing in business for the forseeable future, and if so it will be perfectly proper to prepare the accounts as those of a 'going-concern'.

25.3 The 'consistency' concept

One of the chief purposes of preparing accounts is to see how our business is doing, and this implies that we compare the present accounting period with past accounting periods. To make these comparisons meaningful we must prepare the accounts in the same way from year to year; in other words we must be consistent. We should not change the way in which we prepare the accounts, and if we do we must draw the attention of the interested parties to the different approach we are adopting. For example if we use the equal instalment method of depreciation one year and the diminishing balance method another year (see Chapter 17) the two sets of results will not be strictly comparable. If we treat 'wages' as a Trading Account item one year and a Profit and Loss Account item the next year the figures for the Gross Profit will be on a different basis in the two years, and the inconsistency may lead us to wrong conclusions about our business and its development over the years.

25.4 The 'objectivity' concept

When preparing final accounts we should view the business situation from the point of view of a disinterested outsider. This is called taking an objective view — a view that is not coloured by the viewpoint of the people in the business which is the subject of examination. An insider takes a biased, subjective view. For example, consider the question 'Should this business be allowed to carry on, or should it be closed down and the resources be used in some different business altogether?'. Here the subjective views of the insider will almost always be 'Let it continue!'. Nobody wants the business in which they work to close down, and make them redundant, and therefore unemployed.

Looked at objectively, the views of a disinterested outsider might be the same. The outsider might say 'Keep it going because it is making excellent profits; it is very efficiently run and it employs a lot of people, etc., etc. On the other hand the outsider might be of the opinion that the products made were old-fashioned, that demand for them was declining and that the same resources employed in some quite different enterprise would create more wealth and be of greater use to everyone. Whether the business is approved of or disapproved of, the objective view is unbiased and therefore better than the subjective view of the insider.

25.5 The 'prudence' concept

We have already noted this concept in the chapter on adjustments, Chapter 24. In business we must be prudent, that is cautious. Expect the worst, not the best that can happen. Never take a profit before you have actually made it. That is why we value stock at cost price, or net realisable value, whichever is the lower. Even if our stock is worth more now than when we purchased it, we do not value it at its present value because that would mean taking the profit now when we have not actually realised it. If we sell the stock at present prices then of course we can take the profit, because we have actually made it.

Similarly, we always take a loss when we know we have suffered it, because that is the prudent thing to do. If a debtor is never likely to pay we write off the bad debt. We don't keep it on our books and pretend it is still a good debt. The prudence concept says 'Always take losses into account if you suspect you have suffered them, and never anticipate profits; they may not materialise.'

25.6 The 'matching' concept (sometimes called the 'accruals' concept)

This concept is the basis of the preparation of final accounts. It holds that we must match the revenues (income) we receive with the expenses incurred in earning those incomes, so that the profit figure we arrive at is correct. If we have included all the income received in a given accounting period and have set against these revenues all the expenses that have been incurred (including any that have accrued and are due for payment) in the same time, we shall arrive at the correct profit figure. Since we have studied this closely in the chapter on adjustments in final accounts (Chapter 24) we are familiar with this concept.

25.7 The 'materiality' concept

The aim of our book-keeping is to present a true and fair view of the affairs of our business. What profits have we made? What assets and liabilities do we have at the end of the year, as we move into the next financial period? However, we do not need so much detail that we cannot see the wood for the trees. If a thing is of sufficient importance we say it is a material item, and should appear as a separate item in the accounts. If it is not an item of great importance we say it is 'immaterial' — not of any real consequence. We cannot leave such things out, but we can merge them with other items so that they do not appear separately. A few examples will illustrate the point:

1 Mr Smith has 34 debtors, to a total value of £2763. We need not show any one of these items separately — the fact that one of the debtors is Miss Prendergast who owes Smith £13.50 is immaterial. We merge them all as a single item 'Debtors £2763'.

2 The Helpful Bank PLC has 2784 branches, each in its own premises, to a total value of £104 725 000. We need not show any of these items separately — the single item 'Premises £104 725 000' is all we need.

3 Helena Massowa spends £84 in the year on advertising expenses. It is such a small item she merges it into 'General Expenses' which amount to £7256 and the item appears on her Profit and Loss Account as 'General Expenses £7340'.

4 The Industrial Finance Company has loans outstanding at the end of the year of £8 million. However, one of these loans is for £250 000 made to one of the directors T. Smith. Now finance companies should not regard a loan to a director as an immaterial item, because loans of this sort are rather special. The Board therefore agrees that the item is material and must be shown separately:

Loans:

Commercial	£7 750 000
A. Director (T. Smith)	250 000
	£8 000 000

25.8 The 'stable-money' concept

This is a very important concept, especially in inflationary times when prices are rising and the value of money is falling. The general idea is that money is stable in value. If I buy goods worth £100 today and agree to pay in one month's time (the usual credit period for trading purposes between businesses) we both expect that the value of money will remain the same, and when I pay you the £100 it will be a fair payment for the goods supplied. If this is not the case, and the value of money has halved in the credit period, so that I repay you with money that is only worth £50 in real terms (i.e. in terms of what it will buy today) this is unfair.

All sorts of strange things happen in inflationary times. For example debtors delay payments, since the longer they delay the less they will really have to pay. Rates of interest rise, since those who loan money demand more compensation for the use of their funds — part of the interest payable is really compensation for the changing value of the money that is being returned. Prices are raised frequently. People do their shopping early in the morning, before the shop-keepers have time to go round and change the prices on the items on display. Those eating out in restaurants pay for their meals as they go in, for fear the prices have risen by the time they leave the restaurant. In some countries workers have had to take a suitcase to work just to take home their wages, because the money was worth so little.

What is done in book-keeping in inflationary times is a very complicated story. It is called 'inflation accounting', and is too difficult for a book of this kind. The basic thing is that the traditional methods of accounting no longer work. The traditional method is called 'historical cost' accounting because we record things at the value they had when we purchased them at some time in the past. This has to be changed to one where we record the value of things at today's date, as inflation 'raises' their value in money terms. A small reference to one aspect of it has been made in Section 23.7 about FIFO, LIFO and AVCO. The reader might like to re-read this section and think about the basic problems of book-keeping in inflationary times, when the value of money is falling, and everyone prefers to hold goods rather than money. At the end of World War 2 in Germany money ceased to have any value, and the nation's business was carried on in cigarettes, which became far too valuable to smoke.

25.9 Self-assessment questions

1 What is an accounting concept?
2 What is the concept of business entity?
3 What is the concept of stewardship?
4 What is the going-concern concept?
5 What is the consistency concept?
6 What is the objectivity concept?
7 What is the concept of materiality?
8 What is the prudence concept?
9 What is the matching concept or accruals concept?
10 What is the stable-money concept?
11 What is the concept of duality?

25.10 Exercises on the concepts of accounting

1 What is the concept of stewardship? Explain how Wabenze, the accountant of a Government department in charge of a national park in an African country is a steward of the park's affairs. To whom should he report?

2 Explain the concept of materiality? Which of the following would you say was a material item?
(a) the factory (the only one of its kind) owned by an oil refinery and used to manufacture plastic articles as by-products of the refinery's activities.
(b) a tied garage — one of 3800 similar garages — which sell the oil company's refined products.
(c) a loan of £2000 to the owner of one of these garages; one of many such loans.
(d) a loan of £5 million to the ruler of a country whose crude oil plays a considerable part in the oil company's achievement of prosperity.

3 An item of equipment (a heavy duty crane) is recorded in the records of a Pacific fringe country as a debit in the Plant and Machinery Account and a credit in Bank Account. What concept of accounting do these entries illustrate? Explain the nature of this concept.

4 An investor notices that a company of which he is a shareholder had premises valued at £100 000 this year, although last year they were only valued at £10 000. To his knowledge there has been no change of premises during the year and no mention is made of this in the accounts except for an item 'capital appreciation £90 000'. What principle of accounting has been overlooked in this arrangement?

5 'All businessmen must be prudent — especially when preparing their Final Accounts.' Explain this statement and give an example of prudent behaviour in preparing the Final Accounts of a business.

6 Explain the accruals concept in accounting. Bloggs has started this year to make a new product, which brings in £17 280. Against this he has to set raw material costs of £5000 (but £1000 of this is still in stock) and wages of £8000 — but in addition he owes one employee £65.00 for unpaid overtime. He also advertises this item by mail order with literature that cost him £420 — of which about one third of the leaflets are still in stock. Postage came to £814. What on an accruals basis, is the profit on the new product?

7 Anne Ford is a fashion designer, running a specialist couturier's business. She says she has been told that it is advisable to open a separate business bank account, and asks you whether you think this is necessary. Explain the principle that is involved in such a decision.

8 What is the going-concern concept? Refer in your answer to Heavy Haulage Ltd, who have a number of specialist vehicles, low loaders, tank vehicles, etc., and whose owners are thinking of going out of business in about four week's time at the end of their financial year.

9 Explain the difference between an objective view and a subjective view of a business decision. Use in your explanation the case of a small hotel business which is in financial difficulties. The proprietor is thinking of dismissing half the staff. The hotel has a valuable site which a national supermarket is interested in buying, but it would mean the dismissal of all the hotel staff and the demolition of the premises.

10 Eight years ago Tom Smith purchased a lorry for £12 000. He depreciated it by £1000 every year and put the money in a special deposit account. The fund has now reached £10 500 with interest, and the old vehicle is now worth £1500. However, the same vehicle today costs £27 500. What principle of accounting has he been abiding by, and what can he do to get a new vehicle now this principle has let him down?

25.11 Answers to self-assessment questions

1 A concept is an idea which is fundamental to the project we have in hand. An accounting concept is a fundamental idea which guides us in all our accounting.
2 The concept of business entity holds that every business is a separate unit, which is distinct from the person who owns the business. The owner is just one more creditor to whom the business owes back whatever has been subscribed to the business, and the profit it has earned.
3 The concept of stewardship holds that the the accountant must report back

honestly to the owner or owners of the business to show how it has been managed on the owner(s) behalf.

4 The going-concern concept holds that when the final accounts of any organisation are presented for examination it may be assumed that they are the accounts of a concern that intends to continue for a further trading period. If this is not the case the accountant must draw the attention of all interested parties to this fact, and will use a different set of standards when valuing the assets, etc.

5 The consistency concept holds that we must prepare accounts year after year in the same way as we have always done, so that comparisons may be made between one year and another. If we do change any part of the accounting procedures — for example the method of depreciation used — we should draw the change to the attention of any interested parties.

6 The objectivity concept holds that we should always view the business and the forces at work to influence the business from the point of view of a disinterested outsider, and not from the viewpoint of a biased or prejudiced insider (a subjective view).

7 The concept of materiality holds that when an item is of distinct importance, and interested parties should know about it, it should appear in the accounts as a separate item, but where an item is trivial and has no particular significance it can be merged with other items as immaterial.

8 The prudence concept holds that businessmen should always be prudent, taking a loss into account as soon as it occurs and refusing to take account of a profit until it has actually been realised. Thus if stocks rise in value we do not take these increases into account as profits unless we actually sell the stock and realise the profits.

9 The 'matching' or 'accruals' concept says we should always match our revenues (income) against our outlays (expenditure), so that we arrive at a true profit. This means we must adjust our incomes to take account of sums due and sums paid to us in advance, and similarly we should adjust for expenditures for the present period that have not yet been paid and expenditures for the year ahead that have been paid early.

10 The stable-money concept holds that money always holds its true value, so that £1 borrowed this year may be repaid with £1 next year (disregarding any interest). In fact, in inflationary times money falls in value and this affects the willingness of business people to trade unless account can be taken of the changing value of money. The whole problem is called by the general name of 'inflation accounting'.

11 The concept of duality deals with the fact that every transaction involves two accounts, one of which receives value and the other gives value. If we understand the double entry nature of a transaction we know how to record it in the books of our business.

26 Partnerships

26.1 Why form a partnership?

A partnership is an arrangement where two persons, or more than two persons, carry on business with a view to making profits. There are many reasons for going into partnership but the most common ones are:

1 Two people usually can provide more capital than one person, and therefore the assets available are better, and more numerous than if they were just sole-traders.

2 Two people usually have a wider range of skills and knowledge than a single person, and therefore the service they can offer is more extensive and specialised, with each doing the things he/she is better at.

3 Sole trader businesses are very vulnerable from the point of view of sickness of the proprietor or absence for other reasons, family problems, bereavements, etc. Partners can cover for one another in sickness, holiday periods, etc.

Partnership agreements may be made orally, or in writing, or even just by shaking hands, but it is best to draw up a formal agreement with a solicitor, called a deed of partnership. This will usually state the main points on which the partners are agreed. These include such points as:

1 How much capital is to be contributed by each partner.

2 Whether they are to be equal partners, or whether one is to be senior and the other junior.

3 How the profits are to be shared — usually in some simple proportion ($\frac{1}{2}$ and $\frac{1}{2}$ or $\frac{2}{3}$ and $\frac{1}{3}$, etc.).

4 Whether interest is to be paid on capital, and whether drawings are to be permitted during the year, in expectation of profits made.

5 The date of commencement and the duration of the partnership.

A good solicitor will suggest many more points which will prevent difficulties in the future should a dispute arise between the partners.

The *Partnership Act of 1890* is the Act which controls partnerships and embodies a wealth of experience of partnership difficulties with the law. It does not interfere with a partnership at all provided the partners have reached an agreement on any point, but it becomes important when a dispute arises over a point which they failed to anticipate when they went into partnership. Then it will usually be found that the Act covers the point somewhere, and the partners will be bound by the rules laid down in the Act. For example the Act says that any partner may see and make copies of the books of account, so that if one partner was preventing the other seeing the books the Act would enable the disappointed partner to force the other to deliver the books for his consideration.

26.2 The accounts of partners

With sole traders we saw that the Capital Account of the sole trader shows the amount the business owes back to the trader — his original capital and any profits added over the years, less any drawings drawn out over the years. With partnerships it is not helpful to have Capital Accounts which fluctuate in this way, because the capital contributed at the start is stated in the partnership agreement or deed and it is best to leave that as a fixed sum. To get over the difficulty each partner has two other accounts, a Current Account, which is allowed to fluctuate year by year, and a Drawings Account which collects all the Drawings over the year, but is cleared into the Current Account at the end of the year. Each partner therefore has a *fixed* Capital Account, a Current Account and a Drawings Account. Sometimes these accounts, which are rather private accounts, are kept in a special ledger called the Private Ledger, and are not shown to the ordinary book-keepers in the firm. A 'firm' is the proper name for a partnership business, but in everyday language it is often misused to mean any sort of business.

26.3 The Final Accounts of a partnership

A full set of Partnership Accounts requires:

1 A Trading Account
2 A Profit and Loss Account
3 An Appropriation Section of the Profit and Loss Account, in which the partnership profits are appropriated in the way agreed
4 A Capital Account for each partner
5 A Current Account for each partner
6 A Drawings Account for each partner
7 A Balance Sheet

Parts 1 and 2 are exactly the same as for the sole trader and need not be repeated here, but parts 3, 4, 5, 6 and 7 are illustrated and explained below.

26.4   The Appropriation Account

The word 'appropriate' means 'allocate to a particular use'. When the Net Profit has been found in the Profit and Loss Account it has to be allocated to the partners in the way they have agreed, and this is illustrated in Fig. 26.1. It is usual to transfer the net profit to a separate Appropriation Account but it is sometimes simply brought down and dealt with in an extension to the Profit and Loss Account, which we then call the Appropriation Section of the Profit and Loss Account.

The following things might happen in an Appropriation Account:

1 The net profit will be brought in on the credit side from the Profit and Loss Account (or we could have a net loss brought in on the debit side).
2 The partners might decide to write off an item like goodwill, which

is a capital item and cannot be written down in value in the ordinary way as depreciation. The Appropriation Account will be debited and Goodwill Account credited to reduce its value on the books.

3 One of the partners might be entitled to a salary. This is often done when a young person teams up with an older person. The young person is given a small salary to help him/her survive the early years, but it is not an employee's salary, it is an appropriation of the profit, and has first call on the profits.

4 One, or both, partners may be entitled under the partnership agreement to interest on capital. This is usually done when the capital contributed has been unequal, so that one partner will not feel he has contributed more without any reward. Usually the rate of interest is chosen at about the same rate as the banks would give on a deposit account.

5 The residue of the profit would then be shared in the agreed way, as laid down in the partnership deed.

6 In each case 3, 4 and 5 above, the Appropriation Account will be debited and the amount due to the partner will be credited in the Current Account.

Here is a typical partnership Trial Balance after the Trading Account and the Profit and Loss Account have been prepared. We will use it to prepare a set of Partnership Final Accounts. Look at it first and the notes below it. Then notice how the Appropriation Account is drawn up in Fig. 26.1, and how it affects the other accounts in Fig. 26.2.

Trial Balance of A. and B. Archer as at 31 December 19. .

	Dr £	Cr £
Goodwill (1 January 19. .)	5 000	
Premises	100 000	
Fixtures and Fittings	8 000	
Motor Vehicles	12 320	
Stock at 31 December 19. .	18 000	
Capital A. Archer		12 000
Capital B. Archer		72 000
Current A/c A. Archer (1 January 19. .)		744
Current A/c B. Archer (1 January 19. .)	1 920	
Drawings A/c A. Archer	10 000	
Drawings A/c B. Archer	14 000	
Net Profit (in Appropriation A/c)		32 600
Mortgage		60 000
Creditors		19 144
Electricity due		218
Debtors	11 000	
Rates in advance	166	
Cash at bank	15 400	
Cash in hand	900	
	£196 706	196 706

Notes

1 The partners share profits one third to A. Archer and two thirds to B. Archer.
2 A. Archer is to have a salary of £4000 per annum.
3 Both partners are to have interest on capital at 10% per annum.
4 The partners agree to write off £1000 of the Goodwill at this date.
5 No interest is to be charged on drawings.

The Appropriation Account for this business will appear as shown in Fig. 26.1. The important points are explained in the notes below it.

Appropriation Account for year ending 31 December 19. .

	£		£
Goodwill	1 000	Net Profit	32 600
Salary A. Archer	4 000		
Interest on Capital			
A. Archer	1 200		
B. Archer	7 200		
	8 400		
Share of residue			
of profit			
A. Archer	6 400		
B. Archer	12 800		
	19 200		
	£32 600		£32 600

Fig. 26.1 An Appropriation Account

Notes

1 In each case where some of the profit is appropriated to a particular purpose it is debited in the Appropriation Account and credited to the account named. If the name given is one of the partners then it is the partner's Currrent Account that is credited.
2 Certain items are entered first, for example a salary has first claim on the profits as far as the partner's shares are concerned and interest on capital is given before the profits are shared. So it is really the residue of the profit that is shared in the ratio $\frac{1}{3}$ and $\frac{2}{3}$.
3 Where the partners agree to write down Goodwill out of the profits it is usual to do that first before either partner gets any share of the profits. The various accounts will therefore be as shown in Fig. 26.2.

Goodwill A/c   L97

19. .			£	19. .				£
Jan 1	Balance	b/d	5000	Dec 31	Appropriation	J71	1000
				31	Balance	c/d	4000
			£5000				£5000
			£				
19. .							
Jan 1	Balancè	b/d	4000				

Current A/c (A. Archer)				L195
19. .	£	19. .		£
		Jan 1 Balance	b/d	744
		Dec 31 Salary	J71	4000
		31 Interest on		
		Capital	J71	1200
		31 Share of profit	J71	6400

Current A/c (B. Archer)				L196
19. .	£	19. .		£
Jan 1 Balance	b/d 1920	Dec 31 Interest on		
		Capital	J71	7 200
		31 Share of Profit	J71	12 800

Fig. 26.2 Double entries for the Appropriation Account entries

Notes
1 The balance at the start of the year on B. Archer's account was a debit balance, in other words an overdrawn Current Account. He had drawn out more in the previous year than he earned in profit.
2 What happened to the Current Accounts in the present year is explained in the next section. Here we can only see the various bits of profit being appropriated to the accounts.

26.5 Exercises: Appropriation Accounts

1 Brett and Walker are in partnership sharing profits two thirds to Walker and one third to Brett. The partnership agreement provides that Brett shall have a salary of £5000 per annum and that both partners shall have interest on capital at the rate of 8% per annum. At the end of their trading year on 31 December 19. ., the net profit is £37 256. They agree to reduce Goodwill Account by one third. It stands on the books at £4800. Their respective capitals are £5000 (Brett) and £20 000 (Walker). Draw up the Appropriation Account for the year ending 31 December 19. .

2 Dee and Kadar are in partnership sharing profits in the ratio of 1 to Dee and 3 to Kadar. The partnership agreement provides that Dee shall have a salary of £8500 and that both partners shall have interest on capital at the rate of 10% per annum. At the end of their trading year the net profit is £46 252 and they agree to reduce Goodwill Account by one half. It stands on the books at £7600. Their respective capitals are £14 000 (Dee) and £40 000 (Kadar). Show the Appropriation Account for the year ending 31 December 19. . .

3 A, B and C are in partnership sharing profits in the ratios 3, 2, and 1 respectively. The partnership agreement provides that B and C shall each have a salary of £5200 and that all partners shall have interest on capital at the rate of 8% per annum. At the end of their trading year the net profit is £42 502 and they agree to reduce Goodwill Account by one third. It stands on the books at £5700. Their respective capitals are A = £60 000; B = £3200 and C = £4800. Show the Appropriation Account for the year ending 31 December 19. . .

4 Major and Minor are in partnership sharing profits two thirds and one third respectively. The partnership agreement provides that Minor shall have a salary of £5200 per annum and that both partners shall have interest on capital at the rate of 10% per annum. They started business on 1 April 19. . and by 31 December the net profit is £28 542. They agree to reduce Goodwill Account by £1500. Their respective capitals are £24 000 (Major) and £10 000 (Minor). Show the Appropriation Account for the nine month period ending on 31 December 19. . .

5 Singh, Chan and Raffles are in partnership sharing profits equally, except that the partnership agreement provides that Singh shall have a salary of £5000 per annum and Chan shall have a salary of £4500 per annum. It also provides that all partners shall have interest on capital at the rate of 8% per annum. They started in business on 1 July 19. . and by the end of that year the net profit for the six month's trading period was £37 490. Their respective capitals are Singh £5000; Chan £2000 and Raffles £18 000. Show the Appropriation Account for the six months period ending 31 December 19. . .

26.6 The partnership Balance Sheet

The Balance Sheet of a partnership business is only slightly different from the Balance Sheet of a sole trader. The partnership Balance Sheet has two Capital Accounts, which do not vary from year to year, instead of one. The variable part of the Capital Account is now found in the Current Accounts of the two partners, which receive all the profits appropriated to them from the Appropriation Account and also suffer the deductions from the Drawings Account. If we complete the Current Accounts shown in Fig. 26.2 by transferring the drawings into them, we can see how these accounts are cleared to give the figures shown on the Balance Sheet (see Fig. 26.4 below). Naturally the starting point for a partnership Balance Sheet is the residue of the Trial Balance left over after preparing the Trading Account, Profit and Loss Account and Appropriation Account. Look back at Section 26.4 and remind yourself of the figures we are using — and follow them through to the accounts shown in Fig. 26.3 and the Balance Sheet of Fig. 26.4.

		Current A/c (A. Archer)						L195
19. .			£	19. .				£
Dec 31	Drawings	J72	10 000	Jan 1	Balance	b/d		744
31	Balance	c/d	2 344	Dec 31	Salary	J71		4 000
				31	Interest on			
					Capital	J71		1 200
				31	Share of profit	J71		6 400
			£12 344					£12 344
				19. .				£
				Jan 1	Balance	b/d		2 344

Current A/c (B. Archer)   L196

19. .			£	19. .			£
Jan 1	Balance	b/d	1 920	Dec 31	Interest on		
Dec 31	Drawings	J72	14 000		Capital	J71	7 200
31	Balance	c/d	4 080	31	Share of		
					profit	J71	12 800
			£20 000				£20 000
				19. .			£
				Dec 31	Balance	b/d	4 080

Fig. 26.3 Completing the Current Account of the partners

Notes

1 The Drawings Accounts are cleared into the Current Accounts, since the partners have received these sums already, and are no longer entitled to them.

2 This year B. Archer has been more careful with his drawings and has not drawn out more than he earned. So the account has a credit balance, not a debit balance as it did last year.

3 The business owes the partners the balances shown, as well as the amount shown on their fixed Capital Accounts. The partners are creditors of the business for these amounts, as shown by the credit balances on the accounts.

4 Although they are not shown here, the Drawings Accounts are now clear and disappear from the Trial Balance.

We are now ready to do the Balance Sheet which is shown in Fig. 26.4 below.

Balance Sheet of A. Archer and B. Archer as at 31 December, 19. .

	£	£			£
Capital	£		*Fixed Assets*		
A. Archer	12 000		Goodwill		4 000
B. Archer	72 000		Premises		100 000
		84 000	Fixtures and Fittings		8 000
			Motor Vehicles		12 320
Current Accounts	£				124 320
A. Archer	2 344				
B. Archer	4 080				
		6 424			
Long-term Liabilities			*Current Assets*		
Mortgage		60 000	Stock	18 000	
			Debtors	11 000	
Current Liabilities			Cash at Bank	15 400	
Creditors	19 144		Cash in Hand	900	
Electricity due	218		Rates in advance	166	
		19 362			45 466
		£169 786			£169 786

Fig. 26.4 A partnership Balance Sheet

Notes

1 Notice that the Capital Accounts are now fixed and are simply added together on the Balance Sheet.

2 The fluctuating part of each partner's capital is now in the Current Account, and only the final balance needs to be brought onto the Balance Sheet.

3 If one of the partner's Current Account has a debit balance (i.e. it is overdrawn) it will appear on the assets side of the Balance Sheet. As it will always be settled in less than a year, by earning profits in the year ahead, it is shown as a Current Assets, preferably below 'debtors'.

26.7 Exercises on partnership Final Accounts

1 The following figures appear on the partnership books of Butler Brothers (Abel and Charles Butler) who share profits and losses in the ratio of 2:1, Abel taking the larger share.

Capital Accounts as at 1 January 19. . :	Abel £26 000; Charles £10 000
Current Accounts as at 1 January 19. . :	Abel £7160 (credit);
	Charles £180 (credit)
Drawings Account at 31 December, for drawings in the year:	Abel £21 515; Charles £9265

Net Profit for the year £41 562

Charles is entitled to a salary of £5200 a year and both partners get 10% interest on capital, and on Current Account balances at the start of the year. Draw up the Appropriation Account, the two Current Accounts, and the two Drawings Accounts and show how these figures would appear on a Balance Sheet at the end of the year.

2 The following figures appear on the partnership books of Haji and Kabiri, who share profits and losses in the ratio of 3:1.

Capital Accounts:	Haji £42 000; Kabiri £14 000
Current Accounts:	Haji £2874 (credit); Kabiri £1120 (debit)
Drawings Accounts:	Haji £21 260; Kabiri £18 250

At the end of the year the net profit on trading was £42 956

Kabiri is allowed a salary of £8500 per year and both partners get interest of 8% on capital at start, including the Current Account balances (debit balances are deducted from the capital for calculating interest of course). Calculations to the nearest £1. Draw up the Appropriation Account, the two Current Accounts, and the two Drawings Accounts and show how these figures would appear on a Balance Sheet at the end of the year.

3 Here is the Trial Balance of A. and B. Perkins as at 31 December 19. . after the Trading and Profit and Loss Account have been completed. Their partnership agreement holds that B. Perkins is entitled to a salary of £6000 per annum and both partners are entitled to 10% interest on capital at the start of the year, including any balances at the start of the year in the Current Accounts of the partners (debit balances to be deducted for this calculation). Apart from these arrangements profits are to be shared 2:1 (A. Perkins having the larger share). Draw up the Appropriation Account, the Current Accounts and the Balance Sheet as at 31 December 19. . .

	£	£
Premises	46 000	
Plant and Machinery	12 500	
Furniture and Fittings	7 500	
Motor Vehicles	6 250	
Closing Stock	7 150	
Capital (A. Perkins)		24 000
Capital (B. Perkins)		12 000
Current A/c 1 January (A. Perkins)		6 000
Current A/c 1 January (B. Perkins)	2 000	
Net Profit for year on Appropriation Account		46 600
Debtors and Creditors	2 300	4 860
Mortgage on Premises		22 800
Cash at Bank	3 010	
Cash in Hand	160	
Investments (current assets)	8 600	
Advertising materials in hand	540	
Rates in advance	165	
General Expenses due		85
Drawings (A. Perkins)	11 500	
Drawings (B. Perkins)	8 670	
	£116 345	116 345

4 Here is the Trial Balance of Shah and Singh after the completion of their Trading Account and Profit and Loss Account for the year ending 31 December 19. . . The terms of the partnership agreement are that profits and losses will be shared two thirds and one third, Shah taking the larger share. Singh is allowed a salary of £10 000 per annum and both partners get 10% interest on their Capital Account balances at 1 January and their Current Account balances on 1 January. Draw up the Appropriation Account, Current Accounts and Balance Sheet of the partnership.

	£	£
Capital (Shah) at 1 January		50 000
Capital (Singh) at 1 January		15 000
Current A/c (Shah) at 1 January		2 600
Current A/c (Singh) at 1 January		100
Drawings A/c (Shah)	17 290	
Drawings A/c (Singh)	10 000	
Premises	65 000	
Plant and Machinery	18 000	
Furniture and Fittings	12 500	
Motor Vehicles	10 500	
Debtors and Creditors	4 265	5 140
Mortgage on Premises		35 210
Cash at Bank	5 816	
Cash in Hand	729	
Closing Stock	11 720	
C/fwd	155 820	108 050

		£	£
	B/fwd	155 820	108 050
Wages Due			285
Rates in Advance		360	
Commission Due			724
Net Profit			47 121
		£156 180	156 180

5 Here is the Trial Balance of Sue and Nicola Kingham, who are partners in a boutique. The deed of partnership says that profits shall be shared three quarters to Sue and on quarter to Nicola, but that Nicola shall have a salary of £12 500 per year. Both partners will have interest at 10% per annum on their capitals, but not on any balance left in their Current Accounts. Taking into account the adjustments shown below the Trial Balance you are asked to prepare the Trading and Profit and Loss Account of the partnership, the Appropriation Account and the Current Accounts of the partners, and a Balance Sheet as at 31 March 19. . .

Trial Balance as at 31 March 19. .

	£	£
Capital (Sue)		60 000
Capital (Nicola)		20 000
Furniture and Fittings	5 250	
Motor Vehicles	6 250	
Opening Stock	47 250	
Purchases and Sales	125 000	208 000
Sales Returns and Purchases Returns	4 000	5 000
Current A/c (Sue)		4 250
Current A/c (Nicola)	1 250	
Salaries	27 560	
Drawings (Sue)	18 750	
Drawings (Nicola)	15 000	
Rent Payable	12 500	
Light and Heat	2 420	
Telephone Expenses	1 750	
Debtors and Creditors	12 500	8 640
Loan from Bank		5 000
Cash at Bank	27 084	
Cash in Hand	560	
Commission Received		1 650
Advertising	1 240	
Rates	1 350	
General Expenses	2 826	
	£312 540	312 540

Notes
1 Closing Stock is valued at £51 500.
2 Salary is due to an employee £104.
3 Rent Payable has been paid in advance £500.
4 A Bad Debts Provision of £1250 is to be created.
5 Commission Receivable is due £120.

6 Here is the Trial Balance of Sorrel and Willow who are partners in a factory manufacturing electronic units. The deed of partnership says that profits shall be shared two thirds to Sorrel and one third to Willow, but that Willow shall have a salary of £6500 per year. Both partners will have interest at 8% per annum on their capitals, but not on any balance left in their Current Accounts. Taking into account the adjustments shown below the Trial Balance you are asked to prepare the Trading and Profit and Loss Account of the partnership, the Appropriation Account and the Current Accounts of the partners, and a Balance Sheet as at 31 March 19. . .

Trial Balance as at 31 March 19. .

	£	£
Premises	45 000	
Plant and Machinery	19 500	
Furniture and Fittings	3 600	
Motor Vehicles	12 250	
Opening Stock	13 265	
Purchases and Sales	37 285	146 385
Sales Returns and Purchases Returns	1 285	1 400
Carriage In	726	
Wages (Trading Account)	39 265	
Salaries (Profit and Loss Account)	21 520	
Discount Allowed	1 480	
Discount Received		1 652
Rent Received		800
Light and Heat	1 720	
Telephone Expenses	840	
Debtors and Creditors	8 500	3 763
Mortgage on Premises		26 500
Cash at Bank	10 222	
Cash in Hand	460	
General Expenses	13 592	
Advertising	1 800	
Rates	1 720	
Capital (Sorrel)		55 000
Capital (Willow)		20 000
Current A/c (Sorrel)		5 264
Current A/c (Willow)	2 325	
Drawings A/c (Sorrel)	12 654	
Drawings A/c (Willow)	11 755	
	£260 764	260 764

Notes
1 Closing Stock is valued at £11 585.
2 Wages of £150 are owing to an employee in the factory.
3 Advertising of £125 has been paid in advance.
4 A Bad Debts Provision of £1700 is to be created.
5 £200 Rent Receivable is due from a tenant.

27 Clubs and other non-profit-making organisations

27.1 Non-profit-making organisations

Many organisations are not set up to make profits but to provide some useful service either to a particular group of people or to the general public if they wish to join the organisation. For example cricket and football clubs, tennis clubs, gardening societies and similar bodies are non-profit-making. Similarly the Automobile Association and the Royal Automobile Club are non-profit-making and exist to help members whose vehicles break down on the road. Another large group are the charities, of which there are several thousand. Age Concern, Dr Barnardo's Homes and the RSPCA are names that spring to mind.

Although these bodies are not primarily commercial organisations, they do collect funds, either in the form of subscriptions from members or as charitable donations, and it is important to be able to account for them honestly. The usual method is for the person in charge of the funds, the **Treasurer**, to submit accounts to the **Annual General Meeting** (AGM) where the members are usually given a copy and have the opportunity to question the Treasurer about any matters they consider important.

One group of non-profit-making societies — the Co-operative Societies — handle over £3000 million pounds each year, so these organisations are not all small. Similarly the motoring organisations may handle £100 million a year and employ hundreds of staff.

There are two methods of presenting the accounts of such bodies, a simple method and a more detailed method. They are:

1 A Receipts and Payments Account.

2 An Income and Expenditure Account (which is really like a Profit and Loss Account) and a Balance Sheet.

27.2 The Receipts and Payment Account of a club

A Receipts and Payment Account is presented by the Treasurer to the members at the Annual General Meeting. It is an analysed cash book of the club. This term is explained later, but if we first look at a typical Receipts and Payments Account we shall be able to follow the Club's activities. The illustration in Fig. 27.1 is taken from a book which is available from George Vyner Ltd, Simplex House, Holmfirth, Huddersfield, HD7 2TA. It is called The Accounts Book for Club Treasurers and is a cash book for one year's club records.

RECEIPTS and PAYMENTS A/c
Annual General Meeting
Year ending 31ˢᵗ March   19 87

Receipts		£	p
Opening Balances at Start of Year:			
	Cash in Hand	3	54
	Cash at Bank	86	45
Col. 1	Subscriptions	142	50
Col. 2	Donations	5	50
Col. 3	Refreshment Sales	286	45
Col. 4	Trip to France	735	60
Col. 5	Xmas Parties	48	24
Col. 6	—		
Col. 7	—		
Col. 8	Miscellaneous	1	84
		£ 1310	12

Payments		£	p
Col. 1	Equipment	62	50
Col. 2	Refreshment Purchases	250	00
Col. 3	Trip to France	719	25
Col. 4	Xmas Parties	56	50
Col. 5	Funeral Expenses	5	25
Col. 6	O.A.P. Charity Donation	10	00
Col. 7	—		
Col. 8	Miscellaneous	3	64
Closing Balances at end of year:			
	Cash in Hand	4	62
	Cash at Bank	198	36
		£ 1310	12

Auditors' names
and Signatures:

Treasurer's Name
and Signature:

Fig. 27.1 The Receipts and Payments Accounts of a club (courtesy of George Vyner Ltd)

Notes

1 The account is in the form of a Cash Account, but for this purpose cash and cheques received are treated as being the same, and payments might have been made either in cash or by cheque.

2 We start with the opening balance of cash in hand and at the bank.

3 Then all the receipts for the whole year under a particular heading are shown. For example subscriptions would have been collected over the year, but the Treasurer has analysed the receipts and collected all the subscriptions together. That is why we say the Receipts and Payments is an *analysed* cash book of the Club.

4 The members can see the various receipts and the various payments, and they can also see the balances in hand at the end of the year.

5 The Treasurer might add a few notes to explain points members might find difficult to understand or wish to check. For example:

(a) The Cash of £4.62 would be available at the meeting — also the Bank Statement and Bank Reconciliation Statement for inspection by members wishing to see them.

(b) On refreshments, it appears that very little profit was made but as the purchases also covered entertainment to visiting teams this is not surprising.

(c) A stock of refreshments valued at £26 is available (at the start of the year stocks were only £4). Other assets include camping equipment valued at £350, stored on the premises.

(d) Creditors. A debt for repairing windows broken in the recent burglary is outstanding £7.25.

(e) There are no debtors.

6 When the members have had an opportunity to discuss the accounts the Secretary will ask that someone proposes that the Accounts be accepted as a good record of the Club's affairs and on this being proposed, seconded and passed the Chairman or President will sign the accounts as being accepted by the members.

27.3 Drawing up a Receipts and Payments Account

In real life the Treasurer has quite a lot of work to do to analyse the Cash Book of the Club, which may be just a simple cash book purchased at any stationer's shop. If the book referred to above is used it will be slightly easier, since the book is already ruled up in analysis columns and they can easily be totalled to give the figures for the year.

In examinations when preparing Receipts and Payments Accounts we have a very simple task, for the opening balance and any receipts go on the debit side, and the payments, and the final balance at the end of the year, go on the credit side. If the accounts have been carefully kept the two sides should balance. You should now try some of the exercises in 27.4 below.

27.4 Exercises: Receipts and Payments Accounts

1 The following sums of money were received and paid by the Treasurer of Whitewaves-on-Sea Sailing Club during the year ending 31 December 19. . . On 1 January 19. . the club's cash Balance was £143.12.

Payments: Rent & Rates £204.52; Refreshment Expenses £182.20; Printing £19.25; Prizes (for Draw) £236.40; Sundry Expenses £188 .69; Purchase of dinghy £840.

Receipts: Subscriptions £1180; Refreshment Sales £420.40; Draw Ticket Sales £440.00; Sundry Receipts £12.25.

Draw up the Receipts and Payments Account for year ending 31 December 19. . And thus find the balance of cash in hand at that date.

2 Draw up the Receipts and Payments Account for The Borrowdale Cricket Club for the year ending 31 December 19. . from the following:

Cash Balance 1 January 19. . £215.60
Bank Balance 1 January 19. . £450.75
Payments: New Games Equipment £1176.50; Printing & Postage £112.15; Rates £276.20; Repairs to Club House £357.80; Light & Heat £136.75; Dance Expenses £45.60; Refreshments Expenses £223.90.
Receipts: Subscriptions £1580.00; Visitors Fees £360.00; Donations £425.75
Dance proceeds £290.90; Refreshment Sales £750.10.
Closing balances: Cash in hand £314.20 Balance at bank £1430.00.

3 As treasurer of the Lakeside Football Club prepare the Receipts and Payments Account for the year ending 31 May 19. ., from the following information. Cash/Bank Balance 1 June last year was £465, of which £430 was in the Bank Account.

Payments were: Wages; Groundsman £1040; Barman £1572.
Bar Expenses (Supplies) £2446. Coach Hire £1280. Rates £160.
Dance expenses £149; Insurance £152; Trophies £30. and the General Expenses amounted to £425.
Receipts were:
Subscriptions £4420; Bar Sales £4836; receipts from Dances and Socials £475; donations £86.
The closing balances were: Cash £136; Bank £2892

4 The treasurer of the Lake District Climbing Club analyses his cash records and finds as follows:

Balances in hand at 1 January: Cash £84.25; Bank £497.50.
Receipts during year: Subscriptions £276.50; Donations from rescued climbers £485.00; Proceeds of dances and socials £376.50; open day proceeds £1725.65.
Payments during year: Purchase of new equipment £725.62; Refreshment expenses £227.50; Vehicle expenses £386.55; Postage etc £14.25; Expenses of dances and socials £71.25; open-day expenses £114.20; purchase of vehicle £1500.
Balances in hand at 31 December: Cash £42.50; Bank £363.53.

Draw up his Receipts and Payments Account for the Annual General Meeting.

27.5 More detailed Club Accounts

The trouble with a Receipts and Payments Account is that although it is an adequate method of reporting to the club members of a very small club it is not really satisfactory for a large organisation, particularly one that has a great many assets and liabilities. For such clubs we need a more detailed account of the club's affairs. The starting point will still be the Receipts and Payments Account, because it is these figures that enter into our final accounts, but we go on to present a fuller record. For this full record of a club's affairs we need:

1 The Receipts and Payments Account

2 We may need one or more Trading Accounts — for example, we could have a Bar Trading Account to show us whether we made a profit on the bar.

3 We need an account called an Income and Expenditure Account, which is really the Profit and Loss Account, but we can't call it that because we are dealing with a non-profit-making organisation. Ciubs don't call any profits they make 'profits' — they call them surpluses because they are really surplus contributions which the members need not have made. The Club could have managed with a smaller subscription. Similarly a loss is not called a 'loss', it is called a 'deficiency'. The members did not contribute enough, and the deficiency that resulted should really have been met by a larger subscription.

4 Finally we need a Balance Sheet, which shows the assets and liabilities of the club. There is one very important point here, and that is the 'Capital' which normally appears on any Balance Sheet. Clubs are not 'capitalistic' organisations which are profit-motivated. They are non-profit-making. As such it is not usual to call the capital by that word — instead we call it the Accumulated Fund. This is a good name, because the funds have been gradually collected over the years — accumulated by running events such as socials, dances, etc.

We know that capital is what a business owes back to the owners of the business. If the Accumulated Fund is the same as the capital, to whom is it owed? The answer is it is owed back to the members, who are entitled to share it if the Club ceases to function.

To follow this fairly difficult set of Club Accounts we will imagine the following example:

EXAMPLE 27.1   The Valley Young Farmers Club has the following assets and liabilities at 1 January 19. .

> Assets: Club house £8500
> Games equipment £3250
> Bar stocks £7525
> Club house equipment £336
> Subscriptions due £24 (6 members at £4 each)
> Cash in hand £114
> Deposit Account at Bank £1650
> Liabilities: Loan from A. Member £5000 (interest free)
> Creditors £126 (for bar supplies).

The Receipts and Payment Account at the end of the year is shown below.

Receipts and Payments A/C for year ending 31 December 19. .

Receipts		£	Payments	£
1 Jan	Cash in Hand	114	Bar Purchases	12 500
	Subscriptions	1 560	Rates	378
	Donations	224	Light & Heat	296
	Dances/takings	1 206	Purchase of new	
	Refreshments/	1 242	club equipment	344
	takings		Postage & Printing	89
	Bar takings	14 758	Dance Expenses	353
			Refreshment	
			Expenses	467
			Clubhouse Repairs	1 202
			Transfer to	
			Deposit Account	900
			Bar wages	2 100
			Cash in Hand c/d	475
		£19 104		£19 104

			£
Balance	b/d		475

From these figures and the following information prepare a Trading Account for the Bar, an Income and Expenditure Account and a Balance Sheet as at 31 December 19. . . . .

1 The bar stocks at the end of the year were worth £9258.

2 At the end of the year subscriptions were due from 11 members at £4 each and three members had been paid in advance for next year.

3 At the end of the year £194 was owing for bar supplies, and a printing bill for £18 was due and unpaid.

4 All the subscriptions for last year were eventually paid, and we expect this year's outstanding subscriptions to be paid in due course.

5 The member who made the loan last year did not ask for any repayment in the year.

To solve this problem there are several points we must first sort out:

1 *The Accumulated Fund at the start of the year* At the start of any year, just as with an ordinary business, we can draw up a Balance Sheet of the club and the Accumulated Fund will be in the same position as the capital of a business. If we list the assets and liabilities of the club at the start of the year we find:

Liabilities	£	Assets	£
Loan	5 000	Club house	8 500
Creditors	126	Games equipment	3 250
	£5 126	Bar stocks	7 525
		Club house equipment	336
		Subs due (debtors)	24
		Deposit Account at bank	1 650
		Cash in hand	114
			£21 399

It is clear that the missing item is the Accumulated Fund — the capital of the club. It is £21 399 — £5126 = £16 273. Putting in the Accumulated Fund on a liabilities side will make the two sides balance.

2 *Adjustments* We can have adjustments in Club Accounts just as we do in an ordinary business. Once again the rule is to make every penny of this year's income be included in the accounts for this year, and every penny of this year's expenses be borne by this year's accounts. So for example on subscriptions we have the following points to consider.

Subscriptions received in the year £1560.
This would include £24 from last year's subscriptions.
£44 is due from this year's late payers.
£12 has been received in advance for next year.

To find the subscriptions actually received for *this* year we must deduct the £24 for last year and the £12 for next year, and count in the £44 due from the late payers who have not yet paid.

$$\text{Subscriptions} = £1560 - £36 + £44 = £1568.$$

Note that at the end of the year the subscriptions due will be an asset (the members are debtors for £44) but the subscriptions in advance will be a liability (we owe the members a year's entertainment).

3 The creditors for bar stocks at the beginning of the year present a problem. If payments for bar purchases in the year were £12 500 this must include the money owed for last year, £126. The amount owing at the end of the year is for this year's stocks and must be counted in. So the purchases in the year are £12 500 − £126 + £194 = £12 568.

The Final Accounts will now be prepared as follows:

1 Everything in the opening Balance Sheet must appear somewhere in the Final Accounts. This includes the Accumulated Fund at the start.

2 Everything in the Receipts and Payments Account must appear somewhere in the Final Accounts.

3 All the adjustments given in the extra information must appear twice in the Final Accounts, once in the Final Accounts and once in the Balance Sheet as they are carried over to next year.

The final accounts of the club are as shown in Fig. 27.2.

Bar Trading A/c for year ending 31 December 19. .

	£			£
Opening Stocks		7 525	Bar takings	14 758
Purchases	12 500			
Less Last year's	126			
	12 374			
Add This year's due	194			
		12 568		
		20 093		
Less Closing Stock		9 258		
		10 835		
Bar wages		2 100		
		12 935		
Surplus on bar		1 823		
		£14 758		£14 758

Income and Expenditure Account for year ending 31 December 19. .

	£			£
Rates		378	Subscriptions	1560
Light and heat		296	less subs due at start	24
				1536
Postage and printing	89		*add* subs due	44
Add sum due	18			1580
		107	*less* subs in advance	12
Dance expenses		353		1568
Refreshment expenses		467	Donations	224
Repairs to clubhouse		1202	Dance takings	1206
		2803	Refreshment takings	1242
Surplus for year		3260	Surplus on bar	1823
		£6063		£6063

Balance Sheet as at 31 December 19. .

Accumulated Fund	£		Fixed Assets		£
At start	16 273		Club house		8 500
Add Surplus for year	3 260		Games		
			equipment		3 250
			Club house		
	19 533		equipment	336	
			Add new items	344	
					680
					12 430
Long term liability			Current Assets		
Loan from A. Member	5 000		Bar Stocks	9258	
Current Liabilities			Deposit		
Bar supplies	194		Account	£1650	
Printing bill due	18		Add new		
Subs in advance	12		deposit	900	
		224		2550	
			Cash in hand	475	
			Subscriptions		
			due	44	
					12 327
		£24 757			£24 757

Fig. 27.2 A full set of Club Accounts

You should now try some of the exercises given below.

27.6 Exercises: the Final Accounts of Clubs

1 From the information below prepare (a) the Receipt and Payments Account (cash items only), (b) the Income & Expenditure Account and (c) a Balance Sheet for the Lea Valley Social Club for the year ending 31 December 19. . .

Accumulated Fund at 1 January   Cash at Savings Bank £109
                                        Cash in Hand   £ 48

Receipts: Subscriptions £1473
                 Net income from socials £243.

Payments: Rent £274.
                 Rates £163.
                 Light & Heat £175.
                 Purchases of club furniture £560.
                 Transfer to Savings Bank £540.

Notes
1 £33 of the subscriptions were in advance for next year.
2 £14 rent was due to the landlord on 31 December.

3 £21 of the rates were paid in advance.
4 A bill for light and heat was due for payment £25.
5 The interest on savings was £12 in the Savings Bank.

2 Prepare Final Accounts for The Suburbia Tennis Club for the year ending 31 December 19. . . On 1 January the Cash in Hand was £35 and Subscriptions due from the previous year amounted to £20. Other assets of the club on 1 January were the Club House £8200, the courts £7560, nets and other equipment £1580 and a bank balance of £3500. The club had two liabilities; it owed for work done on resurfacing the hard court £2250 and an electric light bill of £72 was also due.

Cash payments in the year were as follows:

Rates for the courts and clubhouse £460; Heat and light £148 (including the (£72 due for last year); new equipment £240. Refreshments for visiting teams cost £285; annual donation to Local Association £100. Paid to Bank £1000. The treasurer paid by cheque £3000 for repairs to the courts (including the £2250 owing from last year).

Cash receipts in the year were as follows:

Subscriptions £1650; profit from dances £460; Donations £250; Fees from members for special events; £230.

At the end of the year subscriptions for the present year were due £280 and subscriptions paid in advance for next year amounted to £25.

3 On 1 January 19. . the Leyfarers Cycling Club had a Cash Balance of £60, and equipment worth £500. Subscriptions due were £20. There was one liability, a repairs bill £48. During the year receipts were: from subscriptions £360; competition fees £80; Socials and dances £340.

Payments were: postage £48; competition prizes £36; socials and dances £52; purchase of new equipment £275; repairs £84.

Other points the Treasurer bore in mind were:
(a) The original equipment was to be depreciated by 20% in the year.
(b) A bill for £60 printing expenses was unpaid at the end of the year.
(c) Subscriptions due at the end of the year were £40 and subscriptions paid in advance for next year were £15.

Prepare a Receipts and Payments Account and an Income and Expenditure Account for the year and a Balance Sheet as at 31 December 19. . .

4 From the information below produce a full set of Final Accounts for the Photographer's Club for the year ending 31 December 19. . .

On 1 January 19. . equipment was valued at £1230, and the Cash Balance was £283. Subscriptions due amounted to £25 for the previous year and Subscriptions paid in advance were £50. During the year there were the following receipts:

subscriptions £1625; sales of refreshments £266; competition fees £125 and from collections £45.

Payments were made for: rent and rates £447; insurance £46; wages of part-time staff £282; postage and printing £53; refreshments £69; prizes £34; repairs £141 and new equipment £467.

Additional information is as follows: On 31 December Rates were due £42; wages due £46; subscriptions due £40. The insurance payment inclues £23 for next year and subscriptions in advance for the year ahead were £75. Old equipment is to be depreciated by 20%.

5 The Wanderers' Cycling Club has assets and liabilities as follows at the start of its financial year, 1 April 19. . .

Assets: Club premises £35 000; practice machines £485; furniture and fittings £3250; subscriptions due £80; stock of spare parts £864; balance at bank £425 and cash in hand £42.

Liabilities: Subscriptions in advance £45; telephone expenses £23; mortgage on premises £15 000.

During the year receipts and payments in cash were as follows:

Receipts: Subscriptions £1652; competition fees £429; refreshment sales £425; sales of spare parts £2659.

Payments: Purchases of spare parts £156; prizes for competitions £124; refreshment expenses £129; premises expenses £384; repairs £266; payment to bank £4000.00.

Receipts and Payments by cheque were:

Receipts: Rent from sub-tenant £1000; subscriptions £240; payment from cash (as above) £4000.

Payments: Rates £246; purchases of spare parts £1150; Telephone Expenses £195; mortgage interest £1592; mortgage repayments £1360;

At the end of the year subscriptions of £84 were due and £135 had been received in advance for the next year. Stocks of spare parts were valued at £755.

Show the calculation of the Accumulated Fund at the start of the year, a Receipts and Payment Account (Cash) and a Receipts and Payment Account (Bank), a Trading Account for Spare Parts, an Income and expenditure Account for the year and a Balance Sheet as at 31 March 19. . .

28 The Final Accounts of companies

28.1 What is a company?

A company is a business organisation, usually registered under the Companies Act 1985, which is given a separate legal entity by the authority of the Queen in Parliament. Such an organisation is called an 'incorporation', a word meaning 'given a body' — a separate body distinct in law from anyone else. Such an incorporation can do all the things an ordinary human being can do, it can own land and property, employ people, sue and be sued in the Courts, etc. Of course it cannot do personal things: it cannot get married, have children or die of old age. Just as it only came into existence by the force of law, it can only go out of existence by a legal process called **liquidation**. The assets of the company are sold off — turned into cash (liquid assets) and the money is given back to the members (shareholders) who are entitled to it. Then the company ceases to exist.

The reasons companies are so popular as business organisations (there are about two million companies in the UK alone) are these:

1 The shareholders of companies have limited liability — they cannot lose more than the money they paid for the shares they purchased — the capital of the company.

2 Companies are separate legal entities from the people who form them (the founder members or promoters of the company) and from the shareholders (who may be the original founder members or may have bought their shares later once the company was successful). If a company gets into financial difficulties the owners of that company, its shareholders at the time, are not affected — except that they may lose the money they have invested in that company. They are not, as are sole traders and partners, liable to the full extent of their wordly wealth, because shareholders have limited liability. Also, when a member (a shareholder) dies the company does not die, and is not subject to inheritance tax. The company continues — it cannot die. The shares in the company are either passed on in the dead member's will to the heirs, or they may be sold to pay the member's personal inheritance tax and a new owner becomes the shareholder.

We are not expected at this level of our studies to know much about the accounts of companies. We know an enormous amount anyway, because the book-keeping for companies is the same as the book-keeping for sole traders and partners. All the books of account, the day books, the Ledger, the Cash Book and the Petty Cash Book are the same —

though they are nearly always computerised as far as big companies are concerned. The Trading Account and the Profit and Loss Account are the same and the only changes are in the Appropriation Account (where the profits are shared up among the shareholders) and the Balance Sheet. We will learn how to do these in this chapter. The difficult part of accountancy for companies is in complying with the many detailed requirements of the Companies Act 1985. This we cannot learn at this stage.

What we are expected to know at this stage, and as we move into employment in companies it is extremely useful to know, is the background vocabulary of business life as far as companies are concerned. Very briefly, the chief features are given in Section 28.2.

28.2 The background to companies

The names of companies

The capital of companies is raised by selling shares to those who wish to be connected with the company. For private companies the shares may be sold only to the original founder members and their friends, but if a company 'goes public' and asks the Council of the Stock Exchange to allow its shares to be dealt in on the open market shares can be sold to the general public. The shareholders have limited liability, as explained above. If a company gets into difficulties (which means it cannot pay its debts), and the shareholders have limited liability and cannot lose more than they originally contributed, who *are* likely to lose their money? The answer is the creditors of the company. To warn anyone who supplies goods and services to a company the name of the company must end in the word Limited (or the Welsh equivalent) if it is a private company, or the words 'Public Limited Company' (PLC) if it is a public company. This is a warning — don't think companies are always big, reliable organisations. They are often reliable, of course, but they do have limited liability and they can get into difficulties. When they do it is the creditors who suffer.

A company might therefore be called something like Thomas Brown (Thames-side) Ltd, or Thomas Brown (Thames-side) PLC. As every company has to have a name that is different from every other company it is often necessary to put in a place name in the title to reduce the chances of having someone else with a name the same as your name.

The types of shares issued

The most important shares in a company are called **ordinary shares**. They are entitled to share equally in the profits (and the losses) of the business, so they are often called **equity shares**. When you hear anyone talking about **equities** they simply mean ordinary shares. However, as ordinary shares also carry the losses of the business, whereas other shares may not (see preference shares below) the term equity shares is also used to refer to the 'risk-bearing' shares. Ordinary shares are always voting shares; they get a vote (one share = one vote) at the Annual General Meeting.

It follows that anyone with 50% of the Ordinary Shares + 1 more share can outvote everyone else and control the company. Actually in most companies even 30% of the voting shares will give a person control, because so many small shareholders do not bother to vote. In a take-over bid the bidder is trying to get about 30–35% of the voting shares, and thus get a controlling interest in the company.

Preference shares are issued as a way of attracting further capital from people who do not like to buy ordinary shares because they are a little risky. These shares have preference over ordinary shares both as to the dividend paid and for repayment in the event of the company being liquidated. The rate of interest is usually specified in the title so that we might have 9% Preference Shares. If profits are made the preference shareholders get a 9% dividend, after which the ordinary shareholders — if there are any profits left — get whatever dividend is recommended by the directors and approved at the Annual General Meeting.

You might question if the preference shareholders get a safe dividend and reasonably certain repayment in the event of liquidation, why does anyone buy ordinary shares? The answer is that ordinary shares, especially in prosperous times do very much better. Thus the directors might recommend 'Pay the preference shareholders their 9% and 20% to the ordinary shareholders.' Even more important, they are also entitled to all the reserves of the company.

The reserves of companies

The directors of companies rarely recommend the sharing out of all the profits made, for that removes money from the company and puts it into pockets of the shareholders. Instead they pay what is considered to be a fair dividend (say 20%) and all the rest is put into reserves. These are called **revenue reserves**, and they can be of two kinds. The first are called **special reserves** where the money is to be used for a particular purpose, such as a Plant Replacement Reserve Account. Here the money will be used to replace plant and machinery as it wears out. The other type is called a **general reserve**, where the money can be used for any purpose. The most common use is to equalize the dividend from year to year. Suppose a shareholder gets a dividend of 40% one year and 2% the next year. He would naturally be annoyed. If the first year the dividend is kept down to only 20% and the rest put in the General Reserve Account, in the second year although the profits have been very low the directors can still pay 20% dividend, using the revenue put away in the General Reserve Account last year. The shareholder is happy, with 20% each year (but actually worse off — because 42% in two years is better than 40%).

A further point is this. When profits are put away into reserves it means we don't pay out the money to the shareholders. All that money in the reserves is lying about loose in the company's accounts. If we don't do something with it someone may decide to spend it — new furniture and new carpets, etc. To avoid this we must either expand the business with it (in which case the share-holders cannot get it back as it has been spent on new machinery etc.) or we can buy investments with it — which will earn dividends for us and can always be sold if we need the money.

What is usually done is to buy a **balanced portfolio of investments**. This is a mixture of shares in other firms, and in Government stocks (gilt-edged securities). A balanced portfolio is one where we don't have 'all our eggs in one basket', but spread the investments around several industries and several companies, balancing some profitable (but risky) investments against others which are less profitable but very reliable.

Another type of reserve is a **capital reserve**. A capital reserve is one that may not be distributed to the shareholders as dividend because it is a capital profit not a revenue profit. We have already learned about one such profit — the capital profit that arises as land and buildings appreciate over the years. If a company up-grades the value of its premises to keep pace with inflation the profit made is a capital profit and is put into a capital reserve; an account such as Premises Revaluation Account.

Sometimes a company is set up to take over and run a business, and has to start doing so at once, even before its 'birth certificate' arrives. This is called a **Certificate of Incorporation**. Since a company is not allowed to make profits before it comes into existence the profits made are called **profits prior to incorporation** and are kept in a Profits Prior to Incorporation Account. They are a capital reserve, and may not be given to the shareholders as dividends because they are a capital profit not a revenue profit.

Debentures

When a loan is made to a company it is usual for a paper security to be issued to those making the loan. It is called a **debenture** and it gives a right to a representative of the debenture holders (usually an accountant or a solicitor) to take certain actions if the interest on the loan is not paid on the due date. This person, the **debenture trustee** has the right to seize certain assets of the company and sell them to get the debenture holders' money back. If it is a **fixed debenture** it is secured on the fixed assets, and the debenture trustee can sieze the premises plant and machinery, etc. in the event of default. If it is a floating debenture it floats over the current assets, the stock, which is moving in and out of the company's warehouses and the money in the bank. If the debenture interest is not paid the floating debenture 'crystallizes' and freezes all the stock movements so that the stock can be sold to find the money for the debenture holders.

There is a class of debentures called 'naked' debentures, which do not have any rights to seize assets in this way. As its name implies the debenture holders in this case are unprotected.

Debenture holders gets a lower rate of interest usually than, say, the dividend on preference shares, but it is very safe, and they rarely lose their money if the debenture trustee is doing his job. Debentures are therefore safe investments for the 'safe' end of a balanced portfolio.

Preliminary Expenses

When setting up a company, and particularly when going public, there are expenses which have to be incurred before the certificate of incorporation is issued. These expenses include fees to the Registrar of Companies, legal fees perhaps and in the case of a public company advertising expenses, administration costs and underwriting costs if the share issue is underwritten by an Issuing House. This means that if the general public do not buy the shares the issuing house will. When we pay these expenses we have very little to show for them except the fact that the company is a going concern. The sums spent are credited in the Cash Book and debited in the Preliminary Expenses Account, but this is a fictitious asset — there is nothing really to show for it. What we do with fictitious assets is explained later in this chapter.

The Ordinary Shareholders' Interest in the company

The last point to note before we prepare Company Final Accounts is this. Who gets what out of company profits? We have seen:

1 The debenture holders are not even shareholders, but creditors of the company who are paid their interest without fail, usually twice a year.

2 The preference shareholders, who were promised a fixed divided, say 9%, always get it if the company is making profits, though they may lose out in a bad year.

3 The ordinary shareholders get the dividend that is approved at the Annual General Meeting, but more of their profits are put in reserves, and there are also some capital reserves as well. Really all this money belongs to the ordinary shareholders not the preference shareholders who always take out their full share of profit. So in company final accounts it is best to show these profits all grouped together in a section called the Ordinary Shareholders' Interest in the Company.

We are now ready to learn Company Final Accounts.

28.3 The Appropriation Account and Balance Sheet of companies

The chief differences between an Appropriation Account for a partnership and an Appropriation Account for a company are as follows:

1 There is always a balance carried down from last year. With partnerships you can always share out the money to the last penny between the partners, but with a large number of shareholders this is not possible. If we have a million shares, even a million pennies is £10 000. In any case the directors do not give away the last penny of the profits to the shareholders; they keep a great deal of the profit to expand the company's activities. This retained profit must appear as a balance on the Appropriation Account, or some of it may be put away in a reserve account, as explained earlier. Since it is owed to the Ordinary Shareholders (it is their profit) it will always be a credit balance on the Appropriation Account (or the Reserve Account).

2 To this balance from last year we add this year's profit.

3 On the debit side we may use the profits earned in a number of different ways. These are:

(a) We first set aside a sum sufficient to cover the Government's share of the profit — the Corporation Tax.

(b) We may then write off any intangible asset (such as Goodwill) or any fictitious asset (such as Preliminary Expenses).

(c) We then transfer to Reserve Accounts whatever sums the directors have recommended should be placed to reserves.

(d) We then give whatever dividend is recommended by the directors and approved by the members (at the Annual General Meeting) to each class of shareholders.

(e) Finally the balance in the Appropriation Account will be carried down to the next year.

The final result will be an appropriation account as shown in Fig. 28.1. It is based upon an example which is given below. The Balance Sheet follows in Fig. 28.2.

Example 28.1

Here is the Trial Balance of ABC Ltd as at 31 December 19. . after the Trading and Profit and Loss Account have been drawn up.

	Dr £	Cr £
Profit & Loss A/c		102 500
Appropriation A/c balance 1 January		1 507
Ordinary Shares of £1 authorised and issued		100 000
9% Preference Shares of £1 authorised and issued		40 000
General Reserve A/c		20 000
Preliminary Expenses A/c	4 000	
Premises	86 000	
Plant and Machinery	25 000	
Fixtures and Fittings	38 000	
Motor Vehicles	19 000	
8% Debentures		20 000
Stock	28 567	
Debtors and Creditors	5 000	8 000
Bank	27 250	
Cash	850	
Provision for Bad Debts		1 000
Rates in advance	420	
Wages due		350
Investments (Current Asset)	58 170	
Insurance in advance	1 100	
	£ 293 357	293 357

Notes
1 The dividend on the preference shares is to be paid.
2 The ordinary shareholders are to have a dividend of 20%.
3 £2000 of the preliminary expenses is to be written off.
4 A reserve for Corporation Tax is to be created of £50 000.
5 £5000 is to be placed in a Plant Replacement Reserve Account.
6 £20 000 is to be added to the General Reserve Account.

Appropriation Account for year ending 31 December 19. .

19. .		£	19. .		£
Reserve for			Balance	b/d	1 507
Corporation Tax		50 000	Net Profit		102 500
Preliminary Expenses		2 000			
Plant Replacement					
Reserve		5 000			
General Reserve		20 000			
Preference					
Dividend		3 600			
Ordinary Dividend		20 000			
Balance	c/d	3 407			
		£104 007			£104 007
			19. .		£
			Balance	b/d	3 407

Fig. 28.1 The Appropriation Account of a company

28.4 The Balance Sheet in vertical style

Because the Balance Sheet of a company is a fairly detailed statement it is sometimes presented in vertical style, with the capital and other liabilities shown first and then the words Represented By: and the assets listed in the usual way. The only advantage in such a presentation is that it gives slightly more room to display all the details. The disadvantage is that it makes nonsense of the words 'Balance Sheet' since the very idea of a balance is of two scales weighed against one another horizontally so that we can see that the two sides are of equal importance.

In the presentation shown in Fig. 28.3 the opportunity has been taken to show two other points:

1 The method of showing depreciation of the fixed assets has been made clear. The figures used are imaginary — in real life we would have needed extra figures on the Trial Balance shown in Example 28.1.

2 Some accountants like to bring the current liabilities over to the assets side and deduct them, to bring out what is known as the **net working capital**. The net working capital is the capital that is left over to run the business after we have purchased the fixed capital. This is explained more fully in Chapter 30. Briefly, after we have purchased the fixed assets we need more funds to run the business, and these are the current assets. However as we have to pay the current liabilities very shortly we must allow for these first, so that the formula for net working capital is:

$$\text{Net working capital} = \text{current assets} - \text{current liabilities}$$
$$= \text{£120 357} - \text{£31 950}$$
$$= \underline{\text{£88 407}}$$

ABC Ltd: Balance Sheet as at 31 December 19. .

Ordinary Shareholders Interest in the Co.	£		Fixed Assets		£
	Authorised	Issued	Premises		86 000
Ordinary Shares of			Plant and Machinery		25 000
£1 fully paid	100 000	100 000	Fixtures and Fittings		38 000
			Motor Vehicles		19 000
Plant Replacement					168 000
Reserve		5 000			
General			Current Assets		
Reserve	20 000		Stock		28 567
Additions	20 000		Investments		58 170
		40 000	Debtors	5000	
			Less Provision	1000	
Balance on					4 000
Appropriation Account		3 407			
			Bank		27 250
		48 407	Cash		850
		148 407	Rates in Advance		420
Less Preliminary			Insurance in advance		1 100
Expenses	4 000				120 357
Amount written					
off	2 000				
Ordinary shareholders equity		2 000			
		146 407			
Preference Shareholders Interest in the Co.					
		Authorised			
9% Preference Shares					
of £1 fully paid	40 000	40 000			
8% Debentures		20 000			
Corporation Tax Reserve		50 000			
Current Liabilities					
Creditors	8 000				
Ordinary Dividend	20 000				
Preference Dividend	3 600				
Wages due	350				
		31 950			
		£ 288 357			£288 357

Fig. 28.2 The Balance Sheet of a company

Notes

1 The assets side is very similar to the assets side of a sole trader's Balance Sheet. However the depreciation would in fact be shown on the fixed assets, though it was left out in this example to save space. For those who would like to see this it is shown in the vertical style Balance Sheet of Fig. 28.3.

2 On the liabilities side the capital has been split into two parts, showing the Ordinary Shareholders' Interest in the company separate from the Preference Shareholders' Interest in the company, as explained in Section 28.2 above. The point is that the preference shareholders always take their full dividend if profits are being made, and never leave any of their entitlement in the business. The ordinary shareholders by contrast leave quite large sums in reserve. The

total value of the 100 000 ordinary shares is actually £146 407, so that each share is actually worth £1.46. This partly explains why shares on sale on the Stock Exchange are often above par — the share value is not only worth the par value (£1) but it is also entitled to a share of the reserves ploughed back over the years. Shares also fluctuate with expectations of the investors, so they may be worth more (or less) than the strict accounting value on the Balance Sheet.

3 The Companies Act 1985 states that fictitious assets such as Preliminary Expenses must not appear as assets on the Balance Sheet. Naturally we write such assets off as quickly as we can in the first few years of the business but until we can do so the debit balance left (a fictitious asset) must not be shown on the assets side but must be deducted from the Ordinary Shareholders' Interest in the Company to show that really this asset is not worth anything to the owners of the business.

4 Study the Balance Sheet carefully before trying some of the exercises given at the end of the chapter.

28.5 Exercises: Company Final Accounts

1 Here is the Trial Balance of Smith Ltd as at 31 December 19. . after the Trading and Profit and Loss Account have been drawn up. Prepare an Appropriation Account and Balance Sheet of the company.

	£	£
Profit & Loss A/c		86 297
Appropriation A/c balance 1 January		1 542
Ordinary Shares of £1 authorised and issued		80 000
9% Preference Shares of £1 authorised and issued		50 000
General Reserve A/c		10 000
Preliminary Expenses A/c	3 500	
Premises	72 000	
Plant and Machinery	35 000	
Fixtures and Fittings	18 500	
Motor Vehicles	19 000	
8% Debentures		15 000
Stock	19 542	
Debtors and Creditors	3 850	4 950
Bank	8 641	
Cash	1 015	
Provision for Bad Debts		385
Rates in advance	360	
Light and Heat bill due		424
Investments (Current Asset)	66 540	
Insurance in advance	650	
	£ 248 598	248 598

Notes
1 The dividend on the preference shares is to be paid.
2 The ordinary shareholders are to have a dividend of 25%.
3 £1750 of the preliminary expenses is to be written off.
4 A reserve for corporation tax is to be created of £35 000.
5 £2500 is to be placed in a Plant Replacement Reserve Account.
6 £15 000 is to be added to the General Reserve Account.

ABC Ltd: Balance Sheet in Vertical Style as at 31 December 19. .

Ordinary Shareholders' Interest in the Company		Authorised £	Issued £
Ordinary Shares of £1 fully paid		100 000	100 000
Plant Replacement Reserve	5 000		
General Reserve	20 000		
Additions	20 000		
	40 000		
Balance on Appropriation Account	3 407		
			48 407
			148 407
Less Preliminary Expenses	4 000		
Amounts written off	2 000		2 000
Ordinary shareholders' equity			146 407

Preference Shareholders' Interest in the Company			
9% Preference Shares of £1 fully paid		Authorised	
		40 000	40 000
8% Debentures			20 000
Corporation Tax Reserves			50 000
			£256 407

Represented by:

Fixed Assets	At Cost £	Less Depreciation £	Value £
Premises	86 000	—	86 000
Plant and Machinery	34 000	9 000	25 000
Fixtures and Fittings	50 000	12 000	38 000
Motor Vehicles	28 000	9 000	19 000
	198 000	30 000	168 000

Current Assets			
Stock		28 567	
Investments		58 170	
Debtors	5 000		
Less Provisions	1 000		
		4 000	
Bank		27 250	
Cash		850	
Rates in Advance		420	
Insurance in Advance		1 100	
		120 357	

Less Current Liabilities			
Creditors	8 000		
Ordinary dividend	20 000		
Preference Dividend	3 600		
Wages due	350		
		31 950	
Net working capital			88 407
			£256 407

Fig. 28.3 The Balance Sheet in vertical style

2 Here is the Trial Balance of Field Ltd as at 31 December 19. . after the Trading and Profit and Loss Account have been drawn up. Prepare an Appropriation Account and Balance Sheet of the company.

	£	
Profit & Loss A/c		75 240
Appropriation A/c balance 1 January 19. .		5 248
Ordinary Shares of £1 authorised and issued		60 000
8% Preference Shares of £1 authorised and issued		60 000
General Reserve A/c		15 000
Preliminary Expenses A/c	4 800	
Premises	86 500	
Plant and Machinery	18 000	
Fixtures and Fittings	16 500	
Motor Vehicles	24 000	
8% Debentures		20 000
Stock	15 750	
Debtors and Creditors	4 850	5 650
Bank	26 838	
Cash	1 240	
Provision for Bad Debts		750
Rates in advance	420	
Wages due		550
Investments (Current Asset)	44 000	
Printing expenses due		460
	£ 242 898	242 898

Notes
1 The dividend on the preference shares is to be paid.
2 The ordinary shareholders are to have a dividend of 10%.
3 £1200 of the preliminary expenses to be written off.
4 A reserve for corporation tax is to be created of £30 000.
5 £5000 is to be placed in a Machinery Replacement Reserve Account.
6 £20 000 is to be added to the General Reserve Account.

3 From the information below prepare the Profit and Loss Account and the Appropriation Account of XYZ Ltd for the year ending 31 December 19. . and the Balance Sheet as at that date.

Trial Balance of XYZ Ltd as at 31 December 19. .

	Dr £	Cr £
8% Debentures		5 000
Stock	35 225	
Ordinary Shares of £1 fully paid		25 000
Debenture Interest for half year	200	
Bad Debts	450	
Discount Received		1 225
Debtors and Creditors	2 900	4 100
Premises	41 000	
Furniture & Fittings	12 200	
Gross Profit		66 975

	Dr £	Cr £
Salaries	22 500	
Bank	12 505	
Rent	4 100	
Rates	1 520	
Appropriation Account 1 January		1 400
9% Preference Shares of £1 fully paid		30 000
General Expenses	1 100	
	£133 700	133 700

Notes
1 Rent is due £100.
2 Rates in advance £220.
3 The rest of the debenture interest is to be paid.
4 Depreciate the furniture and fittings by 10%.
5 Pay the preference dividend and also a 20% dividend on the ordinary shares.
6 Management also decides to put £8000 into a General Reserve Account and to set up a Reserve for Corporation Tax of £15 000.
7 On the Balance Sheet bring out the figure for net working capital.

4 From the information below, prepare Final Accounts for Brown Ltd for the year ending 31 December 19. . and a Balance Sheet as at that date.

Trial Balance of Brown Ltd as at 31 December 19. .

	£	£
Purchase & Sales	25 000	78 000
General Expenses	15 500	
Salaries	18 500	
8% Fixed Debentures		16 000
Debenture Interest, half year only	640	
Motor vehicles	22 000	
Plant & Machinery at cost	14 000	
10% Preference Shares of £1 authorised and issued		30 000
Ordinary Shares of £1, authorised and issued		20 000
Debtors & Creditors	5000	4 000
Stock 1 January	18 250	
Bank	44 750	
Cash in hand	360	
Commission Received		15 600
Appropriation Account 1 January		400
	£ 164 000	164 000

Notes
1 Closing Stock at the end of the year = £16 275.
2 The rest of the debenture interest is to be paid.
3 The Plant and Machinery Account is to be depreciated by 10%.
4 The Motor Vehicles are to be depreciated by 10%.
5 The preference dividend is to be paid and the ordinary shareholders are to have a dividend of 25%.
6 A Reserve for Corporation Tax Account is to be opened with a reserve of £10 000.
7 £8000 is to be placed in a General Reserve Account.
8 Present the Balance Sheet in vertical style in such a way as to bring out the net current assets (net working capital).

29 Manufacturing Accounts

29.1 Basic ideas on accounting for manufacturers

If an enterprise manufactures items for sale it must carry out a range of activities all of which cost money. These costs must be recovered when the product is sold, and therefore they enter into the pricing arrangements for each unit of output, whether it is an item of furniture, a bag of cement or a gallon of petrol. The whole procedure is called **costing** and is a separate subject in its own right, and cannot be covered in this book. However, we must just learn enough to see how the Final Accounts of a manufacturing business are worked out. The first thing to do is to learn some new pieces of vocabulary.

Prime costs and overheads

It is usual to divide all the costs of manufacturing into these two main groups. Prime costs are the costs of items actually embodied in the finished product. For example if we are making motor vehicles we shall need steel of various sorts, aluminium, all sorts of components, wheels, tyres, etc. The word 'prime' means first. Before we can make a car we must have these materials first. For every car we shall need one set of parts, and the number required varies with output. Sometimes prime costs are called variable costs for this reasons, or they may be called direct costs since the items purchased go directly into the product.

The most common prime costs are raw materials, components and fittings bought in to be worked into the finished product (for example hinges and handles in the furniture trade) and the labour of production workers. Some firms treat power as a prime cost, at least the part of the electricity bill that is used to drive machines (lighting will be treated as an overhead cost).

Overhead costs

These are costs which do not go directly into the product, but have to be spread around the various units of output in some fair way. Thus if design costs come to £1 000 000 and we make 50 000 cars the design costs must be carried by each vehicle made — which is £20 per car. Since they do not vary with output they are often called fixed costs, or on-costs or overhead costs. You might like to notice here that if we double the output of cars we double the prime costs, since we need a set of parts for every car, but the overhead costs per car fall, because — for example — the £1 000 000 referred to earlier is now to be spread over 100 000 cars, at

Manufacturing Account for year ended 31 December 19. .
Prime Cost Section

		£			£
Opening Stock (Raw Materials)		16 259	Prime Cost	c/d	97 109
Purchases		42 654			
		58 913			
Less Closing Stock		11 784			
Cost of raw materials used		47 129			
Factory overheads:		38 726			
Fittings used		11 254			
		£97 109			£97 109

Cost of Manufactured Goods Section

		£		£
Prime Cost	b/d	97 109	Cost of Manufactured	
Factory overhead:			Goods	122 657
Light and heat	725			
Rates	1 400			
Supervision wages	17 246			
General expenses	8 184			
		27 555		
		124 664		
Work in progress:				
At start	+8 284			
At end	−10 291			
		−2 007		
		£122 657		£122 657

Fig. 29.1 (a) The Manufacturing Account

Notes
1 The various prime costs are transferred into the Prime Cost Section and this gives us the total prime cost of the goods produced. This is carried into the Cost of Manufactured Goods Section.
2 To this section we add the overhead costs, and we also take the Work in Progress into account.
3 It is important to understand what goes on in the factory as far as work-in-progress is concerned. As soon as production starts up on the first working day of the new year the £8284 of goods which were in progress at the start goes through the production schedule and on into the Selling or Marketing Department. At the end of the year on the last day some of the raw materials and components in the factory are trapped in the factory when work ceases. This work-in-progress does not become part of this year's output — it will be next year's output. So the starting work-in-progress is added to this year's output but the closing work-in-progress has to be deducted. The net result in this case is a deduction, because the closing work-in-progress was greater. So the cost of the manufacturered goods was £122 657.

Trading Account for year ended 31 December, 19. .

	£		£
Opening stock of finished goods	23 528	Sales	196 384
Cost of manufactured goods	122 657		
	146 185		
Less Closing stock	18 764		
Cost of stock sold	127 421		
Warehouse wages	17 268		
Warehouse expenses	3 568		
Cost of Sales	148 257		
Gross profit	48 127		
	£196 384		£196 384

Profit and Loss Account for year ended 31 December 19. .

		£
	Gross profit	48 127

Fig. 29.1 (b) The Trading and Profit and Loss Accounts after manufacturing

Notes

1 In the Trading Account of a manufacturing concern the 'Purchases' line is replaced by the 'Cost of Manufactured Goods' line — since the purchases would be raw materials in the Prime Cost Section.

2 Apart from (a) above the Trading Account is unchanged and the gross profit is found in the usual way, and is carried to the Profit and Loss Account as usual.

You should now try some of the simple Manufacturing Account exercises on page 280.

£10 per time. Of course we might make a little saving on prime costs too by buying in bulk, but generally speaking the main saving is on over-heads which fall per unit of output as we increase production.

The most common overhead costs are factory light and heat, factory rent and rates, supervision wages, management expenses, telephone expenses, forklift vehicle expenses, clearing the production lines, etc.

There are a number of special features in Manufacturing Accounts. They are best studied by working through an example, bearing in mind the matters raised in Section 29.1.

Here is a typical Manufacturing Account exercise.

Work in progress (or semi-manufactured goods)

Accounts have to be worked out on an annual basis, and when work stops on the last day of the year we have a lot of unfinished items going through the factory. Some of them will only have had the very first processes carried out, while others will be almost ready to leave the factory and go to depots to be sold. On average we can say they are half completed, and this work-in-progress has to be treated very much as a kind of stock — we have some items in progress at the start of the year and some items in progress at the end of the year. If we count them and value them at half-cost we get a figure for work in progress.

Stock in Manufacturing Accounts

When we do a set of Final Accounts for a manufacturer we do a Manufacturing Account in two parts — a Prime Cost Section and a Cost of Manufactured Goods Section. These goods are then handed on to the Trading Account to be sold. We therefore have three different sets of stock in Manufacturing Accounts; a stock of raw materials (which are a prime cost), a stock of work-in-progress, or partly-finished goods, and a stock of finished goods. The raw materials go in the Prime Cost Section, the work-in-progress goes in the Cost of Manufactured Goods Section and the finished goods go in the Trading Account.

In examinations it is usual to test students on Manufacturing Accounts by giving them only part of a Trial Balance — otherwise an exercise would take too long. It is usual to ask students to show the Manufacturing Account and Trading Account only — but of course in real life we would go on to do the Profit and Loss Account and Balance Sheet — with an Appropriation Account for partnerships and limited companies.

29.2 A simple example of a Manufacturing Account

The manufacturing Account is shown below, with some explanatory notes. This is followed by the Trading Account, and the opening line of the Profit and Loss Account, with some more notes.

EXAMPLES 29.1

A. Smith is in business manufacturing components for the motor vehicle industry. From the figures given below produce a Manufacturing Account and Trading Account for the year ended 31 December 19. ., and carry the gross profit you find into the Profit and Loss Account.

	£
Opening Stocks:	
Raw materials	16 259
Work in progress	8 284
Finished Goods	23 528
Closing Stocks:	
Raw materials	11 784
Work in progress	10 291
Finished Goods	18 764
Purchases (raw materials)	42 654
Factory Wages	38 726
Fittings (used in product)	11 254
Factory Light and Heat	725
Factory rates	1 400
Supervision wages	17 246
Factory general expenses	8 184
Warehouse wages	17 268
Warehouse expenses	3 568
Sales	196 384

29.3 Exercises: Simple Manufacturing Accounts

1 P. Sinclair is in business manufacturing electrical components. From the following information prepare his Manufacturing Account and Trading Account. Carry the gross profit to the start of the Profit and Loss Account.

	£
Opening Stock at 1 April 19. .	
Raw materials	7 081
Work-in-progress	4 216
Finished goods	17 295
Closing Stocks at 31 March 19. .	
Raw materials	5 504
Work-in-progress	3 214
Finished goods	11 724
Purchases of raw materials	38 257
Direct wages (prime cost)	52 754
Power (prime cost)	3 824
Factory overheads	
Light and heat	1 978
Rates	2 800
Maintenance and repairs	7 342
Supervision salaries	27 584
Product development	9 560
Sales	380 274
Warehouse wages	17 294
Warehouse expenses	9 983

2 Maira Malik is in business manufacturing fashion garments. From the following information prepare her Manufacturing Account and Trading Account. Carry the gross profit to the start of the Profit and Loss Account.

	£
Opening Stock at 1 January 19. .	
Materials	17 256
Work-in-progress	10 525
Finished goods	19 858
Closing Stock at 31 December 19. .	
Materials	14 255
Work-in-progress	16 744
Finished goods	23 851
Purchases of materials	48 816
Direct wages (prime cost)	37 250
Trimmings (prime cost)	8 250
Factory overheads	
Light and heat	1 721
Rates	2 400
Maintenance and repairs	1 510
Supervision salaries	8 250
Product development	3 458
Sales	199 858
Warehouse wages	18 280
Warehouse expenses	17 350

3 Diane Hughes is in business manufacturing safety equipment. From the following information prepare her Manufacturing Account and Trading Account. Carry the gross profit to the start of the Profit and Loss Account.

	£
Opening Stocks at 1 January 19. .	
Raw materials	17 256
Work-in-progress	11 746
Finished goods	23 816
Closing Stock at 31 December 19. .	
Raw materials	19 381
Work-in-progress	9 560
Finished goods	41 726
Purchases of raw materials	168 254
Direct wages (prime cost)	38 175
Power (prime cost)	7 925
Factory overheads	
Light and heat	4 925
Rates	6 500
Maintenance and repairs	8 352
Supervision salaries	17 265
Product development	9 295
Sales	384 726
Warehouse wages	27 850
Warehouse expenses	16 752

29.4 Showing a manufacturing profit

There is one disadvantage about the Manufacturing Accounts discussed already, and that is that they shed no light on the efficiency of the factory. For example in Fig. 29.1 (a) and (b) a gross profit was made of £48 127, but was the profit made by the skill of the manufacturer (the factory's effort) or was it clever selling by the Sales Department? We have really no idea. Perhaps it was a bit of both.

Suppose we can find out what the output obtained by the factory's efforts would have cost us if we had purchased the product from someone else. Suppose for example, we find that we could purchase them for £100 000. Since they cost us (see Fig. 29.1 (a)) £122 657 to make, there would be little point in keeping the factory going because we can buy them for £100 000 and save £22 657. Of course it means dismissing a lot of employees, which we may hesitate to do, but it is the sort of problem management will have to consider. At least, if they know about it, they can consider what to do. See what happens to the accounts when we bring out the loss on manufacture. To save space we will leave out the Prime Cost Section which will be the same as in Fig. 19.1(a). All we are going to do is carry the factory output to the Trading Account at market value (not at manufacturing cost as before).

Cost of Manufactured Goods Section

		£		£
Prime cost	b/d	97 109	Trading Account (market value of manufactured goods)	100 000
Factory overheads:				
Light and heat	725		Profit and Loss (loss on manufacturing)	22 657
Rates	1 400			
Supervision wages	17 246			
General expenses	8 184			
		27 555		
		124 664		
Work-in-progress:				
At start	+8 284			
At end	−10 291			
		−2 007		
		£122 657		£122 657

Fig. 29.2 (a) Taking account of a loss on the factory

Notes

1 Instead of debiting the Trading Account with the cost of the goods manufactured, we only debit it with the market value of the goods as if we had purchased them at market price from another factory.

2 This leaves a balance on this section of the Manufacturing Account which is the loss on the factory. This is carried to the Profit and Loss Account as a loss.

Trading Account for year ended 31 December 19. .

	£		£
Opening stock of finished goods	23 528	Sales	196 384
Market value of output	100 000		
	123 528		
Less Closing stock	18 764		
Cost of stock sold	104 764		
Warehouse wages	17 268		
Warehouse expenses	3 568		
Cost of Sales	125 600		
Gross profit	70 784		
	£196 384		£196 384

Profit and Loss Account for year ended 31 December 19. .

	£		£
Manufacturing loss	22 657	Gross profit	70 784

Fig. 29.2 (b) Increased profits on selling revealed

Notes

1 Since the Trading Account now only has to pay the market price for the goods, and not the manufacturing cost the Cost of Sales is less and the gross profit is more. We can see that the salesmen have been doing a really good job, getting good prices for our products — but previously their good efforts were hidden by the loss on the factory.

2 The profit over-all has not changed, because the profit of £70 784 is reduced by the loss on the factory

$$£70\ 784 - £22\ 657 = £48\ 127$$

This is the same profit as in Fig 29.1 (b).

29.5 'Make or buy' decisions

Part of the purpose of bringing out the profit (if any) on manufacturing is to help us with 'make or buy' decisions. It seems obvious that if someone can supply us with exactly the same item that we are making at a lower price there must be something wrong with our own methods of production. At first glance it might seem we should close our factory and buy-in the product from the more efficient producer. However, it may not be as simple as all that. For example:

1 Our competitor could be cutting the quality in some way — for example by not doing enough inspection work to ensure quality control. If so the complaints will be made to us, not him, and all we shall have bought is a load of trouble.

2 He may be short of work now, and have spare capacity at the moment to make our product, but will this always be the case? At the very least he might raise the price for continuing to make our product and we may not be able to start our own plant up again.

3 The present product will soon date. It must develop and change over the years. Will he put the research and development costs in to keep the product at the forefront of the market?

4 Do we really want to dismiss all our workers and disband the expertise we have built up? What will it do to the workers and their families, and to the town and to our own brand name in the market place?

These are the sort of considerations that need to be taken into account, but the book-keepers have to make the figures available so that management can know what the true position is.

You should now try some of these exercises which show the true value of the factory output in each case. If a profit is made on the Manufacturing Account it will of course be taken to the credit side of the Profit and Loss Account. If a loss is made it will appear as a debit on Profit and Loss Account as shown in Fig. 29.1(b) opposite.

29.6 Exercises: More difficult Manufacturing Accounts

1 M. Neil is in business manufacturing hair driers. From the following information prepare his Manufacturing Account and Trading Account. A competitor offers to make and supply the same number of hair driers to his exact specifi-

cations for £200 000. Produce your Manufacturing Account to bring out clearly the manufacturing profit, or loss and thus help Neil decide what to do about this offer. How would you advise him?

	£
Opening Stocks at 1 January 19. .	
Raw materials	12 060
Work-in-progress	5 214
Finished goods	19 800
Closing Stock at 31 December 19. .	
Raw materials	7 876
Work-in-progress	4 238
Finished goods	17 450
Purchases of raw materials	68 245
Direct wages (prime cost)	36 315
Power (prime cost)	10 214
Factory overheads:	
Light and heat	3 178
Rates	2 400
Maintenance and repairs	3 525
Supervision salaries	18 985
Product development	1 280
Sales	246 725
Warehouse wages	13 295
Warehouse expenses	8 164

2 Anne Mitchell is in business manufacturing leather trimmings for the fashion trade. From the following information prepare her Manufacturing Account and Trading Account. Another supplier has offered to supply the same type of goods in the same quantities for £87 500. Bring out Anne's manufacturing profit or loss, and thus show whether this offer should improve her position. How would you advise her?

	£
Opening Stocks at 1 January 19. .	
Raw materials	3 254
Work-in-progress	2 164
Finished goods	5 984
Closing Stocks at 31 December 19. .	
Raw materials	4 281
Work-in-progress	3 275
Finished goods	6 782
Purchases of raw materials	37 254
Direct wages (prime cost)	28 564
Factory overheads:	
Light and heat	1 795
Rates	2 800
Maintenance and repairs	4 525
Supervision salaries	17 254
Product development	1 160
Sales	149 250
Warehouse wages	17 124
Warehouse expenses	4 925

3 Ken Hom is in business manufacturing beachwear. From the following information prepare his Manufacturing Account and Trading Account. A colleague from Hong Kong offers to supply the same volume of production in a similar range according to his specifications for £180 000. Use this figure to work out a manufacturing profit (or loss) and thus bring out the exact position. What advice would you offer Ken Hom about this proposal?

	£
Opening Stocks at 1 January 19. .	
Raw materials	13 256
Work-in-progress	7 314
Finished goods	29 520
Closing Stocks at 31 December 19. .	
Raw materials	12 995
Work-in-progress	5 815
Finished goods	16 720
Purchases of raw materials	54 621
Direct wages (prime cost)	47 854
Power (prime cost)	1 254
Factory overheads:	
Light and heat	669
Rates	6 400
Maintenance and repairs	4 250
Supervision salaries	16 725
Product development	14 985
Sales	320 000
Warehouse wages	17 265
Warehouse expenses	5 384

30 Assessing the accounts of a business

30.1 Accounting ratios

The whole purpose of book-keeping is to establish control over the affairs of a business and to decide whether they have been economically, honestly and profitably conducted. We should also be able to compare them with similar enterprises and decide whether the capital invested in them was wisely invested, or could it have been more usefully employed elsewhere in some other enterprise or some other industry.

To do this we use a number of **accounting ratios**. These are statistics derived from the figures provided by the book keeping, and show relative performance, not actual performance. Relative figures (ratios) often give a more meaningful set of figures than actual results. For example, suppose the profit made on one business is £20 000 and another business makes £25 000 it might appear that the second business is better run. If we are then told that the first business has a capital of £20 000 and the second business has a capital of £100 000 it is clear that the first business makes 100% profit on the capital invested while the second makes only 25%. It appears that the first business is run better than the second. Relative to the capital invested the profit of £20 000 is better than the profit of £25 000. If asked to make a loan to these two firms a banker would look more favourably on the first business.

To study this section of the work we must use a set of final accounts and since we have used it before we will study the books of K. Marshall, from Chapters 20, 21 and 22. First, the Trading Account.

30.2 Analysing the Trading Account

From the Trading Account we can work out the following ratios:
(a) the **gross profit percentage**
(b) the **rate of stock turn**

The Gross Profit Percentage

This is the ratio which helps us understand how our business is doing as far as the trading activities are concerned, and enables us to compare this year with last year, this quarter with last quarter (or better we could say this quarter with the same quarter last year). Firstly let us remind ourselves of the Trading Account of K. Marshall. This is given in Fig. 30.1.

K. Marshall
Trading Account for year ended 31 December 19. .

	£		£
Opening Stock	6 985	Sales	98 260
Purchases	37 900	*Less* Sales Returns	1 260
Add Carriage In	855	Net turnover	97 000
	38 755		
Less Purchases Return	155		
Net Purchases	38 600		
Total Stock available	45 585		
Less Closing Stock	9 762		
Cost of stock sold	35 823		
Warehouse Wages	13 250		
Cost of sales	49 073		
Gross Profit (to P/L A/c)	47 927		
	£97 000		£97 000

Fig. 30.1 A Trading Account in good style

The formula for the gross profit percentages is:

$$\text{Gross profit percentage} = \frac{\text{Gross profit}}{\text{Turnover}} \times 100$$

$$= \frac{£47\ 927}{£97\ 000} \times 100$$

$$= 49.4\%$$

This might seem to be a very good rate of profit per cent, but we must remember it is *gross* profit percentage not *net* profit percentage. We shall see the net profit percentage later in this chapter. In fact we do need a fairly high rate of gross profit percentage if we are going to make enough profit to cover all the overheads of our business which are of course deducted in the Profit and Loss Account. The biggest single cause of bankruptcies among small businesses is a low gross profit percentage. People who are new to business think that if they add on 10% to cost price they will be making a reasonable profit, but they should be adding on at least 40% — preferably 50% and in many trades even 300% is not unknown.

The chief use of a gross profit percentage figure is to compare this year with last year — to show what is happening to the gross profit percentage. It will rarely be exactly the same from year to year, but it is usual to take a close look if it varies by more than 3%. This is because, as a rough guide the gross profit percentage should be the same from year to year — in other words a constant. To prove this point imagine that next year K. Marshall does twice as much business — £194 000. Of course he will buy more goods (purchases) and employ more labour to handle the extra goods, but the profit should go up as well. So if we imagine that doubles too, we have:

$$\text{Gross Profit Percentage} = \frac{£95\ 854}{£194\ 000} \times 100$$
$$= \underline{49.4\%}$$

Although the figures double the ratio remains the same, because it is a relative figure not an actual figure. The relationship between sales and profit is still the same.

A fall in gross profit percentage

It follows that if gross profit percentage should be the same from year to year, and it isn't, for some reason, we should ask 'Why has it changed'. Suppose it has fallen to 44% from 49.4%. What can have caused the fall? The possible answers are:

1 Someone is stealing the takings. This makes the sales figure smaller than it should be.

2 Someone is stealing the stock. This makes the 'cost of stock sold' higher, but in fact it hasn't been sold it has been stolen, either by shoplifters or by the staff.

3 It could be other types of stock losses; breakages in the china department, food going bad in the grocery department or the greengrocery department.

4 It could be bad buying — we are having to sell goods at cheap prices to clear unfashionable items.

5 It could be inflation — prices are rising but we are slow to pass them on to the customer and as a result our profit margins are being squeezed.

6 It could be competition — we are having to lower our prices to meet competition and consequently the volume of business is the same but the takings are lower because each item is lower in price.

Clearly, all these things require action to put them right. We must find out who is stealing the cash, or the stock. We must do what we can to reduce breakages and other stock losses, and we must make sure we pass increased prices on to the customer as soon as possible.

A rise in gross profit percentage

If the gross profit percentage rises there is no cause for concern; indeed we are delighted. It may be worth while finding out why the improvement has occurred. A new manager may have tightened up on shoplifting, staff thefts, poor buying, breakages, etc. We might feel he/she deserves a bonus for their efforts. It may be that our goods are increasingly popular and that we should do what we can to take advantage of this favourable trend.

The Rate of Stock Turnover

This is a very important ratio. It tells us how many times the stock turns over in a year. By 'turns over' we mean that we buy (or make) a certain amount of stock, sell it, and have to buy a further amount to sell again. Each time we do this we make a profit on the stock sold, so that the more rapid the turnover the more profit we make. Some stock must turn over everyday (e.g. newspapers) or very frequently (e.g. cut meats, eggs, fruit). Other stock may sell more slowly, for example furniture will not deteriorate all that much if kept in stock for three months — but until we sell it we don't make any profit, so a rapid turnover is desirable in every trade.

The formula for finding the rate of stock turnover is as follows:

$$\text{Rate of stock turnover} = \frac{\text{Cost of stock sold}}{\text{Average stock at cost price}}$$

There is another formula:

$$\text{Rate of stock turnover} = \frac{\text{Turnover}}{\text{Average stock at selling price}}$$

but this is not so easy to use since we have to alter the stock figures to selling price.

If we have prepared our Trading Account in good style (see Chapter 20) we have all the figures we need for Formula 1 on the Trading Account. In the case of K. Marshall, the average stock is taken as:

$$\text{Average stock} = \frac{\text{Opening Stock} + \text{Closing Stock}}{2}$$

$$= \frac{£6\,985 + £9\,762}{2}$$

$$= \frac{£16\,747}{2}$$

$$= £8\,373.50$$

Of course, if we do interim final accounts more frequently, say quarterly or even monthly, we could add up the quarterly stock figures and divide by 4, or the monthly stock figures and divide by 12.

Using this figure the rate of stock turnover is:

$$\text{Rate of stock turnover} = \frac{\text{Cost of stock sold}}{\text{Average stock at cost price}}$$

$$= \frac{£35\,823}{£8\,373.50}$$

$$= 4.3 \text{ times}$$

The answer is always a number, the number of times the stock turns over in a year. Is this a good rate of stock turnover or a poor rate? We cannot say, unless we know what merchandise the trader deals in. It would not do for newspapers, or weekly periodicals such as the *TV Times*. It would not do for new laid eggs. It might be quite good for bicycles, storage heaters, or Rolls Royce cars, which we might expect to have on our books for a month or two before a buyer of the right type was found.

We may find this figure easier to understand if we use it to find the number of days, weeks or months the average item is in stock during the year. If we divide 12 months or 52 weeks or 365 days by the rate of stock turnover we get this average time. In this case it is as follows:

12 (months) ÷ 4.3   = 2.8 months
52 (weeks) ÷ 4.3   = 12.1 weeks
365 (days) ÷ 4.3   = 84.9 days

How shall we improve the rate of stock turnover?

There are several ways of improving the rate of stock turnover. We can open more hours in the day, and more days in the week (within the limits set by law). In the United States many supermarkets are open 24 hours a day, seven days a week, and those who suffer from insomnia go out and do the week's shopping. We can advertise in local and national news media; put on special events and promotions; increase goodwill by courtesy, efficiency, competitive pricing and friendly service. Above all we can tighten stock control. Do not buy excessive quantities of slow-moving items!

There are difficulties with all such policies. If we increase advertising will it bring in enough extra business to cover the advertising costs, or is the market almost saturated anyway and likely to be unresponsive to our campaign. If we reduce the stock of slow-moving items will those who buy them go elsewhere and buy all their requirements from some other supplier who is prepared to hold them.

30.3 Exercises: Analysing the Trading Account

These calculations should be done (where appropriate) correct to one decimal place. Calculations may be used where available.

1 Tom Brown's Trading Account shows his turnover to be £283 000 and his gross profit to be £123 105. What is his gross profit percentage?

2 Matilda Moore trades as 'New Arrival'. Sales in the year of babywear, nursery equipment, etc. total £84 000 and the gross profit is £31 500. What is the gross profit percentage?

3 (a) Mohammed Akram trades in woven goods. His sales in the year are £585 650 and his gross profit is £172 180. What is his gross profit percentage (answer correct to one decimal place). (b) Last year the gross profit percentage was 34.2%. Suggest what sort of changes might have caused this fall in gross profit percentage.

4 Ken Ingrams runs a roadside cafe in a lay-by. He and a friend keep it open 16 hours a day, working 8 hours each. The annual takings are £32 240 and the gross profit is £16 894. (a) What is the gross profit percentage? (b) Last year the gross profit percentage was 60%. Is the difference worth investigating and what sort of changes could have occurred to explain it?

5 Maira Sijuwade has an average stock of £4500 and the cost of stock sold last year was £38 250. (a) What was her rate of stock turnover? (b) How many weeks was the average item in stock? (Answers correct to one decimal place, where necessary.)

6 Sandra Patel has an average stock of £13 875 in her grocery store, and the cost of stock sold last year was £144 300. (a) What was the rate of stock turnover? (b) How long was the average item in stock (answer in weeks).

7 Mrs A. is thinking of buying two businesses. She has the following monthly figures about them.

	Business No. 1	Business No. 2
Monthly turnover	£16 500	£19 000
Gross Profit	5 600	6 033
Opening Stock	2 358	5 176
Closing Stock	3 126	7 236
Cost of stock sold	9 520	11 254

(a) Find the gross profit percentage in each case and the rate of stock turnover.
(b) Which business would you say was the better choice.

8 Growing Ltd has expanded until it has four outlets A, B, C and D. The annual turnover and gross profit figures for the year just ended are:

	Turnover	Gross Profit
A	£18 000	£4 500
B	24 000	7 000
C	30 000	6 250
D	16 000	4 950

(a) Work out the gross profit percentage and decide which is the best outlet.
(b) What would you say about the results generally?

30.4 Analysing the Profit and Loss Account

The Profit and Loss Account can also be subjected to analysis and its results compared with the results in previous financial periods. The ratios we can extract from a Profit and Loss Account are:
   (a) the **net profit percentage**, and
   (b) **expense ratios**
To consider these ratios we will use the Profit and Loss Account of K. Marshall as shown in Fig. 30.2.

The net profit percentage
The formula for this ratio is:

$$\text{Net profit percentage} = \frac{\text{net profit}}{\text{turnover}} \times 100$$

In the case of K. Marshall's net profit it is:

$$\text{Net profit percentage} = \frac{£21\ 007}{£97\ 000} \times 100 = \underline{\underline{21.7\%}}$$

K. Marshall
Profit and Loss Account for year ended 31 December 19. .

	£		£
Carriage Out	1 750	Gross Profit	47 927
Rent and Rates	950	Commission Received	758
Light and Heat	684	Rent received	1 000
Insurance	560	Discount Received	790
Salaries	21 460		
Advertising	1 790		
Bad Debts	864		
Discount Allowed	280		
Postage	455		
Travelling Expenses	675		
	29 468		
Net Profit (to Capital A/c)	21 007		
	£50 475		£50 475

Fig. 30.2 The Profit and Loss Account

Students sometimes ask 'Is that a reasonable net profit percentage?', but, while it may be, we cannot judge a business's success on that basis. We try to get as much net profit as we can on our business, not only by charging our customers as much as the competition will allow (if we charge too much they will go elsewhere) but also by reducing our costs as much as possible. If our expenses grow, the net profit percentage will fall. The ratio that really answers the question 'How is our business doing?' is the **return on capital invested**, and a related ratio, the **return on capital employed**. We shall discuss these later. All we can say is that if our net profit percentage is high (and anything over about 15% is reasonable) then probably the business is sound enough.

What the net profit percentage *does* tell us is how we did this year (K. Marshall had a net profit percentage of 21.7%). As with gross profit percentage the net profit percentage tends to be constant from year to year. If nothing is actively changing to influence it then it should be the same. Even if the turnover increases or decreases the ratio should stay constant.

Suppose that last year the net profit percentage was 25%. What can have changed to give us a lower percentage this year?

1 It could be that the gross profit percentage has fallen — because of course a fall in the gross profit will affect the net profit. Assuming the gross profit is constant and not the cause of the trouble it could be:

2 One of the expenses, or several of them, have risen more than proportionally during the year. If the rent or rates have been drastically increased this will reduce the net profit and hence the net profit percentage. Similarly if salaries have increased because we took on more staff (or conceded big salary increases) but the volume of trade did not

rise to earn the profit to finance the increase the net profit will fall, and so will the net profit percentage. Similarly an expensive advertising campaign at the wrong time, or directed at the wrong section of the market, gives extra expense but no increase in sales to pay for the increase. We can check these expenses as shown in the next section on expense ratios.

3 The other adverse change is a fall in the various profits on the credit side — commission received, rent received, etc. If we have earned less of these profits in the year the net profit will fall and so will the net profit percentage. Sometimes we can't help it — for example if we had two rooms let to sub-tenants last year but this year we used one of them for storage space and only let one room we must take a drop in Rent Received Account. Just as we try to keep expenses down we should try to keep these miscellaneous receipts up, and if they have fallen away for some reason we should pursue them more vigorously in the year ahead.

Expense Ratios

To tell if an expense item has risen we need to work out an expense ratio. We usually do this to one decimal place.
The formula is:

$$\text{Expense ratio} = \frac{\text{expense item}}{\text{turnover}} \times 100$$

$$\text{So the salaries expense ratio} = \frac{\pounds 21\ 460}{\pounds 97\ 000} \times 100$$

$$= 22.1\%$$

Suppose last year the salaries expense ratio was 17.4%. This is a serious increase. Twenty-two per cent of our total takings is going on salaries (which is more than the entire profit). We can't do much about it, but if the office staff ask for another rise this year we shall be very tempted to tell them they can't have it.

30.5 Self-assessment questions

1 What is a gross profit percentage?
2 How do we find it?
3 What is special about the gross profit percentage?
4 List four things that could cause a fall in gross profit percentage.
5 What is the rate of stock turnover?
6 What is the formula for it?
7 A firm's average stock is £10 000 and it's cost of stock sold in the year was £180 000. What was the rate of stock turnover?
8 Was that a good rate of stock turnover?
9 What is the net profit percentage and what is the formula to find it?
10 What is an expense ratio, and what is the formula to find it?
11 Name three things that could cause a drop in net profit percentage.

30.6 Exercises: net profit percentage and expense ratios

In each case where appropriate give the answers correct to one decimal place. A calculator may be used on these calculations if available.

1 J. Phillimore has net profits of £31 265 on a turnover of £126 256. What is his net profit percentage?

2 Carla Inglis has a net profit from her boutique of £37 525 on a turnover of £185 562 in the year. What is her net profit percentage?

3 Lewis Cosford has a net profit of £19 286 on a turnover of £112 725. Two of the expenses in the Profit and Loss Account are Salaries £16 850 and rates £4800. Calculate:
(a) the net profit percentage
(b) the salaries expense ratio
(c) the rates expense ratio

4 Hong Ying has a restaurant which yields a net profit of £37 425 on a turnover of £147 256. Two of the expenses in the Profit and Loss Account are rent and rates £3850 and advertising £7950. Calculate:
(a) the net profit percentage
(b) the rent and rates expense ratio
(c) the advertising expense ratio

5 Sanjit Singh has a small factory which yields a net profit of £57 284 on a turnover of £385 260. What was his net profit percentage? He tells you that last year the net profit percentage was 18%, and asks whether you think his expenses of rent and rates £8500 and the salaries cost of £37 285 could be the cause of the poor results. Last year the rent and rates expense ratio was 1.8% and the salaries expense ratio stood at 12.9%.

6 Star Cabs is a small taxi service which at the end of the year has a net profit of £78 256 on a turnover of £285 620. What was its net profit percentage? The five proprietors who run it as a cooperative tell you that last year its net profit percentage was 33.8%? They ask you whether diesel costs £65 260 and radio hire costs £15 850 could be the cause of the decline in profit. Last year these had an expense ratio of 18.5% and 5.4% respectively.

7 Fill in the missing parts of the following table.

	Opening Stock	Closing Stock	Average Stock	Mark-up	Rate of Turnover	Sales Figure	Gross Profit
Jane Smith	£4000	£6000	?	30%	8	?	?
Claire Brown	6000	9000	?	33 1/3%	10	?	?

Now calculate the Gross-Profit Percentage and the Net-Profit Percentage (correct to one decimal place) in each case bearing in mind that general expenses in the Profit and Loss Account are Jane £2000; Claire £2500.

8 Fill in the missing parts of the following table

	Opening Stock	Closing Stock	Average Stock	Mark-up	Rate of Turnover	Gross Profit	Sales Figure
K. Morton	£7000	£9000	?	40%	12	?	?
P. Akram	9000	5000	?	50%	8	?	?

Now calculate the Gross-Profit Percentage and the Net-Profit Percentage (correct to one decimal place) bearing in mind that general administration expenses in the Profit and Loss Account are Morton £14 400; Akram £8500

30.7 Analysing the Balance Sheet

The Balance Sheet is a snapshot of the affairs of a business at a given moment in time. There are a number of terms we need to learn about the Balance Sheet and they then make discussion of the state of affairs much more meaningful. We can then prepare a number of ratios very easily, which answer important questions about the Balance Sheet. K. Marshall's Balance Sheet for interpretation is given in Fig. 30.3. The special terms need to understand are:

(a) Fixed capital
(b) Working capital
(c) Liquid capital
(d) Capital owned
(e) Capital employed
(f) Capital invested
(g) Opportunity cost

The ratios we need to study are:

(a) Working capital ratio (or current ratio)
(b) Liquid capital ratio (the quick ratio or acid test ratio)
(c) 'Debtors to sales' ratio
(d) Return on capital employed
(e) Return on capital invested

K. Marshall
Balance Sheet as at 31 December 19. .

Capital	£	£	Fixed Assets		£
At start		107 990	Land and		
Add net profit	21 007		Buildings		34 500
Less Drawings	9 500		Plant and		
		11 507	Machinery		14 800
		119 497	Furniture and		
			Fittings		8 650
			Motor Vehicles		12 420
Long-term Liabilities					70 370
Mortgage		10 000	Current Assets	£	
			Stock at close	9 762	
			Sundry Debtors	17 250	
Current Liabilities			Bank	38 640	
Sundry			Cash	1 740	
Creditors		8 265			
					67 392
		£137 762			£137 762

Fig. 30.3 A Balance Sheet for appraisal

30.8 The vocabulary of Balance Sheet appraisal

1 *Fixed Capital* When we put capital into a business at the start, or even later when a further injection of capital is required, we can spend the money in two main ways. We can use it to buy land, buildings, plant and machinery, furniture and fittings etc. These are all items that last a long time (more than a year) and we know that they are called 'fixed assets'. Capital that is tied up in this way is called 'fixed capital' because it cannot readily be turned back into cash, and be used in a different way. If we ever do try to sell our fixed assets we usually lose quite a large part of our money — it is very rare for buyers to pay as much for second-hand items as they would for new items.

If we look at any Balance Sheet and ask ourselves 'What is the fixed capital?' it is the total of the fixed assets — £70 370 in Fig. 30.3. That is the amount of our capital which has been fixed by turning it into long-lasting assets for use in our business.

2 *Working Capital* The rest of the capital we have collected for the business is not fixed, but in much more liquid form. In accountancy 'liquid' means 'in cash form'. A business that has liquidity problems is short of cash, and it is one of the commonest causes of bankruptcy — as we shall see in a minute.

However some of our liquid capital quickly gets used up in other ways, for example by buying stock. Stock is not a fixed asset but a current asset. The word current comes from the French 'courrant' meaning running. Stock is always on the move. We buy it, sell it for cash or sell it on credit and use the money received to buy some more stock. Other current assets are debtors, investments (which can be sold on the Stock Exchange fairly easily and turned back into cash), and our bank and cash balances. All these items are said to be 'working capital', because they are available to work the business.

One more thought about these working balances is that they have to be used to pay our **current liabilities** because these are falling due for payment week by week. Therefore we cannot look at a Balance Sheet and say 'Ah-the working capital is the total of the current assets.' Some of these current assets have to be used to pay the current liabilities. So the formula for working capital is:

$$\text{Working capital} = \text{Current Assets} - \text{Current Liabilities}$$

In the present case this is:

$$\text{Working Capital} = £67\ 392 - £8\ 265$$
$$= £59\ 127$$

We saw in company Final Accounts that some people show this figure as 'net working capital' in their Balance Sheets by deducting current liabilities from current assets. This would make the bottom part of the Balance Sheet in Fig. 30.3 look like this:

Current Assets	£
Stock at close	9 762
Sundry debtors	17 250
Bank	38 640
Cash	1 740
	67 392
Less Current Liabilities	
Creditors	8 265
Net working capital	59 127

3 _Liquid Capital_ Having some of our capital in money form is essential if we are to pay wages, settle our debts, buy new stock, etc, and so liquidity is a major concern of all accountants. The only part of our current assets which is in rather illiquid form is the stock, because you cannot compel anyone to buy your stock — though if you lower your prices enough you will usually be able to dispose of it. Investments are regarded as liquid, because we can always sell them easily if they are quoted investments which can be dealt with on the Stock Exchange. Our liquid assets therefore may be defined as follows:

$$\text{Liquid assets} = \text{Current Assets} - \text{Stock}$$

In Fig. 30.3 this gives us:

$$\text{Liquid Assets} = £67\ 392 - £9\ 762$$
$$= £57\ 630$$

4 _Capital Owned_ The 'capital owned' is the capital owned by the proprietor. This is of course the capital owned at the start of the year, plus any profits left in the business at the end of the year after the drawings have been deducted.

We can see that in Fig. 30.3 the figure for capital owned is £119 497, which is made up of £107 990 invested in the business at the start of the year plus another £11 507 of profit left in by the proprietor at the end of the year. This is known as 'profit ploughed back' into the business.

5 _Capital employed_ The term 'capital employed' can be defined in a number of ways but the most popular definition is the one that says capital employed is the long-term capital used by the business, whether it was supplied by the proprietor or was made available by other institutions such as banks, building societies, debenture holders etc.

In the case of K. Marshall's business the capital employed would therefore be the sum of the capital owned by K. Marshall (£119 497) and the mortgage made available to him of £10 000. Capital employed is therefore £129 497.

The term capital employed is chiefly used about companies, by financiers making inter-company comparisons — to see which company is using the capital made available to it in the best possible way. It is not so widely used with sole traders and partnerships.

6 *Capital invested* The capital invested refers to the capital invested by the proprietor at the start of the year. As we have seen in 4 this figure for K. Marshall's busines is £107 990. The figure is important since it is used by the proprietor to see what return he received on his capital invested. This is discussed later, but before it can be dealt with we must study one further point — opportunity cost.

7 *Opportunity Cost* Opportunity cost is a term usually used in Economics to refer to the fact that we cannot use resources in one way without losing their use in another way. The cost of one opportunity taken is the lost opportunity we cannot take. If we carry this idea over into accountancy it is obvious that a businessman who sets out to run a business must give up other opportunities such as employment elsewhere. He must also lose the interest he would have earned on his capital had it been invested instead of being used in the business. In one of the ratios we work out at the end of the year — the return on capital invested, we really should take these lost opportunities into account.

30.9 Ratios derived from the Balance Sheet

(a) Working capital ratio (or Current Ratio)

The working capital ratio tells us how easily the business can pay its external debts. It is found by the formula

$$\text{Working capital ratio} = \frac{\text{Current assets}}{\text{Current liabilities}}$$

In Fig. 30.3 the figures for K. Marshall's business would be

$$\text{Working capital ratio} = \frac{£67\,392}{£\,8\,265}$$

$$= \underline{\underline{8.2}}$$

In other words current assets: current liabilities:: 8.2:1 to express the idea in its mathematical form as a ratio. This means that with his present level of current assets K. Marshall can pay his current liabilities more than 8 times over. This is clearly a very sound position.

The working capital should ideally be about 2:1.

Suppose the figures had been: current assets £8500; current liabilities £15 250

$$\text{Working capital ratio} = \frac{£\,8\,500}{£15\,250}$$

$$= \underline{\underline{0.56}}$$

So the ratio current assets to current liabilities is 0.56:1

In that case the business would not have been able to pay its current liabilities and could easily have been pushed into bankruptcy if some creditor had pressed for payment.

When a business is short of working capital it is called **over-trading**. The proprietor has tried to grow too fast, and has invested too much in fixed assets and not kept back enough capital for working capital. He is said to be **over-capitalised**. It is not an easy position to cure, because you can't sell the extra fixed assets without losing most of the money on them. It requires careful control — restrict expenditure as much as possible, reduce drawings and gradually restore the liquidity of the business.

However K. Marshall is not in this position. As a matter of fact the situation is the very reverse — because he is **undertrading**. He has a ratio of 8:1, whereas the ideal is 2:1. He could expand the business if he wished to do so, using some of the £38 640 in the bank to buy more fixed assets. It is really rather a waste of resources to have such a big balance available at the bank.

(b) Liquid capital ratio (the quick ratio or acid test radio)

If we really want to test the liquidity of a business (its ability to pay its debts with the funds available to it) we can use the **liquid capital ratio**, also called the **quick ratio** or the **acid test ratio**. This is found by the formula

$$\text{Liquid capital ratio} \quad = \quad \frac{\text{liquid assets}}{\text{current liabilities}}$$

Liquid assets are the current assets minus the stock — which is not very liquid because it is not easily turned into cash. In K. Marshall's case this gives us:

$$
\begin{aligned}
\text{Liquid capital ratio} \quad &= \quad \frac{£67\ 392 - £9\ 762}{£8\ 265} \\
&= \quad \frac{£57\ 630}{£8\ 265} \\
&= \quad 7.0
\end{aligned}
$$

So the ratio is:

Liquid assets: Current liabilities:: 7:1

Clearly a 7:1 ratio is a very liquid state of affairs, and the essential figure is at least 1:1, in other words the business can pay its debts in full without any difficulty. K. Marshall can pay its debts seven times over, and is therefore very liquid indeed.

Suppose we re-arrange K. Marshall's figures to demonstrate why this ratio is the acid-test of a business's ability to pay its debts. Suppose the current assets had been:

	£
Stock	59 762
Debtors	2 250
Bank	3 640
Cash	1 740
	£67 392

The stock figure is now much bigger and the debtors and bank balance much smaller.

The working capital is still the same 8.2.:1

The liquid capital ratio is now:

$$\text{Liquid capital ratio} = \frac{\text{Current assets} - \text{stock}}{\text{Current liabilities}}$$

$$= \frac{£67\ 392 - £59\ 762}{£8\ 265}$$

$$= \frac{£7\ 630}{£8\ 265}$$

$$= 0.9$$

The ratio is now 0.9:1, in other words Marshall cannot pay all his debts if asked to do so, and is in an illiquid position. He has purchased too much stock — an illiquid asset — and although a bank would probably help him out if he was put under pressure from his creditors it is a sign of poor management and would reduce his credit-worthiness in the bank's eyes.

(c) 'Debtors to Sales' Ratio

Another important cause of illiquidity in any business is the failure of debtors to pay when they should do so. We usually trade with those we know on monthly credit terms, that is we send the statement at the end of the month showing how much is due, and they pay the amount due within thirty days. If they fail to pay in the agreed time it puts us into difficulty, because we have our own debts to pay. We must keep tight control of our debtors, both in general and individually. Do not let a debtor get deeper into debt every month; refuse further supplies until the last batch are paid for. Keep a general eye on all debts, and we can do this best by taking out a 'debtors to sales' ratio. The formula is:

$$\text{Debtors to sales ratio} = \frac{\text{debtors}}{\text{sales} \div 12}$$

This measures the debtors against the average monthly sales to show how long the average debtor is in debt (sometimes called the **average collection period**). The sales figure is of course the turnover. We can get rid of the awkward division sum re-arranging the formula to:

$$\text{Debtors to sales ratio} = \frac{\text{debtors} \times 12}{\text{sales}}$$

In the case of K. Marshall's business this gives us:

$$= \frac{£17\ 250 \times 12}{£97\ 000}$$

$$= 2.1 \text{ months}$$

The average debtor is in debt for 2.1 months which is more than we would hope, and some measures of credit control seem to be required.

(d) Return on capital employed

If we wish to know how well a business is using the capital it has had provided to it we can work out the **return on capital employed**. The capital employed has been described already as the long term capital available to the business. In K. Marshall's case it was the capital owned by the proprietor and the mortgage funds, and amounted to £129 497.

If we now express the net profit for the year as a percentage of this we have the return on capital employed.

$$\text{Return on capital employed} = \frac{\text{Net profit}}{\text{Long-term funds available}} \times 100$$

$$= \frac{£21\ 007}{£129\ 497} \times 100$$

$$= \underline{\underline{16.2\%}}$$

The figure is chiefly used by bankers and such people to see what rate of return is being earned on the capital employed. In this case it is 16.2% which is not bad — better than the same money would earn if invested in a safe investment such as debentures or gilt-edged securities — but then, of course, the risk is higher too.

(e) Return on capital investment

If we wish to know how well a businessman is really doing by being in business, we can work out the **return on capital invested**. The formula is;

$$\text{Return on capital invested} = \frac{\text{net profit} - \text{opportunity cost}}{\text{capital invested at start}} \times 100$$

The reason we must take the opportunity cost into account is that if the businessman was not engaged in this business he would be able to take up other opportunities, both for his own efforts and for his capital. Suppose that K. Marshall, if not self-employed, could earn £8000 per year as the manager of a small enterprise and suppose the capital invested could earn 7% interest if invested in a safe investment. Seven per cent of £107 990 is £7559.30 — we will call it £7560.

The opportunities lost by being self employed are thus £8000 + £7560 = £15 560

The calculation is therefore:

$$\text{Return on capital invested} = \frac{£21\ 007 - £15\ 560}{£107\ 990} \times 100$$

$$= \frac{£5447 \times 100}{£107\ 990}$$

$$= \underline{\underline{5.0\%}}$$

By being in business K. Marshall is actually earning an extra 5% on his capital, over and above what he could earn anyway if working for someone else and with his money in a safe investment. Clearly, it is not much. That is the sort of figure which might persuade a trader to sell his business and seek employment elsewhere. On the other hand, in judging whether to be self-employed the monetary rewards are not necessarily everything. The non-monetary satisfactions may be important. K. Marshall may dislike intensely being told what to do by an employer; he may like to 'be his own boss'. He may like the status in the community that self-employment brings, and he may like being able to offer employment to others.

30.10 Exercises on the appraisal of Balance Sheets

1 Here is the Balance Sheet of T. Curtis. You are asked to answer the question below it, with calculations correct to one decimal place if necessary.

Balance Sheet as at 31 March 19. .

Capital		£	Fixed Assets		£
At start		50 000	Premises		40 000
Add Net profit	35 000		Rent and		
Less Drawings	16 800		Machinery		12 500
		18 200	Furniture and		
		68 200	Fittings		3 800
			Motor vehicles		16 700
					73 000
Long-term Liabilities			Current Assets	£	
Mortgage	20 000		Stock	15 725	
Loan from bank	5 000		Debtors	3 875	
		25 000	Cash at bank	4 610	
			Cash in hand	390	
					24 600
Current liabilities					
Creditors	4 250				
Wages due	150				
		4 400			
		£97 600			£97 600

(a) What is the fixed capital?
(b) What is the working capital?
(c) What is the capital owned by the proprietor?
(d) What is the capital employed in the business?
(e) What is the return on the capital invested at the start assuming that the opportunities Curtis has given up by being self-employed would have earned him £19 000.

2 Here is M. Lee's Balance Sheet. You are to answer the questions below (with calculations if needed).

Balance Sheet as at 31 December 19. .

Capital		£	Fixed Assets		£
At start		45 000	Goodwill		4 000
Add Net Profit	43 000		Premises		34 000
Less Drawings	17 588		Plant and		
		25 412	Machinery		17 000
			Motor Vehicles		6 000
		70 412			61 000
Long-term Liabilities			Current Assets		
Mortgage		18 000	Stock	14 596	
			Debtors	4 274	
			Cash at Bank	14 381	
			Cash in Hand	72	
					33 323
Current Liabilities					
Creditors	5 614				
Accrued Charges	297				
		5 911			
		£94 323			£94 323

(a) What is the capital owned by the proprietor?
(b) What is the capital employed in the business?
(c) What is the working capital?
(d) What is the liquid capital?
(e) Work out the acid test ratio (correct to two places of decimals).
(f) Work out the return on capital invested (correct to one decimal place) assuming the Lee could earn £15 000 a year in an alternative position with none of the responsibilities of a small businessman, and his capital would also have earned 8% if invested safely.

3 Here is Anne Wood's Balance Sheet. You are to answer the questions below (with calculations if needed).

Balance Sheet as at 31 December 19. .

Capital		£	Fixed Assets		£
At start		60 000	Premises		54 000
Add Net Profit	30 350		Plant and Machinery		18 500
Less Drawings	20 250		Motor Vehicles		17 350
		10 100			89 850
		70 100			
Long-term Liabilities			Current Assets		
Mortgage		37 000	Stock	14 764	
			Debtors	5 176	
Current Liabilities			Cash at bank	3 081	
Creditors	9 950		Cash in Hand	4 275	
Accrued Charges	158		Payments in Advance	62	
		10 108			27 358
		£117 208			£117 208

(a) What is the capital owned by the proprietor?
(b) What is the capital employed in the business?
(c) What is the working capital?
(d) What is the liquid capital?
(e) Work out the working capital ratio (correct to 2 decimal places).
(f) Work out the liquid capital ratio (correct to 2 decimal places).
(g) Work out the return on capital invested, assuming that Wood could earn £16 000 a year in an alternative position with none of the responsibilities of a small businesswoman, and that her capital could earn 10% in a reasonably safe investment. (Answer correct to 1 decimal place.)

30.11 Cash flow

Cash flow presents problems at all times of the year but is included at this point because it is a control procedure — but one that needs constant attention. As the name implies it is concerned with the movements of cash into and out of a business. These occur at all sorts of times, but in an irregular way, and we have to watch the flows to make sure we don't run out of cash (or that we can borrow if we do). Equally when there is plenty of cash we don't want to leave it loose in the system, someone may use it improperly or even steal it. For example many traders stock up in September and October for the Christmas rush in November and December. They may get very short of cash in October (and perhaps need an overdraft) while in November and December takings will be high and cash will be collecting in the tills and bank accounts.

To follow what is happening and estimate what is likely to happen to our cash flow we draw up a cash budget like the one in Fig. 30.4. The trader gets short of cash in October and has to arrange for an overdraft of £5000. The position is a little better in November, but he is still overdrawn by £2765. However, the Christmas sales should bring him back into balance to clear his overdraft during December.

30.12 Exercises: cash flow

1 Mary Estall's cash flow estimates for the month ahead are as follows: cash in hand on 1 January 19. . £326; cash at the bank £4265; cash sales for the month £7245; credit sales for the month £3450; credit sales in December were £6954 and half are expected to pay in January; credit sales prior to December and still outstanding for payment total £5192 of which £4320 are confidently expected in January. Cash purchases are expected to be £725 in January and it is also proposed to pay £2400 for goods received in November and December. Wages are expected to be £3580 in the month, and other overheads £1856. A capital item (a new delivery vehicle) is expected in January and half the price of £6150 will be paid on delivery. Drawings of £600 are to be made in the month.

Work out a cash flow statement for the month of January and the anticipated bank balance at the end of the month assuming cash in hand at that time will be restricted to £150.

(Note: Credit sales for the month will not be paid until next month — and therefore may be disregarded.)

Cash Flow	September Budget (£)	September Actual (£)	October Budget (£)	October Actual (£)	November Budget (£)	November Actual (£)
1 Cash in hand at start of month	150		250		150	
2 Cash at bank	3 850		2 345		−4 555	
3 Total	4 000		2 595		−4 405	
Receipts:						
4 Cash sales	3 750		4 590		8 265	
5 Debts collected	4 250		3 850		4 720	
6 Other receipts	250		250		250	
7 Extra capital contributed	–		1 000		–	
8 Total receipts (add 4–7)	8 250		9 690		13 235	
9 Total cash available (add 3 and 8)	12 250		12 285		8 830	
Payments:						
10 Purchases	2 395		9 870		5 435	
11 Wages	3 250		3 250		3 250	
12 Other expenses	1 760		2 570		1 760	
13 Capital expenditure	1 250		–		–	
14 Business payments (add 10–13)	8 655		15 690		10 445	
15 Drawings of proprietor	1 000		1 000		1 000	
16 Total payments (add 14 and 15)	9 655		16 690		11 445	
17 Final cash balance	250		150		150	
18 Final bank balance	2 345		−4 555		−2 765	
19 Total (Take 16 from 9 or 9 from 16)	2 595		−4 405		−2 615	
			Arrange £5000 overdraft until January.			

Fig. 30.4 Budgeting for cash flow

Notes
We can notice one or two points in this budget. They are:
1 Each month is given a double column, one for the budgeted figures and one for the actual figures. The actual figures put in at the end of the month will let us know how close we came to the budget, and may lead us to adjust our ideas on budgeting in the future.
2 We can do a certain amount of **cash flow smoothing**. This is where we take steps to avoid running short of cash. For example, in October and November when our trader was buying goods to sell in the pre-Christmas period he did not budget to buy any capital items. The money just would not be available. In January, when the overdraft is cleared he might think about using some of the spare cash he should have by then to purchase any capital items required.

2 M. Muhammadu's cash flow estimates for the month ahead are as follows: cash in hand on 1 January 19. . £125; cash at the bank £4095; cash sales for the month £8950; credit sales for the month £7250; credit sales in December were £16 842 and half are expected to pay in January; sales prior to December and still outstanding for payment total £6750 of which £4350 are confidently expected in January. Cash purchases are expected to be £840 in January and it is also proposed to pay £3250 for goods received in November and December. Wages are expected to be £4650 in the month, and other overheads £2150. A capital item (a new till) is expected in January and half the price of £480 will be paid on delivery. Drawings of £800 are to be made in the month by the proprietor.

Work out a cash flow statement for the month of January and the anticipated bank balance at the end of the month assuming cash in hand at that time will be restricted to £250.

3 Alan Seymour's cash flow estimates for the month ahead are as follows: cash in hand on 1 October 19. . £425; cash at the bank £3280; cash sales for the month £3425; credit sales for the month £4865; credit sales in September were £5426 and half are expected to pay in October; sales prior to September and still outstanding for payment total £4265 of which £3500 are confidently expected in October. Cash purchases are expected to be £1660 in October and it is also proposed to pay £4580 for goods received in August and September. Wages are expected to be £5250 in the month, and other overheads £1960. A capital item (a new machine) is expected in October and half the price of £10 500 will be paid on delivery. The proprietor will take drawings of £1000 in the month.
(a) Work out a cash flow statement for the month of October and the anticipated bank balance at the end of the month assuming cash in hand at that time will be restricted to £250.
(b) What would you advise Seymour to do in view of this budget, before the month begins?

30.13 Sources and Applications of Funds

One of the problems with a business is that 'profits' are not the same as money. Many business owners who know their businesses are making good profits are amazed to find that there is no cash available, and consequently they cannot draw out the profits they have made. There can be many explanations of this shortage of money. Some of the common ones are listed below.

1 The proprietor has purchased too many fixed assets, and all the profits made are no longer in cash, they have turned into fixed assets.

2 Similarly the proprietor may buy too much stock and the cash will be turned into stock.

3 The goods sold to customers may have been sold on credit, so that although we have made good profits we have not yet received the money; instead of cash in hand, or money in the bank, all we have are debtors.

A typical problem of this sort is given in the example below:

To explain what has happened to a business with this sort of problem we draw up a statement known as a 'Flow of Funds Statement' which shows the sources of extra funds in the year and how they have been applied.

EXAMPLE

M. Evans complains to you that although his business has made excellent profits in the year he has been very hard pressed for cash and is now overdrawn by £7850. 'Where', he asks 'has all the money gone?' The Balance Sheets of his business for this year and last year are shown below. Explain what has happened to his money. (*Note*: the figures in brackets have been deducted.)

M. Evans Balance Sheet as at 31 December this year — and last year

	Last Year	This Year	Fixed Assets	Last Year	This Year
				£	£
Capital (at start)	29 430	45 430			
Add Net Profit	24 000	26 000	Premises	30 000	30 000
Less Drawings	(8 000)	(8 000)	Machinery	17 000	27 000
			Fixtures & Fittings	3 000	4 500
	45 430	63 430	Motor Vehicles	3 000	8 500
				53 000	70 000
Long-term Liability					
Mortgage	25 000	25 000			
			Current Assets		
			Stock	14 000	23 150
Current Liabilities			Debtors	2 000	8 300
Creditors	1 420	5 420	Bank	2 000	—
Bank Overdraft	—	7 850	Cash	850	250
				18 850	31 700
	£71 850	£101 700		£71 850	£101 700

As we can see Evans has a big bank overdraft and only £250 in cash. Although he earned £26 000 profit he has only been able to draw £8000; there is no money to give him the rest of his profit. What has happened to it? We can see what the source of his funds is this year and how he has used them if we draw up a Sources and Application of Funds Statement, sometimes called a Flow of Funds Statement. Comparing this year's figures with last year we have:

Flow of Funds Statement

Source of funds:	£
Net Profit	26 000
Increased credit by creditors	4 000
Bank balance used	2 000
Bank overdraft made available	7 850
Cash used up	600
	£40 450

Application of these funds:	£
Drawings	8 000
Increased machinery	10 000
Increased fixtures etc	1 500
Increased motor vehicles	5 500
Increase in stocks	9 150
Increase in debtors	6 300
	£40 450

Clearly, all the funds have been used up and the extra profit cannot be withdrawn, unless arrangements can be made to increase the overdraft.

30.14 Exercises: fund flow statements

1 Alice Lumsden asks you to explain why, although she has made more than £17 000 profit she cannot draw out £17 000, because after drawing £8000 she only has £3250 left in the bank. Explain the position with the help of a flow of funds statement. (Figures in brackets have been deducted.)

Alice Lumsden: Balance Sheets for this year and last year

	Last Year £	This Year £		Last Year £	This Year £
Capital	26 700	36 700	Premises	34 000	48 000
Net Profit	16 000	17 100	Fixtures & Fittings	2 500	4 000
Drawings	(6 000)	(8 000)	Stock	12 500	14 000
Mortgage	25 000	25 000	Debtors	2 300	3 300
Creditors	1 300	2 000	Bank	11 250	3 250
			Cash	450	250
	£63 000	£72 800		£63 000	£72 800

2 P. Ramirez cannot understand why, when his business is so profitable, he has so little money. He presents you with the following details. Draw up a flow of funds statement showing him why he is so short of funds. (Figures in brackets have been deducted.)

P. Ramirez: Balance Sheet for this year and last year

	Last year £	This year £		Last year £	This year £
Capital	38 000	39 664	Machinery	17 000	26 000
Net Profit	11 664	21 126	Fixtures & Fittings	2 500	4 500
Drawings	(10 000)	(8 000)	Stock	15 256	27 650
Bank Loan	5 000	10 000	Debtors	3 284	4 726
Creditors	5 420	2 420	Cash at Bank	11 564	1 834
			Cash in hand	480	500
	£50 084	£65 210		£50 084	£65 210

3 Abdul Malik, a dentist asks you to explain why, despite the satisfactory surplus of income over expenditure in the current year he is extremely short of cash. Why, he complains, when his drawings are so modest, does he not have reasonable funds available in his bank account or in cash. From his Balance Sheet draw up a statement of the flow of funds through his business. What advice would you give him to overcome his difficulties? (Figures in brackets have been deducted.)

Abdul Malik: Balance Sheet as at 31 December

	Last year	This year		Last year	This year
Capital			*Fixed Assets*		
At Start	40 000	79 656	Premises	85 000	124 000
Profit	49 656	43 806	Surgical equipment	39 500	62 600
Drawings	(10 000)	(11 000)	Motor vehicles	7 950	12 590
				132 450	199 190
Long-term Liabilities			*Current Assets*		
Mortgage	65 000	90 000	Stocks	1 216	1 519
			Debtors	495	995
Current Liabilities			Cash at Bank	11 725	2 164
Creditors	1 425	1 656	Cash in hand	195	250
				13 631	4 928
	£146 081	£204 118		£146 081	£204 118

30.15 Answers to self-assessment questions (see 30.5 above)

1 The gross profit percentage is a ratio which tells us what percentage of the turnover figure is gross profit of the business.

2 The formula is $\dfrac{\text{Gross profit}}{\text{Turnover}} \times 100$

3 The special point is that even if the turnover increases or decreases the gross profit percentage should be constant. If it is not some force must be at work to change it.

4 Four things that would cause the gross profit percentage to fall are (a) theft of cash from the tills (b) theft of stock (c) breakages of fragile items such as china or glassware (d) bad buying (causing perishable items to go bad before sale, or fashionable items to lose their popularity before sale).

5 The rate of stock turnover is the number of times stock turns over in the year.

6 The formula is: $\text{Rate of stock turn} = \dfrac{\text{Cost of stock sold}}{\text{Average stock at cost price}}$

7 Eighteen times in the year.

8 We can't possibly say unless we know what product is being sold. It would not be good enough for new laid eggs, but very good for kitchen units.

9 Net profit percentage is the percentage of our turnover that is actually net profit of the business. The formula is: $\dfrac{\text{Net profit}}{\text{Turnover}} \times 100$

10 An expense ratio is the percentage of turnover which is used up by an expense item such as electricity, motor vehicle expenditure etc. The formula is:

$$\dfrac{\text{Expense item}}{\text{Turnover}} \times 100$$

11 A drop in net profit percentage could be caused by:
(a) a more than proportional increase in rent
(b) a more than proportional increase in advertising
(c) a fall in miscellaneous profits earned relative to the turnover of the business.

31 Control Accounts

31.1 Keeping track of sections of the books

When a business is large enough to split the accounts it is dealing with into different sections it is often convenient to keep track of the separate sections and devise some way of building in checks and balances. For example, a business may have 100 000 debtors. Senior staff will only be interested in the total debtors position, but office supervisors will have several people handling these accounts; few book-keepers can handle more than a thousand accounts at a time. It is helpful if we can have a system which discovers the mistakes that have been made and for which book-keepers are responsible. We can give such people special help to solve the errors, while other book-keepers whose books are correct can get away for their evening appointments.

Such **control accounts** or **total accounts** are devised to make sections of the work self-balancing, and create what are called self-balancing ledgers. Consider the illustration in Fig. 31.1 and you will see how the system works. Of course the same sort of device could be handled electronically by a computer, with the figures held in the computer's memory.

A–E Debtors Control A/c			
19 . .	£	19 . .	£
Cash	26 524	Balance	12 785
Discount	228	Sales	34 728
Returns	156		
Balance c/d	20 605		
	£47 513		£47 513
		Balance b/d	20 605

A	B	C	D	E
ADDISON, C.B A/c				

A–E Debtors Ledger
(Card index)

A–E Debtors Control A/c			
19 . .	£	19 . .	£
Balance	12 785	Cash	26 524
Sales	34 728	Discount	228
		Returns	156
		Balance c/d	20 605
	£47 513		47 513
19 . .	£		
Balance b/d	20 605		

Fig. 31.1 A Control Account on the A-E Debtors Ledger

Notes

1 The person who keeps the A–E Ledger is entering all sorts of entries, sales invoices, credit notes, cash and cheque payments and discounts in the various ledger cards which are the accounts of the A–E debtors in the card index shown.

2 At the back of the card index is one more card, a Control Account in which the various total figures are entered at the end of the month, on the opposite side to the side which they would normally be entered on the actual customer's accounts. Thus if we sell goods to the customers we would naturally debit the sale on the debtor's account, but the total sales are entered on the Control Account on the other side.

3 The reason why this is done is easy. The chief accountant (or a supervisor) makes these entries, and he/she wants the real debits and credits to be in his version of the Control Account in the General Ledger which is going to be used at Head Office. You can see it in the diagram. It has all the entries on the correct side — the total sales is debited to the Head Office copy just as it would be in the debtor's own accounts, but the double entry for this, on the copy at the back of the book-keeper's tray of accounts is the wrong way round. The result is that the book-keeper's tray is **self-balancing**. All the debit balances on the individual debtor's accounts (provided no mistakes have been made) will be balanced up by the credit balance on the Control Account. At trial balance time a book-keeper whose book balances can go home happy to know that there is no error on the month's work. A book-keeper whose book doesn't balance must look for a mistake.

4 A special point to note is that the chief accountant has, on one page, the whole of the entries on — say — one thousand accounts in the A–E ledger, and when someone rings him to say 'The A–E ledger balances' he can use the figures confident that all is well — there are no errors.

5 A nasty accountant might stoop to an unkind trick. Although he draws up the Control Account he only does one half of the work — he doesn't give the book-keeper the copy at the back of the book which makes it self balancing. Now the book-keeper who has taken out a Trial Balance has to ring the accountant and say 'A–E ledger here — I make the balances total £20 605'. 'Well done', says the accountant — 'so do I'. Or he may say 'Oh — it looks as if you have made a slip — you are £365 out. Have a look for it, will you?'.

31.2 Simple Control Accounts

In examinations it is usual to ask students to prepare a simple control account, or total account, for a specific section of the ledger such as the A–E Debtors or the A–K Creditors. It is usual to draw it up as shown in Fig. 31.1, in the Head Office style with the figures on the correct side as they would be in the individual accounts of the debtors or creditors. A typical account for the Creditors' Ledger might look as shown in Fig. 31.2.

A–K Creditors Control A/C

19..			£	19..			£
Mar 1	Balances	b/d	138	Mar 1	Balances	b/d	3 974
31	Returns	PRB14	1 045	31	Purchases	PDB56	11 586
31	Bank	CB9	5 965	31	Carriage	J27	244
31	Discount			31	Insurance	J30	196
	Received	CB9	472				
31	Balance	c/d	8 380				
			£16 000				£16 000
				19..			£
				Apr 1	Balance	b/d	8 380

Fig. 31.2 A simple Control Account

Notes

1 When asked to draw up an account you simply ask yourself on each item "Where would this go on an ordinary creditor's account. If it is purchases, a purchase from a creditor is credited in his account — he is giving the goods. So purchases goes on the credit side.

2 Opening balances are almost always on the credit side — in this case we owe the creditors £3974 on 1 March. However — we can have an odd creditor who is for just a little while a debtor. This is usually because we paid his account in full but then returned some item. For a short while, until we have a further order, he is a debtor not a creditor. In this example we had an opening debtor of £138 — one of our creditors was temporarily in debt to us.

3 Think about each each line in the account and make sure you understand why it is debited or credited, as the case may be. Then try some of the entries in Section 31.3.

31.3 Exercises: Simple Control Accounts

1 Make out a simple Debtors A–E Control Account for the month of March 19. . using the following total figures which have been extracted from the books of Sims and Partners. Calculate the debit balance outstanding for total debtors at the end of the month and bring both balances down to start the month of April. Opening balances 1 March 19. .: debit £13 243; credit £28. Total figures on 31 March were: Sales £27 353; Sales Returns £859; Cheques received £16 254; Discount allowed £126; Credit balance outstanding at the end of the month £45. *Note:* If a debtor has a credit balance outstanding at the end of the month (i.e. he is temporarily a creditor then this balance will be on the debit side before the book is balanced off, and it is brought down on the credit side.

2 Make out a simple Debtors F–L Control Account for the month of June 19. . using the following total figures which have been extracted from the books of T. P. Bryon. Calculate the debit balance outstanding at the end of the month and bring both balances down.

Opening balances: debit £27 314; credit £426. The figures for the month were Sales £18 295; Sales Returns £1094; Cheques received £16 868; Discount allowed £595; Credit balance outstanding at the end of the month for one debtor £49.

3 Make out a simple Creditors A–K Ledger Control Account for the month of October using the following total figures which have been extracted from the books of M. Mishadar. Calculate the credit balance outstanding for A–K creditors at the end of the month and bring the balances down ready for the start of November.

1 October 19. . Opening balances: debit £72; credit £14 296. The monthly totals at 31 October were: Purchases £17 249; Purchases Returns £2584; Cash paid £187; Cheques paid £18 796; Discount received £1425; Debit balance outstanding at the end of the month from one creditor who was temporarily a debtor £79. (Remember — to come down on the debit side it must start off on the credit side before balancing off the account.)

4 Make out a simple Creditors L–Z ledger Control Account for the month of January 19. . using the following total figures which have been extracted from the books of Janet Symes. Calculate the credit balance outstanding for L–Z creditors at the end of the month and bring the balances down ready for the start of February.

1 January 19. . Opening balances: debit £172; credit £11 896. At the end of January total figures were: Purchases £16 268; Purchases returns £1725; cash paid £396; Cheques paid £11 128; Discount Received £372. Debit balance outstanding at the end of the month from a creditor who was temporarily a debtor; £48.

5 Make out a simple Debtors A–E Control Account for the month of July using the following total figures which have been extracted from the book of T. Brown & Co. Ltd. Calculate the debit balance outstanding at the end of the month and bring both balances down.

July 19. . Opening balances were: debit £14 258; credit £75. On 31 July the total figures for the month were: Sales £18 595; Sales returns £285; Cheques received £14 858; Discount allowed £1245; Credit balance outstanding at the end of the month (from a debtor who was temporarily a creditor) £56.

31.4 More difficult ideas on Control Accounts

The figures for Control Accounts

We have to get the figures for Control Accounts from somewhere, and this means building in extra columns on the day books to capture the figures. If we are using a computerized system we need to write into our programs instructions for the computer to catch the data for each section of the ledger, so that any entries made on an A–E debtors account will be caught by the computer and stored in a register to give the total sales for the A–E ledger. Similarly in the Cash Book when we receive cheques from customers we need extra columns for the A–E, F–K, L–R and S–Z customers. All this gives considerable work to someone to build up the figures we want, or capture the data on a computerized system.

With Journal entries, which are not very numerous, it would not be worth while inserting extra columns to collect the figures we need, but the accountant would look through the journal and extract the figures for each section of the ledger.

Contra entries in Control Accounts

Where we have a simple ledger every person we deal with will have an account in the ledger and every entry affecting that person will appear on the Ledger Account. When we start to split the ledger up into separate sections, with a Debtors Ledger, a Creditors Ledger, a General Ledger and perhaps a Private Ledger, we face a difficulty. Suppose we deal with a person in two capacities, as both a debtor and a creditor. We cannot really run from one department to another making entries especially if the Debtors Ledger is in one building and the Creditors Ledger 250 miles away in another building. The one person must have two accounts, a debtor's account in the debtors ledger and a creditor's account in the Creditors Ledger. We usually speak of these accounts as Contra Accounts, because they are the opposite of one another (contra = opposite (L)). Suppose James Black's account in the Debtors ledger shows that he owes us £248, while his account in the Creditors Ledger shows that we owe him £4725. It is usual to do a journal entry clearing off the smaller entry against the larger entry. This is called a **contra entry**. The two accounts would then look as shown in Fig. 31.3.

James Black A/c (in the Debtors Ledger) DL27

19. .			£	19. .			£
July 15	Sales	SDB1	248.00	July 31	Contra	J29	248.00

James Black A/c (in the Creditors ledger) CL36

19. .			£	19. .			£
July 31	Contra	J29	248.00	July 27	Purchase	PDB49	4725.00
31	Balance	c/d	4477.00				
			£4725.00				£4725.00
				19. .			£
				Aug 1	Balance	b/d	4477.00

Fig. 31.3 Clearing a small debt against a larger debt with a contra entry

Notes
1 The small debt of the debtor James Black, who is also a supplier of ours, is cleared off and reduces the amount we owe him as a creditor.
2 The amount we owe him is reduced to £4477.

The names of Control Accounts

Generally speaking at this level students are only expected to produce Control Accounts from sets of figures which imitate on a single page the whole of a section of accounts, like the A–E Debtors Ledger or the A–K Creditors ledger. In deciding which side of the account to place a particular figure — for example the sales figure — you would ask yourself, 'Where does Sales go on an ordinary debtor's account?' The answer is on the debit side — increasing his/her debt. By contrast, the cash paid by the debtors goes on the credit side because it reduces the debts owing by the debtors.

You may come across the names 'General Ledger Adjustment Account', 'Debtors Ledger Adjustment Account' and 'Creditors Ledger Adjustment Account'. These are Control Accounts where there is a full double entry system. The General Ledger Adjustment Account would be the page at the back of the ledger tray which makes the tray self-balancing (see Fig. 31.1) while the A–E Debtors Ledger Adjustment Account (for example) would be in the General Ledger, and have the whole of the A–E Debtors Ledger on one page, and with the figures the right way round (see Fig. 31.1).

31.5 Exercises: more difficult Control Accounts

Note: In these exercises you will sometimes find that figures have been given to you which affect two different Control Accounts. You have to sort out which entry applies to which Control Account, and if it is a contra entry it will probably affect both. Do not be worried about tackling this type of exercise — think of the double entries in every case and ask yourself — would this be a debit entry or a credit entry.

1 A. Cutler keeps a Sales Ledger Control Account. For the month of January the figures are:

	£
Credit balances at 1 January	29
Debit balances at 1 January	3 825
Sales for month	5 984
Sales returns for month	386
Cheques paid by debtors	3 420
Discount allowed	180
Transfers of debit balances on the Sales Ledger to the Purchase Ledger (contra entries)	225

(a) Draw up the Control Account
(b) Cutler now tells you that the Sales Ledger totals at a figure of £5569. What comment do you make on that figure?

2 Janet Lowe keeps a Purchase Ledger Control Account. For the month of May the figures are:

	£
Credit balances at 1 January	7 189
Debit balance at 1 January	256
Purchases for month	11 529
Purchases Returns for month	1 426
Cheques paid to creditors	6 895
Discount Received	172
Transfers of credit balances on Purchase Ledger to credit side of Sales Ledger (contra entries)	246

(a) Draw up the Control Account
(b) Janet now tells you that the Purchase Ledger totals at a figure of £8995. What comment do you make on that figure?

3 Rajiv Shah keeps a Sales Ledger Control Account. For the month of August the figures are:

	£
Credit balances at 1 January	325
Debit balances at 1 January	8 172
Sales for month	8 586
Sales returns for month	186
Cheques paid by debtors	7 540
Discount Allowed	285
Transfers of debit balances on Sales Ledger to Purchase Ledger (contra entries)	489

(a) Draw up the Control Account
(b) Shah now tells you that the Sales Ledger totals at a figure of £7953. What comment do you make on that figure.

4 T. Marshall keeps a Sales Ledger Control Account and a Purchase Ledger Control Account. For the month of April the figures are:

	£
Credit balances on Sales Ledger 1 April	127
Debit balances on Sales Ledger 1 April	5 895
Credit balances on Purchase Ledger 1 April	4 921
Debit balances on Purchase Ledger 1 April	65
Sales in the month	11 526
Sales Returns in the month	725
Purchases in the month	4 986
Purchases Returns in the month	124
Cheques received from debtors	9 256
Discount allowed	140
Cheques paid to creditors	4 648
Discounts Received	373
Contra entries	127
Debit balances on Creditors Ledger at the end of the month	21
Credit balances on the Debtors Ledger at the end of the month	137

You are asked:

(a) To draw up the two Control Accounts

(b) To say what, exactly, the balances on the Purchases Control Account represent

(c) You are then told that the Trial Balance fails to agree by £100 and that the Sales Ledger totals at £7083 and the Creditors' Ledger totals at £4591. What comment can you make on these figures?

5 Tahira Kadar keeps a Sales Ledger Control Account and a Purchase ledger Control Account. For the month of October the figures are:

	£
Credit balances on Sales Ledger 1 October 19. .	145
Debit balances on Sales Ledger 1 October 19. .	25 745
Credit balances on Purchase Ledger 1 October 19. .	9 866
Debit balances on Purchases Ledger 1 October 19. .	52
Sales in the month	33 816
Sales Returns in the month	1 240
Purchases in the month	7 349
Purchases Returns in the month	126
Cheques received from debtors	22 950
Discount allowed	1 750
Cheques paid to creditors	7 482
Discounts received	183
Contra entries	195
Debit balances on Creditors Ledger at the end of the month	168
Credit balances on the Debtors Ledger at the end of the month	173

You are asked:

(a) To draw up the two Control Accounts.

(b) To say, exactly, the balances on the Sales Control Account represent.

(c) You are then told that the Trial Balance fails to agree by £55 and that the Sales Ledger totals at £33 454 and the Creditors Ledger totals at £9290. What comment can you make on these figures?

6 M. Dickens keeps a Sales Ledger Control Account and a Purchase Ledger Control Account. For the month of March the figures are:

	£
Credit balances on Sales Ledger 1 March 19. .	75
Debit balances on Sales Ledger 1 March 19. .	21 726
Credit balances on Purchases Ledger 1 March 19. .	11 584
Debit balances on Purchases Ledger 1 March 19. .	124
Sales in the month	19 856
Sales Returns in the month	174
Purchases in the month	7 248
Purchases Returns in the month	226
Cheques received from debtors	19 714
Discount allowed	826
Cheques paid to creditors	10 170
Discounts received	248
Contra entries	495
Debit balances on Creditors Ledger at the end of the month	73
Credit balances on the Debtors Ledger at the end of the month	182

You are asked:

(a) To draw up the two Control Accounts

(b) You are then told that the Trial Balance fails to agree by £197 and that the Sales Ledger totals at £20 480 and the Creditors Ledger totals at £7642. What comment can you make on these figures?

32 Accounts from Incomplete Records

32.1 The Increased Net Worth Method of Finding Profits

Before the introduction of income tax in the 1840s there was little need for some people to keep accounts, and many of them did not do so. The success of a business was judged by the gradual accumulation of wealth around the proprietor of the business. The man who one year had a horse and cart and ten years later had a livery stables was proved to be doing well by this increase in wealth which was visible for all to see. Today we tend to keep book-keeping records because it is the easiest way to prove to the Inland Revenue exactly what profits we have made in the year. There are some people who cannot keep accounting records or perhaps cannot even write their own names, yet they still run successful businesses. How do we calculate the profits made by such enterprises? The answer is we use 'the increased net worth method'.

The increased net worth method is one where we draw up a Balance Sheet at the start of the year, showing the assets and liabilities of the business, and then do the same at the end of the year. Since the word Balance Sheet implies that there are accounts with balances on them it is a bad word to use in these circumstances and instead we call it a 'Statement of Affairs'. We draw up an opening Statement of Affairs and a closing Statement of Affairs. On each of these statements we shall have the capital of the proprietor; what the business owes to the owner of the business, in other words the net worth of the business to the owner of the business. The question is, has their been any **increase in net worth** of the business during the year? This must be due to the profit earned. On the other hand, if there has been a decrease in net worth the business must have been running at a loss, and the owner has been 'living on his capital'.

John Briggs: Statement of Affairs at 1 January 19. .

Liabilities	£	Assets	£
Capital (net worth)	3000	Cash	3000

Fig. 32.1 The opening Statement of Affairs

John Briggs: Statement of Affairs at 31 December 19. .

	£	Fixed Assets		£
Capital (net worth)	7 572	Premises		18 000
		Fixtures and Fittings		2 000
		Motor Vehicles		5 000
				25 000
Long Term Liabilities		Current Assets		
Mortgage	15 000	Stock	4 256	
Bank Loan	10 000	Debtors	185	
	25 000	Cash at Bank	3 271	
		Cash in Hand	140	
Current Liabilities				7 852
Creditors	280			
	£32 852			£32 852

Fig. 32.2 The closing Statement of Affairs

Notes

1 We can see that the net worth of the business has increased from £3000 to £7572, which puts our starting figure for the profits at £4572. However, that is not the full story which is explained in the next section, 32.2.

2 We can also see that the actual value of the assets has risen from £3000 to £32 852 — which is an increase of £29 852. A lot of this increase was due to borrowing — £15 000 on a mortgage and £10 000 on a bank loan. Also £280 of the assets were provided by creditors who have not yet been paid. So the actual increase in value of the whole business was due to borrowing £25 280, and increase in net worth £4572 = £29 852 altogether. Now read Section 32.2 for a full explanation of the profit.

32.2 Working out the profit by the Increased Net worth Method

As we saw in the notes to Fig. 32.2 the increase in net worth is:

	£
Closing net worth	7572
Less Opening net worth	3000
Increase in net worth	£4572

This is the amount of increase in the year due to the activities in the business, but is it the correct figure? the answer is 'no', because John Briggs has also lived throughout the year and must have been drawing money to live on. Had there been no drawings this money would have been left in the business and the increase in net worth would have been greater. Suppose Briggs has drawn £120 a week for living expenses. This makes £120 × 52 = £6240 in the full year. Therefore the profit figure is:

	£
Increase in net worth	4 572
Add drawings	6 240
	£10 812

There are one or two things that could have affected this profit, for example Briggs might have put in extra capital — say a legacy or a win on the football pools, or something like that. Clearly it would not be fair to count that as 'profit'. Suppose Briggs had been left £2000 in the will of his uncle, and had put it into the business during the year. Some of the increase in net worth would not be due to the profits but would be due to this new capital contributed during the year. The profit would therefore be:

	£	
Increase in net worth	4 572	
Add drawings	6 240	
	10 812	
Less new capital contributed	2 000	
	£8 812	net profit

It would be this figure which would be used by the Inland Revenue to determine how much tax Briggs should pay in the coming year.

Figures for the Statements of Affairs

How do we discover the figures for the Statements of Affairs? Some of them are easy enough, for example the cash in hand figure and the bank balance are easily found. Assets such as premises and motor vehicles have to be valued, and we may need, if we don't agree about the correct value, to call in an independent valuer. You will find plenty of these valuers listed in your local Yellow Pages. We have to question the trader about his debts to creditors and about who owes him money (his debtors). Clearly this is not as satisfactory as keeping books of account, but if a trader cannot read and write he cannot keep books, and we cannot stop him earning a living in business just because he is illiterate.

32.3 Exercises: simple increased net worth problems

1 M. Lock starts in business on 1 January 19. . with capital of £2500 which is placed in a Bank Account except for £100 which is kept as cash in hand. One year later he has assets and liabilities as follows: Premises £12 000; Fixtures and Fittings £3200; Motor Vehicles £2480; Stock £5350; Debtors £320; Cash at Bank £1854; Cash in hand £246; Bank Loan £5000; Mortgage £11 500 and Creditors £1216.

During the year Lock has drawn £100 per week for living expenses and has also taken home (drawings in kind) goods worth £800. Lock won a prize of £500 for an invention, and this was paid into the business Bank Account as extra capital during the year.

Work out M. Lock's profit (or loss) for the year, showing your calculations, including an opening and a closing Statement of Affairs.

2 Man Lee starts in business on 1 April 19. . with capital of £5000 which is placed in a Bank Account except for £250 which is kept as cash in hand. One year later he has assets and liabilities as follows: Premises £34 000; Fixtures and Fittings

£4500; Machinery £8250; Motor Vehicles £4725; Stock £3650; Debtors £325; Cash at Bank £2825; Cash in hand £160; Bank Loan £10 000; Mortgage £30 000 and Creditors £425.

During the year Man Lee has drawn £120 per week for living expenses. A legacy of £5000 from a relative who died was paid into the business Bank Account as extra capital during the year.

Work out Man Lee's profit (or loss) for the year, showing your calculations including opening and closing Statements of Affairs.

3 Sue Hallett starts in business on 1 April 19. . with capital of £2000 which is placed in a Bank Account. One year later she has assets and liabilities as follows: Premises £27 000; Fixtures and Fittings £3300; Machinery £16750; Motor Vehicles £3850; Stock £9250; Debtors £1340; Cash at Bank £2825; Cash in hand £435; Bank Loan £15 000; Mortgage £25 000; Creditors £1850 and Rates due £230.

During the year she has drawn £80 per week for living expenses and has made herself garments for her own use worth £1200 (drawings in kind). A win of £10 000 on the Premium Bonds was paid into the business Bank Account as extra capital during the year.

Work out Sue's profit (or loss) for the year, showing your calculations, including opening and closing Statements of Affairs.

4 K. Onabanjo is in business on 1 January with assets and liabilities as shown in the table below. By the end of the year they have changed as shown:

	1 January 19. . £	31 December 19. . £
Premises	23 000	23 000
Plant & Machinery	5 800	7 500
Fixtures and Fittings	2 400	3 600
Motor Vehicles	5 840	5 240
Stock	3 784	4 925
Debtors	426	180
Cash at Bank	3 275	4 135
Cash in hand	180	230
Mortgage	20 000	18 000
Bank Loan	4 000	3 400
Creditors	560	1 260

Find the net worth of the business to the owner at 1 January and 31 December. Hence find the profit or loss for the year bearing in mind that drawings totalled £9800 in the year and that £1500 extra capital from a relative had been introduced during the year.

32.4 More difficult cases of incomplete records

Many business owners do keep some sort of records, from which it is possible to draw up a full set of final accounts with a certain amount of ingenuity on the part of the accountant. The essential features for such an exercise are as follows:

1 We must have an opening Statement of Affairs and be able to build up a closing Statement of Affairs from the information provided by the proprietor.

2 We must have a list of cash receipts and payments in the year and a list of cheque receipts and payments in the year. Sometimes these are mixed together in a general list of receipts and payments.

3 We usually need to find the total credit purchases in the year — which can be done by preparing a Total Creditors Account.

4 We also need to find the total credit sales in the year — which can be done by preparing a Total Debtors Account.

With these figures we should be able to draw up a Trading Account, Profit and Loss Account and Balance Sheet.

The best way to follow such an activity is to work through a typical example.

EXAMPLE

On 1 January the following Statement of Affairs was drawn up for M. Capulet's business.

M. Capulet Statement of Affairs as at 1 January 19. .

			£
Capital (net worth)	12 883	Machinery	8 560
Bank Loan	5 000	Furniture & Fittings	3 260
Creditors	472	Stock	4 925
		Debtors	175
		Bank balance	1 285
		Cash in hand	150
	£18 355		£18 355

His notes about cash dealings during the year show:

Receipts from customers £112 724; payments to suppliers £427; general expense items £1425; drawings taken in cash from till £5200; salaries and wages paid £24 250; paid to bank £81 284.

His notes about cheque book dealings show:

Cash deposited £81 284; payments by debtors £1816; payments to suppliers £37 210; purchase of new machine £15 000; payment on life assurance policy (to be treated as drawings) £2400; rent £4520; rates £840; light and heat £1374; telephone expenses £816; bank loan repaid £5000; bank interest £225.

Other facts he is able to give you are as follows:

Discount allowed to debtors came to £48

Discount received from suppliers came to £1054

Closing stock was valued at £3850

Debtors at the end of the year were £595

Creditors at the end of the year were £4278

Machinery was to be depreciated by £1712 and furniture and fittings by £652.

Prepare a full set of Final Accounts from the information provided.

Taking the work in stages we have:

1 The opening Statement of Affairs at 1 January

This has been provided for us, so there is nothing to prepare, but we could usefully say that every item in this opening Statement of Affairs must go on into the new year, and must appear somewhere in the records we are going to produce. Thus the capital will go into the Balance Sheet and become Capital at Start (of the year). The Bank Loan will go into a Bank Loan Account, but we shall find that it is all repaid and therefore does not appear on the Balance Sheet at the end of the year. Look for each of these items as it appears (or in the case of the Bank Loan disappears) during the year.

2 The Cash Receipts and Payments Account

We can prepare this now from the information provided. Don't forget it must start with the opening Cash balance of £150.

Cash Receipts and Payments Account for year ending 31 December 19. .

	£			£
Opening balance	150	Payments to suppliers		427
Receipts from customers	112 724	General expenses		1 425
		Drawings		5 200
		Salaries and wages		24 250
		Paid to bank		81 284
		Balance in hand	c/d	288
	£112 874			£112 874

		£
Balance in hand	b/d	288

3 The Cheques Receipts and Payments Account

We can prepare this from the information provided. Don't forget it must start with the opening balance in the Statement of Affairs at the start of the year.

Cheques Receipts and Payments Account for year ending 31 December 19. .

	£			£
Opening balance	1 285	Creditors		37 210
Cash deposits	81 284	New Machine		15 000
Debtors	1 816	Drawings		2 400
		Rent		4 520
		Rates		840
		Light & heat		1 374
		Telephone expenses		816
		Bank loan		5 000
		Interest paid		225
		Balance	c/d	17 000
	£84 385			£84 385

		£
Balance	b/d	17 000

4

We now need to find the purchases for the year, which we do with a Total Creditors Accounts, as shown below:

Total Creditors Account

19. .			£	19. .				£
Jan–Dec	Cash paid		427	Jan 1	Balance		b/d	472
	Cheques paid		37 210	Jan–Dec	Purchases			?
	Discount received		1 054					
Dec 31	Balance	c/d	4 278					
			£42 969					£42 969
				19. .				£
				Jan 1	Balance		b/d	4 278

Note

We are now trying to find the purchases figure. We know what we paid this year (£427 + £37 210) and we know what discount we received and also what we still owe. The total of these gives us the total paid or due to be paid for the year £42 969. However a small part of this £472 was for last year's purchases, so we must deduct this. The result is that the purchases figure, which should go where the ? appears is £42 497.

5 By a similar process of reasoning we can arrive at the sales figure for the year by doing a Total Sales Account.

Total Sales Account

19. .			£	19. .			£
Jan 1	Balance	b/d	175	Jan–Dec	Cash Receipts		112 724
Jan–Dec	Sales		115 008		Cheque Receipts		1 816
					Discount Allowed		48
				Dec 31	Balance	c/d	595
			£115 183				£115 183
19. .			£				
Jan 1	Balance	b/d	595				

The sales figure for the year is found to be £115 008.

6 We are now ready to do the Trading Account, Profit and Loss Account and Balance Sheet.

Trading and Profit and Loss Account for year ending 31 December 19. .

		£		£
Opening Stock		4 925	Sales (Turnover)	115 008
Purchases		42 497		
Total Stock available		47 422		
Less Closing Stock		3 850		
Cost of stock sold		43 572		
Gross profit		71 436		
		£115 008		£115 008
General expenses		1 425	Gross Profit	71 436
Salaries & wages		24 250	Discount Received	1 054
Discount allowed		48		
Rent		4 520		
Rates		840		
Light & Heat		1 374		
Telephone expenses		816		
Interest paid		225		
Depreciation:	Machinery	1 712		
	Furniture	652		
		2 364		
Net profit		35 862		
		36 628		
		£72 490		£72 490

Balance Sheet as at 31 December 19. .

Capital at start		12 883	*Fixed Assets*		
Add Net Profit	36 628		Machinery	8 560	
Less Drawings	5 200		*add* Additions	15 000	
Life Assurance	2 400			23 560	
	7 600		*Less* Depreciation	1 712	
		29 028			21 848
		41 911	Furniture		
			and Fittings	3 260	
Long Term Liability			*Less* Depreciation	652	
Bank Loan	5 000				2 608
Less repayment	5 000				24 456
		. . . .	*Current Assets*		
			Closing Stock	3 850	
			Debtors	595	
			Bank	17 000	
Current Liabilities			Cash in hand	288	
Creditors		4 278			21 733
		£46 189			£46 189

32.5 Exercises: more difficult accounts from incomplete records

1 Kay Bulmer runs a small fashion business from rented premises. Most of her sales are cash sales but she allows credit to a few established customers. The following figures relate to the business for the year 19. . . . Prepare an opening Statement of Affairs, a Cash Receipts and Payments Account, a Bank Receipts and Payments Account, a Total Debtors Account and a Total Creditors Account, and a full set of Final Accounts for the year ended 31 December 19. . .

	1 Jan	31 Dec
	£	£
Cash in hand	185	?
Cash at bank	2 420	?
Debtors	236	540
Stock	7 956	9 165
Fixtures and Fittings	2 500	2 500
Motor Van	1 850	1 850
Creditors	580	1 426
Cash receipts during the year:		
Debtors		495
Cash sales		57 256
Cash payments during the year:		
Payments for purchases		326
Cleaning		584
General expenses		426
Paid into bank		56 450

	1 Jan	31 Dec
	£	£
Bank receipts during year:		
Amounts paid into bank		56 450
Payments by debtors		500
Extra capital (legacy)		2 000
Loan from bank		2 500
Bank payments during year:		
Creditors		18 528
Rent		2 000
General expenses		5 984
Rates		640
Drawings		7 500
Salaries		4 250

Kay tells you to depreciate the van by 20% and the fixtures and fittings by 10%. She also tells you Discount Allowed was £52 and Discount Received £428.

2 K. Marshall, a retailer, keeps a partial set of records only and asks that you produce for him a Trading and Profit and Loss Account for the year ended 31 March 19. . and a Balance Sheet showing his business position at that date. He pays all cash at once into his Bank Account and settles all debts by cheque only. You ascertain the following:
His assets and liabilities were:

	1 Apr 19. .	31 Mar 19. .
	£	£
Bank	2 580	?
Debtors	765	495
Creditors	1 245	1 880
Salaries owing	165	
Insurance in advance	130	
Stock	5 980	7 950
Fixtures	2 500	?
Van	3 825	?

A summary of his Bank Account shows:

	£		£
Balance 1 April 19. .	2 580	Creditors	11 325
Debtors	1 425	Cash purchases	9 504
Cash sales	48 266	Drawings	9 650
		Salaries	7 965
		Insurance	550
		Other expenses	4 925

You ascertain also:
(a) that he has taken goods for his own use worth £400; these count as sales (goods drawn in kind).
(b) that fixtures are to be depreciated by 10%, and the van by 20% on the opening balances.

Prepare an opening Statement of Affairs, a Total Debtors Account and a Total Creditors Account, his Bank Account and a Trading and Profit and Loss Account and closing Balance Sheet of the business.

3 Isaac Sijuwade keeps only limited records from which he is able to provide you with the following information. Draw up an opening Statement of Affairs, a Cash Receipts and Payment Account and a Bank Receipts and Payments Account, a Total Debtors Account and a Total Creditors Account and a closing Statement of Affairs as at 31 December 19. . .

	1 Jan 19. .	31 Dec 19. .
	£	£
Creditors	1 754	1 584
Mortgage	18 000	14 400
Stock	7 164	12 165
Debtors	3 258	3 286
Premises	24 000	24 000
Fixtures and Fittings	3 850	?
Motor Vehicles	4 600	?
Cash at bank	2 713	?
Cash in hand	117	?

A summary of Sijuwade's cash records shows he has received cash for sales £63 812 and from debtors £3859. He had paid for general expenses £3472, for postage £495 and has drawn in cash £5600. He has also paid into the bank a total of £58 041.

A summary of his cheque book for 19. . appeared as follows:

	£		£
Balance at bank — 1 January	2 713	Cash paid to credit suppliers	23 258
Cash paid in	58 041	Telephone Expenses	490
Extra capital introduced	2 000	Rates	1 200
Cash received from debtors	12 280	Salaries	7 592
		Wages (Trading Account)	11 566
		General expenses	4 320
		Drawings	13 300
		Cash purchases	1 750
		Mortgage payment	3 600

In preparing the final accounts take the following points into consideration:
(a) Depreciate the fixtures and fittings at 10% p.a. and the motor vehicles at 20% p.a.
(b) A provision for bad debts of £786 is to be made.
(c) Rates are overdue £300.
(d) Discount Allowed was £568 and Discount Received was £1216.

33 Sundry other matters

33.1 Household Accounts

Many students and young persons share accommodation these days and it is helpful if some sort of simple Household Accounts can be kept which show all members of the group exactly who has paid, and how much, and what the money has been spent on. Such arrangements call for cooperation between the people who are participating. One person will usually take responsibility for handling the household affairs and 'a volunteer is worth ten pressed men' in such a situation. At the same time the work can be tedious if some people do not readily pay their fair share, and have to be asked repeatedly for their contribution.

Household accounts are very similar to Club Accounts in that they are really an account of receipts and payments, and at the end of the year could be presented in the form of a Receipts and Payments Account, as explained in Chapter 27. A typical example is shown in Fig. 33.1, ruled up to give analysis columns on both sides of the page.

Receipts							Total	Payments						PCV	Total
Date	Details	Bill	Mary	Sue	Peter	Sundries	£ p	Date	Details	Rent	Food	Drinks	Sundries		
27 Sept	Monthly charges	35.00	35.00	35.00	35.00		140.00	30 Sept	Rent	85.00				1	85.00
30 Sept	Collection at party					11.50	11.50		Party						
25 Oct	Monthly charges	35.00	35.00	35.00	35.00		140.00	30 Sept	expenses		17.50	12.00	1.40	2/3	30.90
29 Oct	Telephone	5.00	3.00	10.00	14.00		32.00	6 Oct	Food etc		16.25	3.25		4/5	19.50
31 Oct	Donation Peter's							9 Oct	Cleaning				4.00	6	4.00
	father					50.00	50.00	11 Oct	Food etc		17.85	3.85		7/8	21.70
								15 Oct	Cleaning				5.20	9	5.20
								19 Oct	Food etc		15.40	1.80		10/11	17.20
								23 Oct	Cleaning				3.80	12	3.80
								26 Oct	Food etc		12.86			13	12.86
								29 Oct	Rent	85.00				14	85.00
								31 Oct	Balance				88.34	c/d	88.34
	£	75.00	73.00	80.00	84.00	61.50	373.50			170.00	79.86	20.90	102.74		373.50
1 Nov	Balance b/d					88.34	88.34								

Fig. 33.1 Household Accounts

Notes
The following points about Fig. 33.1 are worth noting.
1 You can rule up as many columns as you like — for example an A4 page for each side would give plenty of room. If you rule up one copy and photocopy a small supply you will have all you need for a year's records.

2 All receipts are entered on the debit side, and each entry appears twice — once in the analysis column and once in the total column.

3 It may be thought advisable to give people a receipt for their contributions. If so a small pad of receipts can be purchased at any stationers, which leaves a carbon copy with the book-keeper and gives the person paying a torn-off perforated top copy.

4 All payments are entered on the credit side, and are similarly analysed off into columns which collect the various items of expenditure together.

5 The book-keeper is well advised to get a petty cash voucher for all sums spent so that no criticism can be made of the records.

6 The balance at the end of the month has to go into one of the analysis columns if they are to cross-tot to the correct figure. This is also true at the start of the next month when the balance is carried down.

You should now try some of the simple exercises in 33.2 below.

33.2 Exercises: Household Accounts

1 Simon, Michael, Sue and Tahira share a flat in suburbia. They agree to pay £120 per month each on the first day of each month but to pay an extra call for any major expenses, telephone bills, celebration parties, etc. No one will pay for his/her own birthday party which will be a present from the others. Tahira will keep the books and will issue receipts for all sums collected and get petty cash vouchers for all expenses. Receipts and payments in the month of January were:

Contributions 2 January, £120 by each person. 15 January £10 from each of the others for Sue's birthday party.
Food: 2 Jan £18; 9 Jan £20.35; 14 Jan £32; 19 Jan £17.50; 25 Jan £18.30.
Rent: 3 Jan £280; Cleaning: 3 Jan £8.50; 10 Jan £9.50; 17 Jan £8.50; 24 Jan £9.00; 31 Jan £10.50.
A telephone bill arrived on the 27 Jan for £23.80 and was paid that day — each person contribution £5 towards it.

Rule up suitable paper to make these entries. Enter all items in date order and balance off the book at the end of the month.

2 Abdul, George, Maira and Sonia share a flat on a college campus. They agree to pay in £140 per month each on the first day of each month but to pay an extra call for any major expenses, telephone bills, celebration parties, etc. Maira will keep the books and will issue receipts for all sums collected and get petty cash vouchers for all expenses carried out. Contributions in the month of May were £140 as arranged on May 1 when there was already a balance of £54.00 in hand.

Food: 1 May £34.60; 8 May £27.50; 15 May £31.20; 22 May £18.70; 29 May £38.50
Rent: 27 May £200
Cleaning: 7 May £12.00; 14 May £13.85; 21 May £12.00; 28 May £14.80.
On 24 May a telephone bill arrived from the College Bursar for £62.50. It was paid and it was agreed it should be met by a special payment of £15.00 each. A special payment for the post-examination Leavers' Ball was paid (£72.00 for the group) on 23 May.

Rule up suitable paper to make these entries. Enter all items in date order and balance off the book at the end of the month.

3 Sara, Joe, Lucy and Alec share a flat in suburbia. They agree to pay in £135 per month each, on the first day of each month, and to pay an extra call for any major expenses, telephone bills, etc.

Alec will keep the books and will issue receipts for all sums collected and get petty cash vouchers for all expenses carried out. Contributions in the month of September were the initial contributions mentioned above and £15 each on 7 September for the purchase of a heating appliance. Expenses were

Food:1 Sept £23.56; 8 Sept £19.54; 15 Sept £22.36; 22 Sept £23.70; 29 Sept £19.22.
Rent: 1 September £220; Rates £26 on the same date.
Cleaning: 6 Sept £5.50; 13 Sept £7.25; 20 Sept £5.95; 27 Sept £9.20.
A party held on the 30 Sept. was paid for by each person contributing £10. Expenditure was on food £19.50 and wine £12.00. Competition prizes cost £8.50.

Rule up suitable paper to make these entries. Enter all items and balance off the book at the end of the month. Carry this balance forward for the start of October.

33.3 Departmental Accounts

We have seen how analysis columns can be used to collect together related items, both in the Household Accounts mentioned above and also in the Petty Cash Book in Chapter 15. This idea is sometimes used, particularly in large organisations, to collect together the various costs associated with particular departments, and thus keep track of the work of each department. Any such system is described by the term 'Departmental Accounts'. This does not really require us to learn anything new, because we already know how to do all the book-keeping concerned, but it is worth while considering a particular example just to think about the whole idea.

Example

Imagine a trader who deals in two chief sets of products, office stationery and educational textbooks. These two sets of products are fairly distinct, people who want office stationery are not likely to order textbooks, and vice versa. He might feel that instead of preparing general accounts covering all his activities it would be worth while preparing Departmental Accounts, so that he could tell how much profit was being made on each department, as well as the total profit on the whole business. Suppose his profit in one year came to £60 000 he might feel very satisfied with the year's work, but if the preparation of Departmental Accounts showed that office stationery yielded £55 000 of the profit and educational books only yielded £5000 he would not feel quite so pleased. 'Is it worthwhile selling books at all?' he might ask himself.

This is the sort of thing we discover from Departmental Accounts. We might even find, for example, that office stationery yielded £85 000 but educational books were losing £25 000, to give a final profit of only £60 000. That would be an even more disturbing result.

Capturing the figures for Departmental Accounts

Thinking about the example described above, to prepare a Departmental Trading and Profit and Loss Account for the business described we would need to separate off the figures we use to give separate figures for each department. This is fairly easy in some cases, for example.

Purchases As these arrive we would record purchases of stationery in one column and purchases of educational books in another, with a total column to take the total purchases.

Sales Sales could be separated off at the tills, or recorded in separate columns on the Sales Account. If we have a computerized till we can use a code to collect each type of sales; the computer capturing the data for each code.

Wages We could easily allocate the wages of those who deal with stationery to one column and those who deal with books to another column.

Some overhead items like Light and Heat, Rent and Rates, insurance etc would not be quite so easy to allocate, and would have to be apportioned on some fair basis — for example if stationery is two thirds of the turnover we might decide to make it carry two thirds of the overhead expenses.

At the level of this book we do not need to know too much about Departmental Accounts, which are really part of a higher level of studies known as **costing**, or **management accounting** (because this kind of account helps management make business decisions about the expansion or contraction of departments, etc). The reader is urged to pursue his/her studies into this sort of area once present studies are successfully completed.

33.4 Purchasing a business

When we purchase a business there are a number of considerations which need to be borne in mind. First, the present proprietor naturally hopes to get a good price for the business, whereas we hope to pay as little as possible. However we do not wish to set our price too low or another buyer may succeed and disappoint us. Buying a business is always a matter for bargaining and many factors must be considered. It is better to take your time, and consider carefully the site, the amount of business it is likely to produce, the past record of the present proprietor, the state of the premises, equipment and stocks, etc. etc.

Goodwill and the purchase price

When we purchase a business we shall often be asked to pay an extra sum for goodwill, which is really a payment for the hard work of the present proprietor in the past. Some of the profit we make in the future will really be the result of his/her hard work in the past, because customers will continue to deal with the business even though the ownership has changed. Naturally we shall not pay more than we can help for the goodwill, and in any case the actual figure to be recorded in Goodwill Account may vary with some of the valuations we place on the assets when we take them over. This is explained in the example below.

EXAMPLE   R. Sanderson is selling his business, whose assets and liabilities are shown below:

R. Sanderson: Balance Sheet as at 31 July 19. .

Liabilities		Assets	£
Capital	60 976	Premises	34 000
		Fixtures and Fittings	12 000
Bank Loan	5 000	Motor Vehicles	5 600
		Stock	14 250
Creditors	1 614	Debtors	160
		Bank	1 542
		Cash	38
	£67 590		£67 590

M. Crabtree agrees to take over all the assets except the Bank balance and the cash. He will also take over the creditors, but not the bank loan. Sanderson will settle this privately. The purchase price is to be £70 000, which includes an element of goodwill. Crabtree decides to value the assets taken over as follows: Premises £48 000; Fixtures and Fittings £4000; Motor Vehicles £4200; Stock £8500. Debtors will be left at their present book value. This gives a total asset value as follows:

	£
Premises	48 000
Fixtures and Fittings	4 000
Motor Vehicles	4 200
Stock	8 500
Debtors	160
	£64 860

From this asset value of £64 860 we must deduct the creditors taken over, which are a liability of £1614. This means that the net value of what is being taken over is £64 860 − £1614 = £63 246. This is the actual value of the business taken over, but the purchaser has agreed to pay £70 000 for it, Therefore the rest of the money he/she is prepared to pay must be the value of the goodwill.

		£
Purchase price	=	70 000
Net value of business	=	63 246
Goodwill value		£ 6 754

33.5 Opening the books with an Open Journal entry (or entries)

We would need to do some Journal entries to record the opening of the books, and the taking over of the various assets and liabilities. If we think about the problem in chronological order we have the following stages.

1 The parties agree about the price. M. Crabtree is to take over the business for £70 000 from the vendor, R. Sanderson. This makes the vendor, Sanderson, a creditor for £70 000. We make the debit to balance this credit in an account called Purchase of Business Account which is opened for a short time to record the purchase. The Journal entry is: debit Purchase of Business Account £70 000; credit the vendor with £70 000. When posted to the Ledger the accounts are as shown in Fig. 33.2.

Purchase of Business A/c   L1

19. .			£		
Jan 1	R. Sanderson	L2	70 000		

R. Sanderson (Vendor) A/c   L2

				19. .			£
				Jan 1	Purchase of Business	L1	70 000

Fig. 33.2 The original agreement to purchase the business

2 We now take the assets on to the books, which calls for a debit entry in all the asset accounts and a credit entry to balance them in the Purchase of Business Account. These entries are shown in Fig. 33.3. Notice that goodwill is also an asset, even though there is nothing really to show for it — it is called an **intangible asset,** because we cannot really touch it; it exists in the minds of customers of the business. We could of course need to know the names and addresses of the individual debtors before we could take them on, and the vendor would need to write to them and tell them to settle their debts with M. Crabtree instead of him. We will imagine there is only one debtor, R. Markham.

Premises A/c   L3

19. .			£		
Jan 1	Purchase of Business	L1	48 000		

Furniture & Fittings A/c   L4

19. .			£		
Jan 1	Purchase of Business	L1	4 000		

Motor Vehicles A/c   L5

19. .			£		
Jan 1	Purchase of Business	L1	4 200		

Stock A/c   L6

19. .			£		
Jan 1	Purchase of Business	L1	8 500		

R. Markham A/c   L7

19. .			£		
Jan 1	Purchase of Business	L1	160		

Goodwill A/c   L8

19. .			£		
Jan 1	Purchase of Business	L1	6 754		

Purchase of Business A/c   L1

19. .			£	19. .			£
Jan 1	R. Sanderson	L2	70 000	Jan 1	Sundry assets	L3–8	71 614

Fig. 33.3 Taking over the assets

3 We now take on the liabilities, which is the creditor figure of £1614. We would of course need to know the names and addresses of the creditors, and would need to write to them explaining the change of ownership, in case they had some objection. If they did object the new owner would probably pay them up at once. The creditors would of course be credited, and the double entry would then be in the Purchase of Business Account. This would close off this account which has now served its purpose. We will imagine there are only two creditors, P. Long (£850) and T. Short (£764).

P. Long A/c						L9
			19..			£
Jan 1			Jan 1	Purchase of business	L1	850

T. Short A/c						L10
			19..			£
Jan 1			Jan 1	Purchase of business	L1	764

Purchase of Business A/c							L1
19..			£	19..			£
Jan 1	R. Sanderson	L2	70 000	Jan 1	Sundry assets	L3 — 8	71 614
1	Sundry Creditors	L9 — 10	1 614				
			£71 614				£71 614

Fig. 33.4 Taking over the liabilities

4 The business has now been taken over but the vendor has not yet been paid, and appears on the books as a creditor, R. Sanderson, for £70 000. The new owner must now contribute the capital, or if arrangements have been made to borrow some of the purchase price these must now be put into effect. We will imagine Crabtree is to contribute £25 000 capital, and is to borrow £50 000 from the bank. This gives him £75 000 out of which he will pay the vendor £70 000. The entries for all these matters are shown in Fig. 33.5.

BankA/c							CB1
19..			£	19..			£
Jan 1	Capital	L11	25 000	Jan 1	R. Sanderson	L2	70 000
1	Bank loan	L12	50 000				

Capital A/c					L11
			19..		£
			Jan 1	Bank	CB1	25 000

Bank Loan A/c					L12
			19..		£
			Jan 1	Bank	CB1	50 000

R. Sanderson A/c   L2

19. .			£	19. .		£
Jan 1	Bank	CB1	70 000	Jan 1	Purchase of Business	70 000

Fig. 33.5 Paying the vendor

All the accounts are now open, the various assets and liabilities have been taken over, the vendor has been paid and the Balance Sheet of the new business is as shown in Fig. 33.6.

M. Crabtree: Balance Sheet as at 1 January 19. .

Capital	£	Fixed Assets		£
At start	25 000	Goodwill		6 754
		Premises		48 000
		Furniture & Fittings		4 000
Long-term Liabilities		Motor vehicles		4 200
Bank Loan	50 000			62 954
		Current Assets	£	
		Stock	8 500	
Current Liabilities		Debtors	160	
Creditors	1 614	Bank	5 000	
				13 660
	£76 614			£76 614

Fig. 33.6 The Balance Sheet of the new business

33.6 Exercises: The purchase of a business

1 R. Smallbridge decides to sell his business, the Balance Sheet of which is as follows:

Liabilities		Assets	
Capital	31 600	Premises	35 000
Mortgage	25 400	Fixtures & Fittings	4 200
Creditors	1 820	Motor Vehicles	3 750
Electric light bill due	35	Stock	9 850
		Debtors	4 250
		Cash at Bank	1 150
		Cash in Hand	655
	£58 855		£58 855

Mary Hughes agrees to buy the business on the following terms:
(a) She will not take over the debtors, cash at bank or cash in hand, nor will she be liable for the creditors (except the electric light bill due).
(b) The mortgage will be settled privately by Smallbridge at the same time as the property is transferred.
(c) The purchase price will be £52 000.
Mary decides to revalue the assets as follows: Premises £40 000, Fixtures &

Fittings £2000, Motor vehicle £1250, Stock £5500. Show the entries on 1 April when the transactions all take place, and Mary contributes £60 000 as capital to her Bank Account. Show all the ledger entries for the opening of Mary's accounts and a Balance Sheet of her new business at the start of its affairs.

2 Yacob Muhammad agrees to take over the business of Yussuf Museveni. The assets and liabilities were as follows on the Balance Sheet provided by Museveni.

Y. Museveni: Balance Sheet as at 30 June 19. .

Capital	£		Fixed Assets		£
At start		35 693	Premises		42 000
Add profit	32 650		Machinery		19 500
Less drawings	12 650		Furniture and Fittings		4 850
		20 000	Motor Vehicles		8 250
		55 693			74 600
Long-term Liabilities					
Mortgage		30 000	Current Assets	£	
Current Liabilities			Stock	9 750	
Creditors		3 725	Debtors	3 250	
			Cash at Bank	1 650	
			Cash in Hand	168	
					14 818
		£89 418			£89 418

Muhammad will take over all the assets except debtors, cash at bank and cash in hand. He will take over one of the creditors, R. Johnson, to whom £625 is owing, but the rest will be settled by Museveni. The purchase price will be £83 000. Muhammad decides to value the motor vehicles at only £6000 and the stock at £7750. Otherwise values are believed to be fair.

Show the ledger entries for the start of the business on 1 July 19. ., and the Balance Sheet on commencement on that date. Muhammad contributed £50 000 from private funds for capital, and borrowed £50 000 from Helpful Bank PLC.

3 Keith Nadarr agrees to purchase the hairdressing salon of Stylish Fashions Ltd, for £74 000. The assets are Premises Account £35 000; Fittings and Equipment £28 000; Stocks £5000 and a deposit for electricity of £500. There is a liability for rates of £850 which Nadarr agrees to honour. Nadarr provides £50 000 capital on 1 March 19 . . and borrows £30 000 from the Generous Finance Co., on that date to provide the balance required and a small amount of working capital. Nadarr proposes to reduce the stock value to only £4000 when opening his books.

Show the Journal and ledger entries necessary to open the accounts, and the opening Balance Sheet of the business.

Answers

1.4 Cashing up at the end of the day
1 £340.70; 2 £942.31; 3 £770.48; 4 £1651.10

1.7 Recording weekly takings
1 £1303.49; £862.17; £500.00; 2 £2468.68; £1818.53; £17.54; 3 £1870.71; £1139.37; £160.00; 4 £2145.57; £706.83; £1000.00

2.2 Recording payments for business stock
1 £31.45; £204.34; 2 £67.03; £41.05; 3 £12.81; £291.99; 4 £56.05; £51.45

2.4 Recording payments other than for stock
1 £158.90; £138.25; 2 £103.44; £409.16; 3 £48.74; £176.04; 4 £24.60; £300.40

3.3 Debtor's Accounts
1 D. Black: debit balance £166.80; 2 Mrs E. Noir: debit balance £145.15; 3 Miss B. Schwarz: debit balance £167.95; 4 T. Zwart: debit balance £103.20; 5 S. Davies: debit balance £199.35

3.5 Creditors' Accounts
1 C. Reid: credit balance £131.65; 2 R. Glover: credit balance £1661.40; 3 E. Roth: credit balance £697.40; 4 D. Rankin: credit balance £762.45; 5 S. Grainger: credit balance £173.60

3.7 Running balance accounts
1 A. Martin: debit balance £636.92; 2 M. Senior: debit balance £898.60; 3 M. Wabenze: account clear; 4 R. Carless: credit balance £1320.60

4.4 Simple Cash Accounts
1 Debit balance £146.22; 2 Debit balance £172.22; 3 Debit balance £229.40; 4 Debit balance £216.14; 5 Debit balance £710.00

4.6 Simple Bank Accounts
1 Debit balance £1763.84; 2 Debit balance £2122.55; 3 Debit balance £3636.60; 4 Debit balance £2819.63

5.4 Nominal Accounts
1 Debit Rates A/c £880 and credit Bank A/c £880
2 Debit Bank A/c £385 and credit Commission Received A/c £385
3 In each case the loss account should be debited and the Bank A/c should be credited, as it has given value.
4 (a) Debit Bank A/c with £325 000 and credit Fees Received A/c
(b) Debit Aviation Expenses A/c with £84 000 and credit Bank A/c.

6.3 Contribution of capital by the proprietor

1 Debit Bank A/c (£1000) and credit Capital (C. Ralston) A/c (£1000).

2 Debit Cash A/c (£500); Debit Bank A/c (£4500); credit Capital (E. Shah) A/c £5000.

3 Debit Cash A/c (£155); Bank A/c (£3825); Computer Equipment A/c (£1750) and Furniture and Fittings A/c (£360). Credit Capital (Margaret Green) A/c with £6090.

4 Debit the four asset accounts, Furniture A/c, Motor Vehicles A/c, Art Equipment A/c and Bank A/c with the amounts given and credit Capital A/c with £3081.65.

6.6 Double entries

1 Debit Purchases A/c and credit Bank A/c

2 Debit Cash A/c with £580 cash received and credit Motor Vehicles A/c, to remove the vehicle from her books.

3 Debit Carriage Out A/c and credit Cash A/c

4 Debit Motor Vehicles A/c (£2300), Purchases A/c (£620) and Equipment A/c (£580). Credit Bank A/c (£3500).

5 (a) Debit Machinery A/c (£3850) and credit Dental Hygiene Ltd (£3850).
  (b) Debit Dental Hygiene Ltd (£3850) and credit Bank A/c (£3850).

7.5 Exercises to the Trial Balance level

1 Total £5875.00; 2 Totals £4356.20; 3 Totals £46 876.10; 4 Totals £9554.55

8.5 The completion of invoices

1 Invoice total £500.50 (VAT £45.50); 2 Invoice total £113.30 (VAT £10.30); 3 Invoice total S$955; 4 Invoice total Z$3375

8.7 The completion of credit notes

1 Total £377.03 (VAT £34.28); 2 Total £472.50; 3 Total £395; 4 Total £140.75 (VAT £12.80)

9.5 VAT

1 (a) £685 (b) £52.50 (c) £346.50 (d) 2 pence (e) 16 pence

2 (a) £21 (b) £5.62 (c) £9.98 (d) £9.71 (e) £54.75

3 VAT due £5152

4 VAT due £4683.75

5 VAT of £1080 is repaid by Customs & Excise to the shopkeeper

6 Debit Purchases A/c £17 520; debit VAT A/c £1752; credit Garden Supplies Ltd £19 272

7 Debit R Akram & Co. with £1242; credit Sales A/c with £1080 and VAT A/c with £162

10.3 The purchase of assets

1 Debit Typewriters A/c £850; credit Electronic Office Supplies Ltd £850

2 Debit Fixtures & Fittings A/c £420; credit Shopfitters PLC £420

3 Debit Restaurant Equipment A/c £319; debit Purchases A/c £120; debit Shopfittings A/c £90; credit Cash A/c £529

4 Debit Machinery A/c £465; credit Bank A/c £465

5 Debit Furniture A/c £845; debit Computers A/c £3000; credit Mitre Furniture PLC £3845

6 Debit Office Furniture A/c £600.90; debit Typewriters A/c £327.50; debit VAT A/c £92.84; credit Business Materials Co. £1021.24

10.6 Purchases Day Book
1 Purchases £7130; Carriage In £130; VAT £726; Total £7986
2 Purchases £4300.50; Carriage In £442.50; VAT £474.30; Total £5217.30
3 Purchases £6531.50; Carriage In £97.50; VAT £662.90; Total £7291.90
4 Purchases £1091.10; Carriage In £68.90; VAT £116.00; Total £1276.00

10.8 Sales Day Book
1 Sales £4591.53; VAT £440.70; Total £5032.23
2 Sales £12 748.60; VAT £1274.86; Total £14 023.46
3 Sales £5999.20; Carriage Out £333.50; VAT £394.18; Total £6726.88
4 Sales £3336.10; Carriage Out £184.15; VAT £352.03; Total £3872.28

10.10 Purchases Returns Book
1 Purchases Returns £3405; Carriage In £75; VAT £348; Total £3828
2 Purchases Returns £564.50; Carriage In £18; VAT £58.25; Total £640.75
3 Purchases Returns £860.50; Carriage In £35; VAT £89.55; Total £985.05

10.12 Sales Returns Book
1 Sales Returns £361; Carriage Out £10; VAT £37.10; Total £408.10
2 Sales Returns £1099.50; Carriage Out £61.50; VAT £116.10; Total £1277.10
3 Sales returns £486.50; Carriage Out £5.50; VAT £49.20; Total £541.20

11.8 No numerical answers for Chapter 11

12.7 No numerical answers supplied for Chapter 12.

13.6 The three-Column Cash Book

	Discount Allowed	Cash Balance	Bank Balance	Discount Received
1	£27.55	£ 465.88	£5953.23	£19.89
2	£42.28	£ 800.82	£5726.92	£86.59
3	£90.87	£498.06	£4440.47	£214.70
4	£17.18	£671.76	£4742.30	£9.72
5	£10.13	£1212.75	£3680.97	£3.27

13.9 Paying-in slips

	Cash total £	Cheque total £	Final total £
1	1 094.40	776.00	1 870.40
2	1 042.30	411.00	1 453.30
3	11 549.55	560.00	12 109.55
4	1 182.90	2 336.35	3 519.25

14.5 Bank Reconciliation Statements
1 Alan Ahlberg: revised Cash Book balance £2818.97; then add back two cheques not yet presented.
2 J. M. Chara: revised Cash Book balance £956.13; then add cheque not yet presented and drawings not yet cleared.
3 K. Grieve: revised Cash Book balance £4798.67; then add back cheque not presented and deduct lodgement not yet cleared.
4 T. Nash: revised Cash Book balance £2894.48; then deduct lodgement not yet cleared.
5 Lee Sim Huatt: revised Cash Book balance £3058.11; then add back cheques not yet presented.

15.3 The Petty cash Book

	Total Expenditure £	Balance carried down £	Imprest restored £
1	68.12	21.73	58.27
2	69.75	18.05	61.95
3	95.46	9.49	90.51
4	82.99	4.81	—
5	77.07	30.28	69.72

16.2 Capital and revenue expenditure
1 (a), (c), (g) and (i) are capital items.
2 (a), (d) and (f) are capital items.
3 —
4 (a), (d), (e), (g), (k), (o), (q), (r), (t) are capital items. (m) the uniforms for the keepers are a debatable point, but probably more revenue than capital, as it is difficult to pass on uniforms to another employee.

16.9 More about capital and revenue expenditure
1 (c) (f) (g) (h) and (i) are capital items.
2 (a) (c) (g) and (i) are capital items.
3 (b) The machine should be valued on the books at £32 980 (Debit Machinery Account). Bank should be credited with £32 480 and Wages Account with £500.
4 Debit Premises Account with £24 000, and Redecorations in Suspense Account with £7500. Debit £2500 in Repairs and Renewals Account for this year's expense. Credit Bank Account with £34 000.
5 Debit Pleasure Boat Account £26 000, Motor Vehicles Account £ 12 600, Camping Equipment Account £1600; Land and Buildings Account £2400 and Repairs in Suspense Account £1200. Also debit Repairs Account with £1200 for this year's share of the loss. Credit Bank Account with £45 000.

17.4 Depreciation by the straight-line method
1 Depreciation A/c is debited with £12 000 and Machinery A/c is credited.
2 (a) £550 per annum (b) Sewing Machine A/c is credited each year with £550 and ends up with a balance of £1400.
3 (a) Depreciation charge is £1600 for the half year.
  (b) By January Year 4 it is worth £28 500
4 (a) Depreciation per annum = £6240.
  (b) At the end of Year 1 value is £29 320 (3/4 of a year depreciation); then falling to £23 080 and £16 840 in next two years.

17.8 More depreciation exercises
1 Thompson Bros: Value falls to £15 000, then £11 250 and then to £8438.
2 Marshall & Co.: Value falls to £45 200, then £36 160 and then to £28 928.
3 Somalia Desert Corporation: Provision for Depreciation Account is credited each year with £15 000.
4 Far East Fuels PLC: Provision for Depreciation Account is credited with £11 720 000 in year 1, with £9 376 000 in year 2 and with £7 500 800 in year 3. At the end of year 3 the tanker is worth £58 600 000 − £28 596 800 = £30 003 200.
5 Farmer Hendrikson: Herd A/c is credited with £5300 for the fall in value; Profit & Loss A/c is debited.
6 Plastic Corporation Ltd: Machine Tools A/c is debited with £24 250 for the increase in value; Profit & Loss A/c is credited.

18.4 Trial Balances
1 R. Patel: Totals agree at £69 164.55
2 Lee Kiang: Totals agree at £64 645.10
3 M. Finch: Totals agree at £131 741.10
4 R. Wylie: Totals agree at £162 563.
5 G. Haji: Totals agree at £90 433.20
6 R. Maples: Totals agree at £133 338.

19.5 Bad debts
1 Debit Bad Debts A/c £150; credit P. Jones £150.
2 Debit Bank A/c £900 and Bad Debts A/c £900; credit Mayotte's A/c £1800 to clear the debt.
3 Debit Bank A/c £297.50 and Bad Debts A/c £552.50; credit the airline with £850.00
4 Debit Bank A/c £320; credit Bad Debts Recovered A/c £210, Legal Expenses A/c £25 and Interest Received A/c £85.
5 Debit Bank A/c £718.52; credit Bad Debts Recovered A/c £420, Legal Expenses A/c £86 and Interest Received A/c £212.52.

19.9 The sale of assets, etc.
1 Debit Cash A/c £120 and Loss on Sale of Equipment A/c £230; credit Kitchen Equipment A/c £350.
2 Debit Bank A/c £23 600; credit Machinery Account £18 000 and Profit on Sale of Machinery Account with £5600.
3 Debit Bank A/c £1000, Workshop Equipment A/c £550 and Loss on Sale of Motor Vehicle A/c £450. Credit Motor Vehicles A/c with £2000 to remove the motor vehicle from the books.
4 Debit Makaria Security Co. with £5800; credit Power Launch A/c with £5600 and Profit on Sale of Launch A/c with £200.
5 Debit Bank A/c £4000 and credit Loan A/c (Helpful Bank PLC) with £4000.
6 Debit Bank A/c with £15 000 and Interest Payable A/c with £4500; credit Loan A/c (Union Finance Ltd.) with £19 500.
7 Debit Bank A/c with £25 000 and Interest Payable A/c with £10 000; credit Loan A/c (Commercial Bankers Corporation) with £35 000.
8 Debit T. Smith A/c with £49.50 and credit Bank A/c to remove the dishonoured cheque.

19.14 The correction of errors.
1 Debit Eastern Chemicals Ltd. with £642 and credit Eastern Chemists Ltd. to clear the incorrect entry.
2 Debit T. Edmunds with £84.50 and credit T. Edwards to restore the full amount owing to him.
3 Debit Motor Vehicles A/c £4950 and credit Furniture and Fittings to clear the incorrect entry.
4 Debit Purchases A/c with £1756 and credit Computers A/c to remove the incorrect item.
5 It is a single sided Journal entry. All we need to do is credit Motor Vehicles A/c with £90 to reduce the value to the correct figure.
6 Debit Suspense A/c with £90 to clear the account and credit Millers Ltd. A/c with £90 to get the full amount owed recorded properly.
7 (a) Debit Suspense A/c with £121.40 and credit Interest Received A/c
   (b) Debit Loan A/c £1000 and credit Suspense A/c £1000
   (c) Debit Suspense A/c £156.90 and credit R. Higgs A/c.

8 (a) Debit S. Iskander with £81.00 and credit Suspense A/c.
(b) Debit A. N. Archer A/c with £42.50 and credit Anne Archer A/c.
(c) Debit Suspense A/c with £5.50 and credit Bank A/c.
(d) Debit T. Heron & Co. A/c with £350 and credit Suspense A/c.

20.8 Trading Accounts

		Gross Profit	Total of Trading A/c
		£	£
1	M. Shute	52 568	66 000
2	K. Lawal	75 936	119 000
3	R. Phillipson	105 916.95	141 000.00
4	M. Ankor	129 539.07	172 000.00
5	M. Stevenson	38 530.20	98 381.10
6	M. Tully	21 417	44 000
7	F. Dearborn	34 605	83 000
8	T. Honeywell	58 030	116 411

21.4 Finding the Net Profit

		Net Profit	Total of Profit & Loss A/c
		£	£
1	G. Vyner	22 361.77	48 221.55
2	T. Calthorpe	44 448.94	67 886.54
3	T. Boake	34 430	60 531
4	Kenya Fashions (Baragoi) Ltd.	28 755	97 082
5	Tina Price	22 552	43 640
6	Isaac Adeleye	88 164	124 924

21.6 The Trading and Profit and Loss Account

	Gross profit	Trading A/c totals	Net profit	Profit & Loss A/c totals
	£	£	£	£
1	44 761	68 000	19 492	46 211
2	110 731	135 411	50 312	113 581
3	66 566	123 000	18 826	68 473

22.6 Preparation of Balance Sheets

The assets side only has been given in Questions 1–4

		Fixed assets	Current assets	Balance Sheet total
		£	£	£
1	R. Seagrave	35 185	33 615	68 800
2	T. Sillitoe	52 700	13 787	66 487
3	I. Olaleye	86 285	9 615	95 900
4	G. Franklin	38 800	15 546	54 346

	Gross profit	Net profit	Balance Sheet totals
	£	£	£
5	—	32 560	76 710
6	42 648	15 133	85 965
7	67 478	37 431	71 606

23.3 Bin Cards

1 Final balance 17 pumps
2 Final balance 47 reams

3 Final balance 410 copies
4 Stock value £11 199.45
5 Stock value £10 580.

23.10   Stock-taking

1 (a) Stock is valued at cost price or net realisable value, whichever is lower.
(b) £37
2 Stock at close = £5050
3 R. Bayford: Stock at close = £6960
4 Mumtaz & Kadar: Stock value = £16 819
5 Colby & Co. Stock value = £33 274
6 New Arrival: Stock value = £12 977
7 Peter Farmer: Stock value = £7354

24.4   Payments in advance

1 M. Nolan: (a) £560; (b) Insurance in advance £270
2 W. Akram: (a) £579.75; (b) Rates in advance £193.25
3 Industrial Properties Ltd.: (a) Profit element to Profit & Loss A/c £172 000;
(b) Balance on liabilities side of Balance Sheet £115 000.
4 Helpful Bank PLC: Balance carried forward £9 989 989 liability.

24.7   Payments in advance and accrued expenses

1 T. Philips: (a) Rent £2400; Rates 645; Insurance £540 to Profit & Loss A/c.
(b) Balances: Rent due from sub-tenant £50 asset; Rates in advance £215 assets;
Insurance in advance £180 asset.
2 A. Garage owner: £2850 to Profit and Loss A/c; £465 to Balance Sheet (asset).
3 Yosemite Wholesaling Co.: Trading A/c £95 044; Profit & Loss A/c £47 522;
Wages due on Balance Sheet £11 966 (liability).
4 Joseph Chicoh: Amount to Profit & Loss A/c £4783.50; Balance Sheet items
Rates in advance £312.50 (asset). Rent received in advance (liability) £400.
5 R. Chequeurs: Charge to Profit & Loss A/c £2001.

24.9   Final Accounts with adjustments

	Gross Profit £	Net Profit £	Balance Sheet Totals £
1 M. Jaffrey:	44 156	22 222	64 508
2 Young Alert:	80 862	56 549	94 862
3 Peter Osborne:	45 654	19 926	82 754

24.11   Provisions for Bad debts

1 M. Lark: (b) Debit Profit & Loss A/c £202; credit Provision for Bad Debts
£202; (c) Debtors £2020 − £202 = £1818.
2 (a) £17 269 − £629 = £16 640; £16 640 ÷ 10 = £1664
(b) Debit Profit & Loss A/c £1664; Credit Provision for Bad Debts A/c £1664
(c) Debtors £16 640 − £1664 = £14 976
3 B. Scrivenor: (a) Bad Debts Account total £432; (b) Carried to Profit & Loss
A/c £452; (c) Debtors £3000 − £300 = £2700
4 W. Mathai: (a) Bad Debts Account total £611; (b) Carried to Profit & Loss A/c
£673; (c) Balance Sheet Debtors £4820 − £482 = £4338.

24.14   More adjustments

1 Depreciated by £500 each year.
2 Goodwill came to £3500. Advised to write it off over 5 years by equal
instalments.

3 No numerical answer.

4 £3000.

5 £5500 per year.

6 Leone Ogbara: Gross profit £88 124; Net profit £53 605; Balance Sheet totals £95 600.

7 Helen Cartwright: Gross profit £46 725; Net profit £34 680; Balance Sheet totals £97 235.

25.10 Concepts of accounting
Numerical answers are as follows:

2 (a) and (d) are material items.

6 £4121 profit.

26.5 Appropriation Accounts

1 Brett and Walker: residue is shared £9552 to Brett; £19 104 to Walker.

2 Dee and Kadar: residue is shared £7138 to Dee; £21 414 to Kadar.

3 A, B and C share the residue A; £12 381; £8254; C: £4127.

4 Major and Minor: share of residue. Major £13 728; Minor: £6864.

5 Each partner's share of the residue of the profit is £10 580.

26.7 Partnership Final Accounts

1 Current A/c balances: A £10 313; C £7809.

2 Current A/c balances: Haji £7581 credit; Kabiri £2381 debit.

3 A & B Perkins: Shares of residue A £24 400; B £12 200; Current A/c balances A £21 900; B £8530; Balance Sheet totals £94 175.

4 Shah & Singh: Shares of residue Shah £20 234; Singh £10 117; Current A/c balances Shah £10 804; Singh £11 727; Balance Sheet totals £128 890.

5 Sue & Nicola Kingham: Gross profit £88 250; Net profit £39 520; shares of residue: Sue £14 265; Nicola £4755; Current A/c balances: Sue £5765; Nicola £3005; Balance Sheet totals £102 514.

6 Sorrel & Willow: Gross profit £67 394; Net profit £25 799; Current A/c balances: Sorrel £5876 credit; Willow £1547 debit; Balance Sheet totals £111 289.

27.4 Receipts and Payments Accounts

1 Cash in hand £524.71: Receipts and Payments Account totals £2195.77.

2 Totals of Receipts and Payments Account £4073.10.

3 Totals of Receipts and Payments Account £10 282.

4 Totals of Receipts and Payments Account £3445.40.

27.6 Final Accounts of Clubs

1 Valley Social Club: Cash balance £52; Total of Receipts and Payments A/c £1764 Surplus for year £1065; Total of Income and Expenditure A/c £1695; Total of Balance Sheet £1294.

2 Suburbia Tennis Club: Cash in hand £392; Total of Receipts and Payments A/c £2625; Surplus £1154; Total of Income and Expenditure A/c £2825; Accumulated Fund at start £18 573; at end £19 727; Balance Sheet total £19 752.

3 Leyfarers Cycling Club: Cash in hand £345; Surplus £453; Total of Income and Expenditure A/c £785; Accumulated Fund at start £532; at end £985; Balance Sheet totals £1060.

4 Photographers' Club: Cash in hand £805; total of Receipts and Payments A/c £2344; surplus for year £668; Accumulated Fund at start £1488; at end £2156; Balance Sheet totals £2319.

5 Wanderers' Cycling Club: Accumulated Fund at start £25 078; Cash in hand £148; Receipts and Payments A/c total £5207; cash at bank £1122; Receipts and Payments (Bank) totals £5665; Trading A/c Gross profit £1244; Income and Expenditure A/c surplus £1991; Balance Sheet totals £40 844; Accumulated fund at close £27 069.

28.5 Company Final Accounts
1 Smith Ltd.: Appropriation A/c balance £9089 and totals £87 839; Balance Sheet totals £244 713.
2 Field Ltd.: Appropriation A/c balance £13 488 and totals £80 488; Balance Sheet totals £237 348.
3 XYZ Ltd.: Net profit £37 030; Appropriation A/c balance £7730; Balance Sheet totals £90 730.
4 Brown Ltd.: Gross profit £51 025; Net profit £27 745; Appropriation A/c balance £2145; Balance Sheet totals £86 145.

29.3 Simple Manufacturing Accounts
1 P. Sinclair: prime cost £96 412; cost of manufactured goods £146 678; gross profit £200 748.
2 Maira Malik: prime cost £97 317; cost of manufactured goods £108 437; gross profit £59 784.
3 Diane Hughes: prime cost £212 229; cost of manufactured goods £260 752; gross profit £97 282.

29.6 More difficult Manufacturing Accounts
1 M. Neil: prime cost £118 958; manufacturing profit £50 698; gross profit £22 916. Advice: There is no point in taking up the offer; the factory is profitable and should be kept going.
2 Anne Mitchell: prime cost £64 791; loss on manufacturing £3714; gross profit £40 499. Advice: The factory is inefficient and should be better managed but the gain by closing it is only going to be small and this is not worth doing.
3 Ken Hom: prime cost cost £103 990; profit on manufacturing £31 482; gross profit £104 551. Advice: No point in closing factory — it is well run and should be continued.

30.3 Analysing the Trading Account
1 43.5%; **2** 37.5%; **3** 29.4%; **4** 52.4%; **5** (a) 8.5 times (b) 6.1 weeks;
6 (a) 10.4 times (b) 5 weeks;
7 Business No. 1. 33.9% No. 2 31.8%; Rate of stock turn No 1. 3.5 times per month No 2. 1.8 times per month.
8 Gross profit percentages: A 25%; B 29.2%; C 20.8% D 30.9%.

30.6 Net profit percentage and expense ratios
1 24.8%; **2** 20.2%; **3** (a) 17.1% (b) 14.9% (c) 4.3%
4 (a) 25.4% (b) 2.6% (c) 5.4%
5 (a) 14.9% Rent and Rates have risen to 2.2% — part of the cause; salaries have fallen to 9.7% — not part of the cause.
6 Net profit percentage 27.4%; diesel 22.8% — Yes!; radio hire 5.5% No!
7
Name	Av. Stock	Sales	Gross profit
Jane	£5000	£52 000	£12 000
Claire	£7500	£100 000	£25 000

Gross profit %: Jane 23.1%; Claire 25%
Net profit %: Jane 19.2%; Claire 22.5%

8

Name	Av. Stock	Sales	Gross Profit
K. Morton	£8000	£134 400	£38 400
P Akram	£7000	£ 84 000	£28 000

Gross profit % K. Morton 28.6% P. Akram 33 1/3%
Net profit % K. Morton 17.9% P. Akram 23.2%

30.10 Appraisal of Balance Sheets

1 T. Curtis: Fixed capital £73 000; working capital £20 200; capital owned £68 200; capital employed £93 200; ROCI = 32%.

2 M. Lee: Capital owned £70 412; capital employed £88 412; working capital £27 412; liquid capital £18 727 acid test ratio 3.17:1; ROCI = 54.2%.

3 Anne Wood: Capital owned £70 100; capital employed £107 100; working capital £17 250; liquid capital £12 594; working capital ratio 2.71:1; liquid ratio 1.25:1, return on capital invested 13.9%.

30.11 Cash Flow

1 Mary Estall: Bank balance £7247.

2 M. Muhammadu: Bank balance £13 761.

3 Alan Seymour: Bank overdraft £6607 Advice to Seymour: he should arrange an overdraft at once with his bank manager.

30.13 Fund Flow statements

1 Alice Lumsden: Total sources £26 000, spent on extra premises, fittings, stocks and debtors, and on drawings.

2 P. Ramirez: Total sources £35 856, spent on reducing creditors, on extra machinery, fixtures, stock and debtors and on drawings. He also has £20 extra cash.

3 Abdul Malik: Total sources £78 598, spent on extra premises, equipment, vehicles, stocks and debtors. He also has £55 extra cash. Advice: Malik should not buy any more fixed assets until his liquidity improves, and should watch *all* types of expenditure.

31.3 Simple Control Accounts

1 Sims & Partners: Balances £23 374 (debit) £45 (credit).

2 T. P. Byron: Balances £26 675 (debit) £49 (credit).

3 M. Mishadar: Balances £79 (debit) £8560 (credit).

4 Janet Symes: Balances £48 (debit) £14 419 (credit).

5 T. Brown & Co. Ltd.: Balances £16 446 (debit) £56 (credit).

31.5 More difficult Control Accounts

1 A. Cutler: (a) Debt balance £5569 (b) We tell him the book-keeping has been done correctly.

2 Janet Lowe: (a) Credit balance £9723 (b) We tell her there is an error somewhere of £728.

3 Rajiv Shah: (a) Debit balance of £7933 (b) There is an error somewhere of £20.

4 T. Marshall: Sales balances £7183 (debit) and £137 (credit). Purchases balances £21 (debit) and £4591 (credit). (b) The debit balance is a creditor who is for a short time a debtor. The credit balance is the total we owe to all our creditors. (c) The error is in the Sales Ledger somewhere.

5 Tahira Kadarr: Sales balances £33 454 (debit) and £173 (credit). Purchases balances £168 (debit) and £9345 (credit) (b) Sales balances represent the total owed to us by our debtors and one odd debtor who is temporarily a creditor. (c) The error is in the Creditors Ledger somewhere.

6 M. Dickens: Sales balances £20 480 (debit) and £182 (credit); Purchases balances £73 (debit) and £7642 (credit). (b) The comment is that wherever the mistake is it isn't in either the Debtors Ledger or the Creditors Ledger. Must be in the General Ledger or the Private Ledger.

32.3 Simple increased-net-worth problems
1 M. Lock: Increase in net worth £5234; net profit £10 734.
2 Man Lee: Increase in net worth £13 010; net profit £14 250.
3 Sue Hallett: Increase in net worth £20 670; net profit £16 030.
4 K. Onobanjo: Increase in net worth £6005; Net profit £14 305

32.4 More difficult incomplete records
1 Kay Balmer: Capital at start £14 567; Cash balance £150; Bank balance £24 968; Sales on credit £1351; Purchases on credit £19 802; Gross profit £39 688; Net profit £25 560; Balance Sheet totals £38 553.
2 K. Marshall: Capital at start £14 370; Bank balance £8352; Credit Sales £1155; Credit purchases £11 960; Gross profit £30 327; Net profit £15 907; Balance Sheet totals £22 107.
3 Isaac Sijuwade: Capital at start £25 948; Cash balance £180; Bank balance £7958; Sales on credit £16 735; Purchases on credit £24 304; Gross profit £47 928; Net profit £28 616; Balance Sheet totals £53 948.

33.2 Household Accounts
1 Balance in hand £74.05; totals of book £530.00.
2 Balance in hand £136.35; totals of book £674.00.
3 Balance in hand £217.72; totals of book £640.00.

33.6 Purchase of a business
1 R. Smallbridge: Goodwill £3285; Balance Sheet totals £60 035.
2 Y. Muhammad: Goodwill £3525; Balance Sheet totals £100 625.
3 K. Nadarr: Goodwill £7350; Balance Sheet totals £80 850.

Index